Breaking Barriers

HARVARD EAST ASIAN MONOGRAPHS
163

BREAKING BARRIERS

Travel and the State in
Early Modern Japan

CONSTANTINE NOMIKOS VAPORIS

Published by the COUNCIL ON EAST ASIAN STUDIES, HARVARD
UNIVERSITY and distributed by HARVARD UNIVERSITY PRESS,
Cambridge (Massachusetts) and London   1994

The Council on East Asian Studies at Harvard University publishes a monograph series and, through the Fairbank Center for East Asian Research and the Reischauer Institute of Japanese Studies, administers research projects designed to further scholarly understanding of China, Japan, Korea, Vietnam, Inner Asia, and adjacent areas.

Library of Congress Cataloging in Publication Data

Vaporis, Constantine Nomikos, 1957–
    Breaking barriers : travel and the state in early modern Japan / Constantine Nomikos Vaporis.
       p. cm. – (Harvard East Asia monographs ; 163)
    Includes bibliographical references and index.
    ISBN 0-674-08107-2 : $55.00
    1. Transportation–Japan–History. 2. Transportation and state–Japan–History. 3. Travel restrictions–Japan–History. 4. Travel–Japan–History. I. Title. II. Series.
HE277.V36 1995
388'.068–dc20

94-37981
CIP

Index by Constantine Nomikos Vaporis

For Maria

Preface

The idea for this book arose out of a graduate seminar paper written at Princeton University in 1981 on the system of alternate attendance (*sankin kōtai*). In carrying out that research, I was impressed by the amount of movement on Tokugawa roads and imagined how colorful life on them must have been. George Tsukahira's monograph, *Feudal Control in Tokugawa Japan: The Sankin Kōtai System*, provided the inspiration for that paper and thus this book owes him a great intellectual debt. The fact that I have since then returned to the subject in my current research only reveals the depth of that debt.

Although I am, of course, responsible for the errors of fact and interpretation in this book, I would like to acknowledge the kindness and assistance of many people on both sides of the Pacific over the past years. In the United States, warmest thanks go to Martin C. Collcutt and Marius B. Jansen of Princeton University, the latter of whom directed the research for this study in its dissertation phase. Professor Collcutt's unwavering moral support over the years was invaluable, and his invitation to return to Princeton in the summer of 1991 as a Visiting Research Staff member proved instrumental in allowing me to complete this manuscript. Gilbert Rozman, also of Princeton, read and gave substantive comments on the entire manuscript in this early period, as did William B. Hauser (University of Rochester), James L. McClain (Brown University), Ronald P. Toby (University of Illinois, Champaign-Urbana), Conrad Totman (Yale University), and Anne Walthall (University of California, Irvine). Sheldon Garon (Princeton University) and George Akita (University of Hawaii) each kindly read and commented on several chapters. Personal thanks also go out to Bob Tadashi Wakabayashi (York University), Luke S. Roberts (University of California, Santa Barbara), James Mohr (University of Oregon, Eugene), Jo Ann Argersinger and John Jeffries (University of Maryland Baltimore County).

In Japan, I wish to acknowledge the kindness of Kanai Madoka, whose sponsorship in 1984–1986 enabled me to work in comfort in an office at the Historiographical Institute of Tokyo University. My deepest gratitude goes to Kodama Kōta, former Dean and Professor Emeritus of Gakushuin University and now Head of the Edo-Tokyo Museum, one of the foremost historians of the early modern period, whom it has been a true honor to know. His introduction to the community of scholars working on communications history (*kōtsū shi*) greatly facilitated and enriched my research. Two of these scholars, Watanabe Kazutoshi (Aichi University) and Yamamoto Mitsumasa (National Museum of History), have been extremely generous with their time and ideas; Professor Watanabe, moreover, was instrumental in obtaining a number of photographs of wood-block prints from the Arai sekisho shiryōkan (Arai Sekisho Historical Museum) which appear in this volume. Michael Cooper, Editor of *Monumenta Nipponica,* carefully nurtured my first draft article into publishable form ["Post Stations and Assisting Villages: Corvée Labor and Peasant Contention," *Monumenta Nipponica,* vol. 41, no. 4, pp. 377–414 (Winter 1986)] and gave permission for that material to appear here, with some revisions, as Chapter Two. Hashimoto Ken'ichirō, Curator at the Kanagawa Prefectural Library in Yokohama, also kindly provided me with a number of the photographs of wood-block prints from the wonderful Tamba Collection which adorn some of the pages of this book. Personal thanks also go out to Shindō Kazuyuki and Kayoko, Kurumada Hiroyuki, Ishida Yuri, Kawasaki Masami, Dr. and Mrs. Okamune Shigehisa, Moriguchi Kōji, Yorimitsu Kanji, Takahashi Shirō, Hosokawa Shimako, Yasuhara Taeko, and Ishizu Kazuko.

I am grateful as well to those institutions and organizations that helped support my work financially: Princeton University, which provided not only a variety of scholarships (University Fellowship, National Defense Foreign Language Fellowship, National Resource Fellowship, Japan Government Fund), but employment for a year as a Lecturer in the Department of History as well as a summer visiting research fellowship; the Japan Foundation, for a language grant to attend the Inter-University Center for Japanese Studies in 1981–1982; the Historiographical Institute, where I was a Foreign Guest Researcher (*gaikokujin kenkyūin*) (1984–1986); Fulbright (IIE), for twenty-one months of support on a dissertation research grant; the Reischauer Institute and its then-Director, Harold Bolitho, for a most stimulating nine months in residence as a post-doctoral fellow; and the University of Maryland, Baltimore County, for two faculty research grants from the Directed Research Initiative Fund (DRIF) during the summers of 1990 and 1991, as well as a subvention to cover the costs of producing the maps and diagrams that appear in this volume.

I probably would not be a historian of Japan today were it not for the accident of making the acquaintance of James R. Bartholomew in an elevator at the International House in Tokyo in 1978. He encouraged me to direct my interest in Japan to the study of its history, which I did briefly under his tutorship at The Ohio State University. Later he suggested that I apply to Princeton, and it is fortunate for me that I followed his advice. That my life's work has had anything at all to do with Japan in the first place is due to my parents, Reverend Dr. Nomikos Michael Vaporis, a Greek Orthodox priest and scholar of Byzantine history and Modern Greek Hellenism, and Mary Konstantine Vaporis, an artist, both of whom first opened my eyes to that part of the world.

To my daughter, Michaela, who asked me not to go to work every day during the summer of 1991 at Princeton, when I was fully engaged in rewriting this manuscript, but who walked me to the street, bidding me "Hurry back, soon," and welcomed me home with open arms when I did return: thank you for your patience and love. Both she and my son, Gabriel Aleydis, have brought immeasurable joy to my family. And, though she would want no place here, to not mention Maria, my wife and partner in life's journey, would be a true sin of omission. The rest will remain unstated here, but not unacknowledged.

Contents

Figures

Maps

Tables

Breaking Barriers

Introduction

Sitting in a comfortable seat on board the "bullet" train in Japan today, speeding from Tokyo to Kyoto, the modern traveler perhaps has little reason to stop and consider what the same journey was like for people living more than a century and a half ago during the Tokugawa, or early modern period (1600–1868). Feet inclined, sipping a soft drink or beer purchased from one of the young women who push refreshment carts down the aisles, the present traveler's mind is no doubt far from thoughts of the weariness that his earlier counterparts experienced trudging over almost the same route by foot or being jostled about in the cramped quarters of a palanquin. As the train crosses a bridge spanning a normally shrunken river, such as the Ōi, it is easy to forget the fear that gripped those who were carried across the raging river on wooden platforms or pick-a-back.

Whereas the passenger on board the bullet train speeds to his destination, perhaps forgetting to look out the window to view Mount Fuji or other sites of natural beauty, in earlier times it was the trip itself, not just the destination, that often drove people to leave the comforts of home in spite of the accompanying hardships. Moreover, the freedom of movement that is enjoyed today as a constitutional right was much more circumscribed in that earlier period. The relative difficulty of travel in Tokugawa times may stand in contrast to the comfort that is the present norm, yet the experience of yesterday and today's travelers is not totally dissimilar; for in Tokugawa times travel first emerged as a form of recreation that reached the commoner masses, meaning the lower three levels in the idealized Neo-Confucian social order of samurai-peasant-artisan-merchant adopted by the political elite.

The purpose of this study is to examine Tokugawa society—one of the most urbanized societies in the early modern world—before the introduction of railroad technology from the West in the late nineteenth century, through the prism of travel and transport. The object of its focus is an examination of this facet of Tokugawa history in terms of the relationship between the state and society. In taking this rather unusual approach to state-society relations, it is hoped that this monograph will appeal more broadly to scholars outside of the field of Japan or East Asia, particularly to those in European history.

Definitions of the state are numerous, but for our purposes here a simple one will suffice. In discussing the Tokugawa "state" I mean a compulsory association that claims control over a territory and the people within it. According to this definition, "administrative, legal, extractive, and coercive organizations are the core of any state."[1] Of course, the state is much more than the government. It is the "continuous administrative, legal bureaucratic and coercive systems that attempt not only to structure relationships between civil society and public authority in a policy but also to structure many crucial relationships within civil society as well."[2]

Since the functioning of the Tokugawa state, which includes the Tokugawa shogunate, or bakufu, and the domains, was predicated upon the assumption that the peasant class, which comprised some 80 percent of the population, would stay on and work the land, it is important for us to ask to what extent the state sought to exert control over its subjects and how that control manifested itself. We must also ask how successful the state was in its efforts, and how in turn the people responded. Furthermore, we must consider whether or not these controls encouraged parochialism, thereby making the modernization of the Meiji years (1868–1912) a more arduous process.

At least three dimensions are important to our understanding of the Tokugawa state and its activities: the specific form the state assumed, the functions it engaged in, and the mechanism or "apparatus" through which these functions were carried out.[3] The dimension of "form" refers to "how and why a specific state is constituted by, and evolves within, a given social formation."[4] The story of the formation of the Tokugawa state has been explored elsewhere, although the nature of that political order remains a subject of some debate.[5] This study, therefore, will be concerned largely with the latter two elements.

"Function" signifies "those activities undertaken by and in the name of the state"—in other words, the state's operational objectives. The goals or objectives of the state are dependent on the existence of an adequate bureaucratic mechanism through which state functions are executed. To understand the Tokugawa state's capacity to execute certain objectives, we will need to examine the resources and instruments it had for dealing with particular problems. This study will explore how the Tokugawa state affected society not only through its interventions, but also through its abstentions. In doing so, it is in line with current research which views the state as "an agent which, although influenced by the society that surrounds it, also shapes social and political processes."[6]

Furthermore, in discussing the concept of social control we should recognize that it can usefully be considered in terms of two categories: namely, coercive controls, which "either use or imply force, legal or extralegal"; and social controls, which "consist of group self-regulation outside the boundaries of force."[7] These coercive controls involve the "successful subordination of people's own inclinations of social behavior in favor of the behavior prescribed by state rules."[8] Together, these two categories constitute a control system; both are important in understanding how Tokugawa society functioned.

By way of introduction to this historical problem of travel and social control (used in the broadest sense of the term), the three examples that follow are particularly instructive.

In the middle of the eighteenth century (1759), three regional village headmen from an area in northern Kyushu applied to the proper domainal officials for permits to travel. On the pretext of making a pilgrimage to Ise Shrine and Hachiman-gū in Kamakura, they were able to obtain a passport, but as they traveled up the Eastern Coastal Highway, the Tōkaidō, which linked Edo (present-day Tokyo) with Kyoto, they failed to stop at either shrine. Instead, they stayed on the main road and headed for Edo, where they had other business.[9]

At the beginning of the next century, a six-year-old boy repeatedly threatened his parents that he would leave with one of the groups of young children that were forming to travel on pilgrimage to Ise. His parents forbade him to go; but while their attention slackened momentarily, the boy pinned on to a pillar in the house one of the fallen amulets which had precipitated the mad rush to Ise and dashed out the door to join the masses. The mother, upon discovering that her son had indeed left, went after him in hot pursuit.[10]

Still later, in the middle of the nineteenth century, the mother of a rural samurai from a domain in northern Japan bid her friends good-bye, telling them that she was going to make a pilgrimage to nearby Kankoku-ji. Instead, she met up with her sister and her son the next day and headed in the opposite direction, south, toward Ise Shrine. Her friends were kept waiting a long time, for she and her relations did not return home for six months, as they traveled around much of the country on an extraordinary journey that included stops at many of the most famous tourist spots in Tokugawa Japan. None of the three, however, had bothered to obtain official permission to travel.[11]

The similarities throughout these stories reveal several important points about travel in Tokugawa Japan. First, we can observe that during this period there was an intimate relationship between travel and pilgrimage. They were to a large extent synonymous—a fact that is readily apparent from a quick perusal of travel permits and diaries. Authorities were much more tolerant of pilgrimage than other types of travel because of its sacred nature as a religious act; and, therefore, travel often fell under that rubric. While pilgrimage was, for many people, a significant religious act, for others, pilgrimage became largely a means or pretext by which to obtain official permission to travel.

Second, travel in the Tokugawa period developed an important recreational character, as long-distance, multi-destinational trips became common. Third, in two of the examples, the pilgrims did not bother to obtain the permission of government officials to travel: for them, pilgrimage became an excuse to leave home without the sanction of either political or household authorities. And finally, these three examples show that the same phenomena occurred throughout the Tokugawa period;

further evidence in this study will reveal that these patterns of travel were established as early as the late seventeenth century.

The findings of this study will reveal a great disjunction between government regulations on travel and the social reality at which they were aimed. Countless persons from all social ranks defied governmental authority by traveling without official permission despite the volumes of legislation intended to regulate or restrict movement. Such legislation appears to have been merely a reaction to the social reality that existed and thus, in a sense, was little more than sumptuary legislation. The social, economic, and political implications of this interpretation necessarily recast our view of Tokugawa society.

This study, furthermore, will show that government policy regarding travel was, on the whole, positive rather than repressive; the application of regulations was far more flexible than suggested by statute. This growing flexibility in a system that originally had been more rigid allowed for—and in fact promoted—the increasing mobility that characterized Tokugawa Japan from the eighteenth century on.

As we look at Tokugawa society through the prism of travel and communications, we will have to discard certain assumptions and viewpoints. For example, legalistic or authoritarian views of Tokugawa Japan assume that government by nature seeks to be intrusive, to regulate closely all aspects of society. With regard to the regulation of physical mobility, it has been asserted that, in the Tokugawa era, "free movement was severely restricted."[12] The historical record will reveal that the situation was far more complicated than this. While the legal structure did not change dramatically during the early modern period, the application and interpretation of the law most certainly did; the government reacted to and tried to keep pace with the changing economic and social landscape.

The assumption of a closely regulated society is also related to the view that villages were static entities: in other words, that peasants were "immobile" and "mutually dependent," "captives of the demands of the rice cycle itself, strapped to the land by the registries, and defenseless in a world of sword-wielding warriors."[13] The demands of the rice cycle did not prevent peasants from engaging in travel and other recreational activities. They worked around those demands, traveling during the off-season or lulls in work. Furthermore, cooperative arrangements allowed many to leave the village to travel while others cared for their fields. At other times all responsibilities were ignored with reckless abandon as peasants and townsmen alike literally dropped what they were doing and engaged in *nukemairi* (lit., "stealing away on pilgrimage") or "pilgrimage for thanksgiving," *okagemairi*.

If we were to accept a legalistic interpretation of Tokugawa Japan, then we would be led to believe falsely that peasants were "in general not allowed to leave their villages except for pilgrimages to the Ise Grand Shrine or the Zenkō-ji Temple."[14] Furthermore, we would have to accept as factual the limitations on mobility implicit in the view that peasants faced draconian punishments if they traveled without the required permits. We would also have to believe that permits were indeed strictly inspected at the barriers (*sekisho*) found on the bakufu's central road network, the Gokaidō.[15] The evidence presented here will show a much more varied pattern. In fact, quite paradoxically, the system that the ruling class devised to control commoners actually ended up restricting themselves more.

A legalistic interpretation also overestimates the state's authority. For example, scholars who argue that travel restrictions caused local isolation to remain the rule in the nineteenth century overemphasize the strength of political controls and minimize the considerable energy, ingenuity, and consequent mobility of people in the preceding two centuries. It is not the case that, "for about two hundred years . . . feudal controls were strong and the various edicts and checking stations [i.e., *sekisho*] performed their functions of restricting the movement of people."[16] Official sanctions did not so much restrict travel as constrain or discourage it and make it harder. In fact, one can argue that the lack of bite behind the government sanctions actually stimulated travel. As noted, since governmental authorities were much more tolerant of pilgrimage than other types of travel, most recreational travel fell under that category.

This study will examine not only the legal walls surrounding the state, that is, bakufu and domain restrictions on travel, but also the physical barriers, or sekisho, constructed on the major roadways to regulate traffic and the documentation that travelers were sometimes required to carry to pass through them. The evidence presented here will demonstrate that, while sekisho did affect the flow and pattern of travel throughout Tokugawa Japan, they did not significantly impede travelers. An examination of the diaries kept by officials at Hakone and Arai sekisho, the two strictest in the land, reveals that the requirements for passage generally were not as onerous as previously believed. Moreover, sekisho officials were often known to facilitate commoner passage through—or around—the barriers, when, according to the letter of the law, they should have been stopped.

To determine which restraints acted on travel, we must, as has been suggested here, look beyond monocausal, political explanations. It will become evident that the cost in terms of money spent and productive time lost, as well as the social pressures within the community and the household, restrained travel more than political controls did.

The literature on early modern transport and communications is quite limited in volume. Most general studies of transport deal with the subject as an aspect of the economy; and within this field, according to one scholar, "there has been outright neglect of the pre-industrial economy as if it uses no form of transport at all."[17] The more general, pre-industrial studies that do exist tend to be highly descriptive, lacking much qualitative analysis.[18] According to Michael Robbins in his review article on research in communications history, "what is now wanted is essentially *transport* history; not history of roads, or vehicles, or railways, or ports, or shipping or airlines. We need history of the movement of people and things between places." Moreover, he states, "the business of tourism is wide open for historical treatment."[19] This monograph seeks to fill a part of this need and to stimulate further research.

A few scholars of Japan have studied the problem of migration and have used the population registries kept by the Tokugawa government as part of its anti-Christian policy, the *shūmon aratamesho* ("Registries of the Investigation of Sect Affiliation and Population"), to show that "far more migration took place than would be expected" and that "peasants sometimes migrated without taking any of the required procedures."[20] While migration for employment, marriage, and adoption were important factors in accounting for greater mobility during the Tokugawa period, they are only a partial explanation. Moreover, the quantitative, inductive methodology used by these historians will, by the nature of the sources used, produce limited results.

This study does not attempt to discredit what is pathbreaking historical inquiry; yet for us to discover the social reality behind the façade of government regulations, we will have to examine other types of source materials in order to differentiate between the seemingly harsh laws of the Tokugawa government and how those laws were, or in many cases, were not, actually enforced. While making ample use of government documentation, such as official notices and diaries, this study delves into the rich resources of contemporary travel diaries, travel literature, road and travel guides, as well as popular songs, poetry, and wood-block prints. Unlike medieval travel diaries, those of the early modern era often give realistic descriptions of road conditions and the human experience of wayfaring.[21] These sources will play a major part in the arguments that follow. Literature, which is not employed by historians of Japan for its social content as frequently as it could be, is also integrated—when it can be substantiated by other historical sources—to add color and texture to our picture of Tokugawa times.

Important as background for this study of travel in early modern Japan is an examination of the system of overland communications that the Tokugawa government, or bakufu, established during the first half of the seventeenth century. We will examine how the communications system—with its infrastructure of roads, bridges, river-crossings, post stations, barriers (bakufu-constructed sekisho and domainal tolls or *bansho*)—developed in central Japan as well as regionally, beyond the great Tōkaidō.

But discussion of the system of overland communications will serve as more than background, for the transmission of ideas and the transportation of physical objects, both people and commodities, are the threads that hold a society together. Transport, the material means of communication between two places, physically organizes a society.[22] Without efficient communications, an early modern economy, based on the division of labor as well as on regional and national markets, could not survive.[23] The more efficient the transport system, the wider the scope is for the division of labor, and the more highly developed an economy can become.[24]

Efficient communications also make it possible for large or geographically fractured areas to be politically unified and for the internal security of that area to be maintained. Road conditions reflect the degree of national cohesion and thus are a measure of the vitality of any government. Furthermore, territorial expansion and the scope of the road system are guides to the political aims and actual extent of control of the state. That is, an examination of the communications system can illuminate the pattern, aims, character, and scope of power of a government. Another major aim of this book then is an examination of the Tokugawa state as revealed through the key institution of overland communications.

The establishment of a centralized system of communications contributed to the construction of the Tokugawa state and the bakufu's assertion of controls on the daimyo. Not only did the bakufu usurp daimyo authority, but it also prohibited daimyo from interfering with the flow of traffic on the central highway network, as they had done during Japan's earlier period of Warring States (*sengoku jidai*). It should be noted, however, that the central government tacitly accepted their existence by another name, *bansho* (domainal tolls), within the domains—that is, anywhere but on the Gokaidō.

As in many other areas of governance, in administering its network of fifty-three barriers on the central road system, the bakufu did not assume direct control. Instead, it relied heavily on the efforts of its vassal daimyo (*fudai daimyō*), sending general regulations to officials at the barriers, but leaving the definition of day-to-day operations to the individual administrative authorities. Thus the domains were an important component in the early modern, or *bakuhan*, order.

The Gokaidō network was created out of political necessity. Its function encompassed the entire continuum of political concerns, from a symbolic presence of Tokugawa authority, to active surveillance of traffic and an instrument of military strategy. Having emerged from the turbulent period of civil war, culminating in the decisive but, from a contemporary point of view, not necessarily final battle at Sekigahara in 1600, it is not surprising that the system the Tokugawa forged reflected a consciousness of the military threat the other daimyo posed. In addition to this political function, the Gokaidō provided an efficient means for official communications and a control mechanism for the movement of potential violators of the law; it also made possible the circulation of commodity goods as well as a large number of people throughout the country.

Given its principal functions, it is not surprising that the transport system was geared towards official use; that is, official, rather than private, traffic and communications were given top priority. Moreover, the Tokugawa "rigged" the costs of using the system to their own advantage and therefore, by necessity, were required to create a system of transport corvée labor (*sukegō*) to support it. When increasing levels of official traffic, corruption, and abuse of the transport system threatened to bankrupt it, the government increased the tax level and spread the costs by increasing the number of villages assessed the transport corvée levy.

Although the Gokaidō was established for official rather than private use, the commoner class was able to take full advantage of the infrastructure, giving what had been essentially a military/political system an overwhelmingly plebeian character. The transport system was unexpectedly transformed in character through its use by the common people, particularly for travel as recreation. Travel-related facilities specifically geared for commoner use proliferated on the Gokaidō network during the seventeenth century, and a system developed by merchants for relaying correspondence (*machi hikyaku*) was so efficient that even political authorities turned to it for routine business—one further indicator that the character of communications had changed.

Despite their lower social status, commoners were not required to travel on shank's mare while their superiors rode horses or were carried in palanquins. Surprising though it may seem for the status-conscious society that Tokugawa Japan was, the mode of transport available to individuals on the highways was determined by economic rather than social considerations. Thus, with their improving economic lot, the common people could enjoy the same privileges as their social betters. This occurred, paradoxically, despite a legal proscription on commoners' riding horses that remained in effect until after the Meiji Restoration of 1868.

Throughout Japan's pre-industrial history, overland communications consisted primarily of the transport of people and their personal goods. One reason for this was the country's natural, physical characteristics. Unlike China or the Low Countries in Europe, Japan had few great rivers, and scarce wide lowlands over which canals could be constructed, suitable for the transportation of people. Mountainous terrain and an abundance of rapidly flowing rivers made the transport of heavy or bulky goods overland difficult and costly.[25] Roads, therefore, served an auxiliary rather than a principal role in the movement of commodity goods by serving as a conduit by which these goods were transported to river or ocean ports, where they could be transshipped. In addition to this auxiliary role, recourse was made to overland transport only where water routes were unavailable or when loads were either too small, too valuable (as in the case of gold), or were being moved over short distances. This study will focus on the central functions of overland transport and thus deal almost exclusively with the transport of people and their personal goods.[26]

The popular image of overland communications in Tokugawa Japan is essentially negative. Thus far, most scholars have emphasized their slow and unsatisfactory nature, relating them frequently to the bakufu's desire to limit lateral connections between the domains. This study will seek to correct this view. In part, the poor image exists because the lack of wheeled traffic on the main roads and the consequent reliance on transport workers and pack horses are seen by some scholars as evidence of a backward system. According to the author of the introduction to, and translation of, Shimazaki Tōson's novel, *Before the Dawn* (Yoake Mae), which revolves around life in a post station on the Kiso kaidō, "The roads remained unsuitable for wheeled traffic as a matter of national policy."[27] In other words, the lack of wheeled traffic is misconstrued as evidence of a backward system and a reactionary government; in fact, conscious restrictions on that traffic actually resulted in good road conditions. Without carts tearing up the road, spilling their cargo, or causing traffic accidents, as occurred in urban centers, communications were able to flow, free of any interruptions.

The alleged scarcity of bridges is offered as yet further evidence that Tokugawa communications were primitive. One has only to look at contemporary maps and art work to realize that this was not true. There were many reasons why some rivers were bridged and others were not (see Chapter One), but it is important to note that the Tokugawa tended to retreat from the use of available technology when the trade-off in terms of travel and road conditions, as well as the economic costs, appeared too dear.

This study will dispel the notion that Tokugawa communications were backward. A well integrated system of major post roads made possible the steady growth of communications. Carts were kept off the principal roads as part of a conscious policy to maintain the roads in good condition for pedestrian traffic. A number of foreigners praised the integrated system of well-maintained and much-traveled main roads in Tokugawa Japan, comparing them quite favorably with conditions in Europe.

The misperception of Tokugawa communications as underdeveloped is a result, perhaps, of a lack of comparative analysis: e.g., the crossing of streams and rivers by fording or ferrying, as was common in Japan, was the norm, not the exception, in the preindustrial world. Furthermore, in reading some accounts written by foreign visitors in the nineteenth century, we must remember that the writers came from a newly industrialized Europe and were therefore judging Japan by criteria totally different from those of earlier travelers. For example, while they found the shogunate in decline to be rigid and repressive, earlier, seventeenth-century observers found Japan "harshly but well governed."[28] Similarly, some Westerners who visited Japan late in the Tokugawa period and in the early years of the Meiji government found fault with the roads because they were not macadamized and therefore unfit for wheeled traffic.[29] Their criticism, however, should not obscure the fact that for almost two centuries the infrastructure of overland communications more than met the perceived needs of the times.

During the Tokugawa period the roads were filled with all types of travelers, from all social stations. First there were the "Princes and Lords of the Empire," the daimyo who were required to make annual trips of alternate attendance to wait upon the shogun. Their trips were made with "pomp and magnificence," the train of some of the most eminent filling up the road for some days.[30] The early modern era, however, became the age of the commoner; it was this traffic, rather than that of the daimyo and bakufu, that set the character of the road. With the improving economic conditions of the early Edo period, for the first time, commoners were able to travel in great numbers for recreational purposes; the roads filled with pilgrims headed for Ise, the Saikoku and Shikoku circuits, and Zenkō-ji. There were also merchants and hawkers plying their trade, begging orders of young and attractive nuns, transport workers in their minimal attire, and the poor and destitute; all combined to give the road a distinctly plebeian character.

The emergence of travel as a significant social phenomenon was made possible only by the elimination of many of the impediments to physical mobility that existed during Japan's medieval era, such as political fragmentation, warfare, social instability, mountain bandits, pirates, and the proliferation of economic tolls. The three political unifiers of the late sixteenth and early seventeenth centuries, Oda Nobunaga, Toyotomi Hideyoshi and Tokugawa Ieyasu, went a long way towards removing these obstacles; and the Tokugawa rulers that followed continued that effort with great success.[31] As Reinhard Bendix has noted, "Japan's external security stands in obvious contrast to the European powers during the seventeenth and eighteenth centuries."[32] Instead of the pandemic warfare that afflicted Europe, Japan was blessed with peace for almost two and a half centuries. With the Tokugawa peace as a historical given, however, it is easy for us to underestimate the tremendous social impact that the cessation of warfare and local violence had. Just how fundamental the changes in the early modern order were is evident from the fact that in 1658 Asai Ryōi, author of *Tōkaidō meishoki* (An Account of Famous Places on the Tōkaidō), could write about "sending a cherished child on a journey" to gain experience "in all manner of things."[33]

The removal of these impediments to physical mobility alone would not have been sufficient to spur the masses to travel. It also required the economic growth that came with peace. Rising productivity, coupled with the declining ability of the political authorities to tax away surpluses in the eighteenth and nineteenth centuries, left peasants with more disposable income.[34] A rising standard of living, in turn, allowed them to pursue recreational activities such as travel. The rapid development of urban centers during the seventeenth century, which grew and were sustained by the inflow of migrants from rural areas, was a further sign of economic growth. Less permanent forms of migration were common, too. Rural people traveled for occupational reasons, not only to the big cities and castle towns, but to rural towns as well, as those developed from the eighteenth century on. The development of improved transport facilities, which will be an important focus of our discussion in Chapters One and Two, provided the infrastructure necessary to support the economic activity of travel. In addition to roads and the transport services available at the post stations on them, rest stops, inns, tea houses, and other merchant enterprises for the benefit of travelers sprang up, dotting the highways. Moreover, the widespread use of silver and gold—which could be converted to copper, as needed, at any post station—made it possible for the first time for travelers to venture far from home without being weighed down by strings of heavy copper coins.

The better economic position of many commoners partially explains the increase in travel, but the proliferation of religious confraternities (*kō*) and the proselytizing efforts of priests (*oshi*) were also quite important in popularizing pilgrimage. The existence of confraternities and the institutionalization of the practice of alms-giving meant that a wider spectrum of the population could engage in the social activity of travel. Rich and poor, samurai and commoner: all could meet on the same road. Despite the great social pressures and legal sanctions restricting their movement, women, too—for the first time in Japanese history—were able to travel in significant numbers.

Not only were people traveling more during the Tokugawa period, but they were also staying on the road for longer periods of time. By the nineteenth century extended trips of two to three months were not unusual. As a result, the geographic range of the lives of commoners expanded greatly.

The creation of a "culture of movement"[35] was an important stimulus for travel. By the late eighteenth century prospective wayfarers would already have had a substantial knowledge of the experience of travel from word of mouth. They would also have seen a number of printed sources related to the experience, such as mass-produced woodblock prints, travel literature (*tabi nikki* and *kikō bungaku*), commoner temple school textbooks, travel board games (*dōchū sugoroku*), maps, travel guides (*annaiki* and *meisho zue*), and how-to-travel handbooks. All encouraged people to travel and told those who could not—the armchair travelers—what the experience was like. The physical evidence of a culture of movement is enough to indicate that travel during the Toku-gawa period had become a form of recreation, or *yusan tabi* ("pleasure-seeking travel"), an escape from the rigid pattern governing day-to-day living, a time when, according to the early-nineteenth-century author Jippensha Ikku, one could flee from the bill collectors at the end of the month and cleanse one's life of care.[36]

Tokugawa Japan, as it emerges in this study, is neither uniform nor static. In response to the needs of the seventeenth century, a communications system developed which, by the end of the same century, was outgrowing its initial objectives. Government authorities reacted to the changing social reality and attempted to create a better system, but there was no one system per se—proof of the diversity that was the early modern political order. As suggested, the interpretation and application of law with regard to communications changed dramatically in response to overwhelming social transformations. Japanese society by the nineteenth century was far more flexible than it had been a century and a half earlier; mobility, in physical, social, and economic terms, was far less restrained.

Many factors which will be discussed in the following pages contributed to the rise of travel and its emergence as a national pastime among the masses. As early as the late seventeenth century, authorities were taken aback by the large numbers of people traveling on the roads. The German physician Englebert Kaempfer, who was employed by the Dutch traders residing on Deshima in Nagasaki, was also startled by the heavy traffic. In 1696, he remarked, "It is scarce credible, what numbers of people daily travel on the roads in this country, and I can assure the reader from my own experience, having pass'd it four times, that [the] Tokaido . . . is upon some days more crowded, than the publick streets in any [of] the most populous town[s] in Europe."[37] Surely no one in government then could have imagined how popular travel would become. With as many as an estimated five million (out of a population of about 30 million) converging on the sacred Ise Shrine in 1830,[38] by the beginning of the nineteenth century we can speak of a veritable "travel boom" taking place.

ONE

The Arms and Legs of the Realm

A Tokugawa official wrote in the early eighteenth century that the Gokaidō, or Five Highway, system, and the post stations on them were the "arms and legs of the realm." To take his analogy further, we might say that the Tōkaidō, the greatest of the routes, which linked Edo with Kyoto, was the "main artery" through which the lifeblood of early modern Japan coursed.[1] Early in the seventeenth century, the Tokugawa regime had realized the importance of overland communications and made a centralized network a top priority in its agenda. The establishment of a unified communications system under bakufu authority stands as a major achievement which usurped daimyo sovereignty in a number of areas, thus reflecting the broad scope of Tokugawa power. The assertion of these prerogatives belong in any catalogue of expanding central powers asserted over the domains: for example, control of foreign policy, the authority to settle disputes among the daimyo, the alternate attendance system, and the one-castle-per-province (*ikkoku ichijō*) regulation.[2]

The bakufu created a network of overland communications in order to fulfill political and strategical needs rather than economic needs. The shogunate required command of the country's major highways for the passage of its martial forces, the movement of its officials, and the conveyance of official communications. A central aim of its policy was to keep traffic flowing; and the bakufu tried to achieve this by nationalizing the central road system, the Gokaidō; abolishing private sekisho; promulgating regulations which prohibited and discouraged the disruption of transport services; and giving top priority to its own transport needs. In doing so, however, the Tokugawa created a monopoly and thus its efforts to maintain the economic solvency of that system at times worked at cross-purposes with its efforts to promote the uninterrupted flow of traffic.

Although the communications system was initially developed to meet the central government's transport needs, new demands arising from the creation and maintenance of the Tokugawa order altered the system's scope and character. When, for example, alternate attendance became institutionalized in 1635, the movement of daimyo between Edo and their domains became routine, necessitating an expansion of the work force maintained at stations. The requirements of periodic attendance also spurred the development of transport infrastructures within the domains for the transport of the daimyo's retinue to and from Edo as well as for the shipment of rice to the Osaka market, where it could then be converted to the cash needed to cover the weighty costs of the daimyo's duty to the shogun. Through these policies on communications and the system of alternate attendance, the Tokugawa attempted to shift the center of the realm from Kyoto, where it lay during the Warring States period, to Edo.

The Tokugawa constructed a well-integrated system of overland communications that was much praised by visitors from abroad, who compared conditions in Japan quite favorably with those that they experienced at home in Europe. Thus the assertion by some scholars that conditions in Japan were retarded in development does not take into account the early modern experience worldwide.

The Gokaidō post system was created to meet Tokugawa needs, but stations were allowed to service commoners when not undertaking official duties. Although bakufu transport planners did not foresee this outcome, in fact, the Gokaidō network, together with the years of peace and internal stability and the early expansion of the economy, made it possible for commoners to take to the roads in large numbers and contributed to the development of travel as recreation.

GROWTH AND EXPANSION OF THE TOKUGAWA SYSTEM

Shortly after his victory at Sekigahara in 1600, Tokugawa Ieyasu moved quickly to take control of overland transportation. He ordered that an expanded version of the system he had employed in his former domainal holdings centered in Mikawa (Aichi prefecture) be implemented on a national basis. In the first month of 1601, Ieyasu dispatched two of his most influential officials (Ōkubo Nagayasu, a Senior Councilor and Hikosaka Motomosa, a Chief Intendant) to tour the Tōkaidō, the central artery linking Edo and Kyoto. They inspected local conditions and granted certain post stations official status. Each station was instructed to maintain thirty-six pack horses and, although the decree issued referred only to horses, it is reasonable to believe that a proportionate number of porters was also maintained there. The larger number of horses maintained at Tokugawa period stations in comparison with stations established by daimyo during the Warring States (*sengoku*) period reflected the wider scope of bakufu control and its centrist inclinations.[3] Within a few years, similar systems were established on two other major roads, the Nakasendō and Ōshū dōchū; and existing regional transport networks were integrated into what became known as the Gokaidō.[4] In its completed form, the Gokaidō consisted of the Tōkaidō, Nakasendō, Ōshū dōchū, Kōshū dōchū, Nikkō dōchū, and eight auxiliary roads (see Map 1). Just as a number of Warring States daimyo had done, Ieyasu ordered that the pack horses maintained at post stations in his domains be dispatched only to persons holding a document bearing the stamped mark of his personal post-horse seal (*tenma shuin*).[5] Misuse of the system was strongly discouraged: anyone trying to procure post horses without the proper documentation, either by suasion or force, was to be held at the post station while the proper authorities were notified. Bakufu instructions to one station in 1602 went so far as to order villagers there to assemble and physically strike down any offender who attempted to obtain horses and porters illegally.[6]

As with other major Tokugawa institutions, the post-station system was, by the end of the fourth decade of its existence, generally in the form it would retain for the remainder of the Tokugawa period. Thirty-three stations on the Tōkaidō were granted official status in 1603 and twenty

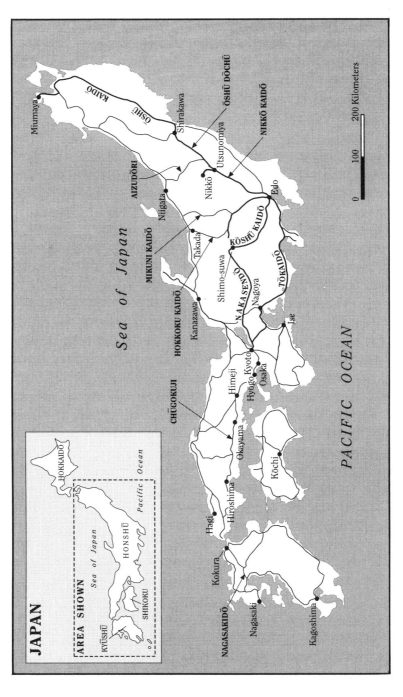

Map 1 Gokaidō Network and Other Major Roads

more were to follow over the next twenty-nine years in a process of con-solidation.[7]

The latter twenty stations were selected for official status in order to decrease the distance between stations that were spaced particularly far apart; similar efforts were also exerted for the other roads in the Gokaidō network. On the Tōkaidō, for example, Totsuka (1604) was established to reduce the sixteen-kilometer distance between Hodogaya and Fujisawa. Kawasaki (1623) was similarly created to reduce the stretch of almost twenty kilometers between Shinagawa and Kanagawa.[8] In the unusual case where no settlement existed, an artificial one was created: certain designated residents from Odawara and Mishima, for example, were forced to relocate to Hakone, which lay between the two stations on a very difficult stretch of road.[9]

In order for an official system to be created, therefore, non-essential stations had to be eliminated: in 1603, for example, there were over twenty stations on the stretch of Tōkaidō from Odawara to Edo alone; but only two, Totsuka and Kawasaki, would be integrated into the official system.[10] The other eighteen stations were ordered to stop operating because they refused to provide the required transport services for official travelers; but the bakufu's desire to maintain fairly uniform distances between stations no doubt influenced its decision to close down particular stations. In its final configuration, the post system between, but not including, Edo and Odawara consisted of eight stations, each spaced at an average distance of about eight kilometers.

While the transport network was being consolidated, some post stations exhibited aggressive behavior in protecting their economic self-interests, even when that was incompatible with bakufu policy. For example, Fujisawa on the Tōkaidō issued complaints to the bakufu that the next station, Totsuka, was operating illegally: that is, it was refusing to provide horses for official travelers. Totsuka was thereupon ordered to cease operating and the local intendant (*daikan*) instructed to seize any horses found at the station.[11] Even though Totsuka promised to provide the required number of horses in the future, Fujisawa, in an effort to retain sole right to post operations on the sixteen-kilometer stretch of road to Hodogaya, continued to oppose its efforts to acquire official status. The bakufu, however, ignored Fujisawa's protests and granted

Hodogaya approval of its application.[12] Only through these efforts was the shogunate able to establish transport monopolies for the stations in its official communications network.

In its completed form, the Gokaidō network consisted of 248 post stations, which were, depending on the road, spaced from four to twelve kilometers apart (see Table 1). According to the written accounts that contemporary travelers have left us, as well as the pictorial evidence presented in wood-block prints, each station seemed to have its own distinct personality. Each offered its own speciality product (*meibutsu*) for sale: for example, the grated yam soup (*tororojiru*) of Mariko, the dyed cloth of Narumi, the crude prints of Ōtsu (*Ōtsu-e*), and even the prostitutes of Akasaka and a number of other post stops.[13] All stations fulfilled the various functions of rest stop, transport center, information communications center, and recreation area. The primary responsibility of post stations was to provide transport services for official travelers and cargo. These services were obtained at the office of the station manager, or *ton'ya-ba* (the manager himself was referred to as a *ton'ya*), which was usually located near the center of the station.[14] Many stations had more than one manager and central office, and in those cases duty was rotated between men and locations. The manager was assisted by a small staff of men who dispatched horses and porters, kept the official account books, and performed miscellaneous tasks.[15] Stations were also required to maintain at least one designated inn, known as *honjin*, for travelers on official duty, and many maintained auxiliary inns (*waki-honjin*) to handle the overflow of guests. The central location of the *honjin*, as well as their impressive size and construction, signified the political function of the post station.[16] There were, however, many more inns which catered to commoners (*hatagoya*) than there were *honjin*.

Post stations characteristically assumed a long, narrow shape along both sides of the road, but they nevertheless encompassed a variety of settlement patterns.* On the Tōkaidō, for example, at one extreme there were small stations along mountain passes such as Sakanoshita. Its pop-

---

*I use the term "post station" (*shukueki*) to refer to both the station where the transport services were offered and to the larger settlement of which it was sometimes a part (referred to at times as *shukubamachi*). Both Japanese terms are used interchangeably, although the distinction is important in large, multi-functional settlements.

TABLE 1 Gokaidō Statistics

Road	Number of Stations	Average Distance Between Stations (km.)	Average Population Per Station	Average Number of Commoner Inns (Hatagoya) Per Station
Tōkaidō	57	8.4	3,950	55
Nakasendō	67	5.2	1,165	27
Nikkō dōchū	21	5.0	2,264	39
Ōshū dōchū	10	7.9	1,186	27
Kōshū dōchū	45	4.2	779	11
Sayaji	4	4.6	946	15
Minoji	7	5.0	2,836	13.7
Mibudō	7	5.0	892	17
Reiheishidō	13	4.7	1,411	21
Mito-Sakuradō	3	5.1	1,141	13
Nikkō onaridō	5	8.4	1,567	7
Honzaka dōri	3	12.1	504	4
Yamazaki dōri	6	8.0	2,089	24

Source: Based on data from Kodama Kōta, *Shukueki*, pp. 177–230.

Note: The data is based on a bakufu survey from 1843.

ulation of 564 (1843) was supported almost entirely by travel-related services such as transport, entertainment, food and drink, and lodging; hence, once the post station system was abolished in 1872, Sakanoshita became a virtual ghost-town. A second type of small station was barely distinguishable from any other agricultural village except that as a sideline some farmers offered limited services to travelers. Ishiyakushi (pop. 991) and Shōno (pop. 855) are typical examples of this type of station.[17] Other types of post stations, however, served many purposes, the station itself occupying only a small part of the physical space of the settlement. For Yokkaichi (pop. 7,114), which doubled as a port town, its function as a post station played a minor role in the economic life of the urban center itself. In fact, most Tōkaidō stations with commercial facilities supported populations of at least 3,000.

A fourth type of station was located in castle towns, and, like the third category, played a minor economic role, which was reflected by the small amount of physical space it occupied. Post station functions were assigned to a number of wards lining the road—in the case of Hamamatsu, to six out of a total of twenty-four wards in the city.[18] The Tōkaidō boasted nine castle towns (Fuchū, Kuwana, Okazaki, Hamamatsu, Odawara, Numazu, Yoshida, Kakegawa, and Kameyama) and their populations varied according to location as well as the nature and extent of any auxiliary functions performed. Inland castle towns like Kameyama (pop. 1,549) were dwarfed by more advantageously located settlements such as Kuwana (pop. 8,848), which also doubled as a port. (For details on Tōkaidō post stations in 1843, see Appendix 1.)

There was great variation among post stations in economic function, and the range in population varied according to function, but a majority of stations on the main arteries of the Gokaidō (not including branch roads) supported fewer than 1,000 residents.[19] Almost one-third numbered 1,000–2,999 residents and the remainder realized larger totals based on other, largely commercial and administrative, functions and occasionally as entertainment for nearby large urban centers as well. Tōkaidō stations, however, supported larger populations than those on other roads. On the main road and its extension to Osaka less than 16 percent of the stations had populations less than 1,000 while the remaining 84 percent were divided evenly between the 1,000–2,999 and the 3,000+ ranges. The villages, post stations and other urban settlements along the Tōkaidō seemed so populated that another German physician with the Dutch in Japan, Philipp Franz von Siebold (1826), remarked that, "Except for a small portion of the Tōkaidō which passes through a mountainous region, the road consists of almost a continuous line of towns, villages, and teahouses."[20] In comparison, a majority of the stations on the other Gokaidō roads supported populations of under 1,000. Stations off the Gokaidō network were smaller, supported smaller populations and, as Kaempfer and other travelers noted, offered fewer services.

Although the primary purpose of post stations was to service official traffic, it would have been prohibitively expensive to maintain the post system if the work force was allowed to sit idle between periods of official use. Thus commoner use of its transport services was allowed and, in fact, encouraged. The bakufu also gave post stations different types of economic support in order to further offset the costs of providing services for official travelers. The stations were initially granted tax-free land, the amount varying according to the distance between the stations as well as the degree of difficulty of the stretch of road between them.[21] The amount of land exempt from taxation was subsequently increased proportionately in the 1630's when the stations were ordered to maintain larger numbers of porters and post horses.[22] The bakufu also paid the salaries of post station managers.[23] It further provided a small rice stipend to all stations on the Tōkaidō, Minoji, and Sayaji, as well as to eleven stations on the Nakasendō, for maintaining a messenger service (*tsugi hikyaku*) for official communications.[24]

To provide economic support to the post stations, the bakufu instituted a relay method of transporting people, goods, and written communications. Without any revolutionary technological advances, communications could be made more efficient only by an effort to make the "best use of the already existing means of conveyance . . . and [by] organizing a more efficient and intensive circulation."[25] Efficiency was achieved on the Gokaidō by employing a relay system and by spacing the nearly 250 post stations at an average interval of eight kilometers. Like Europe in the following century, the economic take-off in Japan during the 1600s "coincided with the peak achieved by traditional methods of circulation."[26]

The use of this relay method assured every station its share of business. The prohibition against skipping any post station obliged travelers to change at each post stop: they switched palanquins or horses and goods were transferred to another horse that worked the stretch of road to the following station.[27]

The bakufu was concerned about the smooth operation of the system. Post stations were ordered to perform the relay "without delay, day or night, rain or shine."[28] They were further instructed to dispatch horses as soon as they were relayed to the station according to demand, rather than holding them in reserve for any private user of the system. Nevertheless, stations were required, of course, to reserve porters and horses for official travelers and cargo.[29] Should no horses be immediately available, the post-station manager was to establish a numbered order for waiting travelers in order to expedite the dispatching of horses as they arrived.[30]

Foreigners complained about the inconvenience of the relays, but the system was created in part to prevent porters and horses from being worn out.[31] Load limits were also established and served the same purpose.[32] Nevertheless, the primary intent behind the relay system was economic: hence the bakufu's policy of discouraging sea transport, which would have allowed travelers to skip post stations and would reduce the amount of revenue they could raise through provision of transport services. For example, on several occasions the authorities prohibited pilgrims to Mount Fuji or Ōyama from traveling by water from Edo to Kanagawa because this route bypassed Shinagawa and Kawasaki stations.[33]

The focus here has been on the central government; but the private domains, particularly those of the vassal, or *fudai*, daimyo, had always tended to follow the bakufu's lead in overland communications: they established domainal post station systems, employed the relay method, and required official users of the system to carry written documents of authorization for transport services.[34] Even the wording of regulations that some domains sent to their post stations was quite similar to that of the bakufu's regulations.[35]

For transport services offered at post stations, the bakufu established a three-tiered system of rates that reflected the official nature of the Tokugawa communications network. The first tier allowed free (*muchin*) transport for more than seventy-nine categories of travelers and goods, including those with the authorization of the shogun, the Office of Senior Councilors (*rōjū*), the Kyoto Deputy (*Kyōto shoshidai*), and the Finance Magistrate. A wide range of people and goods traveled or were transported at no cost: certain bakufu officials and messengers, court nobles, members of shogunal processions and foreign missions, letter boxes with official bakufu and daimyo correspondence, the shogun's tea from Uji, the tatami covering (*tatami omote*) for Edo Castle coming from Bingo province, and so forth.[36]

The second tier in the rate system offered transport services at a fixed rate (*osadame chinsen*) set by the bakufu for seventeen categories of travelers and goods. These categories included many ranking bakufu officials, such as the Keeper of Sunpu Castle; the guards for Nijō, Osaka and Sunpu castles; and bakufu messengers to the Three Houses (*gosanke*). More importantly, daimyo and their retainers were also granted the privilege of using a designated number of porters and pack horses at the fixed rate.[37]

The third tier was for the masses and offered transport services at a negotiable rate (*aitai chinsen*). Instead of being charged the fixed rate available at the post station transport center, or *ton'ya-ba*, commoners were obliged to negotiate directly with porters at the roadside for their services. The negotiated rate fluctuated with the price of commodity goods, but was usually about twice that of the fixed rate.[38]

Transport rates and load limits for transport services were first set early on, in 1602.[39] Fees for transport labor varied from station to station according to distance, the difficulty of terrain, and local grain costs. Prices for the various transport services offered were listed on a placard posted near both entrances to each station. Rates charged on the Tōkaidō were about one-third more expensive than those on the Nakasendō, while those on other Gokaidō roads were, in turn, around one-third less than on the Nakasendō.[40]

Load limits were standardized to protect transport workers and regularize the income earned by the stations. A porter was allowed to carry up to 5 *kan* (18.8 kilograms) for a designated fee; if the traveler's baggage weighed just slightly more, a tip was usually necessary.[41] A load much in excess of 5 *kan* could be transported by hiring more than one porter or by hiring a pack horse. These horses were specially bred for strength and, by regulation, could carry up to 40 *kan* (150 kg.), a capacity comparable to that of any eighteenth-century English pack horse.[42] A traveler could also ride a horse from station to station and was allowed to carry with him up to 5 *kan* of personal baggage. Rates for this type of load, known as *karajiri*, or "light load," cost about one-third more than hiring a porter.[43] Like Yaji and Kita, Jippensha Ikku's peripatetic characters in *Hizakurige* (*On Shank's Mare*), commoners of no great financial means could obtain much less expensive rates by negotiating with porters returning to their base station with no rider or load to carry.

To be able to offer transport services for official travelers and their goods, post stations were required to maintain a designated number of porters and horses. These were supplied by households in the station and obligations were generally assessed on the basis of road frontage and location.[44] The land-tax exemption granted to many stations was divided among roadside households that provided transport services for official cargo and travelers. Some households provided horses; others provided porters; and they all rotated their duties on a regular basis.[45] But soon after the establishment of the transport network on the Tōkaidō, it became clear that the current system could not meet the growing demand for its services.

After the Battle of Sekigahara, Ieyasu moved quickly to take control of overland communications as part of his effort to bring the country under his hegemony. Perhaps one reason why he exerted so much effort to establish the Gokaidō system, with its roads, bridges, river crossings, and lodging facilities, was the knowledge that a well-developed system of transport would be necessary in order to mobilize a large army for his eventual showdown—at Osaka, in 1614-1615—against the forces aligned with the Toyotomi. Hideyoshi, and Nobunaga before him, had also expended much effort in improving roads for military purposes.

Daimyo began to call on Ieyasu and his successor, Hidetada, at Fushimi, Edo, and Sunpu shortly after the Tokugawa victory in 1600. Later, in 1635, these daimyo trips to the shogun's capital would be regularized as the system of alternate attendance. Daimyo brought such large numbers of retainers in their entourages and paraded them so conspicuously up the highways to Edo that the bakufu admonished them repeatedly to reduce the size of their entourages.[46] The Tōkaidō was the most traveled route, used by nearly three-fifths of the daimyo; and this fact spurred its continual development.[47] Ieyasu himself, since 1601, had followed a routine of commuting, which took him back and forth along the Tōkaidō between Edo, Kyoto, and Fushimi; during the spring of 1603 and the autumn of 1606 he made four such round trips.[48] Sunpu served as a second center of administration during Ieyasu's retirement from 1606 until his death in 1616; this arrangement resulted in a stream of bakufu officials scurrying between Sunpu and Edo.

Eleven bakufu processions to Kyoto between 1605 and 1634, climaxed by Iemitsu's procession of more than 300,000 men, brought about the realization that the existing system required expansion and gave rise to efforts to improve the transport infrastructure.[49] Before each trip the bakufu ordered the repair of roads and bridges on the shogunal route, the Tōkaidō, in all domains, regardless of whether they were house (bakufu) or private lands.[50] The need to amass a large army to suppress the rebellion at Shimabara in 1637–1638 only further emphasized the need to expand the system.

In response to the increased demands for transport services brought on by official traffic, daimyo alternate attendance, and economic expansion, post stations on the Tōkaidō were ordered sometime during the late 1630s or early 1640s to increase the transport work force maintained there almost threefold to 100 porters and 100 horses. Those on the Nakasendō were ordered to keep 50 of each, and all others in the Gokaidō network were ordered to keep 25.[51] On all roads post horses were accompanied by one attendant each. Some stations were already maintaining more than the required number of horses and porters. Hamamatsu, on the Tōkaidō, for example, had already increased their horses to 75;[52] not all post stations, however, were able to maintain the required 100 horses, and some never even attained that figure.

As part of its centrist policy to control overland communications, the bakufu assumed jurisdiction over all roads in the Gokaidō system. This assumption of power helped to establish the bakufu's political authority over the daimyo and distinguishes the Tokugawa polity from its predecessors. As another foreign visitor to late-Tokugawa Japan, Sir Rutherford Alcock, noted, "There is an arrangement in this country already alluded to, by which certain high roads, the great arteries of the empire, leading to and from Miaco [Kyoto] and Yeddo [Edo], are made imperial [i.e., bakufu] property. . . . The road between there and from them, to the other imperial cities on the coast, although passing through the domains of the several Daimios, are in no sense considered as a part of their territories, or under their jurisdiction."[53] Unlike roads in Tokugawa Japan, English roads in the mid eighteenth century were maintained not by a government department, but by turnpike trusts, local, statutory bodies created by Parliament, which managed sections of the road and charged travelers tolls in return for their services; the turnpike trusts took over from the older system of parishes, which were often unable or unwilling to pay for adequate upkeep of the roads.[54]

The Tokugawa usurped domainal authority by assuming jurisdiction over the central road network and post stations, regardless of the territory covered by the system. Domains, however, were largely held responsible for the upkeep of the transport infrastructure, which included roads, bridges, river crossings, and roadside trees. Domains were also required to supplement—and at times to provide the major share of—the work force of porters and post horses maintained at stations.

By usurping domainal prerogative and declaring all Gokaidō roads bakufu territory, the bakufu was able to assure that communications would not be disrupted by individual daimyo, as they had been in the Warring States period. As Alcock said, nationalizing the Gokaidō "was a very needful reservation . . . as otherwise they [i.e., the daimyo] could stop all traffic and communications throughout the empire . . . [and] levy a tax *in transitu* upon produce, as did our barons of yore in the good old time, and so arrest all development of trade."[55] To prevent this problem, the shogunate ordered in 1617 that, "Roads, post-horses, boats and bridges shall be used freely, without interruption." It further prohibited the erection of private barriers on roads and the detention of vessels in ports.[56]

The post stations and the land tax exemptions that assisted them were both elements in the assertion of bakufu authority through the Gokaidō network, and both infringed on domainal prerogative. Although, according to one bakufu source, about one-half of all Gokaidō post stations lay in Tokugawa territory and the other half in private, or daimyo, lands,[57] requisition orders for transport services issued by the bakufu for officials traveling anywhere in the country had to be honored at local cost.[58] Moreover, shogunal transport received priority in the domains over that of any local daimyo.[59]

The transport of Tokugawa written communications also received top priority. Official messengers (*hikyaku:* lit., "flying feet"), who always traveled in pairs, one carrying the lacquered message box (*gojōbako*) and the other a paper lantern on a pole for use at night, were given right of way on the roads. In Kaempfer's words, all travelers, even daimyo, "must retire out of the way, and give free passage to those messengers, who carry letters or orders from the Emperor [i.e., the shogun], which they take care to signify at a due distance, by ringing a bell."[60] Moreover, when the waters of flooded rivers receded to acceptable levels, they were the first to be allowed across.

The domains, no doubt, resented the various prerogatives concerning communications that the bakufu took unto itself. This is evident, for example, from the fact that daimyo, in the closing decades of bakufu rule, disputed the right of foreign representatives to deviate "a single step to one side or the other" from the main roads. In every town where he stopped, Alcock noted that "curtains bearing a Daimio's arms were raised, not only preventing any passage, but shutting out the view of the streets branching off."[61] For more than two hundred years, the Tokugawa system of alternate attendance required daimyo to pass through others' territories on the way to and from Edo, again infringing upon their prerogatives as domainal rulers.

While overland communications were a top priority of the early Tokugawa government, a specialized administrative post, the Magistrate of Road Affairs (*dōchū bugyō*), was not created until 1659. This Magistrate served concurrently as one of a small number of Inspectors General (*Ōmetsuke*).[62] A second position was added before the turn of the century, and this official was chosen from among the Magistrates of Finance (*kanjō bugyō*); he too served in a double capacity.[63] Finance Magistrates were already involved in road affairs in that they were charged with administration of bakufu lands, which included the Gokaidō, as well as finances. Thus, this order only meant that one of them would become more specialized. The Magistrate of Finance, however, continued to have jurisdiction over all roads not administered by the Magistrate of Road Affairs. The major responsibilities of these officials included the overseeing of the upkeep of the road infrastructure and the processing of petitions presented to the Magistracy.[64]

Communications policy was implemented by the Magistrate of Road Affairs through bakufu intendants (*daikan*), who were required to report on all matters concerning roads, post stations, travelers, and any other pertinent matters in their areas of jurisdiction.[65] In the 1720s, administration was centralized further by taking road affairs out of the hands of intendants and placing them solely under the care of the Magistrate of Road Affairs, who was assisted by a number of auxiliary officials (*dōshin* and *yoriki*).

THE ROAD INFRASTRUCTURE

The nature of the early modern order in Japan, often referred to as "centralized feudalism" because of the balance of tension between the centripetal force of the bakufu and the centrifugal force of the daimyo, was actually conducive to the development of an integrated road system. The central government, motivated by military, administrative, and economic rationale, created the main arteries, or the Gokaidō. The domains, on the other hand, created the secondary network out of the need to establish the castle town as the economic center of their territories, to provide adequate conditions for the passage of Tokugawa officials, to guarantee the passage of daimyo on alternate attendance to and from Edo, and, if possible, to establish overland links to the commercially developed Kinai area. The first Tokugawa shogun, after moving to his new domain in eastern Japan in 1590, followed the pattern set by daimyo of the Warring States period; he centered his domainal transport network around his administrative center, Edo. This pattern continued after the establishment of the shogunate in 1603, as Edo remained the focal point in the bakufu's central road network. Four major thoroughfares radiated directly outward from that city, and a fifth branched off from one of the other four. Like the great roads of the Roman Empire, which all began at the Forum, the Gokaidō began at Nihonbashi—the "Bridge of Japan"—which was the symbolic center of the land.

The Tōkaidō linked Edo, the new administrative capital, with the older capital at Kyoto. Between Edo and Odawara, the Tōkaidō followed the coastline, except where it crossed the Miura peninsula. One can sense the closeness of the ocean in the 1689 diary account of Inoue Tsūjo, the daughter of a Marugame (Sanuki) samurai, who, on her way home down the Tōkaidō, describes the loud sound of waves echoing in the wind that blew through the roadside trees.[66] In fact, for most of the way between Edo and Kanagawa, the road was near the water's edge, necessitating the construction of sea walls. After passing through a mountainous area around Odawara, Hakone, and Mishima that surely tested the traveler's stamina, it then crossed the Sagami peninsula and skirted along the coast of Suruga Bay, before turning inland after Ejiri. The ocean was again visible more than ten stations down the road, around Maisaka, Arai, and

Shirasuka, and then again at Miya, Kuwana, and Yokkaichi (the crossing between Miya and Kuwana was a distance of almost thirty kilometers over the open sea). Past Yokkaichi, the Tōkaidō headed inland, north-west, towards Kyoto. The Tōkaidō was extended by seven stages and fifty-one kilometers, as Tokugawa power increased with the fall of Osaka Castle in 1615, adding to the 53 stages and 488 kilometers that made up the main route. The extension from Fushimi to Osaka thus provided Edo with a direct link to that important commercial center.

It was common for Tokugawa travelers to take the Nakasendō, which also connected Kyoto with Edo, on the return leg of a journey to the Kinai from the Kantō or other points east. The change in scenery, the cheaper rates for transport-related services and the fewer number of river crossings on the Nakasendō no doubt had a lot to do with this. This "road through the mountains," as its name denotes, followed the same line as the Tōkaidō from Kyoto to Kusatsu. After Kusatsu it moved north and east through Sekigahara and Tarui, across Mino and into Shinano province by way of Shimo-Suwa, Kutsukake, and Karuizawa. Then, bending towards the southeast, it passed through Kōzuke and Musashi before reaching its terminus at Edo, sixty-seven stations and 527 kilometers later. Although in contemporary times it was frequently called the Kiso kaidō, in the strict sense the latter refers only to the stretch of road passing through eleven stations, from Niekawa to Magome.

The third member of the Gokaidō, the Kōshū dōchū, was named after the mountainous province of Kai through which it passed on its 211-kilometer route from Edo to Shimo-Suwa in Shinano, where it then connected with the Nakasendō. The entire road was lined with the domains of fudai daimyo. It provided direct access to the gold mines developed by the Warring States lord Takeda Shingen, which had helped enrich bakufu coffers early in the Tokugawa period. Moreover, the Kōshū dōchū provided an escape route for the shogunate in the case of an attack from the north or the west. A retreating party could pick up the road right at the Hanzōmon Gate of Edo Castle. At Naitō Shinjuku, on the western outskirts of the city, a 100-man musket unit was kept ready. Further west, at Hachiōji, a 1,000-man samurai unit (the *Hachiō-ji sennin dōshin*), organized from the surviving retainers of the Takeda family, was strategically placed to cover the escape route.[67] Continuing west, the castle of Kōfu, which was in fudai daimyo hands, provided still more protection. From Kōfu, the escaping party had two possibilities. The first was simply to continue north to the Nakasendō; the second was to travel by boat down the Fuji River to Sunpu, a bakufu-controlled stronghold on the Tōkaidō.[68]

The last two roads in the Gokaidō network gave the bakufu a direct line of communications with which to meet a possible threat from the northern daimyo. The Ōshū dōchū branched off from the Nikkō dōchū at Utsunomiya (Shimotsuke province) and went as far as Shirakawa (Iwashiro), a castle town under Tokugawa fudai daimyo control. The Nikkō dōchū stretched almost 145 kilometers from Edo to its terminus at Nikkō Tōshō-gū (Shimotsuke).[69] Filling out the system were a total of eight branch roads.[70]

In addition to the Gokaidō and its branch roads, there were a number of other roads of some importance to the bakufu which were drawn under the administration of the Magistrate of Road Affairs. Foremost among these was the Chūgokuji, known since Meiji times as the San-yōdō. This route ran west from Kyoto along the shore of the Inland Sea through Okayama and Hiroshima to Shimonoseki on the southern tip of Honshū. Three roads, the Hokkoku kaidō, Mikuni kaidō, and the Aizu dōri, provided the bakufu with important links to the gold and silver mines of Sado.[71] A fifth road, the Iseji, branched off from the Tōkaidō at Yokkaichi and ran to the sacred precincts of Ise Shrine, one of the principal sites for pilgrimage in the Edo period.

The Nagasakidō, which ran from Kokura to Nagasaki, was the only major road in Kyushu and served as the lifeline leading to Nagasaki, Tokugawa Japan's principal window to the outside world. There were other, smaller roads in this area, such as the Satsuma kaidō, Hyūga kaidō, and Karatsu kaidō.[72] Shikoku, on the other hand, had only a small number of minor roads. There were two principal routes in northern Japan, the Ōshū kaidō (not to be confused with the Ōshū dōchū) and the Matsumae dōri, which branched off the Ōshū dōchū. Hokkaidō was, of course, largely uncharted territory.

During the course of an overland journey, Tokugawa travelers would have found it difficult to avoid stepping into a boat at some point to cross a body of water. Water crossings at rivers, as well as an open-sea crossing (between Miya and Kuwana) and passage across a lake, Lake Hamana (between Maisaka and Arai stations), were integrated into the Gokaidō network.

A trip down the Tōkaidō, for example, involved crossing twelve rivers and possibly the two longer stretches mentioned above as well. Jippensha Ikku's characters Yaji and Kita make the trip by boat from Maisaka to Arai. Ikku describes the situation at Arai, where "all the passengers got off the boat with cries of thankfulness that they had arrived in safety."[73] Travel by boat was more dangerous than going overland. In fact, not traveling by sea was one of the precepts the doctor Tachibana Nankei (1753–1805) followed when away from home.[74] The alternative, land routes, however, were circuitous and therefore took longer. Two routes connected to the Tōkaidō, the Sayaji and the Honzaka dōri, were also dubbed "*hime kaidō*" (lit., "princess roads"), supposedly because women, having less "stomach" for water travel, opted for them more often than did men.

Back on land, travelers like the National Learning scholar Sugae Masumi (1754?–1829) and the loyalist Takayama Hikokurō (1747–1793) might have observed that roads largely conformed to the natural contours of the land. For the most part, Tokugawa thoroughfares passed along the bases of mountain masses and crossed rivers at right angles. In mountainous or hilly areas, highways tended to be straight with steep inclines, rather than being graded for motor vehicles as are modern-day roads. In Englebert Kaempfer's words, the roads "go over hills and mountains, which are sometimes so steep and high, that travelers are necessitated to get themselves carried over them [in palanquins]."[75]

The road leading to and from post stations was often square-shaped, involving one or more 90–180 degree bends at each approach, as at Fujisawa post station, where the Enoshimadō branches off from the Tōkaidō. These bends, known as *masu kata*, were found at many post stations, particularly those on the Tōkaidō, such as at Fujisawa. They were defensive: their L-shapes were designed to bottle up an invading force as it approached the station. Although there is no direct evidence that the bends in the roads were a Tokugawa invention, it seems unlikely that such a widespread engineering feat could have been carried out during the Warring States period. It seems more likely that they were, like sekisho, an example of early Tokugawa preoccupation with military deterrence; this interpretation is supported by the fact that the *masu kata* were also a standard feature in Edo-period castle towns. Both *masu kata* and sekisho were concerns which, by the end of the seventeenth century, would seem anachronistic in an age where, according to one contemporary writer, "the sword remains forever sheathed and peace reigns eternal."[76]

No bakufu documentation exists prescribing widths for specific routes, yet the reply of the Magistrate of Road Affairs to a daimyo query on the matter stated that "while road widths are not fixed, they generally should be 2–4 *ken* [3.6–7.3 meters]."[77] Walking requires little in the way of a path; riding on horseback or driving a pack-horse necessitates a track which is slightly broader and better prepared. Kaempfer found Tokugawa highways "broad and large," wide enough that "two companies, tho' never so great, can conveniently and without hindrance, pass by one another."[78] The Gokaidō was made for pedestrians rather than vehicular traffic and therefore it was not necessary for it to have particularly wide or straight roads. In general, a minimum of almost four meters was necessary for pack horses to pass one another safely,[79] and because this minimum was safely met on almost the entire Gokaidō network, the bakufu does not appear to have been particularly concerned with road widths there.

Since Tokugawa roads were largely determined by geography and followed the natural contour of the land, many stretches of road, particularly off the Tōkaidō and Nikkō dōchū, were not completely straight. Road widths, therefore, necessarily varied. For example, between Fujisawa and Hiratsuka, two stations on the Tōkaidō, different stretches of road fluctuated in width between 5.5 and 11 meters. According to a bakufu survey of the roads taken sometime during the beginning of the nineteenth century, road widths on the Tōkaidō as a whole ranged from 2.7 to 14.6 meters, but the two extremes were rare and in fact most stretches were 5.5 to 7.3 meters.[80] Roads tended to be wider near castle towns and quite narrow in mountainous areas.[81]

The daimyo, like the bakufu, were motivated to improve transport facilities in order to promote the flow of commodity goods into urban markets as well as to establish the castle town as the economic center of the domain. Road systems were devised, using main highways to connect the castle town with all important points of communication, both within and outside the domain; secondary road systems branched off the main routes to reach even remote villages. In Kaga, for example, "the domain straightened and repaired a twisting roadway which ran from the port of Miyanokoshi to the northwest entrance of the castle town, thus speeding deliveries of fresh fish and other foodstuffs to the city." Throughout the domain, new roads were built and existing ones repaired or upgraded, such as those connecting Kanazawa with both sides of the Noto peninsula.[82] In Okayama, the Sanyōdō was rerouted through the castle town and the use of alternate routes was discouraged by domain policy.[83] New routes—often called *kome kaidō*, or "rice roads"—were opened up across the country to transport tax rice; many of these routes led to river or ocean ports, where the goods were shipped to the domain castle town, Edo, or Osaka.[84]

Economic considerations alone, however, do not account for the development of transport routes. Those roads used by other daimyo on alternate attendance trips had to be maintained in good condition, lest a domain risk incurring the wrath of the bakufu. The dispatching of bakufu inspectors to the domains early in the seventeenth century also led directly to the improvement of road conditions and travel facilities.[85] Those routes used by bakufu officials and daimyo on alternate attendance were, not surprisingly, maintained better than other domain roads.

Compared with early modern France, where "local initiative in improving communications was meagre,"[86] the domains in Tokugawa Japan played a large part in developing a communication system. Or as one authority put it, "Tokugawa regional institutions—the administration of many *han*—achieved considerable efficiency in contrast to the frequent immobility of European local administration."[87] An isolationist sentiment, or the fear that better links with the provinces would facilitate the dominance of the center—Paris in France and Edo in Japan—was not widely present in Japan's case.[88] In England, too, the people did not want central control of the roads, "because it would have added considerably to the power of the government as well as leading to an increase in taxation," which accounts for the development of local turnpike trusts in the eighteenth century.[89] Even if isolationist sentiments were present in Japan, the fear of possible reprisals from the Tokugawa early on, as well as the realization that the economic benefits of the system outweighed any possible dangers, caused most domain leaders to overcome these sentiments. Here, *sankin kōtai* was an important factor, for the domains' need to export in order to finance the costs of that feudal duty precluded the possibility of isolationism and self-sufficiency.[90] With the combination of all the individual efforts of the domains, who had such a stake in developing transport within their own realms, Tokugawa Japan found itself with a well-integrated system rather than a mere skeleton of a highway network.[91]

MAINTENANCE AND GENERAL ROAD CONDITIONS

The Gokaidō infrastructure, far from being backward, was well-developed and drew almost universal praise from Western visitors, who compared conditions in Japan quite favorably with those in their native lands. The road system was in this admirable state because of the concerted efforts of the Tokugawa to keep at least the most heavily traveled routes in top condition, for as the bakufu ordered, "The roads, post-horse relays, ferries and bridges must be carefully attended to, so as to insure that there shall be no delays or impediments to speedy communications."[92]

The Gokaidō was symbolic of the Tokugawa state and reflected its authority. How effective would it have been, for example, to parade the foreign representatives from Korea and the Ryukyuan kingdom, both of whom were used as "legitimizing propaganda" for the bakufu, up pot-hole-riddled highways?[93] Similarly, for the passage of government officials, Tokugawa family members, and other grand personages, poorly kept roads would not reflect well upon bakufu authority; thus orders were routinely given to repair roads and bridges on these occasions.[94] Daimyo, too, for reasons of prestige, had incentive to keep up with maintenance on those roads used by other daimyo on alternate attendance as well as by shogunal Inspectors sent to examine local conditions. Careful attention to maintenance of the road infrastructure by bakufu and daimyo alike kept conditions impressively good.

One might expect then that conditions would deteriorate as the grip of Tokugawa controls eased. There were some complaints about the roads in places close to Edo in the last years of the bakufu, but the evidence indicates that, in general, the condition of roads did not decline.[95] Although maintenance of the road infrastructure was, in effect, a tax imposed on the domains by the bakufu, it was in a domain's best economic interest to allow communications to flow unimpeded.

For contemporary descriptions of the state of the Tokugawa transport infrastructure we must, to a large extent, rely upon the written records that foreign visitors to Japan have left us. Native travelers were not as likely to comment unless road conditions were extraordinary. That foreigners did frequently commit their impressions to paper attests to the fact that they found road conditions different—and, as we shall see, better— than in their own countries. Charles Thunberg, the Swedish doctor attached to the Dutch commercial outpost on Deshima, made one trip to the capital in 1776 and spoke positively of the general state of Tokugawa Japan's thoroughfares: "The roads in this country are broad, and furnished with two ditches, to carry off the water, and [are] in good order all the year round; but especially at this season [spring], when the Princes of the country, as also the Dutch, take their annual journey to the capital. The roads are, at this time, not only strewed with sand, but, before the arrival of travelers, they are swept with brooms; all horse dung, and dirt of every kind, removed, and in hot, dusty weather, they are watered."[96]

In comparison, contemporary English roads were in a poor state. One authority writes, "The appalling state of the roads in the seventeenth and eighteenth centuries is evident from most contemporary accounts. For much of the year, the soft roads remained impassable. They were often so narrow that two pack-horses could only pass with difficulty, and in winter became so flooded that they were turned into permanent bogs, strewn with big boulders."[97] The turnpike trusts of the eighteenth century were responsible for some improvements, but general mismanagement by local bodies was detrimental to the condition of roads.[98] It was only with the onset of the industrial revolution in England in the 1830s that road conditions there improved rapidly, largely thanks to a new technological development, the process of macadamizing roads.[99]

Foreign visitors to Tokugawa Japan have also left us specific comments about road conditions on the Tōkaidō. It is not surprising that a thoroughfare of such importance was so well-maintained (see Figure 1). Writing very early in the seventeenth century, the Englishman John Saris reported that the road to Suruga, "for the most part is wonderfully even. . . . This way is the mayne Roade of all this Countrey, and is for the most part sandie and gravell."[100] In the middle of the same century, the Swedish physician Olof Willman was so impressed with the infrastructure on the Tōkaidō that he wrote, "Probably no other road in the world costs as much as this."[101] Later, in the middle of the nineteenth century, when an industrializing Europe was in many ways far more technologically advanced than Japan, the Swiss envoy Aimé Humbert wrote, "Compared with the great roads of Europe, the Tōkaidō is not the least bit inferior." In terms of the conveniences it offered the pedestrian traveler, he noted, "it is in certain respects, superior."[102]

It is, in fact, difficult to find outright criticism of conditions on the Tōkaidō by contemporary visitors from abroad. Any criticisms that were expressed were usually lodged after a heavy rainfall. One foreign observer noted that the Tōkaidō and the Nagasaki dōri (referred to in the text as the Saikaidō) was "at all times good and pleasant, unless it be just rainy weather and the ground slimy."[103] More usual were comments like that made by Townsend Harris in 1857: "[We] left Fusisawa [Fujisawa] at seven A.M. The road is very pleasant, as the plain gradually widens as we approach Yedo."[104] Alcock and Kaempfer frequently remarked that the road on different stretches of the Tōkaidō was a "beautiful sanded avenue" or "straight and even."[105]

Their comments are not surprising, for the Tōkaidō was the flattest of the Tokugawa roads running from east to west. The entire length of the road, with the exception of three stretches (the Satta Pass near Yui, the mountainous road near Seki, and Hakone), was under 200 meters in altitude. In earlier times, roads tended to cut vertically across hilly areas, whereas in the Tokugawa period, with advances in agricultural and riparian technology, villages moved from the highlands to low-lying areas and roads generally followed suit.[106]

The three mountainous sections of the Tōkaidō were often difficult to traverse. A trip up and down the many steep inclines of the Hakone area, for example, rarely failed to elicit complaints from travelers, particularly after a heavy rainfall, when the stone-paved road was wet.[107] It was safer to walk rather than ride over the Hakone mountain range, as a number of travelers who fell on the rocks discovered. The fall could be particularly painful for those riding in a palanquin, as Ōta Shokusanjin and the

Figure 1 The Tōkaidō Near Kanagawa. Felix Beato. 1860s. Courtesy of Yokohama Kaikō Shiryōkan.

Dutchman Van Overmeer Fisscher recorded.[108] Inoue Tsūjo, the erudite daughter of a samurai from Marugame, wisely opted to walk: on the inclines she "gasped for breath" as if she was "about to collapse," while on the descents she felt as if she would "surely tumble down."[109]

Particularly steep areas on a number of roads were paved with stones both to facilitate passage when the road was dry and to prevent mudslides when it was raining.[110] For example, about one-third of the road between Mishima and Odawara (the stations on either side of Hakone) was paved, and there were at least eight stretches of paved road on the Nakasendō.[111] These rocks were not simply laid in place: recent, preliminary excavations have revealed that careful attention was paid to the underlying surface as well as to drainage.[112]

To aid travelers on these difficult stretches of road, alms-huts (*segyō-sho*) were established through private initiative in the early nineteenth century. The abbot of a temple in Hakone established such a place on a difficult stretch of road near that post town. At this alms-hut, and at two similar establishments on the Nakasendō, poor travelers and porters were offered firewood and rice gruel during the cold winter months. When the abbot at Hakone was unable to continue operating his alms-hut, he solicited the economic assistance of a dry-goods merchant from Edo. The merchant petitioned both the bakufu and domanial authorities in Odawara to participate in the scheme, but was rejected by both.[113]

Although the bakufu refused to help provide alms for travelers and transport workers, it did pay close attention to maintaining road conditions. Early on, in 1612, instructions were issued to bakufu intendants that:

1. Areas worn down by the weight of traffic, on both major and minor roads, should be filled in with either sand or stones to give them a hard surface and water should be drained off into ditches dug on both sides of the road. Muddy sections should be treated in the same manner.
2. Grass on the road embankments must not be removed.
3. In all areas, whether under shogunal or private control, bridges, large and small, in poor condition must be repaired by the authority of an intendant or his deputies.[114]

As indicated by this directive, damage to roads due to rainfall was minimized by ditches and outlets dug on both sides of the road, which carried

off the water towards low fields; sometimes a mountain stream was diverted alongside a road to provide travelers and horses with refreshment. Grass on road embankments was not to be cut, for it prevented rain and mud from flooding the road. Moreover, as Kaempfer noted, strong dikes were cast up to keep rain water from coming down from higher places.[115] Officials from the Magistrate of Road Affairs were dispatched periodically to inspect the thoroughfares and report on whether repair and maintenance work was being performed adequately. Repairs were carried out according to orders by bakufu intendants or by daimyo, depending on the section of road in question.

Villages lying along or near the highway, regardless of domain, were assessed corvée labor to repair and clean assigned sections of roads.[116] Like the *sukegō* tax, demands for corvée to repair and clean roads were greatest during the agricultural season, when the volume of official traffic on the highways was at its highest.

While there are ample descriptions of road conditions on the Tōkaidō in written travel accounts that foreigners have left us, descriptions of the other routes in the Gokaidō network are not so easy to come by. What evidence there is, however, tells us that the Nakasendō, and particularly the Kiso kaidō portion of it, was a difficult, mountainous road.[117] A samurai from Nabeshima who wandered around Japan for two years (1853–1855) training in swordsmanship found the Kiso kaidō "as difficult as rumor had it to be."[118] Another samurai traveling at the same time (1855) was, however, much less critical: He said, "Some people are afraid of traveling on the Kisoji [i.e., the Kiso kaidō], but that is a thing of the past. Today the road is level and there is no problem procuring horses or palanquins. Daimyo and court nobles travel it just as they do the Tōkaidō. The only 'difficulty' one encounters is the lack of fresh fish available."[119] Furukawa Koshōken, a geographer traveling with a group of bakufu inspectors in 1788, found the Nikkō dōchū a "flat, sanded avenue." From Utsunomiya, however, where he branched off onto the Ōshū dōchū, the road was rocky, the roadside trees (*namiki*) were few in number, and the houses on both sides of the road were shabby-looking.[120] On the Nagasakidō, a Gokaidō branch road quite distant from Edo, Alcock, in the closing years of the bakufu, commented, "During the first five days [from Nagasaki to Kokura—a nine-day journey], the roads, without being as

bad as cross-roads in many European countries to this day, were nonetheless in striking contrast to the fine broad avenues which constitute the
Tocado [i.e., Tōkaidō] of Nipon."[121]

A mistake made by Griffis in 1871 confirms that conditions on Gokaidō branch roads were not necessarily inferior to the main thoroughfares.
Coming from Fukui in Echizen on secondary roads, he hit the Minoji,
a branch artery that linked the Nakasendō and the Tōkaidō. The
improvement led him to believe that he had reached the Tōkaidō itself,
and his reasoning tells us how good the conditions in the Gokaidō network actually were: "We are now on the Tōkaidō. This I see at once,
from its width, bustling air, and number of tea-houses."[122]

The shogunate was concerned with more than road conditions. In
between towns and villages on the Gokaidō, rows of firs and Japanese
pine trees were planted, which helped define the road and "by their agree-
able shade" made traveling "both pleasant and convenient."[123] According
to one late eighteenth-century traveler, the roadside trees not only
helped prevent erosion of the road surface, they also provided shade and
protection from rain and snow.[124] In at least one area another wayfarer
reported that the trees "overarch and interlace . . . like a great cathedral
aisle."[125] Although trees did not line every inch of all Gokaidō roads, an
examination of the historical records—contemporary wood-block prints,
scrolls, the road maps of the Gokaidō that the Tokugawa compiled early
in the nineteenth century, as well as bakufu orders to repair or plant trees
on certain segments of road—reveals that trees were common along
many stretches of road.[126] Daimyo too followed the bakufu's lead and
planted them on major domainal roads.[127]

To further aid the traveler, Kaempfer noted, all the highways were
divided into measured units, known as *ri* (equivalent to 2.44 miles), beginning from Nihonbashi in Edo. "By this means," he said, "a traveler, in
whatever part of the Empire he be, may know at any time, how many
Japanese miles it is from thence to Jedo, the Imperial [shogunal] residence."[128] As is evident from maps and wood-block prints, the "miles"
were "marked by two small hills, thrown up on each side of the way,
opposite to one another, and planted at the top with one or more
trees."[129] These distance markers were erected in the first years of the

shogunate, about a century and a half before they were a regular fixture on English roads.[130]

Road markers, or guideposts (*dōhyō*), were found at many of the junctions of two or more routes: for example, at Utsunomiya, where the Nikkō dōchū and Ōshū dōchū met; or at Oiwake, where the Tōkaidō and the Nakasendō met. Although the markers were erected on private initiative, it appears that official approval was needed. Markers on the roads to major pilgrimage sites were often donated by religious confraternities (*kō*) belonging to that particular temple. Not surprisingly, then, many of the markers doubled as stone Buddhas that watched over travelers passing by. From Hiroshige's prints, and bakufu-sponsored maps, we know that both wooden and stone markers were erected, although only the stone variety remains today.[131]

Stone lanterns (*jōyatō*) were also erected on private initiative, rather than by government directive, and further added to the comfort and safety of travelers: many remain today. The oil-light lanterns were initially donated by religious adherents of a particular shrine and temple and placed along the roadway to illuminate the path leading to the sacred precincts. By extension, some were placed on the roads leading to the shrine and temple complexes themselves and at the forks where these roads branched off from the main thoroughfares.[132] Residents of post stations frequently erected them at both ends of the settlement as well.[133]

Another major reason that road conditions on the Gokaidō were good was the relative absence of the wheeled traffic that caused contemporary European roads to fall into disrepair. In England, carts and wagons created deep ruts which were further widened by surface water, often making the road impassable "except by waggons with teams powerful enough to drag them through 'on their bellies.'"[134] Charles Thunberg explained, "The roads here [in Japan] are in the better order, and last the longer, as no wheeled carriages are used, which do so much damage to the roads."[135]

While there is no documentary evidence for a statutory ban on the use of carts on the Gokaidō, such a law may nevertheless have been in effect. The reason for this ban cannot be attributed to allegedly poor road conditions or geographical constraints, as is often asserted;[136] rather, it lies with the problem of keeping traffic flow free of interruptions and roads in optimum condition for official travelers and communications. While not conclusive, the evidence suggests that another objection may have come from post horse operators who saw the carts as a threat to their livelihood. If so, Tokugawa Japan would not be unique in such a conflict of economic interests, for in the early history of the United States, pack-horse operators opposed the making of wagon roads for the same reason.[137] To explore this point from a slightly different perspective, let us first look at the use of carts in urban areas, which is well documented.

The use of carts, both ox-drawn (*ushi guruma*) and hand-drawn (*daihachi guruma*), was allowed in a number of cities, such as Edo, Kyoto, Sunpu, and Sendai. In Edo, carts were slow in coming into use after their introduction in 1636 to transport goods for the repair of Edo Castle. The use of ox-drawn carts dropped off at the end of the seventeenth century (from a level of 600 units in the Kan'ei period, 1624–1643, to 250 in the Jōkyū era, 1684–1687), but by the end of that century there were over 2,000 hand-drawn carts on the streets of Edo, prompting the stiff resistance of pack-horse operators in the city.[138] In both Edo and Osaka, the pack-horse operators were able to convince bakufu officials to impose a tax on the carts as well as to limit their size and loads, but efforts to restrict the operation of carts were not, on the whole, very successful.[139] City officials in Osaka in 1824 tellingly complained that "despite past orders to reduce the number of hand-drawn carts, they have in fact increased in number and continue to interfere with the business of pack-horse drivers and merchants operating boats."[140]

Restrictions on carts in urban centers were not, however, entirely based on the opposition of pack-horse operators. City officials were very concerned that carts might interfere with the flow of traffic. The top-heavy loads were prone to spills which held up traffic—not surprising if one examines Edo-period popular art, which frequently depicts the carts, piled high with rice bales, "propelled by four powerful fellows, who work in pairs, and have scarcely more clothing than there is harness on a horse [or an oxen, for that matter]."[141] Cart operators were warned to be careful, but in many cases, workers' carelessness and reckless steering resulted in human death.[142] That the problem became serious is evident from the increasingly severe penalty—exile or death—applied from around the turn of the eighteenth century in cases of injury or death.[143] There was also concern that the heavily loaded carts would damage the bridges over which they were hauled or pose a public health risk, as they (in Osaka, at least) continued to be used to transport night soil through the city streets despite a ban on the practice. Moreover, the noise produced by the creaking, overladen carts being pushed through urban streets prompted officials to prohibit their use at night.[144]

Carts were allowed to operate freely on certain stretches of road outside of urban areas, and therefore it cannot be argued that carts were kept off the roads on account of poor road conditions. Around the time of the Battle of Osaka (1614–1615), a special edict was issued allowing cart operators from Kyoto, Fushimi and a number of neighboring localities free reign to ply their trade.[145] Throughout the Edo period carts were allowed to work the stretches of road between the three cities of Kyoto, Fushimi, and Ōtsu. Conditions on the road between Kyoto and Ōtsu were so bad (to Thunberg, writing in 1776, the road "seemed much broke up")[146] that a "kind of stone tramway" was finally built in 1805 for the "heavy, broad-wheeled bullock carts" used to transport rice.[147]

The bakufu could see the effect that the operation of carts had in both urban centers and on limited stretches of road and this, no doubt, was an important factor in the de facto prohibition on their widespread use on the Gokaidō. Late in the Tokugawa period, carts were allowed on another stretch of road, the Nakasendō at Tarui and Imasu. These two post stations petitioned the bakufu and were granted permission to use a type of man-powered cart (*ita guruma*) in 1849.[148] The size and number of carts allowed, however, was severely restricted to prevent an adverse effect on post-station revenue. Permission was apparently granted because the heavy volume of official traffic hampered the ability of the stations to handle private transport, particularly merchant goods, upon which their livelihood depended. The order also provided for the construction of new bridges, so that the carts would not obstruct traffic.[149] There are no records of other stations petitioning for similar rights, but only thirteen years later, in 1862, the shogunate allowed the free use of wheeled vehicles on all roads, with the caveat to use only small carts in order not to obstruct the flow of traffic or damage bridges.[150] Even with that order, there was no mad rush to use carts on the Gokaidō, no doubt because of the negative economic impact that their widespread use would have had on local labor. However, the bakufu was toppled from power only six years later, and therefore we have no way of accurately assessing the real economic effect the freeing of restrictions on carts would have had on post stations.

BRIDGES AND RIVER CROSSINGS

The notion that rivers were not bridged for military reasons has been uncritically accepted as fact. Without basis, statements such as the following have been allowed to stand unchallenged: "One manifestation of the strategy of defense was the reluctance of the Tokugawa to provide bridges over certain of the large rivers in the Kantō area," or "A further method of securing the road was to restrict the number of permanent bridges which crossed the numerous rivers, thus preventing easy access to Edo by potential invaders."[151] Others have offered a second, equally inadequate explanation: "Bridge building on the Tōkaidō was discouraged for military reasons and inhibited by topographical difficulties."[152] While both elements, military and topographical, are germane, they are only partial explanations. Moreover, these explanations are misleading.

There were forty-one river crossings in the Gokaidō network, more than a third of which were on the busiest two roads, the Tōkaidō and the Nakasendō. The greatest number of large-scale rivers had to be traversed on the Tōkaidō.[153] In addition to the eight ferry-boat crossings there, the traveler was compelled to ford four major rivers. Unlike these water crossings, which could be both costly and inconvenient, the bridges built to span the Toyokawa and Yahagi rivers were spectacular.

The accounts of some contemporary foreign visitors to Japan offer various reasons for the fact that major rivers were infrequently bridged. Kaempfer, on one of his trips to Edo, noted, "Several of the rivers we are to cross over, chiefly upon Tookaido, run with so impetuous a rapidity towards the sea, that they will bear no bridge nor boat, and this by reason partly of the neighboring snow-mountains, where they arise, partly of the frequent great rains, which will swell them to such a degree, as to make them overflow their banks."[154] The Ōi, which was the natural boundary between Suruga and Tōtōmi provinces, was the wildest and most feared river in Tokugawa Japan. A pack-horse driver's song that all Japanese schoolchildren still learn today tells of the difficulty of crossing that river: *Hakone hachiri wa / uma demo kosu ga / kosu ni kosarenu Ōi-gawa*. Roughly translated, the lyric relates that, "Even if you have made it over the difficult stretch of road around Hakone on horseback, the 'uncrossable' Ōi River still lies ahead of you." A popular *senryū*, or humorous haiku, of the time conveyed some of the fear that contemporary travelers experienced: "Even if one is carried across on a wooden platform, what lies below is still hell!" (*Rendai ni notte mo, shita wa jigoku nari*).[155] Siebold commented that the Ōi "has so much of the torrent character that neither bridges nor ferry-boats are practicable, and it must consequently be passed by fording: an operation rendered dangerous, as well as difficult, by the unevenness of the bottom, which is thickly strewn with large blocks of stone."[156] When the Korean envoy Sin Yu-han crossed it in 1719, he noted that the river was divided into three streams and that even though the water level was low, only just over the knees, it "flowed like an arrow," making it impossible to bridge the river, even with a pontoon bridge.[157]

People crossed these large rivers, where, according to the Swede Charles Thunberg, "no bridge can be built," in a number of ways.[158] Where the shallow rivers were sufficiently deep and slow enough to allow boats to operate, travelers were ferried across in vessels with "flat bottoms made of thin planks, or boards, which, if in the passage the boat runs on a stone or shallow, will yield, and let it slip over."[159] Ferry boats were more practical than pontoons, or "floating bridges" (*ukibashi*), since rivers swelled during the rainy season and washed out pontoons more often than regular bridges. The pontoon bridges were only used for shogunal travel and for the foreign missions from Korea.[160]

Shallow, variable or multiple currents made it difficult to operate a ferry-boat service. When the fictional characters Chikusai and Niramino-suke reached the Ōi, they saw the currents shift "before their very eyes." Where the river "was deep one minute it suddenly became shallow the next."[161] On her trip home from Edo in 1689, Inoue Tsūjo had to get out of her boat when crossing the Tenryū River so that it could be pushed to a deeper spot. Because the second stream was too shallow for the boat, she and her traveling companions were forced to ford across it.[162] Boats

did not operate on other rivers such as the Sakata, Okitsu, Abe and Ōi;
and travelers there, as at the Tenryū River above, had to be carried across
(see Figure 2 for Hiroshige's wood-block rendition of travelers fording a
shallow river). As Alcock recorded, "Stout porters carried us without
demur across, though the water was surging around their hips in many
places; but they seemed to know perfectly well where to pick their steps,
and taking us in a zig-zag line up the stream made their way without
much difficulty."[163] Important personages, such as foreign dignitaries and
daimyo, were carried across on short, wooden platforms (*rendai*), but
most commoners went across "pick-a-back" on the shoulders of "strong,
brawny men—innocent of all drapery but a loin cloth."[164] Or, as another
humorous lyric put it, the traveler crosses the Ōi "using both ears [of a
porter] as a bridle" (*Ryōmimi o tazuna ni shitaru Ōigawa*).[165]

While it was not possible, at least according to foreign reports, to build
bridges over many of the rivers on the Tōkaidō, they did exist in some
places. Kaempfer noted that "strong broad bridges are laid over all other
rivers [i.e., the Tenryū, Fuji, Banyū], which do not run with so much
rapidity, nor alter their beds."[166] The Yahagi Bridge on the Tōkaidō at
Okazaki was the largest in the realm, spanning almost 300 meters (see Figure 3).[167] The bridge at Nihonbashi, by comparison, was only 67 meters
long. Other major bridges included: the Yoshida (near Yoshida station),
216 meters long; the Seta, near Ōtsu, 324 meters long; and the Senjū ōhashi, 119 meters long. There were also a larger number of bridges on a
more modest scale of 10–50 meters, such as the Tsurumi Bridge between
Kawasaki and Kanagawa, which was 45 meters long, or the Fujisawa
Bridge, between Fujisawa and Hiratsuka, measuring 19.8 meters. There
were an even larger number of bridges on a still smaller scale.[168]

To better understand why certain rivers were bridged and others were
not, it is important to investigate specific cases in detail; the Rokugō and
Ōi Rivers are particularly instructive examples. Between Shinagawa and
Kawasaki, only eighteen kilometers from Edo on the Tōkaidō, the Rokugō was bridged from at least late in the Warring States period. In fact,
the Rokugō Bridge was one of three known as the "Three Great Bridges
of Edo" (*Edo no san ōhashi*), the others being the Senjū Bridge over the
Arakawa River and the Ryōgoku Bridge over the Sumida. According to
one early nineteenth-century observer, it was dismantled by the Go-

Figure 2 Travelers Being Carried across the Seto River at Fujieda. Hiroshige, *Tōkaidō gojūsantsugi*. Sackler Art Museum, Harvard University. Gift of the Friends of Arthur B. Duel.

Hōjō daimyo in 1569 as part of a defensive strategy against the onslaught of the Takeda forces; he further explained, "[It] was subsequently rebuilt in 1605, only to be washed away in a flood in 1688. Since then a ferry boat has been in operation."[169] The Englishman Griffis found no bridge there early in the Meiji period, however, and mistakenly assumed there had never been one.[170]

A bridge over the Rokugō River had, in fact, been washed away in floods brought on by heavy spring rains several times before 1688: in 1612, 1643, 1647, 1659, 1671, and again in 1680. The wash-outs necessitated large-scale repairs; and these costs were borne by the bakufu.[171] For example, in 1612, lumber had to be requisitioned from the Kiso area in Shinano province to rebuild the 216-meter-long bridge.[172] When a flood washed out the bridge again in 1688, the bakufu made the decision not to rebuild, and instead opted to run a ferry-boat crossing.[173]

Although some scholars would say that the existence of a ferry rather than a bridge over the Rokugō River was a sign of the reactionary character of the Tokugawa bakufu, even the Meiji government, which rebuilt the bridge in 1868, experienced similar problems. Soon thereafter, when floods washed it away, the government made the same decision as its predecessor and opted for a ferry service. Not until 1925 was a permanent bridge finally constructed.[174]

The problems the Tokugawa experienced with bridges are quite similar to those of contemporary France. One noted scholar writing about conditions in nineteenth-century France remarked:

> The old sacred awe of rivers and the fear of their murderous ire remained alive throughout the Second Empire. But rivers did not need to rage and ravage. Even at their most placid, many were hard to negotiate. In the Garone valley, almost 300 kilometers from Toulouse to Bordeaux, there was not a single bridge until the mid-nineteenth century. Fords were rare, dangerous and practicable only at low water. When bridges were attempted (at Agen, for instance) they were washed away—and, not surprisingly, there were many second thoughts about reconstructing them.[175]

Thus, it seems that geographical and technological issues, rather than political philosophy, lay at the heart of Tokugawa policy towards rivers and bridges.

Figure 3 View of the Yahagi Bridge at Okazaki. Hiroshige, *Tōkaidō gojūsantsugi*. Sackler Art Museum, Harvard University. Gift of the Friends of Arthur B. Duel.

Even though the river crossing close to Edo, the bakufu's administrative center, was a considerable impediment to communications, economic conditions were paramount in the bakufu's decision not to rebuild the Rokugō on the same scale. From 1703, however, a smaller, temporary bridge (*kari bashi*) was built annually over the shrunken streams during the fall and winter months (the ninth through the third month) and this practice was followed widely elsewhere.

Still, scholars have debated why it was that more rivers were not bridged; and the Ōi has been a center of that controversy. As we noted, the Ōi sometimes flowed as a single torrent, carrying away huge trees and rocks, and at other times it separated into a dozen streams across its riverbed, which was over three kilometers wide. Since most travelers dreaded the trip across the river, one can understand why it was said that the Ōi was "as large a river as you'll find in this world or the next."[176]

Despite the accounts of the natural conditions which impeded the bridging of the Ōi, most scholars believe that military factors were paramount. In other words, the unbridged river acted as a natural barrier—a "sekisho river" (*sekisho gawa*)—and played a part in the bakufu's policy to prevent daimyo rebellion.[177] Proponents of this argument usually cite the incident—of dubious authenticity—from the *Tokugawa jikki* in which Tokugawa Iemitsu punished his brother, Tadanaga, the Keeper of Sunpu Castle, after the latter constructed a pontoon bridge over the Ōi on the occasion of the shogun's trip to Kyoto in 1626.[178] This account, however, seems quite problematic, since Iemitsu himself used the "floating bridges" on many occasions when on pilgrimage to Nikkō; furthermore, the severe penalty imposed on Tadanaga (escheat of his domain and house arrest) suggests that Iemitsu used this incident as a pretext to disgrace Tadanaga, who had been his rival to become heir to their father, the shogun Hidetada. If a bridge over the Ōi posed a strategic security risk, then it made no sense for the Tokugawa to bridge the Arakawa (at Senjū) and the Rokugō rivers, both of which were much closer to Edo. Tadanaga, incidentally, although subsequently given a smaller domain to administer, committed suicide two years after building that ill-fated bridge over the Ōi.

It appears that topography and economics were mostly responsible for the lack of a bridge or any ferry service across the Ōi. While some scholars stress the technological limits of bridge building, the most convincing argument is economic. Whatever the reason for not bridging the Ōi early in the Tokugawa period, by the Genroku period, opposition to bridges was purely economic. For example, Kanaya and Shimada, the two post stations which operated the river crossing, fought petitions sent to local bakufu intendants by Edo merchants who wanted to operate a ferry crossing; they opposed these petitions on four separate occasions in thirteen years. In one case, the petition got as far as the Magistrate of Finance before being refused. The statement presented to the Magistrate by the two post stations played upon the potent myth of strategic defense in order to protect their economic interests; it said, "If the prohibition which has been in effect up until now is lifted, then it will endanger the strategic natural defense of the realm (*goyōgai wa yabure*) and we will no longer be able to operate our river-fording services."[179] The opposition of the two stations is natural, for a ferry-boat operation would have put many of the river-crossing porters out of work.[180] Moreover, charges for ferry-boat services on the Gokaidō were considerably lower than for fording; thus a switch in the type of service offered would have had an adverse effect on the principal business on which the economies of the two post stations depended.[181] In the history of the development of communications in Japan and elsewhere, we find that every improvement in method has been opposed by those whose occupations depended on maintenance of the status quo.

TWO

The Social Organization of the Gokaidō Network

One day during the Hōreki era (1751–1763) a requisition order for horses and transport workers was sent by officials at Warabi post station on the Nakasendō to a number of villages charged with providing this service. Some of these villages—known as *sukegō,* or assisting villages—intentionally dispatched their men and horses late, while others completely refused to obey the order. Their action was tantamount to a work slowdown or stoppage.[1] In cases like this, baggage piled up at the post station and official travelers were sometimes kept waiting. What did the peasants hope to accomplish by their actions? Did they not fear the potentially harsh measures that the state might take against them? In general, how did political leaders deal with the contentiousness of villages in the *sukegō* system? Furthermore, what do such incidents tell us about the interaction between the state and village society, or the limits on state authority?

Although a popular image persists of Tokugawa peasants armed with farm implements, resisting excessive taxation or other political injustices by marching en masse to the residence of their overlord to demand redress of their grievances, recent studies have shown that Tokugawa peasant movements were not very violent.[2] In other words, there were many other methods besides violence—such as those used by Warabi's assisting villages—by which peasants could resist excessive claims, through taxation, on their means of livelihood. If we content ourselves only with an examination of the conspicuous acts of violence, we stand to lose sight of the more routine, but no less important, forms of collective action.[3]

This chapter will examine the overland transport corvée labor tax, the *sukegō* tax, which was imposed on villages lying within a certain designated distance from official post stations. This form of taxation has received little discussion in the literature on agrarian Tokugawa Japan,[4] but it is crucial to a full understanding of how taxes were imposed and how heavy a tax load the peasants bore.[5] The means by which peasants fought and eroded the *sukegō* tax are also part of the story.

Through a seemingly continuous process of signaling, negotiation and struggle, peasants in the affected villages attempted to resist excessive taxation imposed on them by a government that sought to support its own transportation system, a system increasingly unable to maintain itself. Their protest must have had some effect; for from the late seventeenth century on, efforts to eliminate some of the abuses of the system and discover new ways to minimize the dependence on assisting villages increasingly preoccupied Tokugawa transport policy planners. Indeed, the constant contention and the efforts of government at all levels to deal with it reveal much about how both government and village society worked.

SUKEGŌ *TAXATION*

Although post stations were ordered by the bakufu to maintain a certain minimum number of porters and horses, they clearly found it difficult to do so. In 1724, for example, only nine out of fifty-seven stations on the Tōkaidō and its extension to Osaka were maintaining the required number of one hundred porters and one hundred horses.[6] Five of the nine were rewarded for a second time in 1787 for "meritorious service," indicating how rare it was for post stations to fulfill their transport obligations.[7] Some, in fact, probably never attained the full required level. Tarui post station on the Nakasendō was able to muster only twenty-six of the required fifty porters in 1681; the figure rose to thirty-five in 1689, but dropped to thirty-one in 1703.[8] Another Nakasendō station, Annaka, maintained its full complement of porters and horses for only twenty-four years of its existence.[9]

Similar deficits were, in fact, widespread throughout the entire Gokaidō network and were sizeable at many stations by 1724: two Tōkaidō stations were deficient by more than seventy porters and horses; twelve were deficient by fifty or more of each; and twenty-seven were short by twenty porters and fifty horses.[10] A notice issued by the Magistrate of Road Affairs in 1821 reproached post stations for not maintaining enough porters and horses, further reminding them that the bakufu had granted them tax-free land, rate increases, and other financial support to enable them to carry out their transport obligations.[11]

This discrepancy in the actual number of porters and horses available to post stations would have posed no particular problem had the volume of traffic on major roads remained low. Once the alternate attendance system was finalized, however, the routes became crowded with daimyo traveling from their home provinces to Edo and back. As will be shown later, official traffic on the whole increased rapidly during the seventeenth century, peaking during the Genroku through Kyōhō periods (1688–1735), and then again during the Bunka-Bunsei periods (1804–1829). Commoner traffic is less quantifiable because post stations did not keep records of non-official travelers; but the remarkable growth in guidebooks and travel literature indicates it, too, increased as the Tokugawa peace set in and the economy began to expand. Consequently, the resources of the post station system were insufficient to handle the demand for transport services.

The bakufu officially established the *sukegō* system in 1694, but peasants and horses were already being requisitioned for transport services from villages located near post stations. As early as 1616, the Senior Councilors had issued an order to the stations that, whenever necessary, pack horses should be hired from neighboring villages so that goods could be delivered on time, even in inclement weather.[12] At that time, no provision was made for requisitioning peasants as transport workers; but whether villages could, in fact, refuse a post station's request for help is debatable.[13]

To obtain a reliable and adequate supply of horses at post stations, the bakufu decreed an order in 1637 that *sukeuma*, or "assisting horses," could be requisitioned from nearby villages whenever needed. Thus compliance became compulsory for specifically designated villages whenever a shortage arose at post stations.[14] Up to that time it had been the post station's responsibility to maintain an adequate supply of horses, but thereafter much of the burden shifted to the designated villages.

Documentation for the 1637 decree exists for only a limited number of post stations on the Tōkaidō and Nakasendō;[15] but according to the post-station manager at Kawasaki, Tanaka Kyūgu, at that time, each Tōkaidō post station was assigned a number of villages whose total estimated yield of rice (*kokudaka*) was 2,000 *koku* (about 10,000 bushels).[16] The only information available on the nature of the levy, however, is from Hamamatsu, where five neighboring designated villages were required to provide a total of 50 horses, or 2.5 horses per 100 *koku* of estimated yield.[17] In the same year, Nakatsugawa post station on the Nakasendō was given permission by the bakufu to requisition, whenever necessary, not only horses but villagers as well.[18] It thus appears that even before the official *sukegō* system, corvée labor was already playing an indispensable role in the transport of official traffic by the end of the 1630s on the Tōkaidō and Nakasendō, the two busiest arteries, and the road connecting the two, the Minoji. On other roads, additional porters or horses were supplied to post stations by daimyo, rather than bakufu, authority.[19]

The 1637 decree is generally interpreted as the actual beginning of the *sukegō* system. Although there is a lack of agreement on a suitable definition of the term *sukegō*,[20] for the purpose of examining the overall system, it may be defined as obligatory labor owed by designated villages to a specific post station or group of post stations. Technically, *sukegō* may refer to either the transport corvée labor tax or the village assessed the tax; for the sake of clarity, we will refer to the tax as *sukegō* tax and to the villages as "assisting villages" or "*sukegō* villages." The debates on interpretation, while important in themselves, will no doubt persist because of the limited knowledge of transport corvée labor prior to 1694.

In that year the bakufu initiated a major reform of the corvée labor system for overland transport through both private lands (that is, land belonging to the various daimyo) and Tokugawa house lands (*tenryō*). The reform measure systematized the requisitioning of transport workers and horses from villages, which were officially labeled *sukegō* villages for the first time.[21] Registers were compiled, based on a 1689 census taken by the bakufu, recording the station's name, the names of all the villages assigned to it for *sukegō* duty, the names of each of the village headmen, and the villages' estimated yield of rice.[22] This last item was listed because the tax was assessed on the basis of a calculated percentage of the *koku-daka;* the rate at that time was generally two porters and two horses per 100 *koku* each time the village was requisitioned for duty.[23] While the initial act, known as the Genroku Reform, centered on the Tōkaidō, Nakasendō, and Minoji, it was soon extended to the Nikkō dōchū in 1696 and the Kiso kaidō in 1712. The Ōshū dōchū and Kōshū dōchū were not officially included until the 1740s. But, as we have noted, this does not necessarily mean that transport corvée labor was not being requisitioned for post stations on these roads prior to then.

As a rule, before 1694, only villages lying within bakufu territory were levied *sukegō* corvée, although there seems to have been an exception in Mino province, where a particularly strong intendant was able to designate villages for corvée duty from both bakufu and private domains.[24] The Genroku Reform, however, removed local authority from the *sukegō* system, giving the manager of the post station (*ton'ya*) the authority, through the Magistrate of Road Affairs, to requisition corvée labor from villages regardless of their domain status.[25] Of course, as we noted in the previous chapter, the post stations themselves, and bakufu financial assistance to them in the form of land tax exemptions, represented an infringement of daimyo prerogatives; for the Gokaidō and all its post stations were considered bakufu territory regardless of the domain that they happened to traverse. *Sukegō* tax represented a further infringement of domainal rights because the levy imposed both financial and corvée burdens on the lord's peasants, thereby restricting his ability to tax them for his own purposes.

The elimination of independent private authority over corvée labor on the Gokaidō was necessary to assure the smooth operation of the system, particularly in areas with complicated political boundaries. This was important because after the Genroku Reform, assisting villages served post stations in other domains more frequently, particularly in economically advanced areas where the volume of traffic was higher.[26] An extreme case, Mitsuke station on the Tōkaidō used 109 assisting villages (1842) which came under the administrative authority of no less than twenty-seven overlords. Each overlord had from one to eleven villages under his partial or full administration, and one particular village was divided among as many as five overlords.[27] To give another example, half of the 113 assisting villages servicing Odawara post station, part of a vassal (*fudai*) domain, were located in other domains, notably those of the bakufu and its bannermen (*hatamoto*).[28]

Thus the *sukegō* tax was no longer determined by domain borders. Some villages formerly in Utsunomiya domain refused to fulfill their transport corvée duty when, through a daimyo transfer in 1749 and shifting of domain borders, they found themselves belonging to a new domain (Hitotsubashi). In response, the bakufu ordered the villages to continue providing porters and post horses since it "is a duty owed to the bakufu, and not to a private overlord (*jitō*), since ancient times."[29] As the net of villages encompassed by the *sukegō* levy was thrown wider, from the eighteenth century on, infringements on domainal sovereignty became increasingly common.

Under the Genroku Reform, each post station was assigned a designated number of assisting villages within an area that usually extended about eighteen square kilometers around the station. Fujisawa was granted a total of forty-three villages possessing a combined estimated yield of 11,878 *koku;* Odawara, another Tōkaidō station, was assigned villages worth 32,955 *koku*.[30] Around 1761, Tōkaidō post stations were assigned assisting villages averaging an estimated total yield of 14,002 *koku*, not an excessive figure for the nation's busiest road. Post stations on the Nikkō dōchū were assigned villages with a high average yield of 12,726 *koku*, no doubt because of the heavy burden imposed by pilgrimage traffic to Nikkō. The averages for the other three major Gokaidō roads were much lower.[31]

Assisting villages were divided into two classifications, *jōsukegō*, or regular assisting villages, and *ōsukegō*, or auxiliary ones. The latter were located at a greater distance from post stations and were called upon to provide transport corvée labor only when the regular assisting villages could not meet the existing demand.[32] Within a few decades, however, it became apparent that the labor provided by assisting villages was insufficient to meet the growing demand for transport services. Consequently, in 1725 the twofold classification was eliminated in favor of a single designation, *jōsukegō*, that was applied to all assisting villages.[33] By making this simple change in designation, whereby all villages within a certain distance from post stations were taxed according to the same standard, the bakufu effectively raised the amount of taxable income to draw on.[34] Villages were not necessarily assigned to only one post station, and in a number of cases they were assigned to two to more. No stations on the Tōkaidō shared assisting villages, but after a reorganization of the *sukegō* system in 1746, eight pairs of stations and three groups of three stations on the Nakasendō used the same villages. Some stations on the Kōshū dōchū and Nikkō dōchū, as well as on a few branch roads, did the same. This sharing system obviously involved a proportionately heavier corvée burden for the assisting villages.[35]

Another way of raising the amount of taxable revenue available to post stations was to create new categories of assisting villages. This was done from the 1720s on in order to cope with the increasing demand for transport services. Although post stations used different classifications for their villages, certain categories of new, auxiliary villages seem to have been standardized. *Daisukegō*, or "relief assisting villages," was a twofold designation for a village assessed a *sukegō* tax on a temporary basis, such as for shogunal pilgrimages to Nikkō, or when a natural disaster or extreme impoverishment rendered the regular assisting villages unable to meet their tax obligations. *Mashi sukegō* and *ka sukegō*, i.e. "supplemental assisting villages," were also used–and often up to one hundred were assigned to a single post station–to lower the tax burden of ordinary assisting villages during times of special processions. On the Tōkaidō, most post stations were assigned these supplemental villages from the 1730s to the 1760s.[36] In the closing decades of the Tokugawa period yet another category, *tōbun sukegō*, or "temporary assisting village," was created to draw more villages into the system in order to cover the extraordinary demand for transport services at that time.[37] All of the villages falling under the various auxiliary categories were located at a greater distance from the post station than the regular villages. For example, while all of the regular villages for Fujiwara in the mid-eighteenth century were within an area of eight kilometers, the supplemental villages all lay beyond that distance, eight to fourteen kilometers away.[38]

THE NATURE OF THE SUKEGŌ LEVY

The *sukegō* tax burden could cause serious economic hardship to a peasant farmer by keeping him away from his fields at a time when he most needed to be working there. Although the amount of service required during the year varied considerably, peasants were generally called upon to provide corvée labor from the third to the tenth months, the period of the busiest agricultural activity.

Four villages that regularly serviced Ōiso post station on the Tōkaidō complained to a bakufu magistrate in 1680 that the *sukegō* levy was interfering with their economic livelihood. After noting that they had been performing the service for over forty years, the petition for relief continued:

> Because we must dispatch our horses every day there have been delays in planting and harvesting, and consequently we have suffered losses in yield. The peasants have grown steadily weaker, and are practically starving.
>
> Ōiso is a very busy post station where many travelers stop for the night. We are required to perform corvée service day and night; this causes us great difficulties and wears out our men and horses. Even though we receive some monetary compensation for our services, with the increase in prices for rice and soybeans, it is not enough. The post station receives land, rice and monetary stipends, as well as loans, but we receive nothing—despite the fact that the faithful performance of our corvée levy is steadily impoverishing us.[39]

Another example illustrates the point more precisely. On the occasion of Shogun Ieharu's pilgrimage to Nikkō in 1776, one village was called on to provide fifty-one days of assistance to Tokujirō post station on the Nikkō dōchū. As a result, the rice crop was delayed twenty days and upland crops thirty-five days. Moreover, ten acres of land normally used for rice cultivation went unplanted. The crops that were eventually planted were done so only with the assistance of children and old people.[40]

The nineteen assisting villages servicing Oiwake-Kutsukake post stations on the Nakasendō, all located within a range of 10 to 18 kilometers from Oiwake, worked 189 days a year.[41] No labor was required of them in the first month of 1849, while the fourth and fifth months, the peak season for daimyo travel due to alternate attendance, were the busiest in terms of agricultural work.[42] During these two months, the assisting villages provided more horses for transport service than did Oiwake station itself.[43]

The ten assisting villages servicing Hodogaya on the Tōkaidō worked eighty-five days out of the seven months for which there are records in 1672, or 40 percent of the time. The fourth and sixth months were the busiest, during which they worked twenty-one and twenty-three days out of the month, respectively. During the seven-month period, the ten villages, worth an estimated yield of 2,494 *koku*, provided 1,046 porters and 961 horses. The actual daily range was 7–15 horses with one man for every horse plus a group leader. When mean averages are worked out for comparisons with other villages, the rate comes to 41.9 porters and 38.5 horses per 100 *koku*.[44]

Kitabori, for instance, one of Honjō's assisting villages, provides a contrast. In 1694, its rate per 100 *koku* was only 18 porters and 15 horses. Kitabori also, however, supplies data that show how dramatically the *sukegō* tax burden increased during the late seventeenth century and through the eighteenth. In 1783, it petitioned the bakufu, complaining that the startling increase in corvée duty since the Genroku era was forcing them to neglect their work in the field: "At the beginning, we were required to provide twelve men and nine horses per 100 *koku* of our village's estimated yield, but thereafter the demands grew more intense, and we petitioned during the Hōei [1704–1710] and Shōtoku [1711–1715] eras for relief." In specific terms, the rate of 18 porters and 15 horses had risen to 100 porters and 67 horses per 100 *koku* by 1709 and did not level off until it reached 140 porters and 191 horses in 1773.[45]

During the last years of the Tokugawa period and the early years of the Meiji, the *sukegō* tax burden continued to increase, until the entire assisting village and post-station system was overhauled by the imperial government and then finally abolished in 1877.[46] It has, in fact, been suggested that both would have fallen apart had the bakufu not been defeated first.[47] Assisting villages and post stations were pushed to their limits by the increase in traffic after the coming of Perry in 1854, the suspension of the alternate attendance system in 1862, the enormous retinue accompanying Princess Kazunomiya to Edo for her marriage to the shogun Iemochi in 1862, the shogun's procession to Kyoto in 1863, and most especially by the bakufu's punitive expeditions against Chōshū in 1864 and 1866 and the Boshin War (1868–1869).[48] To provide the necessary transport workers and horses, the new Meiji government had to extend *sukegō* tax levies to the land of court nobles and that of the Imperial Court itself.[49] Just a few months later, the tax was extended to the "entire realm." The order stated that this "unprecedented" act had become necessary because "the financial problems of the post stations and assisting villages have gotten progressively worse." The tax, it noted, was to be in effect for only one year.[50] There is no evidence, however, that the new government was able to carry out such an ambitious order at that particular stage in its development.

Sukegō duty could, depending on local conditions, mean that a village was obliged to provide only horses, or perhaps a greater number of either porters or horses. It was not, however, necessarily limited to porters and horses. Villages in areas that surrounded post stations responsible for a river or other water crossing were often assessed a *sukegō* tax in terms of boatmen and boats.[51]

The labor required of the peasants belonging to an assisting village was performed only by men between the ages of 15 and 60; village officials, clergy, villagers away on temporary migration for employment, and the sick were exempted. For Honjō's assisting villages, 1,931 men from 2,015 households were responsible for carrying out the levy.[52] Loss of this valuable work force could, as noted above, have serious economic consequences for a village.

Two to four days of a peasant farmer's time could be consumed by one turn of service for corvée labor. If requisitioned for duty beginning from the morning, the designated villagers would be required to arrive by dusk the night before.[53] After the day's work had been finished, it was often too late to return home that evening, requiring an additional night's lodging. Peasants on *sukegō* duty for Oiwake had to walk an average of ten to eighteen kilometers to the post station, requiring a total of perhaps thirty-two to forty-eight kilometers to fulfill their corvée duty. Oiwake and Kutsukake post stations shared assisting villages, and therefore a peasant might have to work the entire 8.6-kilometer route from Oiwake to Kutsukake and then to Karuizawa during peak periods of travel, thus adding on about ten kilometers.

For ordinary levels of traffic, in order to minimize the disruption of their toil in the fields, villages owing labor to more than one post station would divide up the work, each being responsible for one segment of the trip. They would also, for the same purpose, divide their numbers into smaller groups, each being responsible for *sukegō* duty during some agreed-upon period of rotation.[54]

The documents do not give a very human picture of how *sukegō* duty affected the individual peasant, but the example of Hanejima at least allows a glimpse of how the levy affected one particular village. Located less than eight kilometers from Fujisawa on the Tōkaidō, Hanejima was one of forty-four regular assisting villages serving the station. It was of medium size, containing perhaps forty-eight households.[55] During the period 1729/2/15–5/4, it provided ninety-one men and an equal number of horses. Most of the levy was concentrated in the third month, normally the time for rice planting, when seventy-one men and seventy-one horses were dispatched. Twenty-eight of the men served only once, but the burden on the remaining fifteen was heavier—three of them were assessed duty as many as seven times. Those who were called upon for such frequent service were no doubt wealthier peasants (assessments being based on the estimated yield of a man's land); and they probably hired someone else to perform the actual work. Horses were also probably dispatched several times each, accounting for the large total.[56]

Although compulsory, *sukegō* duty was not, strictly speaking, corvée labor; for, as indicated by the petition from Ōiso station, post stations sometimes paid for the labor of the men and horses in money. Whether or not a wage was paid depended on the type of goods to be transported. According to bakufu regulations, *sukegō* service was supposed to be used only for the category of fixed-rate travel[57] (i.e., travel of lower-ranking bakufu officials, various castle guards, and daimyo); and in these cases, wages were paid. Nevertheless, if demand was excessive and the post stations shorthanded, porters and horses from assisting villages could be employed for free transport as well, in which case no remuneration was offered.[58] Whether *sukegō* labor was used for fixed-rate or free transport, therefore, was an obvious potential source of abuse and contention.

Porters from Shimo-Mariko, an assisting village servicing Shinagawa post station on the Tōkaidō late in the Tokugawa period, could receive eighty to ninety-five copper coins (*mon*) for a full day's work, whereas a regular post-station porter would earn the same amount in one trip from Shinagawa to Edo or to Kawasaki; in other terms, it was equivalent to one-fifth of the daily wages for a carpenter and could purchase three slabs of tofu.[59] The villager was not compensated for the distance that he had to travel to and from the post station, nor for food and lodging costs. And if the post station over-requisitioned—as it usually did to cover itself in the case of unexpected demand—nothing would be paid for the assisting villages' porters and horses that were left idle. Since wages were pooled, this economic loss would be shared by all workers from a village. During a busy travel period when over-requisitioning was likely, therefore, porters from assisting villages might receive only two or three copper coins a day for all their work. If there was a river stoppage or delay in the expected traffic, the villagers could be sent home without even one coin; that is what happened to Hanejima village when the Banyū River was flooded on ten out of the ninety-one workdays for which its men and horses were requisitioned.[60] It is clear that wages were in no way proportionate to the labor performed and did little to make the levy seem less of a burden.

To make up for the low *sukegō* wages, assisting villages paid those who performed the services a supplemental wage (*tachisen*). This was paid from a special levy, the village expenditures tax (*mura iriyō*), that the village itself imposed on its members to cover the food and lodging costs incurred by porters and horses sent on *sukegō* duty.[61] At Shimo-Odagiri, which serviced Odai and Iwamurada post stations on the Nakasendō, *sukegō*-related costs for most of the years 1839–1867 for which there is evidence accounted for more than 35 percent of the village's budgeted expenditures. These costs increased significantly from 1853, the year of Perry's arrival, an event that marked the beginning of a period of feverish activity on the Gokaidō. *Sukegō* costs were the highest in 1863, 74 percent of the village's budgeted expenditures, because of Iemochi's shogunal procession to Kyoto. In the village of Tsubaiso, which serviced Kameyama post station on the Tōkaidō, *sukegō* costs for many of the years 1785–1866 accounted for about 60 percent of budgeted expenditures.[62] Such examples bear out the statement, "Peasants living in assisting villages were financially the most hard-pressed."[63]

Regular assisting villages on the Tōkaidō were granted exemptions from the "three levies" (*san'yaku,* or *takagakari san'yaku*) at different times during the years 1637–1697.[64] The exemption, however, was slight and did not do much to alleviate the tax burden of the villages. The rising tax burden bore heavily on assisting villages; therefore we need to reassess the idea that "peasants in house lands were under less compulsion from above," and that their tax rates "were generally lower than rates on private lands."[65] While this may be true for the annual land tax, it is not true overall.

The original purpose of the *sukegō* tax was to provide corvée labor to post stations. But from the mid-eighteenth century until the Meiji government abolished the post-station and *sukegō* systems, it became necessary to requisition that labor from increasingly distant villages. The widening scope of the areas around post stations drawn into the *sukegō* system and the varying impact of the commercializing economy on agrarian society make it extremely difficult to generalize about the overland transport corvée labor tax and its impact. These two factors, however, had a tremendous effect on the *sukegō* system.

A trend towards monetization of the *sukegō* levy occurred during the second half of the Tokugawa period, and particularly during the nineteenth century. Part of the reason for this trend was the search for an equitable tax. *Sukegō* corvée did not necessarily take into account certain variables, such as the distance of a village from the post station, or the resources available at that village. Monetization was in theory, then, a means of making *sukegō* duty a more equitable form of taxation.[66] Officials under the Magistrate of Finance, in fact, proposed the abolition of the *sukegō* system, as well as the imposition of a "national" tax, which would affect all bakufu lands and would support the post-station system. Arai Hakuseki's opposition, however, defeated the plan in 1711. Arai saw the economic problems of post stations and assisting villages as the result of official malfeasance; he sought instead to strengthen the system through legal action and financial aid to individual post stations.[67] The defeat of the plan for a tax on all Tokugawa lands meant that more villages had to be brought into the *sukegō* system; it was from this point on that various types of designations for auxiliary assisting villages were created.

A number of factors were involved in the gradual monetization of the *sukegō* levy. As the scope of the *sukegō* system grew wider, many auxiliary assisting villages made agreements with post stations to convert all or part of their duties into cash payments. They made rational decisions to do so after an evaluation of the relative cost of performing the actual service and commuting the levy. For example, one-third of Shinagawa's regular assisting villages were paying a money tax in 1865.[68] Distant assisting villages assigned for "temporary" duty were even more likely to pay in cash.

The availability of horses and eligible workers (that is, healthy males between the ages of 15 and 60) also affected the manner in which a village might carry out the *sukegō* levy. The assisting villages of Tarui station on the Nakasendō could not provide enough porters and horses on their own to fulfill these high quotas and were obliged to hire additional labor from neighboring villages. During the years 1816–1817, Tarui's assisting villages hired 30–35 percent of the porters and 17–31 percent of the horses that they were required to supply. Major processions caused labor costs to rise, placing an additional strain on the budget of the assisting villages.[69] The cost of maintaining horses was prohibitive, particularly in areas where peasants could not grow fodder and had to purchase it. Such places would dispatch workers but commute all or a portion of the levy requiring them to provide horses.[70]

The straight commutation of the overland transport corvée labor tax into a cash payment appears to have been a widespread practice on the Tōkaidō, and on some parts of the Nakasendō from the beginning of the nineteenth century. The nature of the *sukegō* levy had been changing even earlier, however, owing to the impact of a commercializing economy and the availability of labor pools. First, on an individual level, if a wealthy peasant was charged with providing a horse as well as his own labor for a turn of *sukegō* duty, he might hire a substitute because he was too busy or simply did not want to perform the manual labor himself. Also, as *sukegō* levies increased during the second half of the Tokugawa period, he might be exacted a double or triple levy, depending on his relative wealth, making it physically impossible to perform the corvée levy himself. Usually, his replacement would come from the lower strata of village society, a landless peasant or tenant worker.[71] Some villagers specialized in performing *sukegō* duty as substitutes for those actually levied with the tax.

On a grander scale, however, an entire village could hire a private labor contractor to assume responsibility for fulfilling the village's *sukegō* duties. Such was the case in 1714 when Yamanishi, an assisting village of Ōiso station on the Tōkaidō, contracted a man named Kyūsaburō for one year at eight *ryō* to provide the post station with the village's quota of porters. Such contractors built holding areas (*ninsoku beya*) at the stations where the workers who formed the labor pools would gather. The available evidence shows that this phenomenon occurred on a wide scale only on the Tōkaidō, which was by far the most economically advanced of the Gokaidō routes.

The high but variable cost of converting the *sukegō* levy into a tax payment meant that a village's ability or desire to pay in cash would depend not only on local conditions, such as its distance from the station, but on its financial state and involvement in the cash economy.[72] Consequently, many villages continued to perform the corvée labor while others could afford to commute only a portion of the levy.[73]

Not all villages, however, wanted to pay their *sukegō* tax in cash. In one case, a village, unable to make cash payments, requested permission to perform the actual labor service even though the post station was located nearly thirty-two kilometers away.[74] Assisting villages for Kurihashi post station on the Nikkō dōchū, which managed a river crossing, also asked permission to perform the actual corvée labor rather than continue paying the tax in cash as they had been doing. Being unaccustomed to the difficulties involved in performing transport services across a river, however, the villages quickly changed their mind, apologized, and asked to pay the tax in cash again.[75]

The expansion of the assisting village network and the intrusion of the commercial economy altered the original character of the *sukegō* levy; its transformation created a variety of economic responses which contributed to the complex nature of life in agrarian society.

ECONOMIC PROBLEMS OF THE POST STATIONS

As post stations came to perceive themselves as increasingly impoverished, they tried to shift the burden of providing porters and post horses onto their designated villages, largely because the special transport rates

TABLE 2 Percentage of Porters and Horses Performing Free
Transport Service

Year	Station	Percentage of Porters	Percentage of Horses
1803	Arai	25	1
1804	Hodogaya	29.6	2.2
1806	Ōiso	27	3
1838	Maisaka	55.8	4.6
1839	Kumagaya	33.1	2.9

Source: For Arai, see Watanabe Kazutoshi, *Kaidō to sekisho*, pp. 126–128; for Hodogaya and Ōiso, see *Kanagawa ken shi shiryō hen*, vol. 9, *Kinsei 6*, no. 60, pp. 98–99 and no. 119, pp. 195–196; for Maisaka, see *KKSS*, vol. 9, no. 776, pp. 255–256; for Kumagaya, see *Shinpen Saitama ken shi shiryō hen*, vol. 15, *Kinsei 6*, p. 25.

granted to official travelers were a major factor in their poor financial condition. The many years of free and fixed-rate transport exhausted the resources of both the post stations and their assisting villages.

The percentage of free transport performed varied from station to station (see Table 2). While the evidence is fragmentary, it does show that over 25 percent of post-station transport service involving porters was performed free, although a much smaller percentage of horses (1–5 percent) was used for the same purpose. Even though fixed-rate transport was performed for a fee, the low charges, as noted above, were only about one-half the market rate. While it is difficult to find documentation detailing the volume of fixed-rate transport, available figures for the growth of all official transport at Oiwake post station are provided in Table 3 and provide a useful index. Despite the large gap in the data, the evidence shows that the volume of porters used at the fixed rate increased more than eight-fold and the number of horses almost fourfold between 1702 and 1858.

Other evidence of the drain on transport resources is available from Edo, where the number of porters used for free transport more than tripled while the number of horses used for the same purpose doubled between 1663 and 1681.[76] In addition, records from Arai on the Tōkaidō show that the number of porters used there for official (that is, free and fixed-rate) transport increased more than fivefold between 1740 and 1808.[77] Further evidence of the rising volume of official transport will be

TABLE 3 Number of Porters and Horses Used for Official Transport at Oiwake

Year	Porters	Horses
1702	2,310	4,335
1830	14,742	18,197
1831	17,797	17,987
1833	16,128	17,832
1849	14,564	15,436
1855	21,498	18,355
1858	19,648	17,324

Source: Kodama, *Kinsei shukueki*, p. 229.

examined later in connection with a discussion of the shifting burden of servicing that transport.

The problem of the bakufu's monopoly system was similar to that in Tudor and Stuart England, where the king enjoyed the prerogative of "purveyance." He could, in other words, demand the use of pack horses from the countryside and "pay for them at a rate fixed (in practice) by his own assessors."[78] This system

> seems to have worked well as long as the volume of dispatches remained moderate and reasonably constant. As long as a post could forecast the amount that was the king's prerogative [i.e., work at the cheaper rate] that he would have to do, he could calculate the number of horses he must keep in order to retain his hold on the private passenger traffic. But it was an inherent defect of the scheme that any large and sudden increase in the volume of official correspondence might produce a situation in which the post would be compelled to keep all his horses at work at a penny a mile [i.e., the cheaper rate], while all the profitable jobbing went to hackneymen [i.e., transport merchants] in the town.[79]

This situation in England mirrors that in Tokugawa Japan; the irony for post-station business was that an increase in the volume of transport services, provided at the cheaper rate granted official traffic, caused only further debt. In Japan, for example, an eruption of Mount Asama (Shinano province) in 1783 caused many travelers, official and commoner, to switch from the Nakasendō to the Kōshū kaidō. Therefore, instead of boosting income, the rise in volume of official traffic created economic difficulties for both post stations and assisting villages. Hard-pressed, the stations were driven to petition for a 20 percent rate increase.[80]

There is also other evidence to show that the high volume of official traffic was an economic drain on post stations. Even as the bakufu was regularizing the alternate attendance system in 1635, it began to advise daimyo that their retinues were too large, and such remonstrances continued for most of the Tokugawa period.[81] These excessively large and ostentatious processions were causing economic hardship not only to their own domains, but to Gokaidō post stations as well, as frequent complaints attest. Attempts were made to limit the numbers allowed daimyo and other official travelers, but daimyo were constantly applying for and obtaining additional porters and post horses far in excess of their daily quotas.[82] Kaempfer observed that "the train of some of the most eminent among the Princes [i.e., daimyo] of the Empire fills up the road for some days."[83] Perhaps economic belt-tightening rather than sumptuary legislation was responsible for generally smaller—but from the bakufu's point of view, still over-sized—entourages after the Genroku era. Nevertheless, as Furukawa Koshōken noted in the late eighteenth century, the size of an important daimyo's procession could still be startling.[84] When official travelers went over their quotas for porters and horses, they were supposed to pay more for the excess numbers than the favorable rate to which they were normally entitled: free travelers were to pay the fixed rate, and fixed-rate travelers, the negotiable rate. But there is evidence of the inability or reluctance of post stations to carry out the official policy as dictated by the Magistrate of Road Affairs. Stations had to be reminded throughout the Tokugawa period to collect the proper fees "without fail" from official travelers who exceeded their quotas.

It was undoubtedly difficult to deny the importunate demands of official travelers for additional services, especially in the case of grand personages such as the imperial envoy to Nikkō (*Nikkō reiheishi*). Around 1736, the envoy and his retinue were limited to 8 porters and 5 horses, but they regularly used no less than 390 porters and 27 horses and did not pay for the extra numbers.[85] Threatening to cut short his journey and return to Kyoto, he usually succeeded in obtaining free porters and horses (*gochisō jimba*).[86] Sometimes official travelers would offer promissory notes of payment to the post station for the additional number of porters and horses used, but they frequently failed to carry through with the payment.[87] According to an official of one post station, even the lowliest of people on official travel abused their authority, and as a result the volume of official goods transported increased "tenfold" during the seventeenth century.[88]

Not only did official travelers use excessive numbers of porters and horses, but they often ignored the established regulations regarding load limits.[89] Daimyo and others were given a leeway of about 59–66 kilos for pack-horse loads, but even these limits appear to have been routinely flouted.[90] To ensure compliance with the regulations, five weigh stations were set up as part of Arai Hakuseki's Shōtoku Reform in 1712, three on the Tōkaidō and two on the Nakasendō. Later, in 1743, additional weigh stations were established on the Nikkō dōchū, Kōshu dōchū, and Hokkoku kaidō.[91]

Despite these measures, officials at weigh stations were subject to bribes and travelers discovered ways to beat the system. A commonly used method involved removing the excess weight of baggage before passing through the weigh station and carrying it by hand until the inspection was over. Transport workers in post stations were admonished not to pass on this "secret" to travelers for a tip.[92] The bakufu even tried appointing special officials, intendant deputies who were known as Weight Verification Officers (*kanme aratamesho shutsuyaku*), to the weigh stations in an effort to clamp down on abuse of the system.[93]

Another trick was practiced by merchants and other commoners: They passed off their goods as baggage belonging to a daimyo, court notable, temple, or even the imperial family in order to qualify for the cheaper fixed rate instead of the negotiable rate that commoners were supposed to pay.[94] Daimyo or court officials were even known to rent to merchants the wooden placards (*efu*) bearing the seal that served as identification for official travelers' goods; it is on record that even the powerful and prestigious daimyo of Owari and Kii indulged in this practice.[95] A mid-nineteenth century travel handbook for merchants instructed them that obtaining the wooden placards was, in fact, indispensable to their success.[96]

The bakufu seemed inert in the face of such widespread and varied abuse of the post-station system and the corruption within it. In its final spurt of reform in 1867, the government did implement a major measure that abolished free transport: Those officials who had formerly traveled gratis were required to pay the fixed rate. Despite the professed "unprecedented nature" of these decrees to assist post stations in financial distress, the measures proved to be too little, too late.[97]

To subsidize the free and fixed-rate transport services, the bakufu granted post stations a monopoly on transport. Despite this monopoly, stations had to make money on negotiable-rate transport in order to at least balance their budgets. Yet by giving priority to official travelers and cargo—commoner transport was undertaken only when the post-station labor force was not handling official transport—the system discouraged private but potentially profitable traffic.

The delays imposed on private individuals as second-priority users of the system prompted merchants to seek the right to have their commodities transported as "official" goods. When it came time to transport merchant goods, post-station officials would sometimes claim that there were no horses available and try to exact a temporary-storage fee.[98] Even when transported without initial stoppage, merchant goods had to be relayed—unloaded and reloaded at each post station—with considerable delay and risk of damage. As a result of this contradiction in the system, competition emerged between the official system and illegal private ones. Most of the latter was done on side roads, but some was carried out stealthily on main routes.[99] Private transport became a problem for the bakufu, particularly in the Shinano region, where private operators set up their own transport network, known as the *chūma* system; in that system one transport operator could lead a train of as many as four or five horses, instead of being limited to just one horse, as on the Gokaidō. Ironically, the unofficial system was more efficient because goods were carried directly to their destination without constant unpacking and repacking.[100]

Although the bakufu was unable to stop the *chūma* operators, it managed to tax them and limit the type of goods they could carry, thereby making the system quasi-official.[101] Nevertheless, conflict between post stations and private operators over transport rights erupted rather often

in Shinano from the late seventeenth century on.[102] Similarly, in the case
of at least one Tōkaidō station, Kakegawa, the volume of merchandise
transported there began to decline in the mid-Tokugawa period. It is
hardly surprising that in some areas the slow, cost-inefficient government
system began losing out to private overland and sea transport from the
late seventeenth century on.[103]

Efforts to keep travelers on the bakufu road system were essential to
the transport monopoly of official post stations and the economic survival of the transport system as a whole. Yet the availability of short-cuts
often proved irresistible. Just as Eugen Weber has found for nineteenth-
century France, in Tokugawa Japan, government did not always build
roads where the people found them the most useful; the state's purposes
in building them and the people's needs did not necessarily coincide.[104]

The practice of using side roads had been going on for a long time, but
early in the nineteenth century the bakufu was feeling particularly hard-
pressed financially and tried to take a firm stand on the issue.[105] Travelers
and merchants in Kōzuke were using one such route, which bypassed
three post stations on the Nakasendō (Kutsukake, Karuizawa, and Sakamoto), and in 1825 the bakufu ordered that this practice cease immediately.[106] In another case, in 1824 the bakufu ordered the local overlord to
close down a side road in Shinano which bypassed Iwamurada station.
This short-cut caused the station great financial hardship, and the overlord was ordered to build a palisade across it to prevent travelers from
using it illegally.[107] Travelers from Edo and Kazusa were also choosing to
travel by boat for part of the pilgrimage to Ōyama, near Fujisawa station,
and were bypassing Shinagawa and Kawasaki post stations. This prompted
complaints from the stations and the issuance of prohibitory edicts
by bakufu intendants.[108]

From these examples we can see that the bakufu transport system
could be quite inflexible when it felt its monopoly threatened: it attempted
to impede the free movement of travelers by prohibiting them from
using the most direct routes available. That it was not very successful in
doing so is evident from the litany of complaints that its officials issued
against the use of side roads. Even within the Gokaidō network, the
Tokugawa enjoined the daimyo to make less use of that system's second-

ary roads: "If the number of travelers using branch roads increases, there will be no meaning to having a main road. Henceforth, use the main road as much as possible."[109]

The bakufu's policy of economic protectionism is further evident in its prohibition of the use of side roads even when a river's waters rose to flood level, stopping all traffic for days.[110] According to one edict (1822), "It has been reported that in recent years travelers for convenience sake have been using side roads. When there is a river stoppage, for example, instead of waiting at the post station for the water-level to drop to an acceptable level, travelers have been breaking the law by using side roads. From now on, this is to cease."[111] Stranded travelers were, at times, forced to stay as long as two weeks at riverside stations, waiting for the waters to recede to an acceptable level.[112] Some even had to backtrack in order to find available lodging. Forcing travelers to stay days on end and spend a lot of money was such a temptation that riverside stations sometimes declared a river impassable when it was not or prolonged the stoppage unnecessarily.[113] According to one post station record at Shimada there was an average of fifteen river stoppages a year during the period 1825– 1830—mostly during the third through fifth months. River stoppages lasted, on average, about three days, and the longest stoppage during the five years was thirteen days.[114] One nineteenth-century traveler complained that villagers intentionally washed out a bridge near Iida on the Kiso kaidō to trap travelers.[115]

Post stations lost their monopoly not only on transport but on travel-related services as well, and were thus deprived of more of the income necessary to subsidize transport of official travelers and cargo. In theory, no travel services were supposed to be performed by villages between post stations. However, with the increase in volume of traffic by the end of the seventeenth century, tea houses, inns, and post-horse operators opened for business in villages without post stations, sometimes referred to as *chaya machi*, or "tea towns," along travel routes.

Some of the villages between post stations were officially recognized as rest stops (*tateba*); there were, for example, five such places on the stretch of road between Edo and Odawara. In 1715, the bakufu prohibited them from operating lodging services and threatened punishment for lodge operator, village headman and elders, and traveler alike. In 1858, though, Ōiso was still complaining that the inns and teahouses at a rest stop located between it and the next stop, Odawara, were maintaining many women who wore fine clothing and played the three-stringed shamisen, attracting not only travelers but local villagers. Moreover, some teahouses were lodging guests on the second floor.[116]

Although the intent of bakufu regulations (i.e., to preserve the economic monopoly of the post stations) was good, the regulations themselves were unrealistic. When a river stoppage occurred, travelers were expected to backtrack to the post station where they spent the previous night, when it was more convenient for them to lodge at nearby villages and wait until the water level dropped. Similarly, the bakufu instructed one village near Fujisawa that it could lodge pilgrims traveling to Ōyama for a five-day period (1829/6/27–7/2) during that shrine's annual festival, but unreasonably insisted that the same practice was prohibited at all other times.[117]

In the late-Tokugawa period, daimyo, financially hard-pressed themselves, began to use private inns rather than those officially designated for their use, or avoided staying in the post stations altogether. Post stations complained, the bakufu fulminated, but the practice nevertheless continued.[118] Even when daimyo stayed in the inns designated for their use, they cut corners on travel expenses by paying the inns insufficient compensation for services rendered. Inns derived income from two sources, lodging and gratuities, and prices were standardized and artificially low. Financially hard-pressed daimyo naturally cut back on gratuities and this practice gravely damaged inn business.[119]

In light of all the problems plaguing the official transport system, it comes as no surprise that most stations operated in the red. The sharp increase in official traffic during the first decades of the nineteenth century, and then again in the 1850s, pushed, for example, Oiwake's annual deficits in the period 1856–1860 from 528 to 737 *ryō* on an income varying from 240 to 260 *ryō*.[120] Such financial problems were compounded by the high interest rates that had to be paid on loans. In 1733 almost one-quarter of the budget of Naitō-Shinjuku on the Kōshū kaidō went toward paying the interest on its outstanding loans. As an increasing proportion of their budget went toward repayment of loans, Naitō-Shinjuku and other stations were swept up in a vicious circle of accelerating debt.[121]

It should be noted, however, that a deficit budget for a post station did not necessarily mean that all merchants there were suffering financial hardships. In fact, it has been suggested that scholars reevaluate post-station budget ledgers because of the possibility that many were "fixed" to support post-station claims of impoverishment.[122]

As noted in the previous chapter, the bakufu tried to help the post stations financially in a number of ways. Grants and loans, the latter particularly after periodic fires had ravaged the stations, were the two main forms of aid offered.[123] We also have noted that many stations were granted exemptions from land taxes when they were first established—an infringement on domainal economic sovereignty—and that later, when the system was expanded, the exemptions were increased proportionately. Yet even with this increase, the exemptions were small in real terms. For example, Oiwake, according to one late-Tokugawa source, was exempted nearly 10,000 *tsubo*, but that amounted to a reduction of only slightly more than 13 percent of its land tax.[124] The bakufu tried to clamp down further on official abuses by issuing regulations concerning the proper functioning of the transport system. A torrent of proclamations came flowing from the brushes of bakufu officials, particularly during the Shōtoku and Bunsei reforms at the beginning of the eighteenth and nineteenth centuries respectively. The repeated reissuing of the regulations meant that they were the equivalent of sumptuary legislation and were, therefore, very hard to enforce.[125]

But as the bakufu's own financial position worsened, it turned to various forms of aid other than loans and grants. For example, it deposited at intendant headquarters sums of money that were later lent out to bakufu liege vassals (*hatamoto*) and peasant villages in their domains. The interest from the loans was then turned over to post stations as a form of income. This source of income became an important part of the post station's budget; in the case of Sekigahara on the Nakasendō, this money comprised 36 percent of the station's income in 1837 and 63 percent in 1841. The smooth functioning of the system, however, depended on regular repayment by borrowers, mostly samurai, who generally spent the money on consumer goods and experienced difficulty in paying it back. Villages to which money was also lent often turned out to be a poor investment risk. Interest rates were lowered in an attempt to retrieve some income, and by 1865 interest income accounted for only 5 percent of Sekigahara's total income.[126]

Another form of aid to stations was a tax on prostitution in the post town. Although the bakufu gave official sanction only to some twenty gay quarters in major urban centers across Japan (e.g., Yoshiwara [Edo], Shimabara [Kyoto], Shinmachi [Osaka]), harlots (*yūjo*) were a regular feature of most post stations. In 1660 the Tokugawa government outlawed them, since the practice of prostitution, like gambling, was deemed disruptive of morality and the social order.[127] The prohibition was strictly enforced at first and severe punishments, such as beheading and crucifixion, were imposed on managers of large-scale operations.[128] The bakufu's hard-line position soon softened, however, and commoner inns were allowed to keep two prostitutes each, although they were now designated as *meshimori onna*, or "serving girls," because of their auxiliary function serving food and drinks to guests. Not surprisingly, the bakufu was hard put to enforce the prescribed limits and repeatedly issued prohibitions in vain.[129] Shinagawa, for example, was supposed to maintain a maximum of 500 women, but was reportedly keeping as many as 1,358 in 1844.[130] In the words of one post-station manager: "Some stations have serving girls and others don't; those with them prosper, those without them suffer economic decline."[131] The bakufu taxed prostitutes' income (inn harlots were considerably cheaper than their counterparts in urban licensed quarters) and from the available evidence it appears that these funds made up close to 7 percent of post-station income on the Tōkaidō in the mid-nineteenth century.[132]

The easiest solution to the bakufu's need for more income was to raise transport fees, yet there was a limit to the number of increases they could enact without discouraging use of the post-station system. Although capable of doing so, the bakufu was not willing to close the gap between the fixed and negotiated rates, and so fixed-rate fees were maintained well below market value. Fees as of 1711 became the base rate and subsequent price hikes, which were usually for a limited period of five to ten years, were expressed as a percentage increase over it. Between 1716 and 1803, prices rose by 20 to 50 percent for long periods of time, and after 1794 they never returned to the original base rate. In fact, for most of the remainder of the Tokugawa period, the fees remained about 50 percent

TABLE 4 Transport Costs (in *mon*) at Odai Station

Year	Cost for one Horse	Cost for Light Load[a]	Cost for one Porter
1606	42	—	—
1643	32	23	16
1666	38	24	19
1681	55	—	—
1690	41	27	21
1711	49	32	25
1815	71	46	36
1863	100	62	49
1868	379	248	191

Source: Kodama, *Kinsei shukueki*, p. 256.

Note: [a]"Light load" refers to *karajiri*, a type of load that a pack horse carried, consisting of either a rider with up to 20 kilos of baggage or up to 71 kilos of baggage without a rider.

higher than the base rate.[133] Transport costs for Odai, as presented in Table 4, provide a representative example of the general trend of increases.

Through price increases and other measures outlined above, the bakufu attempted to keep post stations economically solvent, but its efforts were not enough: ten stations on the Tōkaidō, from Shinagawa to Hakone, petitioned the Magistrate of Road Affairs in 1820, 1821, 1825, 1836, and 1841 asking for more financial aid. In their petitions, they complained that they had been obliged to take out loans merely to survive, leaving no money to repair their buildings. On each occasion, however, their application was ignored, for there were limits on how much the bakufu could help.[134] Moreover, none of the government's measures were able to offset the loss of income from free and subsidized fixed-rate transport, the erosion of the system's monopoly rights, and the rampant fraud and abuse practiced.

CONTENTION AND CONFRONTATION

Assisting villages were first established, as their name suggests, to support post stations when the volume of official traffic was high. With the resources of post stations limited and fixed—no expansion of the system was made after the early 1640s—any increase in volume above the level that stations could handle themselves became the responsibility of assisting villages. Over time these villages lost their supplemental role and assumed a more central function in the post-station system. While there are marked regional differences in the number of porters and horses provided by assisting villages, the central role that these villages came to play is clear. A sampling of the data reveals that, for example, Oiwake's assisting villages provided 70.9 percent of the horses and 45.1 percent of the porters which serviced official traffic at that post station in 1703; Ōiso's villages provided 24.8 percent of the horses and 42.6 percent of the porters for that post station in 1804; Kumagaya's villages provided 32.6 percent of the horses and 45.8 percent of the porters for that station in 1820.[135] In addition, the data for Hodogaya post station for the years 1820–1856 show that, during that period, its assisting villages contributed 47.8 to 63.5 percent of its porters and 2.2 to 12.9 percent of its horses.[136] These figures demonstrate that villages provided an increasing proportion of the steadily growing number of porters needed. Initially the villages played only a supportive role in supplementing the labor force, but from 1821 on they supplied more porters than the post station itself. During the years 1848–1851 the gap between the two sources of manpower was particularly large. In terms of horses, however, the villages provided a much smaller and relatively unvarying percentage.

Just how much the roles of post stations and assisting villages had been reversed by the late Tokugawa period is evident from conditions at Shinagawa. The contribution of porters from its assisting villages jumped from 31.1 percent in 1819 to 83.2 percent in 1861; their percentage of horses rose even more abruptly over the same period, from 2.8 percent to 18.1 percent. The feverish pitch of activity on the Tōkaidō during the closing years of the Tokugawa period is evident from the increasing number of porters (62,704 in 1819 to 263,736 in 1865) and horses (15,583 to 40,021 over the same years) used.[137] The burden placed on the assisting villages would have been considerably alleviated had post stations maintained the stipulated number of porters and horses established by the bakufu for official transport services. But, as noted above, the stations were generally unable to do so. From time to time the government would admonish them about their non-compliance, but its efforts were infrequent and not entirely whole-hearted.[138]

In fact, the bakufu approved further increases in the number of porters and horses that post stations could keep in reserve. As a result of Shinagawa's 1775 petition for such an increase, that Tōkaidō post station was allowed to hold back an additional 25 porters and 15 horses, bringing the total in reserve to 30 porters and 20 horses.[139] In real terms this meant that Shinagawa station could requisition villages when more than 70 porters and 80 horses were to be used in a single day. Other Tōkaidō stations applied for and were granted similar rights during the late eighteenth and early nineteenth centuries.

The number of reserves allowed on other roads varied considerably, but through this legal means the stations were able to transfer to assisting villages more of the burden for servicing official transport.[140] The reserve system was a source of contention between post stations and their assisting villages: the villages made petitions against it, but the bakufu upheld the demands of the stations.[141] Even with the increases in the number of reserve porters and horses allowed, however, post stations still held back additional labor, causing conflicts with their assisting villages.[142]

As early as 1637 post stations were told not to requisition porters and horses from assisting villages until the stations had completely exhausted their own supply. Strictly speaking, according to regulations, assisting villages were not to be used to provide free transport, for this was the responsibility of post stations; they were supposed to assist only with fixed-cost transport when needed.[143] In addition, the stations were instructed repeatedly not to act "in a selfish manner" by relegating official, low-rate, and unwieldy goods to assisting villages, while reserving higher-paying merchant and easy-to-transport goods for the post station's own work force.[144]

In 1658 the bakufu circulated an order that post stations must not request excessive numbers of horses and keep them unnecessarily at the station all day long, nor were they to hide horses when the volume of traffic was high. This injunction was included in a formal written pledge that the government required post stations and the headmen of assisting villages to sign. The villages, on their part, were told to dispatch the requisitioned porters and horses—able-bodied men and strong horses—punctually. The pledges were repeated again in 1665, 1787, and 1836, and declarations reaffirming their basic principles were also issued periodically.[145] The pledge was a statement of principles regarding the economic relationship between post station and assisting village, and either side would petition for redress of its grievances if the other party failed to fulfill its part of the agreement.

Repeated abrogation of these pledges by both parties obliged the bakufu to re-issue the declaration with some frequency. The government announced from time to time, "We hear that post stations have been requisitioning porters and horses from assisting villages before using up their own supply." In 1821 an admonition circulated to Tōkaidō and Nakasendō post stations declared that the stations were offering excuses and charged that they had been requiring assisting villages to provide transport "for sick travelers and for unexpected goods, but it is for these very reasons that they are allowed to maintain a certain number of porters and horses in reserve." Post stations, they were told, should not use assisting villages for these purposes.[146] Assisting villages routinely complained about post-station abuses, but cash compensation was rare; the cash settlement paid to the assisting villages of Shinagawa in one case was exceptional. More often than not, efforts of the post station to extract more than was their due from assisting villages resulted in other forms of contention and collective action.

Just as the bakufu ordered post stations not to use assisting villages for free transport, it repeatedly censured them for requisitioning "unnecessary" (*muda*) porters and horses. This practice, it declared, was causing hardship to the villages and prompting them to appeal to the government for relief.[147] Post stations clearly were over-requisitioning. The twenty-eight assisting villages servicing Kumagaya provided 21,731 porters and 11,874 horses in 1839; of this number, 5,428 porters (25.9 percent) and 4,548 horses (38.3 percent) were not used, and consequently no compensation was provided for them. The villagers had earlier, in 1824, formed a cooperative body to help prevent over-requisitioning, but conditions fifteen years later were evidently still bad.[148]

The bakufu recognized the problem and in 1704 appointed officials from intendant headquarters to oversee post-station business.[149] Too often, however, these officials, known as *shuku yakunin*, colluded with the officials of post stations and increased, rather than decreased, the excessive requisitioning. According to Arai Hakuseki, they were taking two to three times more than the number actually needed. The labor of assisting villages was used to cover free or fixed-rate official transport, and the money made by the station's work force on negotiated-rate traffic was pocketed by corrupt officials.[150] Thus, through the bakufu's inability to curb the rampant abuses of its officials, the experiment with centrally appointed overseers ended in failure. In 1712, only eight years after their appointment, all of them were dismissed.[151]

Post stations attempted to alleviate the constant, disruptive friction with their assisting villages by allowing the villages to appoint their own overseers, or *sukegō sōdai*. It was the responsibility of these peasant officials, who were appointed at different times during the eighteenth century, to prevent illegitimate requisitioning of assisting village porters and horses. At the offices established for them at post stations the overseers routinely examined procurement notices and were required to stamp their seal in the post station ledger, thereby indicating that there was no malfeasance.[152]

The appointment of peasant overseers was perceived to be at least a partial solution to the tension between post stations and their assisting villages because it removed the station manager as the sole authority in determining the division of labor quotas among the villages. The creation of this post was part of a process of what one scholar has called a redefinition of public and private in agrarian society. Just as peasants in late-eighteenth century Tokugawa villages demanded to verify the accounts for the land tax (a demand which "implied a new limitation of the headman's privileges"), those in assisting villages demanded to do the same for the transport corvée labor ledgers. Their actions removed the ledgers from the post station manager's "private realm" and established them in "public space."[153]

This was the theory, at least, behind peasant demands for the appointment of overseers. Their appointment, however, did not insure an end to conflict between post stations and assisting villages. The overseers appointed by the villages, like those designated by the government, proved to be highly corruptible. Rather than representing the interests of the villages that had selected them, they often colluded with station officials, allowing them to over-requisition in return for a secret payment. In fact, they sometimes became the target of complaints in assisting villages' petitions and thus worked contrary to their intended function. A Meiji government decree issued in 1868 formally abolished the position of assisting village overseers, having found that they had "been guilty of much injustice in the past."[154]

Post stations defended their over-requisitioning as necessary "in order to prepare for the [large number of] official travelers who do not submit prior notice of their transport needs."[155] Although encouraged to do so, official travelers often did not send advance notice of their needs to post stations. Therefore, in order to cope with this unannounced traffic, it was necessary for stations to have supplemental porters and horses on standby, and this policy appears to have enjoyed tacit official approval. On the Nakasendō, it was common for stations such as Oiwake to requisition 30 percent more porters and 20 percent more horses than were needed on paper.[156]

The *sukegō* tax, in essence, represented a conflict of economic interest between the state, represented by post stations, and assisting villages. This conflict lasted over a long period, but did not produce a continuous state of open contention. In the words of one authority, contention comes sporadically, "partly because organization and opportunity fluctuate as the parties to conflicts of interest lead their regular lives" and "partly because the parties constantly make strategic adjustments to each others' moves."[157] Through a continuous process of signaling, negotiation, and struggle, assisting villages resisted the insatiable demands of post stations that encroached on both their time and livelihood. Their challenges to post stations ranged from passive resistance to remonstrance to open rebellion.

Assisting villages employed a variety of means to express their dissatisfaction, but different forms of passive resistance were generally the first methods to be used. Villagers signaled their discontent by arriving late for work, by sending old men or young children instead of able-boded men, and by providing insufficient numbers of porters and horses.[158] Tarui post station, for example, complained three times (in 1681, 1689, and 1703) that its assisting villages were not sending the required numbers of horses; reportedly, only seven out of every ten requisitioned were brought to the station. It was only after Tarui petitioned yet another time, in 1718, that the intendant would hear its case. The assisting villages, in turn, censured "the unlawful activities" of the station officials, who, they claimed, were over-requisitioning and making illegal use of labor from assisting villages for free transport.[159]

The discord between Tarui and its assisting villages was not easily resolved. In 1758/4 a compromise agreement was reached that allowed its assisting villages to appoint an overseer to examine the station's ledgers. Despite this accord, the forty-odd assisting villages failed to provide the agreed-upon number of porters and horses, thereby disrupting the station's relay service. A petition to the Magistrate of Road Affairs by the post station in 1758/10 resulted in an order for both sides to appear before him in Edo. An agreement was reached in 1759/4, but the two sides interpreted the terms differently, requiring still further negotiations. Two months later the differences were settled and disputes between the two parties subsided for a while.[160] But the settlement, as was true of most judgments issued by the Magistrate of Road Affairs, was basically a restatement of the way in which the *sukegō* system was supposed to function rather than an assessment of guilt of one or both parties. The period of calm was therefore but an intermission in the long struggle between post station and assisting villages.

Assisting villages could, of course, send a strong signal to their post station by failing to show up for service at all. Kumagaya petitioned the Office of Road Affairs in 1775, asserting that the failure of its assisting villages to perform *sukegō* duty correctly—they were arriving late or failing to show up at all—was hindering its ability to transport official travelers and goods. Its assisting villages, in response, requested a reduction in the number of reserve porters and horses maintained at the post station.[161]

Similarly, the assisting villages of Warabi post station on the Nakasendō failed to dispatch any of the porters and horses requisitioned during the few days before the daimyo of Kaga was due to pass through in 1818, causing a pile-up of baggage at the station. The failure to provide the required services manifested the assisting villages' strong dissatisfaction with the post station's refusal to pay them their share of a recently implemented wage increase. With the indispensable role that assisting villages came to play in the transport system, their demands could not be easily denied, as this case shows. The station had no choice but to pay if it wanted the baggage transported.[162]

The first evidence of refusal by Warabi station's assisting villages to perform their *sukegō* duty dates from the mid-eighteenth century. Declining to perform the duty became so habitual that the local bakufu intendant sent notices to the assisting villages, threatening to report the matter to the Magistrate of Road Affairs if they did not desist. As a result of negotiations, it was agreed that the assisting villages could appoint overseers who would assemble at the post station when porters and horses were requisitioned. These meetings, however, became merely another opportunity for evasion. Village officials failed to attend or sent representatives in their place, thus causing further work delays. The breakdown in the authority of station officials over assisting villages is evident here; the intendant had to intervene and threaten recourse to higher authority merely to get village officials to attend the meetings at the station.[163]

Refusals to fulfill the levy appear early in the repertoire of resistance to *sukegō* taxation, but they occurred with increasing frequency from the mid-eighteenth century on. Moreover, with the monetization of the tax for more distant villages, it became possible to avoid the levy by refusing or delaying payment. Shinagawa complained in 1831 that its assisting villages were often late with payments, thus causing a cash-flow problem.[164] By 1866 Kusatsu post station on the Tōkaidō had not yet received, and probably never would, a total of 13,000 *ryō* in *sukegō* tax payments.[165]

Non-compliance, however, usually was only a temporary measure until a new accommodation could be made between post stations and their assisting villages. The most common way by which the villages resisted increased demands on their resources was through legal petitions to higher authority, meaning to an intendant or the Magistrate of Road Affairs, for a reduction or cancellation of their tax. In many cases, especially in the last century of the Tokugawa period, villages were drawn together, at times without regard to domain boundaries, by a common economic interest (e.g., *sukegō* duty to the same post station or linkage to the same irrigation system) into cooperative groups (*kumiai*). Legal petitions therefore were often, but not always, made by these groups instead of by individual villages.[166] Their petitions would include an overview of each village, a record of its assets and liabilities, and a list of responsibilities for irrigation and other maintenance work. The document often included a statement regarding the unique conditions of the petitioning villages that made their case particularly worthy of consideration. An official investigation was then necessary before a decision could be made.[167]

The Magistrate of Road Affairs, whom assisting villages and post stations could petition, moderated the potentially serious disruption which demands for *sukegō* levies created. Yet, at times, the legal system became overloaded by the volume of petitions submitted. A village official from Katata (Ōmi province) named Nishigori Gohei, who traveled to Edo in 1865 to obtain an exemption from *sukegō* service to Ōtsu station, reported that on the day he arrived at the Magistrate of Road Affairs office, thinking that he had come early in the day, there were already some "seven or eight hundred people" there.[168] Indeed, so many villages were applying for exemptions from *sukegō* duty owed to Tōkaidō post stations that on at least two occasions the Magistrate of Road Affairs explicitly discouraged further applications: "In the future," it announced in 1761 and 1851, "we will not easily grant your petition." Villages were advised, moreover, to refrain from petitioning because of the "wasteful" travel and other expenses involved.[169] Of course, as the case from 1865 just cited indicates, few were, in fact, sufficiently discouraged to not apply. It seems that when the bakufu warned of wasteful expense, they had in mind officials like Nishigori, who spent two months in Edo. He and his companions did not seem to be in any hurry to get home, for after learning that their petition had been accepted on 1865/4/14 they remained in Edo for more than a month, until 5/25, to enjoy the city.[170] Still, the significant cost incidental to petitioning the bakufu in Edo could be a positive force in that it most likely encouraged many assisting villages to try and resolve their disputes privately, outside of the formal courts.

Regular assisting villages applied for reductions in their tax burden by requesting appointment of auxiliary assisting villages. These villages were located further from the post station than the regular assisting villages; those assigned to Oyama on the Nikkō dōchū, for example, were more than twenty-four kilometers away.[171] By the turn of the nineteenth century, regular assisting villages were declaring themselves impoverished and applying for reductions and exemptions in such great numbers that the system seemed in danger of collapse. Many regular assisting villages were granted exemptions or reductions for five to as many as twenty years; to compensate for the loss in taxable income, the bakufu had to expand the geographic sphere of taxation, appointing new, and more distant, villages (*daisukegō* or *tōbun sukegō*) to replace them.[172] In one case, nine regular assisting villages servicing Suzumenomiya post station of the Nikkō dōchū petitioned for relief in 1820 and were granted a reduction of about 25 percent in tax duty. In their place, twenty-four other villages were designated to fill the exempted duty.[173]

Toward the end of the Tokugawa period, the sphere of taxation necessarily spread quite far in order to draw on enough taxable income to support the *sukegō* system. By 1862, 132 villages, with an estimated yield of 37,606 *koku*, were taxed in order to support official transport demands at Mitsuke post station on the Tōkaidō; the same station had required only 68 villages, with 21,484 *koku*, less than forty years earlier. It has been estimated that if, in fact, the situation was similar for the other eight post stations in Tōtōmi province, every village in the province would have been taxed for *sukegō* duty.[174] The trend of expansion was continued by the new Meiji government, which taxed, for the first time, the lands of religious institutions and the imperial court.[175]

The *sukegō* system caused problems not only for post stations but for assisting and non-assisting villages as well. For example, the *sukegō* tax caused tension and conflict between villages when the Magistrate of Road Affairs granted some villages a partial or total tax reduction without appointing any replacements, thereby effectively increasing the tax rate for the other assisting villages.[176] Further tension was created when, in their attempts to reduce or evade *sukegō* taxation, assisting villages petitioned to have other, untaxed villages take their place; the villages so designated were known as *sashimura*. This tactic was resorted to with increasing frequency from the mid-eighteenth century on.[177]

Nine villages located near Fukaya post station on the Nakasendō, for example, were exempted from *sukegō* tax duty because of their traditional obligation to provide personnel for the Tokugawa ancestral shrine at Serada in Kōzuke and to provide porters and horses for official travel to that shrine. Despite these responsibilities, the thirty-six assisting villages servicing Fukaya repeatedly petitioned the bakufu to have the nine villages also perform *sukegō* duties for Fukaya. The thirty-six villages continued to pressure the other nine to provide one horse for every 100 *koku* of their estimated yield. This pressure was so persistent that in 1837 the group of nine villages finally, in self-defense, petitioned the Magistrate of Road Affairs to grant them "explicit and permanent exemption for all future time." The conflict was resolved by an order to the nine villages to make annual payments of 70 *ryō* for an exemption that had hitherto been traditional and without charge. These annual payments came to an end in 1857, when the nine villages paid a lump sum in order to be completely released from any further *sukegō* obligations to Fukaya.[178] While this conflict was resolved peacefully through petition, it demonstrates that villages hard-pressed by taxation sought through collective action to reduce their burden, even if it meant doing so at the expense of other villages.

The process by which assisting villages designated other villages, not necessarily in the same district or even in the same domain, to replace them reveals that the peasants had a surprisingly detailed knowledge of local conditions. To designate another village as a replacement, an assisting village petitioned the Magistrate of Road Affairs, detailing the reasons why the other village, or villages, should perform *sukegō* duty in its place. Usually the rationale was that the other village was closer to the post station and that it was in far better financial condition. The petition normally included an account of the "unique conditions" (for example, extraordinary demands on the village for riparian maintenance work, or its location far from the post station) that made it difficult for the village to meet its tax obligations.[179]

Not all such petitions were successful, for the targeted villages understandably resisted attempts to impose an additional economic burden on them. Even if unable to stave off what amounted to economic aggression on the part of another village, the targeted village itself could later apply for exemption.[180] This aggression could result in interdomainal economic warfare when assisting villages attempted to have villages in another domain replace them.[181]

There were times, however, when the process of signaling, negotiation, and non-violent struggle broke down. Whether because of misread or ignored signals, deadlocked negotiations, or other reasons, *sukegō* taxation was a major cause of at least twenty-one occasions of violent collective action during the Tokugawa period. These outbursts first began around the middle of the eighteenth century,[182] when levies were rapidly increasing. In fact, only one *sukegō*-related disturbance occurred during the century and a half before 1764, the year when the most serious peasant rebellion in the Tokugawa period rocked nine domains and bakufu territories in four provinces. The uprising, known as the *Meiwa tenma sōdō*, or Meiwa Post Horse Rebellion, marked a turning point in the relationship between government, through post stations, and assisting villages.

During 1763 the Magistrate of Roads ordered surveys of supplemental assisting villages in the area from the outskirts of Edo to Shinano, with the intent of increasing their tax burden by changing their status to regular assisting villages. In addition, an ad hoc tax (*kuniyakukin*) was imposed on villages in Musashi and other provinces in the spring of 1764 to defray the costs of the Korean envoy's visit to Edo. To add insult to injury, shortly after this, the bakufu called for a census of villages lying within an area of almost forty square kilometers from post stations on the Nikkō dōchū; the census was ordered in preparation for the pilgrimage of Ieharu, the tenth shogun, to Nikkō to commemorate the 150th anniversary of Ieyasu's death. The rate of taxation was set at six porters and three horses per 100 *koku* of estimated yield. Distant villages could convert the levy to a money tax at the rate of 6 *ryō* per 100 *koku*.[183]

The shogunal pilgrimage was due to take place in 1765/4, but during the last month of the previous year a rebellion was ignited by an uprising of peasants from Seki village in northern Musashi province. Assisting villages from the district designated for service at Honjō post station gathered on 1764/12/16, announced their demands for the remission of the tax, and later joined up with another group from Kōzuke province at Honjō. Avoiding the intendant's headquarters at Okabe, they moved north and then headed south down the Nakasendō to Fukaya and Kumagaya post stations, where peasants from the assisting villages servicing those stations had already assembled. At Kumagaya, the army of peasants clashed with troops the bakufu dispatched from Oshi domain.[184]

At its peak the uprising is said to have attracted more than 200,000 people, making it the largest peasant disturbance of the Tokugawa period.[185] The presence of such a large mass of irate peasants so close to Edo is said to have caused an uproar within Edo Castle.[186] The dispute was settled on 1764/12/30 by the Kantō Intendant, Ina Hanzaemon Tadasuke, who reassured the peasants that the new tax for the pilgrimage would be withdrawn unconditionally. Learning of the success of their campaign, the peasant legion disbanded. At this juncture, the character of the rebellion changed from one directed against bakufu injustice to one aimed at social leveling through the destruction of the homes and storehouses of village officials, rich peasants, *sake* merchants, and moneylenders, and it was not until the sixth day of the New Year that law and order were restored.[187] The Meiwa Rebellion was only one of a number of large-scale outbursts of violence during the years 1726–1764 that rocked the foundation of bakufu rule.[188]

The shock induced by the magnitude of the uprising apparently forced the bakufu to reconsider its policy toward assisting villages. Government authorities recognized that there were clear limits to the usefulness of force in response to peasant contention against the *sukegō* tax. But since assisting villages rarely had to resort to violent means of protest,[189] the use of that option was seldom appropriate. While it occasionally resorted to ruthless suppression when peasants outstepped the bounds of acceptable protests,[190] in general, the bakufu chose to adopt a more conciliatory posture.

In doing so, the bakufu tried harder to resolve the sources of potential conflict between post station and assisting villages. When in 1776 it tried once more to carry out Ieharu's planned pilgrimage to Nikkō, it reduced the tax levy by one-third.[191] In a further attempt to avoid the continuous discord and occasional violent outbursts caused by discontent with the *sukegō* tax, the government encouraged assisting villages to designate overseers to serve at post stations. Although an act of reconciliation, the appointment of these overseers gave assisting villages greater opportunity to resist increased taxation. At Warabi and other post stations the number of delinquent villages increased after 1764.

There were limits to the authority of the bakufu. It could refuse to accept petitions for reductions or exemptions from assisting villages — as it did with increasing frequency in the last decade of its rule — but the result was often a rise in the incidence of villages failing to comply with requisition orders. Once an assisting village refused to perform its *sukegō* levy, the station could threaten to appeal to a higher authority; but that might benefit the village by allowing it a hearing, possibly forcing the post station to compromise. In the meantime, the post station had to cover for the delinquent villages or else watch traffic come to a standstill. The bakufu could impose fines on the assisting villages for their non-compliance,[192] but it seemed extremely reluctant to do so, for increasing the financial burden assessed on peasants did not reduce already existing tensions. Rather, it tried to arbitrate between post stations and assisting villages. Yet the Magistrate of Road Affairs' legal decisions often merely restated the theoretical principles behind the economic relationship between the two; thus the government left it to the two parties themselves to find a modus vivendi. The bakufu courts were, however, an important instrument of conflict resolution beyond their symbolic value as a legal avenue of last resort. The granting of exemptions and reductions, as well as the expansion of the sphere of taxation, were acts of conciliation by the Tokugawa to appease assisting villages. They were also tacit acknowledgment of the vital role assisting villages played in keeping a somewhat precarious post-station system functional.

The Tokugawa bakufu created a well developed network of overland communications for its political and strategical needs that met much praise from Western visitors. It took command of the country's major highways for the passage of its martial forces, the movement of its officials, and the conveyance of official communications, and in so doing usurped domainal authority in a number of ways. The Tokugawa asserted sovereignty over the thoroughfares and the post stations on them and charged the daimyo with the upkeep of the transport infrastructure. The restricted territorial extension of the official Gokaidō system reflects the less-than-national aim and scope of bakufu control.

Beneath the vitality of the post stations that Kaempfer and others found remarkable lay an economic malady that was perhaps invisible to foreign eyes. If Tokugawa roads and post stations were the "arms and legs" of the bakufu, and the Tōkaidō one of the body's "main arteries," then the government was in one sense chronically ill by the middle of the eighteenth century, suffering from hardening of those arteries. Increases in the volume of official transport, which meant an actual loss of income for the stations; inadequate financial aid in relation to the services performed; and the erosion of its monopoly in transport and travel-related services all left the post-station system in serious economic straits. Various schemes, some of them quite imaginative, were attempted in order to aid the stations, but at the same time the bakufu passed up on possible sources of income, such as enforcing quotas and load limits for privileged travelers, which would have enabled the system to survive on its own.

The largest single source of income that the bakufu denied itself was allowing the daimyo use of the lower-priced fixed rate of transport. A government order obliging the daimyo to pay the market price would have reduced the wasteful extravagance of their retinues far more effectively than repeated sumptuary admonitions to economize ever did. It was understandable, perhaps, that bakufu official business should have traveled free, yet it is difficult to understand why the daimyo should have enjoyed the privilege of the reduced, fixed rate. It is possible that the daimyo were initially granted use of the fixed rate early in the Tokugawa period, when the political climate was still unsettled, as an incentive to travel to Edo on alternate attendance. Another possibility is that, early in the Tokugawa period, the difference between the fixed and negotiated rates was not so great (we have no data to support or contradict this), and that subsequent rate hikes increased the gap between the two. Government councils never discussed altering its policy towards the fixed rate, even though such a change would have injected additional finances into the system and eliminated some of the abuses associated with the *sukegō* levy. While one might argue that the bakuhan system was founded on the principle of privilege for the samurai status group, and that to expect daimyo to negotiate prices like commoners was unthinkable, they were already required to do so when they used more than their quota of men and horses at the fixed rate.

When other forms of aid failed to achieve the desired results, the bakufu allowed post stations to transfer much of the burden for servicing official transport onto their assisting villages, and the villages naturally resented and resisted these attempts. Occasionally, they rose up in rebellion to voice their dissatisfaction, but more often, assisting villages had recourse to less spectacular methods of displaying their indignation. Through a seemingly continuous process of struggle, assisting villages attempted to hold off post-station demands for more transport workers, horses, or money. The variety of non-violent methods of contention employed, while more routine and less conspicuous than any acts of collective violence, were as important, and probably more effective in the long run, in defending their interests.[193]

The problems of the post-station system may perhaps be viewed as symptomatic of the malfunctioning of the Tokugawa bakufu as a whole. Retention of the system, essentially unchanged through two and a half centuries, despite its obvious defects and economic weakness, was typical of the bakufu mentality and its determination to preserve the status quo. Perhaps it was because the status quo had acquired an aura of sanctity: to alter it was to violate the legacy created by Ieyasu himself. Piecemeal and inadequate measures with small chance of success were introduced; but when wholesale, organizational reform was suggested—for example, imposing a uniform tax to support the post-station system—it was opposed by scholars such as Arai Hakuseki, who believed that the behavior of human beings and not the system itself should be reformed. Even the proposed reform, however, is suggestive of the limited aims and scope of Tokugawa power, for it never even hoped for a national tax, only one on its home lands.

Official sanctions granted to Gokaidō post stations worked to institutionalize the relationship between overland transport and the bakufu. Authorization of these sanctions reflected a desire to regulate the transport system, limit the proliferation of post stations, and make the system efficient. To a certain extent, however, the creation of an official road network and government-protected stations hindered the development of communications in that the system was created as a result of political and military, rather than economic, considerations. Short-cuts on land and water routes which bypassed stations were therefore prohibited. Nevertheless, higher transport costs on the Gokaidō, the relay method employed on its roads, and the first-priority granted to official traffic, encouraged the use of non-official roads and the development of private transport networks.

THREE

A Curious Institution

Western visitors to Tokugawa Japan invariably remarked on what Lord Redesdale called a "curious" institution:[1] the *sekisho*, or "barriers," as the term is most often translated. Toll-gates were common enough in the West, but not the fenced-in compounds straddling major roads that he found in Japan. Fifty-three of these compounds, however, were erected on the central highway network, the Gokaidō; and the German physician, Englebert Kaempfer, for one, reported on them:

> The goods and baggage of all travellers, but particularly of the princes of the Empire, must be visited in this town by Imperial commissioners appointed for this purpose, who are to take care, that no women nor any arms pass further. This is one of the political maxims which the new reigning Emperors [i.e., shoguns] have found necessary to practise, in order to secure to themselves the peaceable possession of the throne, for the wives and female children of all the princes of the Empire are kept at Jedo [Edo], the Imperial Capital, as hostages of the fidelity of their husbands and parents. And as to the exportation of arms, a full and effectual stop hath been put to that, lest, if exported in any considerable quantity, some of these princes might take it into their heads to raise rebellions against the Government, as it is now establish'd.[2]

In other words, sekisho monitored daimyo compliance with the system of alternate attendance. The passage of women through the barriers was regulated to prevent unauthorized movement of daimyo wives and daughters out of Edo, where they were kept as virtual hostages as insurance against the insurrection of their husbands, the domainal rulers. The movement of guns into Edo was also controlled, to prevent the daimyo from building up a potentially dangerous cache of weapons in the bakufu administrative capital. This two-pronged policy has, in contemporary historiography, become known by the phrase *iri-deppō ni de-onna,* or "inbound guns and outbound women."

The explanation Kaempfer heard was offered to most foreigners by the bakufu. That it was not just an over-simplification, fabrication or half-truth told to satisfy the curiosity of foreigners is evident from the fact that in 1862, when the alternate attendance system was relaxed, the checking procedures at sekisho were also eased. But is this really a sufficient explanation for the function of sekisho? The German physician Franz von Siebold, for one, noted the seeming illogicality of the system: "Why such vigilance is observed in regard to persons visiting Yedo, is nowhere satisfactorily explained; the avowed object of it, however, is to prevent the escape of wives of princes, governors, and other men in high office, whose families are detained at court as hostages for the fidelity of husband and father."[3] Were there not more effective means of preventing daimyo wives and daughters from leaving Edo than by checking all women, from every social status, at each of the barriers across the transport network? The Confucian scholar Ogyū Sorai certainly thought so. In 1727, he proposed that a system of barriers be established on the boundary between the city of Edo and the surrounding countryside to inspect the passes of those leaving (but not entering) the city.[4] Furthermore, if women and guns were the two principal targets of bakufu policy, then why, as the evidence shows, did male travelers also sometimes come under surveillance? To try to answer these questions, it is necessary to analyze the development of sekisho in an historical context.

SEKISHO BEFORE THE INSTITUTIONALIZATION OF ALTERNATE ATTENDANCE

Barriers served different functions before the Tokugawa period.[5] In ancient times they served largely as border military posts to check Emishi invasions of land under Imperial control or to protect the Kinai area, and particularly the Imperial Palace, from attack. By the end of the Heian period (798–1194) they began to assume an important economic role, as the Imperial government, which was feeling the loss of income due to the spread of tax-free estates (*shōen*), began levying tolls on travelers and commerce. Local military powers (*jitō*) likewise erected barriers on estate lands. The number of barriers going up increased rapidly in the Kamakura and Muromachi periods; even religious institutions turned to sekisho as an important source of income to compensate for the dwindling funds they were able to collect from their estates.[6]

The proliferation of sekisho during the Muromachi period was a result of the political instability of the military government, or bakufu, and this pattern continued as political instability progressed into the internecine warfare of the Sengoku age (1477–1567). The military character of the institution became dominant once again, as warlords built armed outposts with high walls and deep moats in mountain passes and on other sites with strong natural defenses.[7]

Nobunaga and Hideyoshi worked hard towards pulling down these barriers in order to promote economic growth and assert their political authority. While they did enjoy a degree of success, the two leaders were not able to eradicate them completely, as most daimyo, including the Tokugawa founder, Ieyasu, were busy erecting sekisho for the defense of their domains during the period of national unification (1568–1600).[8]

While the first barriers on what would later be called the Gokaidō predate the institution of the bakufu, the majority of the fifty-three were put in place during the years of the second shogun, Hidetada (r. 1605–1623). They were established on the two major thoroughfares linking Edo and Kyoto: on the Tōkaidō, at Arai, in either 1600 or 1601, and on the Nakasendō, at Kiso Fukushima, in 1602.[9] An additional sekisho was erected on each of the two roads, and more soon followed on the other roads in the Gokaidō network. The elevation of Ōsasa and Kariyado (Kōzuke) from Numada domain border posts (*kuchidome bansho*) to bakufu sekisho in 1662, and the construction of barriers at Yanagase (Ōmi) and Sekigawa (Echigo) in 1686, completed the network.[10]

The creation of a sekisho network must be seen as the act of a nascent political power to establish and extend its authority over the other daimyo and over a society that had been experiencing tremendous upheaval, particularly during the second half of the sixteenth century. The prerogatives that the shogunate accumulated and the control system it created are for the most part well documented:[11] The bakufu gave and took land at will, built up and maintained military superiority over its likely opponents, prohibited the construction of new castles and required authorization for the repair of old ones. It also maintained a system of direct surveillance of the domains through centrally appointed inspectors, assumed direct control of key commercial cities, and supervised both domestic and foreign trade. While a comprehensive list of bakufu powers would be much longer, we should add to it here the establishment of a centralized transport network and the imposition of a system of corvée labor tax to support it, as previously outlined. The shogunate also asserted in its *Laws of the Military Houses (Buke shohatto)* of 1635 (Kan'ei 12) that, "No private barriers may be erected nor any existing ferry be discontinued,"[12] but as will become clear later in the chapter, it never attempted to fully enforce this area of authority to which it laid claim.

Bringing stability to the realm, however, required more than devising methods to control the daimyo; for the many social, economic and political changes instituted by the bakufu and domains resulted in general dislocation in Tokugawa Japan. Samurai were, for example, drawn off the land and required to live mostly sedentary lives in castle towns; merchants and artisans, and a variety of other people followed in their footsteps as part of a process of rapid urbanization that may have no parallel elsewhere.[13] The inactivity of the samurai contributed to the civil unrest present in many castle towns during the early days of the new political order. Young bushi, dressed in outlandish clothing, formed gangs known as *kabukimono* and strutted through the streets with their swords dangling by their sides, looking for trouble.[14] Crime was epidemic in the cities and on the highways.[15] According to one authority, "The violence of the early seventeenth century symbolized a society that was still relatively open and undergoing profound changes. The fighting at kabuki theaters in 1611 and 1612, the murders in the streets, and the trouble that came when kabukimono loitered on the street corners illustrated the degree to which the Maeda daimyo [of Kaga domain] were unable to extend a full measure of police control over the urban population [of Kanazawa]."[16]

The same was true in most major urban areas and government authorities found it necessary to construct physical barriers, *tsuji bansho,* within the cities.[17] Wooden gates blocked off sections of the city and allowed the foot soldiers who guarded them to control the movement of people. As many as 110 of these barriers were erected by Nagoya authorities in that city by 1624 and there, as elsewhere, nighttime passage through the gates was generally prohibited.[18]

A large number of samurai lost their masters through defeat in the warfare of 1600–1615; these unemployed warriors, known as *rōnin,* posed a real security risk to the Tokugawa government. An estimated 17,000 such warriors were rendered masterless after the Battle of Sekigahara alone. Exercise of Tokugawa power through escheat, reduction, or transfer of domains during the first half of the seventeenth century also caused approximately 398,000 samurai to become *rōnin.*[19] Because these figures have been calculated on the basis of the total rice production (*kokudaka*) of the domains that were confiscated by the Tokugawa, failing to take into account the fact that many *rōnin* did find employment with another lord, we cannot take them at face value. Nevertheless, they are an indication of the number of warriors dislocated through warfare and measures of political control.

The bakufu did not want these idle warriors causing trouble in urban areas. In 1610, four years before the Osaka campaign, orders were issued to a number of major temples in the Kinai region not to harbor *rōnin.* After Osaka, great numbers of *rōnin* collected in Kyoto, prompting the bakufu's highest-ranking official in that city, the Kyōto shoshidai, to issue orders in 1623 to drive them out of the area. One article of the ordinance read: "All *rōnin* trying to enter into the employ of another daimyo should be expelled." Even those former warriors who had settled down into some business and were living as townsmen were not exempt, for it was feared that they would soon long for warfare once again.[20]

In the eastern provinces of Shimōsa, Kōzuke and Musashi, the bakufu constructed temporary sekisho at sixteen water crossings in order to solidify its control in the Kantō as well as to prevent the defeated forces of the Toyotomi camp from escaping into northern Japan, where they could regroup and later stir up more trouble. At the same time, it issued the "Regulations Concerning Ferry Crossings" (*Fune watashi sadame*) of 1616:[21]

1. It is forbidden to cross without special permission at any other but the designated crossing place.

2. Women, people with wounds, or any suspicious looking persons without a pass from the Keeper of Edo Castle [*orusui*, or the bakufu official in charge of Edo Castle in the shogun's absence] must be detained and immediate notification sent to Edo. The above people who do have travel permits may pass through freely.

3. Even with a permit from the Keeper of Edo Castle, it is still forbidden for women, people with wounds, or suspicious looking persons to cross at any other than the designated crossing place.

4. Travelers heading in a direction towards Edo need not be checked.[22]

Ferry crossings were allowed only at designated spots, where the flow of traffic could then be directed and controlled more easily. The 1616 order had an earlier counterpart in a 1607 law governing overland transport, which prohibited travel on any but the main roads. Both sets of regulations were intended to direct traffic into channels that could be monitored more effectively.[23] Without these laws the establishment of sekisho would have had little effect as anyone could have bypassed them on alternate routes.

All sixteen ferry crossings were located on the Edo and Tone Rivers, both of which at that time provided direct access routes from Edo to Kōzuke and Musashi. Because the bakufu was concerned with preventing the defeated forces of the Toyotomi camp from escaping north, only traffic heading in a direction away from Edo was monitored. To catch absconding masterless samurai, inspection at sekisho focused particularly on wounded persons: Without a special permit from the Keeper of Edo Castle, they were denied passage at ferry crossings and arrested.

In addition to these sixteen river sekisho, some river crossings without official designation acted as unofficial sekisho. Government authorities at the river crossing at Nakasemura, for example, checked travelers' permits and prohibited crossings during the night.[24] Located upstream from Shingō-Kawamata, and downstream from Goryō, Nakasemura acted, in effect, as an auxiliary sekisho.

THE STRATEGIC ROLE OF SEKISHO

The mature network of Tokugawa sekisho consisted of fifty-three barriers spread out over nine provinces, ranging from Ōmi in the Kinai region to Echigo in the Hokuriku area (see Map 2).[25] Twenty-four of the fifty-three were classified by the bakufu as "very important" (*omoki*), and were reputed to be the strictest in their requirements for the passage of women travelers. The remainder were classified as "less important" (*karuki*). In the first category, Hakone, Usui, Kiso Fukushima, and Arai were the most important.

The distribution of sekisho reflects the nature and scope of Tokugawa power and reveals the political concerns of that government. Also taking the classification of sekisho into consideration, we can say that the bakufu was an Edo-centered power which was most concerned with the control of the central portion of Honshu island, and was particularly attentive to the threat from the daimyo of northern and northwestern Japan. Reflecting this concern, an inner ring of sekisho was located along the outer boundaries of Musashi and Kōzuke provinces, blocking all the major and minor roads leading to and from Edo. These sekisho lay within territory held by fudai daimyo and served to cut off the fiefs of the hypothetical enemy in the north, such as the Maeda of Kaga, from the Kantō and Tokugawa headquarters in Edo.

Eleven sekisho lay to the south of Edo, in the Tōkaidō region. The three in Tōtōmi cut off any western daimyo approaching the Kantō on the coastal Tōkaidō. The eight in Sagami covered the Tōkaidō closer to Edo and its various branch roads. Sekisho in northern Kai province controlled movement between outer daimyo in Shinano and the northern Kantō. Suruga province, bordered by Tōtōmi, Sagami, and Kai, mostly consisted of bakufu territory and no sekisho was therefore established there.

The sekisho established in Echigo and Ōmi province lay at great distances from Edo and make us wonder what function the bakufu intended for them. The line of sekisho in Ōmi could in fact control traffic between Kyoto and the fiefs of the outer daimyo in the northwest. The bakufu was particularly interested in keeping an eye on all traffic going to and from Kaga domain. That domain's productivity was assessed at a

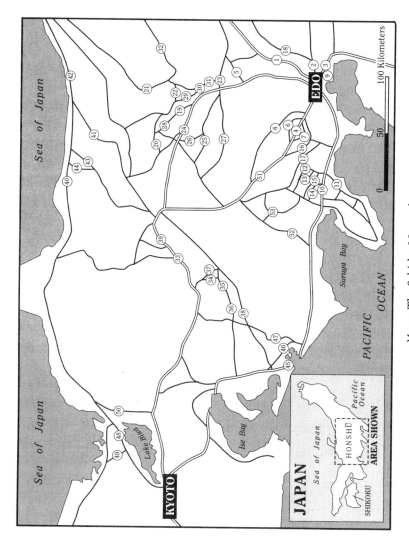

Map 2 The Sekisho Network

Key to Map 2

Sekisho	Province	Administrative Authority
1 Kurihashi*	Musashi	daikan
2 Kanamachi-Matsudo*	Musashi	daikan
3 Koiwa-Ishikawa*	Musashi	daikan
4 Kobotoke*	Musashi	intendant
5 Shingo-Kawamata*	Musashi	intendant
6 Kami-Oshikata	Musashi	Kantō intendant
7 Kami-Kunigida	Musashi	Kantō intendant
8 Hinohara	Musashi	Kantō intendant
9 Nakagawa	Musashi	bannerman
10 Hakone*	Sagami	Odawara
11 Nebukawa*	Sagami	Odawara
12 Kawamura	Sagami	Odawara
13 Tanigamura	Sagami	Odawara
14 Sengokugahara	Sagami	Odawara
15 Yagurasawa	Sagami	Odawara
16 Nenzaka	Sagami	intendant
17 Aonohara*	Sagami	intendant
18 Seki*	Shimosa	intendant
19 Odo*	Kozuke	intendant
20 Ōsasa*	Kozuke	intendant
21 Sarugakyo*	Kozuke	intendant
22 Mokugahashi*	Kozuke	Takazaki domain
23 Goryo*	Kozuke	Maebashi domain
24 Usui*	Kozuke	Annaka domain
25 Nanmoku	Kozuke	intendant
26 Saimoku	Kozuke	intendant
27 Shirai	Kozuke	intendant
28 Kariyado	Kozuke	intendant
29 Ōwatari	Kozuke	Maebashi domain
30 Sanemasa	Kozuke	Maebashi domain
31 Fukushima	Kozuke	Maebashi domain
32 Tokura	Kozuke	intendant
33 Kiso Fukushima*	Shinano	intendant
34 Seinaiji	Shinano	Iida domain
35 Onogawa	Shinano	bannerman
36 Namiai	Shinano	bannerman
37 Kokorogawa	Shinano	bannerman
38 Obigawa	Shinano	bannerman
39 Niekawa	Shinano	intendant
40 Ichifuri	Echigo	Takada domain
41 Sekigawa*	Echigo	Takada domain
42 Hassaki*	Echigo	Takada domain
43 Yamaguchi	Echigo	Itoigawa domain
44 Mushigawa	Echigo	Itoigawa domain
45 Imagiri (Arai)*	Tōtōmi	Yoshida domain
46 Kega*	Tōtōmi	bannerman
47 Kanazashi	Tōtōmi	bannerman
48 Kennokuma*	Ōmi	Koriyama domain
49 Yamanaka*	Ōmi	bannerman
50 Yanagase*	Ōmi	Hikone domain
51 Tsuruse	Kai	intendant
52 Manzawa	Kai	intendant
53 Motosu	Kai	intendant

Source: "Shokoku gosekisho oboegaki," in KKKS, vol. 10, pp. 67–70.

Note: * denotes key sekisho designated as omoki (lit., "very important") by the bakufu.

figure in excess of one million *koku,* and its lord was second in power only to the Tokugawa. Thus, the establishment of sekisho in remote Echigo was an integral part of the bakufu's policy of monitoring the Maeda, a policy which also involved the placement of vassal domains around Kaga. The establishment of Yanagase (1686) and Sekigawa (1687) sekisho at such late dates, however, appears to have been the direct result of a period of agitation between Kaga and the bakufu. Sekigawa was a particularly strict sekisho where only women with a travel permit from the high-ranking Keeper of Edo Castle were granted passage; at all others in Echigo, women needed only a daimyo-issued pass.[26]

Looking at the distribution of sekisho by road, we find two major sekisho on both the Tōkaidō (Hakone and Arai) and Nakasendō (Kiso Fukushima and Usui). These were the four strictest sekisho on the two most important roads in Tokugawa Japan. To prevent detours around these four major sekisho—and this was the pattern for all the major and secondary sekisho—branch sekisho were established on side roads: for example, Sengokugahara, Yagurasawa, Kawamura, and Tanigamura all monitored traffic on roads which bypassed Hakone. It was possible to detour around Arai sekisho by taking the Honzaka dōri, but a sekisho was placed at Kega to monitor that traffic. The same was true of the Nakasendō: minor sekisho were established at Niekawa to monitor traffic on a side road around Kiso Fukushima and at Saimoku to cover a road detouring around Usui sekisho. For this reason we should think of the sekisho network as a group of subsystems, each centering around a major sekisho.

The strategic defensive pattern formed by sekisho in the barrier network can perhaps best be grasped by visually connecting the lines formed by each sekisho subsystem in Map 2. The first line, the farthest to the right on the map, is formed by the sekisho group on the Tone and Edo rivers (nos. 5, 1, 18, 2, 3, and 9 on the map). Another line is formed by connecting the Usui (nos. 20, 28, 24, 26, 25, and 27), Kobotoke (nos. 8, 6, 4, 7, 16) and Hakone (nos. 17, 12, 13, 15, 14, 10, and 11) sekisho subgroups. A third line of defense is formed by connecting the Kiso Fukushima subsystem (nos. 33 and 39) with that of Namiai (nos. 37, 34, 35, 36, and 38) and Arai (nos. 47, 46, and 45). Smaller lines are formed in Ōmi (nos. 48–50), Echigo (nos. 40–44) and Kai (nos. 51–53) provinces.

Both the Honzaka dōri and the road around Usui sekisho, known as the Oiwake dōri, were also referred to as Hime kaidō (lit., "princess road") because women tended to use them. Taking the Honzaka dōri allowed one to avoid the Imagiri crossing, between Arai and Maisaka stations, which involved what was often a rough boat trip of about five kilometers. By taking the Oiwake dōri the traveler avoided the steady uphill climb necessary to cross over the Usui Pass. Although these two roads were time-consuming detours, the guards posted at the sekisho were reputed to be slightly less strict in their inspection of women travelers than those at main-road sekisho, adding to the attractiveness of these routes for women.

Three branch roads leading from the Nakasendō to the Hokurikudō each had two sekisho: The Hokkoku kaidō had Sekigawa and Yanagase; the Mikuni kaidō had Mokugahashi and Sarugakyō; and the Hokurikudō had Ichifuri and Hassaki. The Nikkō/Ōshū dōchū and Kōshū dōchū had only one each, Kurihashi and Kobotoke, respectively. The Kōshū dōchū was regarded as the bakufu's escape route in case of any invasion from either the west or the northeast, and therefore, as noted, in addition to lining the route with fudai daimyo, the bakufu placed the 1000-samurai unit (*Hachiōji sennin*) in Hachiōji to cover their escape route. During any emergency, if the situation warranted it, the entire force could man the sekisho.[27]

During the mid-eighteenth century fudai daimyo administered twenty-two sekisho, while bakufu intendants and bannermen of special rank (*kōtai yoriai*) together were responsible for thirty-one. Arai came under the direct administration of the bakufu through one or two appointed magistrates until 1702, when control of the sekisho was turned over to the vassal domain of Yoshida. To smooth the transition to that domain, which had no experience administering a sekisho, the bakufu permanently left behind seven officials from its staff. The officials, however, drew their stipends from Yoshida, and not bakufu, coffers.[28] The practice of maintaining a hereditary core group of officials with hands-on experience was, therefore, a key to the continuity of policy at individual sekisho such as Usui, which changed administrative hands eight times during the course of the Tokugawa period.[29]

But why would the bakufu turn over the administration of two of its most important sekisho, Hakone and Arai—both on the most heavily traveled road, the Tōkaidō—to fudai daimyo? And why turn over Arai at such a late date as 1702? Why did the shogunate not appoint its own officials, as it did for a century at Arai, to supervise the execution of policy at all sekisho? While the answers to these questions cannot be known conclusively, with so many sekisho under fudai daimyo administration, they must be considered as an organic part of the bakuhan system. Either the bakufu did not have the manpower and finances to maintain direct central control, or with the key administrative role played by its fudai daimyo, did not feel it necessary to do so. By 1702 the Tokugawa peace was well under way and the bakufu probably felt no need to administer Arai itself. Financial belt-tightening might have been another factor contributing to the bakufu's decision to relinquish direct control.

Military and Police Functions

The mountainous character of the land around Edo to the south, west and northwest made it relatively easy to control traffic. The highways ran through the most accessible routes and provided convenient points at which to monitor travelers and cargo. More inconvenient and difficult routes which would not normally be used by the ordinary traveler were controlled by auxiliary sekisho. Most often, sekisho were positioned in mountain passes, in narrow ravines between mountains, or along rivers.

All of the four most important sekisho—Hakone, Arai, Kiso Fukushima, and Usui—were located in strategic geographical positions to control the flow of traffic. Hakone sekisho was located at the western entrance of the first difficult mountain pass west of Edo: In other words, it was the first location on the Tōkaidō heading west where traffic could be easily blocked. The climb up to the sekisho was so treacherous that it was known as *tenka no ken*, or the "impregnable pass of the realm"; it can still be experienced today on a well-preserved hiking path. In the back of the sekisho, to the west, lay Lake Ashi, where no swimming was allowed; the English diplomat Ernest Satow was the only man on record in Tokugawa history to swim there for recreational purposes.[30] The number and movement of boats allowed on the lake was strictly regulated.[31] On its three other sides, the sekisho was surrounded by a number of mountains that were in excess of 1,000 meters, making evasion difficult. To this purpose side roads were covered by minor sekisho. In the words of Kaempfer, who has left us such a vivid picture of Genroku Japan:

> It [Hakone] is stronger than that of Array [Arai], and the people examin'd with more rigor, it being, as it were, the key to the Imperial [i.e, the bakufu] capital, which none of the Western Princes [outer lords] nor indeed any body that comes from those Provinces, can avoid passing through in their journeys to court. For besides that the road on both sides of the Guard-house is very narrow, and shut by several strong gates. Nature herself hath fortify'd this place by inaccessible mountains to the right, and the lake above describ'd to the left.[32]

Kiso Fukushima, on the other hand, was located in a long and narrow ravine running along the Kiso River. (See endpapers. Source: *Kisoji meisho zue.* Tokyo University Library.) Surrounded by mountains, the barrier at Fukushima was located in the narrowest part of the Kiso valley, the best location from which to control the flow of traffic running through the Kiso valley on the Nakasendō. Many sekisho were located in mountain ravines or at the foot of mountain passes, but as we noted earlier, a fair number were also located along rivers, often at places where roads crossed rivers, forming natural barriers where travelers were forced to cross at easily regulated river ferries or fords. The bakufu took advantage of these topographic features and erected a number of sekisho on the Tone and Edo Rivers. Main sekisho were established on the Edo side of the rivers and auxiliary sekisho on the other side in order to discourage detours. This accounts for the hyphenated names of Koiwa-Ichikawa, Kanamachi-Matsudo, Shingō-Kawamata, and Bōsen-Kurihashi sekisho.[33] Arai was the only sekisho located on the coast, or more accurately, on a narrow strip of land which extended into the opening that connected Lake Hamana with the sea; and traffic there was regulated by permitting vessels traveling either east or west to dock or depart only at designated places.[34]

While it is difficult to deny that sekisho were located at points where the flow of traffic could be effectively monitored, it is equally difficult to make the case that the topographical features of the sekisho site imparted any decided military strategic value. Hakone, for example, though in a position to monitor or regulate the flow of traffic on the Tōkaidō, could have its supply lines cut off quite easily if attacked from the west. During the battle between Hideyoshi and the Go-Hōjō daimyo in 1590, when Hakone was actually used strategically, it fell to Hideyoshi's forces in half a day.[35]

As physical structures, sekisho were not meant to be strongholds. Built of highly flammable wood, they usually consisted of one or two simple buildings, each with a number of rooms serving various functions. The physical size of sekisho tended to be directly proportional to the volume of traffic that normally flowed on the road on which they were located. Hakone, one of the busiest sekisho, had two large buildings, facing each other, between which the traveler passed on his way up or down the Tōkaidō. The main building consisted of two guard rooms, a lounge-dining area, a kitchen, a bathing room, and an earthen-floored room leading to a stable. The auxiliary building, which stood directly across from the main one, contained a guard room, a lounge area, and a small jail cell where sekisho offenders could be held.[36] (See Figure 4.)

Sekisho were, with one notable exception (Kega), not enclosed by moats or ditches, but major ones were enclosed by palisades, and passage through them was made via a gate on either end of the enclosure.[37] Projecting from the enclosure or the solitary gate were more palisades, stretching out in various directions as topography dictated to block possible detours around the sekisho. In contrast, minor sekisho usually had only one gate and a much more limited configuration of palisades.[38]

In addition, a number of sekisho also had watchtowers. The one at Hakone, which looked much like a log cabin on stilts, was located to the southeast of the sekisho on a hill about thirty meters above the water level of Lake Ashi.[39] One of its functions was to monitor the lake for unauthorized crossings; this is apparent from orders issued periodically to cut down trees obstructing the view of the water from the watchtower.[40]

GUARD FORCE AND BACK-UP MECHANISMS

The size of sekisho guard forces varied, like the physical size of the barrier building(s), according to the importance of the sekisho. The size and makeup of the guard force at Hakone and its branch sekisho are indicated below in Table 5.

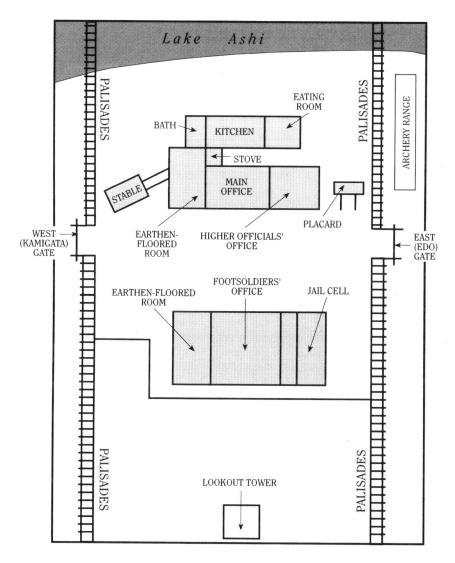

Figure 4 Diagram of Hakone Sekisho.

TABLE 5 Hakone and Its Branch Sekisho Guard Forces (1688)

Sekisho	Head Guards (banshi)	Regular Guards (jōban)	Foot Soldiers (ashigaru)	Attendants (chūgen)	Total Number of Guards
Hakone	5	3	12	2	22
Nebukawa	2	3	2	1	8
Yagurasawa	2	3	2	1	8
Sengokugahara	1	2	2	1	6
Kawamura	1	2	0	2	5
Tanigamura	1	1	0	0	2

Source: Watanabe Kazutoshi, "Edo bakufu no sekisho seido no kakuritsu to kinō," p. 35.

Head guards (*banshi*) were the highest authority at the sekisho; they were officials sent on rotation from Odawara domain. Part of their titular duties included a yearly inspection of the strategic area surrounding the sekisho. In contrast, regular guards (*jōban*) lived near the sekisho, and were the most versed in sekisho affairs. They were the officials actually responsible for the inspection of travel permits and had custody of the key to lock the sekisho gates.[41]

Foot soldiers (*ashigaru*) and attendants (*chūgen*) made up the bulk of Hakone's guard force. Foot soldiers handled travelers' passes (they handed them to the higher officials), captured criminals, and manned the watchtowers. Attendants provided sentry duty at the sekisho gates and performed miscellaneous tasks such as cleaning, taking care of equipment and repairing the palisades. Like the *banshi*, foot soldiers and attendants were sent on rotation from Odawara.[42]

In comparing other sekisho with Hakone we find that Arai, for example, had the largest number of personnel of any sekisho, between fifty-two and sixty-five for most of its history. Of course only a portion of the total force, perhaps eight to ten men, would be on duty on any given day.[43] Usui had a total of eighteen guards and officials, but in contrast with Hakone, all personnel, except the two top officials, who were on rotation from Annaka domain, lived nearby, and their positions were, as at most sekisho, hereditary. The two top officials at Usui were rotated ten times over the years 1749–1834, or about once every eight years.[44] At some other sekisho, however, the period of duty was only a couple of months long.[45]

Except for the four largest sekisho, most others maintained substantially smaller guard forces: Hakone's branch posts maintained a total force of two to eight men; minor sekisho in Kōzuke (Mokugahashi, Sarugakyō, Ōdo, Goryō, Ōsasa, and Kariyado) had from three to six.[46] The same was true of minor sekisho in other provinces as well: The average number of guards maintained was about four, and not all were necessarily samurai. While there was some slight variation in the size of guard forces at different sekisho, the numbers presented here are representative of the mid-seventeenth century on. Unfortunately, however, no records remain of the early Tokugawa period, when the military function of the institution was probably at its strongest.

Middle-size and minor sekisho, usually under the administration of intendants or Tokugawa bannermen of special rank (*kōtai yoriai*), employed peasants as regular or lower guards. At Kariyado, Ōsasa, and Sarugakyō (Kōzuke), peasants with the rights of sword and surname (*myōji taitō*) performed regular guard duty, and their positions were hereditary. At Kariyado, a single peasant with these rights filled the position of regular guard (the equivalent of *jōban* at Hakone) and four peasants without special rights served as lower guards, with two to a shift. Two samurai sent from Numada domain rounded out the guard force.[47] Even at large-scale sekisho such as Usui, however, villagers were used as lower guards: the two men guarding the east gate were villagers without any special rights, while the two who guarded the more important west gate (*tenka no mon*) were commoners with the privileges of sword and surname.[48] Commoners performing guard duty at sekisho were usually granted an exemption from transport corvée labor in exchange for their service.

In addition to the duties described above, guards also manned watchtowers at those sekisho that had them. Their foremost responsibility was to monitor the surrounding area, day and night, being on the lookout for people illegally bypassing the barrier compound. On numerous occasions the watchtower guards at Hakone reported hearing noises in the brush or seeing people trying to sneak by.[49] On such occasions they would alert the sekisho by signaling with wooden clappers.

Watchtower guards at Hakone also patrolled along the palisades three times a month, looking for breaks or areas in need of repair or replacement, and surveyed the strategic area (*yōgai chiiki*) surrounding the sekisho for intruders. All sekisho designated a strategic area, where unauthorized entry was prohibited, even to cut or collect firewood, and at Hakone this area was also observed by boat from Lake Ashi once a month.[50]

Sekisho guards were armed with a variety of weapons, such as guns, bows, spears and staves. Arsenals at a representative sampling of sekisho are listed in Table 6. In addition to these weapons, ammunition—bullets and arrows—was stocked, and manacles and rope kept on hand to bind criminals or insane people.

Most sekisho also maintained on display at one sekisho gate the "three weapons" (mitsu dōgu): a multi-pronged barbed spear (sodegara), a two-pronged, u-shaped weapon (sasumata), and a stave (tsukubō). They were both functional and demonstrative. Placed near the sekisho gate, they were meant as a warning to any person who might be thinking of forcing his or her way through, and they appear to have made quite an impression on travelers. They were also put to use at times to round up criminals or travelers who had mistakenly strayed into the off-limits strategic area, as well as to goad reluctant travelers denied passage away from the sekisho compound.

Sekisho arsenals were not meant purely for show; with the exception of shooting practice, however, one suspects that the guns and bows stored at sekisho were not otherwise used. In the 155 years of guard diary accounts that exist for Hakone, not one mention can be found of either type of weapon's being used on a human being. One notable exception to this, but at a different sekisho, occurred in 1636, when a rōnin cut down a guard at Kiso Fukushima and ran through the barrier compound. The next day a peasant spotted him hiding in a temple not far from the sekisho, and guards were sent to arrest him. The man obviously resisted arrest, and apparently feeling that there was no other recourse, the guards shot and killed him.[51] Nevertheless, among orders to Hakone guards to clean and shine their guns and armaments every month were included the instruction to replace old fuse cords, suggesting that the guns were not used very much.[52]

The military function of Tokugawa sekisho was probably strongest early in the Tokugawa period, when they were called upon to play an active role, but we have no information on armament and staffing levels

TABLE 6 Sekisho Arsenals

Sekisho	Guns[a]	Bows[b]	Spears[c]	Staves[d]
Arai	25	25	10	10
Usui	10	5	10	7
Kiso Fukushima	20	5	15	14
Kobotoke	5	5	5	6
Sekigawa	5	3	5	13
Kega	20	10	15	13
Ichifuri	3	3	5	2
Hassaki	3	2	5	3
Hakone	10	5	15	12

Source: Igarashi Tomio, *Kinsei sekisho seido no kenkyū,* p. 322.

Notes: [a]"Guns" refer to *teppō*, the matchlocks modeled on those first brought to Japan by the Portuguese in the mid-sixteenth century.

[b]"Bows" refer to the native Japanese bow, a graceful weapon made principally of bamboo, which stands over two meters tall.

[c]The category "spears" includes both the long-handled spear and the halberd.

[d]Staves are long, wooden poles, similar to those used in the martial arts today.

until the late seventeenth century. With the onset of the Tokugawa peace, however, there was less and less need for sekisho to play a military role, although that function did not totally disappear.

From the small size of the guard force and the arsenal maintained at Hakone and elsewhere, we may conclude that the forces available were inadequate by themselves to stop a sizeable invasion or civil uprising. Edo period sekisho, however, were similar in some respects to the sekisho of early Japanese history in that they were meant to be manned by a large force only during real or potential emergencies. There was, in other words, an organic relationship between sekisho and the headquarters of the official administrator in which reserve forces could be called up from the headquarters to man the sekisho. In 1631/9, for example, when there was a peasant disturbance in Kōzuke and Musashi provinces, particularly near Oshi, the bakufu ordered that a force of foot soldiers be sent from Tatebayashi Castle to Kawamata sekisho to gather information and prepare defenses against the uprising.[53]

In the case of Hakone and its branch sekisho, reserve forces would be called up from Odawara, located ten kilometers away. Odawara had on standby supplementary guard units for Hakone and its branch sekisho, and in case of need, it is likely that more could have been sent.[54] During the crisis precipitated by Yui Shōsetsu in 1650, the regular guard at Hakone and its auxiliary sekisho was increased and all traffic stopped for a few days.[55] Bakufu intendants or other bannermen appointed as sekisho administrators could have drawn on their limited forces and called upon nearby vassal domains for assistance. The ability of sekisho administrative authorities to send or receive reinforcements in time depended to a certain extent then upon the speed of intelligence received on the movement of an uprising or invading force and the speed with which the reinforcements could be mobilized and dispatched to the sekisho.

Another back-up mechanism that was employed at several sekisho was a peasant-reserve (*gō ashigaru*) system.[56] In this way government sought to use commoners as an apparatus of the state, to control the "activities of civil society through its own infrastructure."[57] At Hakone, for example, 318 villagers from the surrounding area were each assigned one gun by Odawara domain and had orders to assemble at the sekisho gate if anything "suspicious" occurred. The designated villagers, who were granted tax exemptions of up to ten *koku* of rice, were forbidden to sell their guns, lend them to anyone (including relatives), or carry them around.[58] On one occasion Hakone received sufficient warning of a mob of "thousands" of peasants from Suruga province heading towards the sekisho on its way to Edo in time to round up some of its peasant-reserve force. The group of discontented peasants was stopped before passing through the sekisho and persuaded to return home peacefully the next day[59]—evidence that while the size of the guard force maintained at Hakone and elsewhere may not have been large, the threat of the use of force was still a deterrent to civil unrest.

Sekisho were employed for military defense during shogunal trips. For example, guard forces were routinely beefed up and no guns were allowed to pass in any direction towards Nikkō during official pilgrimages to Tōshō-gū. But during the Boshin War, the conflict which brought the Tokugawa to their knees, sekisho did not play an active role. Of the six fudai daimyo that fought with the bakufu at Toba-Fushimi, none were sekisho administrators. Oshi domain, which administered Shingō-Kawamata in Musashi, was important in the bakufu's strategy for the defense of Edo from the northern outside daimyo. Although it did not make the decision to side with the Imperial forces until that army was just outside the town, there was no standoff or military conflict at Shingō-Kawamata or any other sekisho.

Even Hakone was taken over by the Imperial forces in 1868 without a fight. The advance guard of the Imperial Army, which included a group of seventy samurai and gunners from the Kyushu domain of Ōmura, and a small group of Satsuma men reached Hakone on 1868/2/28, where the leader of the Ōmura group got up on the *jōnoma*, the room at the sekisho where the highest officials sat, and declared the shogun, Tokugawa Keiki, a traitor. To the question whether Odawara, the domain charged with administering Hakone, was loyal to the Emperor or not, the head sekisho official gave the only expedient answer, a resounding, "Of course." The sekisho was turned over, without a fight, to the contingent of Satsuma men.[60]

Be this as it may, the peaceful turnover of Hakone to the Imperial forces says more about the nature of the bakuhan system, which relied on the support of fudai daimyo long after it could realistically have expected it, than it does about the military value of Hakone. For, according to Harold Bolitho, the fudai daimyo were "unconvinced that their destinies and that of their Tokugawa master were so closely intertwined that the fall of the one would inevitably bring down the other."[61] While there is no evidence that the bakufu issued orders to its sekisho to stop the invading imperial forces, only four years earlier, in 1864, when orders were sent to Seinaiji (Shinano) to stop a ragged band of about 1,000 Mito samurai and peasants heading for Kyoto, the daimyo in charge there balked, allowing the force to pass through the barrier. The daimyo was, needless to say, punished, but not as severely as one might think. He was removed from his duty and placed under house arrest, yet his domain was not confiscated: It was merely reduced by 2,000 *koku*.[62] This incident reveals the weakness of bakufu authority in the closing years of the Edo period and demonstrates the limitations of the sekisho system, which relied too heavily on the fudai daimyo.

Sekisho Regulations and Policy

Sekisho were used more for routine police functions than as military strongholds. This is made clear by a set of regulations promulgated by the shogunate in 1625 and posted on edict boards at sekisho, providing travelers with instructions on how to pass through safely:

1. All persons must remove their hats or head coverings in front of the guard house before passing through the sekisho compound.
2. All persons in palanquins must open the doors of their vehicle [for inspection] before passing through.
3. Court nobles, temple heads of court rank (*monzeki*), and daimyo have long been exempted from inspection if they have given prior notice of their arrival. If anything seems suspicious, however, any person, regardless of rank, is subject to inspection.[63]

The edict boards later posted at sekisho in 1666 contained the same articles as this earlier set of regulations, but included a new provision: "Guns must be accompanied by the prescribed permit (*shōmon*) or they will not be allowed through the sekisho."[64] Although this represents the first record of an order regulating the movement of guns through a sekisho, we know that they were being inspected well before this.[65] The daimyo who were coming to Edo regularly to wait upon the shogun, a custom that would become systematized in 1635 as the alternate attendance, were required to possess a permit to transport guns into Edo, and it could only be obtained from the bakufu's Council of Elders (*rōjū*).

Bakufu-issued instructions sent to officials at more than a dozen sekisho in 1631 (they were not for public consumption in placard form) read:

1. People with wounds, women, and anyone suspicious are definitely not allowed to pass through the sekisho without a travel permit.
2. If someone passes through the sekisho illegally, even if we find out about it later, the authorities responsible [i.e., the boat man, the official in charge of the river crossing office, etc.] as well as the local residents, will be held accountable.
3. If someone who has passed through illegally is caught, a reward will be given to the person responsible for the arrest, the amount of which will depend on the status of the offender . . .

4. If someone tries to bribe his way through the sekisho, arrest him and send notice of this to us.[66]

In 1711 the bakufu added two more articles to the standardized regulations posted at sekisho, the last change in content or wording that it would make for the remainder of the Tokugawa period.[67] The first of those articles, as found on an edict board at Hakone, stated that "[c]orpses, persons with wounds, and anyone suspicious may not pass through the sekisho without a travel permit."[68] This was nearly the same order issued to sekisho officials back in 1631, yet it was not included on placards posted at sekisho until 1711. This is not unusual, for the content of bakufu-issued notices to its officials typically were not the same as proclamations meant for the public, and judgments about what commoners needed to know could vary over time.[69] The guard diaries maintained at Hakone indicate that the sekisho there was carrying out the instructions received in 1631 at least from the 1680s, when the official diary accounts begin, just as guns were being inspected before the date in which that fact was noted on placards in 1666.

Interestingly, the second new provision issued in 1711 was more specific in its instructions on how female travelers were to be inspected:

1. Women passing through the sekisho must be carefully examined in relation to their travel permits.
2. Women riding in palanquins must be taken to the guard house and inspected by the appointed Inspector of Women (*onna aratame*).[70]

In other words, women presenting their travel permits at sekisho must physically match the person described in the document or else passage was denied. This was done to prevent women from being smuggled out of Edo, especially a daimyo's wife whose husband was about to move against the bakufu in some act of rebellion.

Other orders issued to sekisho regulated night passage, which was generally prohibited. Instructions sent to Hakone, Kega, and Arai specified that only bakufu messengers and post station relay messengers (*tsugi hikyaku*) were allowed passage at night.[71] Later instructions sent to Arai gave this privilege to a larger group comprised of people who carried the sealed documents of the shogun, various high-ranking bakufu officials, daimyo messengers and the Osaka Castle guard force.

These various orders regulating night passage through sekisho were only issued after the Yui Shōsetsu Incident, an attempt to overthrow the bakufu in 1651/7. Yui's ability to pass through or by Hakone undetected before being arrested in Sunpu led the bakufu to reassess its sekisho policies and resulted in the decision to tighten up security by strictly regulating night passage.

From the regulations cited earlier, it is clear that the intent of the bakufu was to monitor outgoing women and incoming guns at sekisho. Instructions sent to officials at Arai said that, "Women and guns are top priority."[72] Daimyo processions, however, were not even inspected if prior notice had been given. The bakufu did reserve the right to do so if anything seemed suspicious, but it appears never to have exercised that right, possibly because it never needed to do so. Its second aim was to control the movement of persons endangering the civil peace.

The bakufu sought to direct the flow of women traveling onto major roads for two basic reasons. The first was consistent with the general policy of directing human traffic onto the main Gokaidō network in order to sustain the system economically. The second was that it was much easier to monitor the movement of women at a fewer number of sekisho on major arteries than to do so at each of the fifty-three sekisho. Consequently, only local women were allowed to pass at twenty sekisho and a number of these applied the same prohibition to men as well.[73]

In Musashi province, for example, only local women were allowed to pass through the sekisho at Hinohara, Kami-Oshikata, Kami-Kunigida, and Nakagawa. Non-local traffic was directed toward the major arteries in the provinces (the Nikkō dōchū, Mito kaidō, Shimōsadō, Kōshū kaidō and Tatebayashidō) where, at five sekisho (Bōsen-Kurihashi, Kanamachi-Matsudo, Koiwa-Ichikawa, Kobotoke, and Shingō-Kawamata), all westbound women were required to hold travel permits from a high-ranking bakufu official, the Keeper of Edo Castle. This pattern of channeling traffic was true in other provinces as well.[74]

It was noted earlier that sekisho were established in Ōmi and Echigo at least in part to enable the bakufu to monitor the activities of Kaga domain. To this purpose women passing through sekisho in Ōmi province heading north were required to apply for travel permits from one of the bakufu's major officials in the Kinai area, namely the Kyoto, Osaka, or Fushimi city magistrates; the Kyōto shoshidai; or Captain of the

Osaka Castle guard. In this way the bakufu could keep track, in part, of who was traveling to Kaga. Travelers from the north heading towards the Kinai area who passed through Ōmi sekisho were not, however, checked for permits. With the exception of the three sekisho in Ōmi and Arai sekisho in Tōtōmi, the bakufu was primarily interested in checking women traveling away from Edo, where they were permanent hostages under the alternate attendance system.[75] We will discuss what form this checking took in detail in the following chapter.

The second half of the bakufu's "women and guns" policy was the checking of weapons heading eastbound towards Edo. Instructions the bakufu sent to Arai stated:

1. Vessels going either east or west anchoring at Arai will be inspected.
2. No eastbound guns will be permitted to pass without a permit issued by the bakufu Elders. It is not necessary to inspect westbound guns.[76]
3. All baggage over three feet being transported either east or west will be examined. Long containers (*nagamochi*) will be examined even when going westbound.[77]

In other words, baggage over three feet long was checked going both ways on the Tōkaidō in order to prevent guns from being smuggled into Edo and daimyo women from being smuggled out of the city.

Englebert Kaempfer noted that his goods "were not opened, but only look'd over." He went on to explain that the weight of his trunk "made them suspect," but that the guards were satisfied with the answers given to their inquiries and did not open it. Granted that the case of a foreigner like Kaempfer might be exceptional, other cases of baggage passing through unchecked make us doubt the strictness with which such examinations were carried out. Ōta Shokusanjin, traveling on official business as a minor official of the Magistry of Finance in 1802, did not have his baggage, which was marked by the characters "*goyō*" or "official," opened. He was required, however, as a formality, it seems, to unlock his baggage, which might have been closed up with chains of some sort, before being allowed to pass through.[78]

A group of three travelers on their way to Edo in 1759 to petition against the transfer of their daimyo also passed through Arai without having their bags opened. The group included a regional village headman (ōjōya) from Karatsu, who most likely had rights of sword and surname; and he was asked what was inside his bags.[79] We are not told how large the baggage was, but if it was large enough for the guard to ask what its contents were, it was probably large enough for guns. From these and other examples we can conclude that the examination of baggage was, to a large extent, an empty formality if the suspicions of the sekisho guards were not aroused.

At Hakone, however, weapons were not checked.[80] Perhaps this was because inspections for guns were made already at Arai and Kega on the Tōkaidō, making it unnecessary to repeat the procedure at Hakone.[81] This reasoning makes sense if one considers that there were no powerful outer lords, whom the bakufu had the most reason to fear, located between Arai and Hakone. While guns were not formally checked at Hakone, it was not permitted for them to be transported through six of the seven other sekisho in Sagami, in effect channeling all guns passing through that province through Hakone and Nebukawa. The same pattern of channeling the transport of weapons through major arteries with large-scale sekisho was repeated throughout the network, just as it was for human traffic.[82] A bakufu record states that "though guns are not checked at Hakone, at Nebukawa they have been checked since olden times."[83] Thus, despite the failure to formally check weapons at Hakone, the bakufu could still monitor gun levels in a rough way. Granted that guns could be smuggled into Edo by vassal daimyo in the Tōkai region, the bakufu still reserved the right to examine anyone or any piece of cargo it deemed "suspicious." Herein lies, it seems, the reason why the bakufu did not feel it was necessary to examine for guns at Hakone as well as Arai.

MAINTAINING CIVIL PEACE

While "inbound guns and outbound women" together were the principal aim of bakufu sekisho policy for most of the Tokugawa era, a second aim was control of the movement of persons posing a threat, real or potential, to civil peace. Sekisho were supposed to act as barriers to fugitives and conspirators, the foremost example of the latter being Yui Shōsetsu, who was mentioned earlier.

Although the sekisho in Sagami province were not effective in catching Yui, Hakone was successful in controlling the movement of some undesirable elements. Sekisho could, for instance, be useful in stopping samurai from fleeing their domain. Usually the domain from which a samurai fled would notify the sekisho that "so-and-so" had absconded and would request that he be stopped at the sekisho should he try to pass through. A physical description of the individual would also usually be included.[84] Because a samurai absconding from his domain or domain residence in Edo would not be traveling with official permission, it was unlikely that he would have had a permit. Sekisho guards would therefore be on the lookout for samurai without permits. The Hakone guard diaries only note the fact that "it has been reported to the sekisho that such-and-such a retainer has absconded" (twelve cases over the years 1687–1746).[85] With no later record stating whether the people were ever caught, it is difficult to judge the sekisho's performance or to even know, for that matter, if the retainer tried or succeeded to pass by Hakone. In the few cases we have of such samurai being caught, they were usually turned over to domain retainers sent to pick them up; if it was a daimyo's retainer, it was up to the daimyo, not the bakufu, to discipline him.[86] Such was the decentralized nature of the Tokugawa political order.

Sekisho were also used to enforce the legal penalty of banishment. In one case, five men banished from Odawara domain were seen approaching Hakone sekisho the following day and were immediately arrested, and thereafter sent off to Odawara for imprisonment.[87]

Samurai or commoners with "suspicious-looking wounds"–in other words, those people without travel permits attesting to the origin of their wound or wounds–were denied passage through sekisho. Records at Hakone note nine cases between the years 1717–1775: as in the case of absconding samurai, not a very common occurrence.[88] Sometimes the person with the wounds would try to "explain" his way through the sekisho, but excuses such as "I fell off my horse"[89] or "This scar on my throat [which impeded the man's speech] is a result of an illness"[90] did not convince the sekisho guards.

Social stability was the foundation of the Tokugawa state. Just as the bakufu could not allow inexplicably wounded people to pass through its sekisho, so, too, it had to control the movement of insane people not accompanied by persons with an appropriate travel permit for them. The guard diaries at Hakone record twelve cases of insane people being turned away between the years 1686 and 1782, either because they had no permit or because the permit was not in proper order.[91] Official, stated policy at Hakone was to send such people back to their place of domicile, if it was known, or otherwise to hold them there and send a letter of inquiry to Odawara, the seat of the administrative authority for the sekisho. However, it appears that the official policy was for bakufu consumption only, for most of these people were simply accompanied a short distance away from the sekisho and set free.[92] If the person got violent or tried to run away, he was tied up and led away with a waist cord to the border of the neighboring village by foot soldiers before being released.[93] This was apparently as far as Odawara domain was willing to go in dealing with these non-domain residents.

Although such cases were extremely few in number, sekisho could also be effective in stopping peasant uprisings from moving forward. In a case discussed earlier, "thousands" of peasants from Suruga province on their way to Odawara to file a petition were turned back at Hakone sekisho, without recourse to violence.[94] But there were limits in jurisdiction even as far as groups of protesting peasants were concerned.

While the peasant groups from Suruga did not try to force their way through the sekisho, there are numerous examples of people trying to evade the inspection of officials there by going around the barriers. With approximately forty known cases during the long years of the Tokugawa peace, however, it cannot be said that it occurred very often. Those accused of this act, known as *sekisho yaburi* or "sekisho smashing," were not just refused passage. Legally the action was treated as a crime, the same as treason, rebellion, or killing one's master or parents. Those found guilty, therefore, were treated harshly, the penalty often being crucifixion.[95]

Influenced as it was by Confucian thought, Tokugawa law differentiated among people not only by status but by gender. In the case of sekisho smashing, if a woman or group of women were caught with a man trying to evade a barrier, the man would normally be crucified, while the woman would be subject only to the lesser penalty of enslavement or forced servitude (*tokei*).[96] The difference in treatment was based on the assumption that women, being socially inferior to men, were induced by men to come along. A woman traveling alone, however, was subject to crucifixion for sekisho smashing. Moreover, any person acting as a guide for an offender was subject to the same penalty as the offender. Trying to pass around a domain barrier (*bansho*), a topic we will come to shortly, was also a crime, though a lesser one. Men were penalized with medium-grade banishment, while women were simply handed over to their appropriate proprietary official for his disposition.

Those caught trying to go around a sekisho were first arrested and held temporarily at the barrier compound or the administrator's headquarters while notification was sent to Edo. Because the crime was committed on the bakufu-controlled road network, Edo had legal jurisdiction over offenders. The arrested party was sent to Edo and placed in one of that city's prisons. After the sentencing was concluded, and the offender found guilty, he was transported back to the place of the crime in a special caged palanquin used expressly for criminals and was crucified at a spot close by the sekisho. The offender suffered thrusts to the body and finally the throat with spears. After death the head was severed from the body and left exposed for three days. A placard was erected beside the head explaining the crime for all passersby to see and left up for a few weeks after the head was buried to serve as a continual reminder. Death in prison before the sentence could be carried out did not spare the criminal: the body was packed in brine and transported to the place of the crime in a vat, where the offender was crucified as if still living.[97] In some other cases, only the severed head was returned and posted on a stake near the sekisho in the same manner.[98] Not only was the criminal himself punished, but in the seventeenth and early eighteenth century, on account of the principle of mutual responsibility, all family and relatives were as well. Fortunately, Yoshimune had the wisdom to end this practice in his 1737 revision of the Tokugawa law codes.[99]

Evaders were caught not only by sekisho guards but also by villagers who were employed in village support systems (*yōgai mura seido*). That is, under the system, surrounding area villages were charged with keeping an eye open for travelers evading the sekisho and rewarded for catching them. Such a support system was established at Kega (1627), a sekisho on the Honzaka road which allowed passengers to avoid the water crossing between Maisaka and Arai, as well as the sekisho at the latter. Arai also employed a similar system, using fifty-six villages on both sides of Lake Hamana to prevent people from crossing the lake on their own and secretly landing at a point other than the sekisho landing area.[100] In this manner, too, political authorities attempted to use commoners as an apparatus of the state.

DOMAIN BARRIERS

In issuing the Laws of the Warrior Houses of 1635, the bakufu prohibited domains from establishing their own sekisho; yet daimyo continued to maintain barriers by a different name, *bansho*, within their own territories. The bakufu was tolerant of these, except on roads that were a part of the official centralized system, the Gokaidō. Some domain barriers predated the seventeenth century, having been established by daimyo for military defense and the regulation of commodity flow, but many were newly constructed. Had the bakufu tried to enforce the letter of the law, as written in the above regulations, prohibiting barriers within the domains, it would have interfered with the ability of daimyo to set their own economic policy, and thus would have entailed an unprecedented intrusion into domainal affairs. Recognizing the impracticality of pursuing such an undesirable policy, the bakufu restricted the application of the statute to the Gokaidō.

A number of differences exists between sekisho and bansho, but the two terms were often used indiscriminately by contemporaries.[101] Some domains referred to their bansho as sekisho for internal purposes while maintaining the semantic status quo by using the term bansho in official contacts with the bakufu.[102] Kaga domain, however, did not even bother to maintain the facade of compliance with bakufu regulations: During the regular inspection tours the bakufu dispatched to the domain, Kaga officials at Sakai bansho responded to inquiries whether it was a bansho or sekisho by asserting, on at least three occasions, that it was in fact a sekisho.[103] Kaga, by virtue of its great land holdings and special relationship to the bakufu, was probably the only domain allowed to openly flout the law.

The difference between sekisho and bansho seems obscure at times, even in bakufu documents;[104] in spite of their imprecise historical usage, for our purposes here, *sekisho* will continue to refer to the bakufu institution and *bansho* to those of a private nature that domains established. Physically, bansho were much like sekisho. Furukawa Koshōken, traveling in Hirosaki (Tsugaru) domain in the late eighteenth century, approached Ikari-no-seki bansho and saw a wooden gate standing in the road with palisades running left and right, blocking possible paths around it, and weapons displayed near the gate—all very much as at sekisho.[105] Sakai bansho in Kaga possessed many of the physical characteristics of a large-scale sekisho such as Hakone: a guard office (*bansho*), dwellings for guards and officials, a watchtower, jail house, and an extensive network of palisades (501 meters) leading from the bansho enclosure to the foot of the mountains on the one side and to a body of water (the ocean) on the other.[106] Its impressive size and layout were due to the fact that Sakai lay along the Sea of Japan coast, effectively blocking access to the Kinai area along the coastal Hokurikudō highway, the only convenient route for the domains in northwestern Japan; most other bansho were not on the same scale as this.[107] As a rule, however, bansho were the size of small- to middle-scale sekisho. The physical placement of bansho also reflected the same attention to topographical value as sekisho.

Despite their similarities, sekisho and bansho differed in function. For example, one of the functions bansho fulfilled was to guard domain boundaries; this is evident from the distribution of bansho. Of Tosa's eighty-six bansho (1781–1788), sixty-two were located on its borders with Sanuki, Awa, and Iyo provinces; these were referred to as border bansho (*sakaime bansho*). The remainder were located inland and like most of the border bansho were located along major transport networks. These "internal bansho" (*uchi bansho*), and the border bansho were known collectively as "road bansho" (*dōbansho*) to contrast them with "coastal bansho" (*tsukuchi bansho*), whose purpose was to regulate commodity goods sent by ship as well as to provide coastal defense.[108] The same pattern of distribution was evident in a number of other domains.[109]

Early in the Tokugawa period, Sendai domain situated many of its bansho on its northern and southern borders to defend territory in boundary disputes with Yonezawa and Sōma (Nakamura) domains to the south and Nambu domain to the north.[110] Five of Kaga's six bansho were in place around 1587, before the onset of the Tokugawa period, but the establishment of Sakai bansho in 1614 is generally interpreted as a precautionary measure for the unrest anticipated during the Osaka campaign.[111]

Sparsely located bansho along a long border would not be able to regulate traffic very successfully. The post at Nishi Mineguchi in Tosa, for example, was responsible for guarding almost twelve kilometers of border with Awa province.[112] In order to do so properly, the Mitani family, who was charged with the administration of the bansho, established seven auxiliary bansho (*shimo bansho*) along its seven miles of territory and appointed its retainers to watch over them. One can only imagine the tedium experienced among guards posted there.

Documentation for bansho early in the Tokugawa period is poor, but the data on personnel and armaments available for later in the period suggests that domains did not as a rule maintain bansho as armed outposts. Like sekisho, these bansho were not meant to stop invading forces. They were better suited to deal with isolated criminals, disorderly people, or other undesirables.

The early military role of bansho gradually ceased as bakufu authority grew. The bakufu prohibited warfare between domains and its role as arbitrator removed the need for constant vigilance against each other. Not all domains, therefore, felt the necessity to guard their borders—or at least all of them—with bansho. Kaga established Sakai on its border with Takada and four on its border with Takayama, but left its borders with Maruoka and Matsumoto domains unguarded. Toyama and Daishōji were branch domains of Kaga, having split off in the 1630s, and placed no bansho on their borders with the parent domain. Similarly, Hachinohe domain split off from Nambu in 1664 and as of 1682, at least, no bansho had been built on their common border.[113]

In addition to their early military role, bansho also functioned as an institution for controlling peasants. More specifically, in the early decades of the Tokugawa period, and in some areas well into the seventeenth century, keeping peasants from running away was a major problem. With the extraordinary amount of political and social upheaval which ensued after Sekigahara it is understandable that peasants felt uneasy about their future. In Tosa, for example, a domain which changed hands from the Chōsokabe to the Yamauchi during 1600–1601, the problem was particularly acute. The fact that twenty-two of the seventy-five articles in the code issued by the Yamauchi in 1612 dealt with peasants running away suggests just how severe the problem really was.[114] Consequently, bansho were set up during the first few years of Yamauchi rule and peasants were prohibited from passing through them without a travel permit.[115] Despite these measures in Tosa and elsewhere, bansho guards were not always willing or able to stop villagers from absconding.[116]

Kaga domain, though it did not change hands, also experienced problems with peasant abscondence early on: In 1601 it issued its first prohibition on the practice, assessed the offending party's village a monetary penalty and imposed on it the burden of assuming the missing person's tax quota.[117] It was necessary to repeat similar prohibitions thereafter, especially once Kaga carried out a set of rural reforms in 1651–1657 which caused the peasantry to panic.[118] It is believed that Kaga women were prohibited from passing through Sakai bansho on the border with Echigo because that was the route used by peasants absconding to Echigo and on, perhaps, to Edo. By prohibiting women from leaving the domain there, officials believed it could prevent men from running away as well.[119]

Bansho also monitored the regular movement of people—samurai, peasants, merchants and artisans, as well as criminals, mendicants, musicians, actors, and outcasts—through domain borders. We will investigate this problem in detail in the following chapter, but in general this was done by requiring travelers to apply for permission to travel and by checking their travel permits at domain barriers.[120]

The movements of a certain highly mobile and free-floating segment of the population came under the particular scrutiny of domains, especially from about the mid-Tokugawa on, when many domains were feeling financially hard-pressed. These people—beggars, flute-playing Zen mendicant priests (*komusō*), Buddhist monks, blind musicians (*zato*), yamabushi, and other types who collected solicitations for temples and shrines—were prohibited from entering numerous domains. Besides draining economic resources, they were often perceived as troublemakers.[121]

Travelers at bansho had to follow regulations similar to those at sekisho in order to pass, such as taking off any headgear and opening the door of the palanquin one might be riding in. The wording of regulations for bansho in Kumamoto domain in 1631 is modeled on those issued by the bakufu in 1625.[122] Time restrictions on passage were observed at bansho as well and nighttime passage was similarly permitted only for those on official (bakufu or domainal) business.[123]

Thus far we have outlined three major functions of domain bansho — that is, military defense, population control, and surveillance of human traffic—and noted that the focus of bansho policy evolved away from defense. Bansho assumed an important fourth function: regulating the flow of commodity goods as peace set in and domain economies began to expand. This economic role is what clearly separates bakufu sekisho and domain bansho, for with one exception (Sekigawa sekisho in Echigo) bakufu sekisho were not involved in the regulation of commodity flow.

The regulation of commodity goods, while evident from as early as the 1630s, assumed even greater significance over time. For example, a domain ordinance from Matsushiro (1713) addressed to its bansho deals with travelers in only one of its five articles.[124] Two out of the eight bansho in Kaga and Toyama regulated commodity goods but did not check travel permits (Nishi Sekibi and Daikanba, both in Kaga). Although travel permits were not checked, only merchants could pass through, leaving ordinary travelers to find alternate routes. Four bansho concerned themselves exclusively with travelers (Sakai, Mizusu, Okunoyama, and Higashi Inotani), presumably because they were not on routes where commodity goods regularly flowed in great numbers.[125]

With the increased economic role played by bansho in the developing domain economy, it is not surprising that in some domains bansho were added or moved.[126] The location of bansho in Aizu domain shifted somewhat over time as certain barriers were abolished on routes no longer frequently traveled and new ones established on busy routes, some of which were opened up as market forces dictated.[127]

Bansho came to play an important role in domain economic policy, especially in domainal efforts to remain as self-sufficient as possible and nineteenth-century efforts to increase income through domain monopolies as well as through the collection of taxes on certain imported and exported goods.[128] The goods to be taxed and the rate of taxation could be adjusted as domainal policy changed. Bansho were thus instrumental in domainal efforts to control commodity flow.[129]

The sekisho and bansho systems became means of channeling goods and people for economic purposes: For the bakufu, this assured that the transport system it had created on the main roads was used and therefore able to sustain itself economically; for the domains, bansho were a mechanism to regulate and tax commodities. However, as the geographic distribution of sekisho suggests, the barriers had originally been meant to contribute to the bakufu's consolidation of military power. That underlying military character persisted in the policy summed up by the phrase "inbound guns and outbound women"; but the sekisho were an inefficient way to keep women hostage in Edo: roadblocks just outside the city would have been simpler and more effective. The elaborate system was instead a measure for bringing general stability to the realm: It allowed the flow of traffic—official, recreational, commercial, and criminal—to be monitored and to a degree controlled by channeling travelers onto only a few roads and allowing them to cross water only at designated points. Within the domains, bansho fulfilled a similar function. Once on the road, travelers were often subject to a system of permits intended to enforce sekisho and bansho policy. These mechanisms, and the extent to which they were successful, are the topic of the next chapter.

FOUR

Permits and Passages

"Fluttering our papers [travel permits]
The spring winds blow,
When through the open barriers
How gratefully we go."[1]

On paper at least, government authorities in Tokugawa Japan appear to have attempted to regulate travel more than any other early modern state. Their efforts reflect the fact that the Tokugawa polity was formed through a lengthy process of warfare and conciliation between rival military powers trying to impose order on a society that had largely lacked it for more than a century: the chaos and destruction which preceded the Tokugawa era led the bakufu and the domains to attend to public order and lay claim to a wide range of powers over the lives of the people. This is not to say, however, that they were necessarily able to exercise those claims; for the increasing concern of political authorities with regulating pilgrimage, the foremost reason for long-distance travel, suggests a disjunction between the state's will and its power.

In Japan, the principal targets of bakufu and domain regulations were the peasants, the backbone of Tokugawa society, who worked the land and produced the taxes which fueled the machinery of government. Obviously from the government's perspective, the more time peasants were away from their fields, the less they could produce taxes; hence, controls were imposed to minimize their movements out of the village. While peasants were the main target of bakufu and domain regulations on

travel, they were by no means the only target. All segments of society—
from the highest samurai to the lowliest outcast—came under some sort
of controls. The tight, well-ordered fabric of Tokugawa society did not
allow, in theory, for people to move freely about, totally at will. Even
when reality contradicted theory, however, polite fictions were maintained: for example, those who received permission to leave their villages
for "temporary work" elsewhere (*dekasegi*) but never returned remained
listed in their village ledgers as if they would.[2]

The alternate attendance system required that travelers be checked at
sekisho established along Tokugawa roadways in order to prevent daimyo wives and children, held as political hostages, from leaving Edo without permission. In one sense, then, commoners might be seen as scape-
goats of a system designed to control daimyo politically; for the system
to be effective, all travelers, not just samurai, needed to be checked. Yet
to hold that commoners were checked at sekisho only as a result of the
alternate attendance system is to miss the point that the Tokugawa and
their fellow daimyo idealized a society where most of the population
remained tied to the land. Thus, to see sekisho only in terms of the alternate attendance system is to overlook the general conditions of social
fluidity and unrest in the early decades of the Tokugawa era.

To regulate movement the bakufu and the domains required most travelers to obtain written permission in the form of a travel permit. While
travel permits or passports were known in other parts of the world, particularly in Stuart and early Tudor England, where they were used to control the movements of the vagrant poor,[3] the Tokugawa system appears to
have been the most developed. In Japan, applying for a permit required
time and, in some cases, money. Central or domainal government could
restrict the number of permits it was willing to issue and discriminate to
whom it would grant them. The authorities could also determine when,
and if, they would grant the permits and their period of validity. The permits had to be shown to designated officials at sekisho and bansho and be
judged in proper order for the traveler to be allowed passage, as suggested in
the quote from Jippensha Ikku's *Hizakurige* that opens this chapter. But
since its Gokaidō network ran through the heartland of Japan, the Tokugawa could exercise these powers not only over people living on its house
lands (*tenryō*), but over anyone who traveled on the bakufu road system.

APPLYING FOR A TRAVEL PERMIT

Tokugawa travelers such as Jippensha Ikku's characters from *Hizakurige*, Kita and Yaji, carried travel permits (*tegata* or *kitte*) with them on their trip to Ise which they presented at sekisho in order to be granted permission to pass. There were two basic types of permits a traveler might carry: sekisho transit permits (*sekisho tegata*) and passports (*ōrai tegata*). Kita and Yaji carried the latter type.

Sekisho transit permits were issued for passage through a particular sekisho. When stopping before the main office for inspection, the traveler handed over the permit and, if it was in order, went on his way. Such permits were issued by designated bakufu officials as well as daimyo and their officials. Passports, on the other hand, could be used for as many sekisho and, in many cases, domain bansho, as the traveler passed through on his journey without surrendering it. Passports were issued by village and post station officials, shrines and temples, and sometimes even innkeepers.

Scholars have not yet been able to clarify the evolution of the two types of travel permits. It is clear, however, that passports did not come into common use until the middle of the Edo period, whereas examples of transit permits can be found from as early as the second decade of the seventeenth century. The eventual emergence of passports points to the growing popularity of travel, and reflects an easing of restrictions on commoner travel as well as the increasing ability of commoners to circumvent barriers erected to check their physical mobility.

Just as we lack knowledge of the steps by which documentation evolved, we have much to learn about the process by which people in Tokugawa Japan applied for travel permits. No article or monograph on the topic has appeared,[4] nor does the most comprehensive survey of Japanese communications history have much to say on the subject of travel documents.[5] Even a reading of several hundred travel permits from across the country reveals only that there are still links missing in the evidence that would allow us to reconstruct the workings of the "permit system." In fact, it becomes evident that there was no one "system" per se, another indication of the extent to which the Tokugawa state was defined by a combination of central, Tokugawa, and individual domain governments, each of which governed their people in generally similar but not identical ways.

Like many urban dwellers across the country, Kita and Yaji obtained their passports to travel on pilgrimage from their family temple, where their identities were on record. Being tenants, they also could have obtained them from their landlord; but since they owed him money, it is doubtful that he would have agreed. They paid a "contribution" of 100 copper coins (*mon*) to the temple and left a small offering of rice in exchange for their permits.[6]

In rural areas administered by the bakufu, sekisho transit permits were issued by intendants (*daikan*). In bakufu cities the designated issuing authority was the City Magistrate (*machi bugyō*). In Edo, however, up until 1659, all urban women were required to apply to the Keeper of Edo Castle (*orusui*), the officer in charge of Edo during the shogun's absence from the city. The 1659/6 order that changed this requirement created a unified system for commoners of both sexes.[7] By allowing commoner women in Edo to obtain their permits from the City Magistrate, a lower ranking official, the bakufu greatly accelerated the application process. The change may have been the result of a steady increase in the number of urban women traveling, prompting the Keeper of Edo Castle to hand over his responsibility for issuing townswomen's permits to the City Magistrate. But, as the evidence from later in the period reveals, townsmen could obtain passports more easily, from a family temple, landlord, or innkeeper.

In private domains, daimyo held the ultimate issuing authority, although it usually passed this power on to a lower authority: in urban centers, the City or Shrine and Temple Magistrate; and in the countryside, the Magistrate of Rural Affairs (*kōri bugyō*). Persons living on land under the jurisdiction of religious institutions would apply to the Shrine and Temple Magistrate; otherwise, urban dwellers applied to the City Magistrate.[8]

For passage through bakufu sekisho, however, women (both commoner and samurai*) needed to have the permit countersigned, hence

---

*For simplicity's sake, female members of the *buke* social status group are sometimes referred to here as "samurai women"; unless so specified, however, "samurai" refers only to male members approved, by a designated bakufu official, thereby adding a further step to the application process. The bakufu designated certain permit-issuers specifically for women (see Table 7); and permits issued by any other authority were considered not valid. No regulations were promulgated regarding permit-issuers for men, largely because that type of documentation was rarely taken out. Women traveling west from sixteen provinces (all provinces north and east of Edo and as far west as Shinano, Kai, Izu and Sagami), with the exception of commoner women from Edo, were required by bakufu statute to apply to the Keeper of Edo Castle for sekisho transit permits. Since applications were made to the office of such a high-ranking bakufu official, no doubt their processing took a considerable amount of time. West of Edo, the permit-issuing authority varied considerably: for example, those women from Suruga heading west (i.e., *de-onna*) obtained their permits from the Sunpu City Magistrate; Tōtōmi women obtained them from the Hamamatsu Castle Keeper (later, issuing authority changed hands to the Yokosuka and Kakegawa Castle Keepers).[9]

Travel permits issued by the Keeper of Edo Castle were required for passage through seventeen sekisho, including the four most important: Arai, Hakone, Kiso Fukushima, and Usui. Permits for women traveling away from Edo were collected at sekisho and returned to the Keeper of Edo Castle every six months, allowing the bakufu to monitor the movements of samurai women as part of its "inbound guns and outbound women" policy.[10]

The bakufu created a complicated process for women applying for sekisho transit permits. Permit-issuers for those traveling towards Edo (i.e., *iri-onna*) differed according to area: In thirty-one provinces in western and central Japan, applications were made through one's overlord to the Kyōto shoshidai, or in his absence, to the Kyoto City Magistrate; in the remaining provinces, applications were made either to a bakufu-designated daimyo, a bakufu City Magistrate, or a bakufu intendant. (See Table 7.) The privileged daimyo of the Three Houses and the Maeda of

---

of that group. Technically, of course, the term refers only to high-ranking (exclusively male) members of a daimyo's retainer corps, or *jōshi*, but in much of the English-language literature the more inclusive definition is used.

TABLE 7 Issuers of Women's Permits for Passage Through Bakufu Sekisho

Province or Area	Issuing Authority
Edo	Orusui
Suruga	Sunpu City Magistrate
Tōtōmi	Hamamatsu daimyo (after 1702, daimyo of Yokosuka and Kakegawa)
Western Provinces	Kyōto shoshidai (if absent, Kyoto City Magistrate)
Kyoto	Kyoto City Magistrate
Fushimi	Fushimi City Magistrate
Ōmi, Tamba	Kyoto City Magistrate
Tangō, Tajima	Kyōto shoshidai (if absent, Kyoto City Magistrate)
Settsu, Kawachi	Osaka City Magistrate
Izumi	Sakai Magistrate
Yamato	Nambu City Magistrate
Eastern Mikawa	Yoshida lord (1701, Nishio lord; 1713, Kariya lord)
Western Mikawa	Okazaki lord (1712, Tawara lord)
Ise	Kuwana lord (1711, Kobe lord; 1711, Kameyama lord)
Shima	Tottori lord (1702)
Mino	Ogaki lord
Wakasa	Obama lord (1683, Kyōto shoshidai)
Owari	daimyo retainers
Kii	daimyo retainers
Kaga, Noto, Etchū	daimyo retainers
Echizen Fukui domain	Fukui lord
Remainder of Fukui	Kyōto shoshidai

Source: *THSS*, vol. 2, pp. 6–20.

Kaga were the only daimyo granted special permission to issue women's travel permits on their own.[11] There were some changes in issuers over time, but an up-to-date list was kept on a placard in all sekisho for the handy reference of the officials there.[12] Still, the system was, apparently, so complicated that even permit-issuing authorities got confused: In one case a group of nineteen women was refused passage at Arai because its permit was issued by the Osaka City Magistrate rather than the Kyōto shoshidai. A male representative had to be sent to Kyoto to get the permit amended.[13] Procedures for travel permit applications varied from domain to domain, but in most cases, commoners obtained their documentation from either the City Magistrate or the Magistrate of Rural Affairs, depending on the applicant's place of residence. Prior to this, of course, they would need the approval of some guarantor, namely the village headman or a local town official, before the permit application could be submitted to the higher authority.

Domain governments simplified procedures later in the Tokugawa period: for example, in Tsuyama domain (Okayama prefecture), regulations issued in 1803 dictated that for an overnight stay one needed only the permission of the Group of Five Households (*goningumi*); for a two- to three-night stay, the permission of the village head or elders; for ten to twenty days, that of the regional headman (*ōjōya*); and for periods of one to two months, that of the rural magistrate.[14] In Fukuyama domain (1821), it was permissible for peasants to take trips of up to twenty days with only the permission of village officials.[15] As will become clear, in simplifying the procedures, they were reacting to the reality around them; and they tried to modify the application process to reflect that reality more closely. Still, the availability of passports, which were easier to obtain, and the widespread practice of *nukemairi,* or making pilgrimages without official permission, suggests that government officials, despite modifying procedures, were still not fully in tune with the times.

This observation is confirmed by actions taken by Owari domain in 1849 to simplify the permit application process. Officials acknowledged that they were changing what had been a "troublesome procedure" by issuing travel permits "on the same day, according to the wishes of the traveler." This was done in an effort to encourage women on pilgrimage to Zenkō-ji (Shinano province) to apply for permits before setting out on their journeys. Many had ignored the permit process, for the ordinance announcing the changes stated that "[f]rom now on be sure to obtain a permit and travel via the main roads."[16] The village headman from Naka-tsugawa post station petitioned the bakufu intendant in whose territory the village lay to change the "troublesome" procedure for issuing women's travel permits. The intendant's headquarters was far away from the post station and hence it was said that one-half of the women setting out on pilgrimage to Zenkō-ji failed to apply for the necessary permit and traveled via side roads to avoid detection.[17] Similarly, the closure of certain sekisho to women was another factor that led women to set out on their journeys without permits.

The permit application process was not as easy in some domains as it was in early nineteenth-century Tsuyama. In Kaga, only men could obtain their permits from the City Magistrate or the Magistrate of Rural Affairs, depending on the applicant's place of residence. All women were required to apply to the *goyōban,* the equivalent of the Domain Elders elsewhere, which meant that it was extremely difficult for commoner women to get permission to travel. Furthermore, the process was not simple for men who were not of the samurai status group. Unlike male members of the warrior status group, who usually applied directly to their overlord, a commoner needed to go through a multi-step process. A peasant, for example, first needed to find a guarantor who would sign his permit request form. The signature of a landlord from a Group of Ten Households (*jūningumi*), known as a Group of Five Households in most other places, would do. Then the request form was taken to the village headman or elder, who would act as a second guarantor. The third step involved presenting the request form to the Senior Village Headman (*tomura*), who presided over a group of villages, ideally ten in number, known as the Ten-Village Group, or *tomuragumi,* a form of village organization particular to Kaga and Toyama.[18] The permit was then endorsed and forwarded to the Magistrate of Rural Affairs, whose office actually issued the permit.

In Kaga and Toyama travelers needed not only a travel permit but also an exit permit; the exit permit was used for passage through domain bansho. Passports issued by family temples, however, were not acceptable as domain exit permits; temple-issued passports were used for bansho and sekisho in other domains after handing over the domain exit permit at a border bansho.[19] Kaga and Toyama were particularly strict in this respect, for most other domains did not require a special exit permit. Non-domain residents leaving Kaga could obtain their exit permits from the domain Travel Permit Office (*tegata ton'ya*) in Kanazawa, which would act as guarantor on the permit request form. That form would then be forwarded to the City Magistrate's Office, where the permit would be issued.[20] According to at least one contemporary traveler to Kaga, this process was "a lot of trouble."[21]

For samurai, procedures were different. Male samurai applied to their immediate superior or overlord for transit permits.[22] Samurai women obtained theirs from a domain official, usually from the Domain Elders or their equivalent. Kaga domain and the Three Houses (*gosanke*) were the only daimyo allowed to issue sekisho transit permits for women belonging to samurai households (*buke no onna*).[23] In other domains these women were required to obtain bakufu approval of their applications (by application to a bakufu-designated permit-issuer). Before that step, of course, the application first had to be approved by the Domain Elders, who acted as the woman's guarantors (see Sekisho Transit Permit No. 1 in Appendix 2). The Domain Elders, however, could issue samurai women's transit permits for bansho without bakufu permission.

TYPES AND METHODS

Although there was no prescribed form that a travel permit had to take, once permit-issuers were regularized in 1661, permits tended to assume a basic, common form and a fairly standardized wording.[24] A typical transit permit might contain the following information: the number of travelers, the purpose of the journey, a destination, a request for safe passage through sekisho or bansho, the name of the permit issuer, the date of issuance, and the name of the sekisho for which the permit was issued. The historical trend was for permits to become more and more abbreviated towards the end of the Tokugawa era as information identifying the traveler was reduced to a bare minimum, again indicating a simplification of the procedures for obtaining permission to travel.[25]

Appendix 2 shows three representative examples of permits. The first permit, a sekisho transit permit, is for four townswomen traveling from Kyoto to Edo and contains a request for safe passage through Imagiri (as the bakufu referred to Arai); the application for the permit was written on a separate piece of paper and is not included in the document. A permit issued for a group could either list all the people's names individually or else only one name representing the group, followed by a notation of the number of people accompanying him;[26] if women or children were in the group, they would be required to have their own permit.[27] For this permit, the travelers' conduct had to be guaranteed by some authority such as the City Elders and the Group of Five Households in Kyoto. The guarantee was a key component of travel permits, because it made a specific individual or group of people accountable for a traveler's behavior. The issuing authority for eastbound women living on Shikoku Island and in the Central and Western Provinces (*Chūgoku* and *Saikoku*), which included Kyoto, was the Kyōto shoshidai; when he was absent in Edo, however, the Kyoto City Magistrate was responsible, as was apparently the case when this permit was issued.[28] As a sekisho transit permit, this certificate had to be surrendered at Arai.

The second travel permit shown in Appendix 2 (see Sekisho Transit Permit No. 2 in Appendix 2) was for four members of a samurai household. Unlike the first transit permit, this permit application contains an endorsement on the reverse side by the Kyōto shoshidai (the issuing authority) with a brief request that travelers be granted safe passage on the roadways. The permit application was signed by the domain Keeper of the Castle (*orusui*), the local official responsible for transit permits. In this case he was not issuing the permit himself, but acted as a guarantor for a retainer's wife and children.

The most salient characteristic of the third permit, a passport (see Passport in Appendix 2), is that it did not have to be surrendered at a particular sekisho; in other words, it was effective for the entire length of a traveler's journey and thereby doubled as an identification card. Such passports usually included a request to sekisho, city, and village officials for benevolent care should the bearer(s) fall ill or die on the road; officials were to notify the traveler's next of kin, administer adequate medical care, and, in the case of death, give the bearer a proper burial. While these might seem to be reasonable requests, Tokugawa travelers without either travel permits or passports who were stricken on the road often received very bad treatment. Villages were known at times to refuse to help them, despite orders to the contrary from government authorities. Some villages refused to forward stricken travelers sent by palanquin-relay.[29] It seems, however, that the lack of a travel permit was merely a convenient excuse for villages not to assume the financial burden imposed on them by an outsider. For these reasons government authorities warned people under their jurisdiction to carry permits when traveling.

Passports were used exclusively by commoners—mostly male—and most frequently by travelers to hot springs or those on pilgrimage. While no statutory evidence has been found to suggest that samurai were not allowed to carry passports, it appears that this was yet another distinction made between the status groups. Passports were not only useful as personal identification, but they were also far less troublesome than sekisho transit permits. Travel from Edo to Kyoto on the Tōkaidō, for example, required transit permits for both Hakone and Arai. But rather than apply for both in Edo, the traveler would hand over his transit permit addressed to Hakone at Hakone sekisho and receive a "transfer permit" (*kakikae tegata*) for Arai. The use of such transfer permits increased from the mid-Tokugawa on as the number of people traveling on the roads grew and a given journey might require three or more of them. Then, of course, there was the return trip, making the use of passports, which obviated the need for transfer permits, all the more attractive.[30]

A transfer permit was written up at the sekisho by an official; it was based on the information contained in the traveler's original permit and also included a notation of the date the traveler passed through. The original was kept at the sekisho and an abbreviated copy of it made in a register.[31] It probably took some time for officials at Hakone and elsewhere to process the transfer permit, particularly on a busy day. Furthermore, any problem with the permit required time to investigate precedents before a decision on passage was made. If the traveler came late in the day, a decision might not be made before the sekisho closed for the day, forcing him to find lodging for the night and return the next day. All of these inconveniences made the use of passports more attractive.

Permits were effective from the date of issuance until the last day of the following month: in other words, for a period from a month and a day up to just under two full months. If the permit was not used before it expired, it was possible to get it updated, rather than to re-apply for another one.[32] Travelers whose permits expired while on their journey were viewed as law breakers, just like travelers without permits. In Tosa, if caught, they were to be expelled from the nearest border; or, in certain cases, if a person appeared suspicious, he was to be arrested.[33] If for some unavoidable reason, such as illness or injury, a traveler's permit expired before the holder could return to his place of origin, he had to obtain a new one at the place where he was held up and explain why he had been delayed.[34]

Pilgrimage to a distant location could require a journey longer than two months, that is, longer than a normal permit would allow. To cover this situation, a traveler carried a travel permit whose wording indicated the purpose of the journey. At a sekisho on the pilgrimage route, it was then handed over to sekisho officials in exchange for a special pilgrimage permit. These permits, which were referred to as *kakikae tegata* (the same term used for transfer permits), were good for up to fifty to seventy days, depending on the traveler's stated wish. Listed on the special permit was the projected date of the traveler's return. On the return trip, the special permit had to be relinquished again at the sekisho where it was issued; there it was compared to the original permit, which was kept on deposit, to ensure compliance with the time limit.[35] Passports, on the other hand, had no expiration date—a feature that added to their convenience and probably accounts for their standard request for benevolent treatment if the bearer were stricken ill.

WHO NEEDED A TRAVEL PERMIT?

The historical record does not make altogether clear exactly who had to carry travel permits nor which kind they needed. According to R. K. Hall, "all who passed through [sekisho] were compelled to carry official passes. All persons and baggage were inspected."[36] Perhaps he was echoing the comments of foreign visitors such as Aimé Humbert, who reported that at Hakone, "all travelers need to present travel permits."[37] While the issue is complicated, for details on travel through Hakone, some helpful correspondence survives. For example, in 1705, the Keeper of Edo Castle sent a letter of inquiry to Odawara concerning procedures for checking different types of travelers at the six sekisho it administered. Such queries were nothing unusual; for although the bakufu routinely sent notices of general instruction (some of which were posted publicly on placards) to sekisho administrators on how to process travelers, they left the details of defining the policy to local officials and periodically sought information on how it was being implemented day to day. The response in this case from Hakone is discussed below and summarized in Table 8. Because it closely resembles another reply to a letter of inquiry sent more than a century later, in 1837, it seems to provide a tentative paradigm for practice during more than a century.[38]

It appears that Hakone sekisho was not much of an obstacle for most travelers. The requirements were strictest for travelers listed in the first group in Table 8. This category consisted of women only and might be divided further into five sub-categories. All women were required to carry a permit from the Keeper of Edo Castle for westbound passage through the sekisho. Those without them were absolutely denied passage. According to this record, women heading in the opposite direction, toward Edo, did not have to present permits for inspection. In such cases, if a man accompanied the woman traveler, he was required only to make an oral report to the sekisho office, identifying himself and the woman, and stating the purpose and destination of their travel. Technically this did not mean that women were not supposed to carry permits, although in some cases it might have amounted to the same thing: the same letter said that permits for "women . . . were obtained from either the Kyōto shoshidai or the City Magistrate from Osaka or Kyoto."[39]

The requirements for those in the second group—prisoners, the wounded, decapitated heads, corpses, and the insane—were the same as for women. In both groups, travelers without permits from the Keeper of Edo Castle were denied passage, and the diary accounts from Hakone give us ample evidence that this was in fact true.[40]

Requirements for the third group of travelers—priests, monks, yamabushi, Ise Shrine clergy, Zen mendicant priests (*komusō*) and young boys who had not yet passed through the rites of manhood—were different. Those with permits from someone with whom they had an established social connection or dependency relationship (*shoen*) could pass. Those without permits who were not suspicious were allowed to pass after "careful inquiry" was made. Members of this group who were traveling towards Edo were not inspected. The same procedures held for the fourth group of people, itinerant entertainers. While entertainers themselves were exempt from the permit requirement, their families were not.[41] For

TABLE 8 Travel Permit Requirements for Hakone (1705)

Classification	Traveling Away from Edo	Traveling Toward Edo
Blind women, *zenni*[a], *bikuni*[b], women with cut hair, other women	Permit required from Keeper of Edo Castle	No inspection; accompanying person reports to sekisho office; permit not inspected
Wounded, prisoners, decapitated heads, corpses, insane	Permit required from Keeper of Edo Castle	Accompanying person reports to sekisho office; permit not inspected
Priests and monks, yamabushi, Ise priests, itinerants, mendicant priests, young boys	Permit from place of residence or *shoen*[c]; those without them who are not suspicious may pass after careful inquiry has been made	No inspection
Blind musicians, actors, puppeteers, monkey trainers	Permit from *shoen;* those without them who are not suspicious may pass after careful inquiry has been made	No inspection
Townsmen, peasants	Permit from village officials, landlord, *shoen;* those without them who are not suspicious may pass after careful inquiry has been made	No inspection
Bakufu direct retainers, the Three Houses	Not required; those with permits, however, present to sekisho office	No inspection
Other samurai	Inspect samurai with permits; those without them who are not suspicious may pass after careful inquiry has been made	No inspection

Source: HGNK, vol. 3, pp. 318–320; THSS, vol. 2, pp. 72–77.

Notes: [a]*zenni* refers to a woman who is the widow or sister of a person of high rank and who has taken religious vows, as indicated by her shaven head the performers themselves, a display of their talent for the amusement of the guards was usually sufficient proof of their identity for them to be granted passage through the sekisho.[42]

Peasants and townsmen could pass through Hakone with a permit from a village headman, landlord, or person with whom they had some dependency relationship. As in the third and fourth groups, peasants and townsmen without permits who were not suspicious were allowed to pass after careful inquiry was made.

Samurai travelers are best considered in two categories. Direct retainers of the bakufu—that is, bannermen (*hatamoto*) and housemen (*gokenin*)—and the retainers of the privileged Three Houses were not required to carry permits; those who did, had them examined pro forma at the sekisho. The requirements were not much different for other samurai: Those without permits who were not suspicious were allowed to pass through after careful inquiry was made. Those with permits, again, had them examined pro forma.

With the exception of Arai, Kega, and Yanagase sekisho, travelers were usually checked only when passing through sekisho in one direction: away from Edo.[43] Travelers passing through two of three sekisho in Ōmi, however, were inspected only when traveling north; in this way the bakufu could monitor traffic heading towards Kaga.

The historical record, however, is not so clear as the evidence just presented might suggest. For example, instructions sent from the Odawara daimyo to Hakone sekisho in 1693 stated, "It has been strictly forbidden for Edo-bound travelers to pass through without a permit ever since the sekisho was founded. All the guards and officials should understand this."[44] The same was true elsewhere: Instructions to guards at Shingō-Kawamata sekisho (Musashi) stated that it was expressly forbidden for travelers without permits to pass through.[45] At Nanmoku sekisho (Kōzuke) guards were instructed to "let no one pass without a permit, except those on official business."[46] Similarly, Kaempfer noted

[b]*bikuni* refers to female attendants of Ise or Zenkō-ji priests, maidservants of widows of high rank, or *kumano bikuni* (members of an order of religious nuns who were known to sell their sexual favors)

[c]*shoen* refers to a person or institution on whom one depends (e.g., an employer, landlord, or benefactor)

that "[p]rivate persons going up to Jedo [Edo], must shew their Passports at this place, otherwise they are kept under arrest for three days, before they are permitted to pursue their journey."[47] His observation was also true for Kobotoke sekisho (Musashi).

It appears that, in the 1693 order from Odawara to Hakone sekisho, which indicated that Edo-bound persons required permits, travelers were treated differently than the information sent from Hakone to the Keeper of Edo Castle in 1705 (and 1837) suggests. It also contradicts a Hakone diary account from 1752, which stated that Edo-bound travelers were not inspected unless they seemed suspicious.[48] There is no other evidence, however, to support an argument that sekisho policy shifted dramatically between 1693 and 1705. In fact, a close examination of the wording of the 1693 order suggests that there were cases when travelers heading towards Edo without permits were being allowed through (hence the reminder to guards and officials about sekisho policy). For example, a group of three village headmen, on their way to Edo in 1759 to present a petition to the Magistrate of Shrines and Temples, did not present permits when passing through Hakone.[49]

The requirements for samurai passing through Hakone are also, despite the information that Odawara officials relayed to the bakufu about its checking procedures, not so clear cut. For example, Nagakubo Sekisui, a Mito samurai traveling to Nagasaki in 1761 to pick up some castaway sailors from his domain, remarked when passing through Hakone that "samurai, even if carrying a spear, do not need a travel permit."[50] If he was referring to samurai traveling on official business, then his statement corresponds with other evidence we have. Ōta Nanpo (alias Shokusanjin, 1749–1823), for example, while traveling to Edo from Osaka where he was working for the bakufu, passed through Hakone sekisho. He observed that if prior notice was given, samurai permits were not inspected. By prior notice we mean that an attendant probably went on ahead, as attendants usually did to secure needed post horses, porters and lodging, and informed the sekisho officials that such-and-such a person would be coming through around such-and-such a time. Having given advance notice, Ōta merely removed his straw rain hat and sandals and passed through the sekisho. It is not written whether he announced himself, but it would seem likely.[51]

Samurai in other cases, however, did need to have travel permits when leaving Edo. There is evidence of this not only for Hakone, but for a number of other important sekisho as well. A retainer named Endō Sōha, for example, left Edo and tried to pass through Hakone in 1780 without a permit. Told that he could not do so, he was escorted back to the border of the next village.[52] In another case (1780), a retainer also tried to pass through Hakone without a permit and was likewise denied permission. Conjuring up a clever way to trick the sekisho guards, he joined in line with a daimyo procession that happened to be about to pass through, but was caught again and held until someone sent from his domain came to pick him up. As it turned out, he had, in fact, absconded from his domain.[53] Many other examples exist of samurai who tried and failed to pass through Hakone heading west from Edo without permits.[54] Unfortunately, in most cases, we do not have sufficient information to determine whether the samurai were refused passage because they somehow aroused the suspicions of the sekisho officials.

In contrast to these examples we have the account of Katsu Kaishū's father, Katsu Kokichi, a bakufu bannerman who set out from Edo for a second time in 1823 without informing anyone. Before leaving, he borrowed a set of equipment for sword-fighting. Approaching the sekisho office at Hakone, Katsu, who did not have a travel permit, told the officials that he was traveling for training in swordsmanship and asked for permission to pass. The official replied, "Show me your travel permit," to which Katsu responded that he did not have one. "The only preparation for the trip I made," he said, "was to put on a pair of leather sandals." The head sekisho official told him: "The law is that no one without a permit may pass. If what you say is true, and you are traveling for training in swordsmanship, we will make an exception and let you pass. In the future make proper preparations." Thanking the official, Katsu continued on his journey to Kyoto.[55]

Another samurai, Takayama Hikokurō (a contemporary of Ōta Nanpo), usually carried a permit when traveling.[56] On one occasion, however, he neglected to do so and was refused passage through a sekisho; thereafter he made a point to carry one whenever he traveled.[57]

In another case, a man named Maki Chūzō, aged twenty-seven or twenty-eight, approached the sekisho wearing a sword. He declared that

he was a retainer of the Hatakeyama daimyo of Shimōsa and was traveling to Kakegawa in Tōtōmi province but had lost his travel permit sometime after leaving Edo. His request for passage through the sekisho was
denied. Hearing this unfortunate news, Maki exclaimed that it would be
most troublesome to have to return to Edo to get one and would they not
please reconsider. Further inquiry by the sekisho guards revealed that
Maki's two "attendants" were, in fact, a day laborer and a worker in a con-
fectionery store in Edo. Asked about their baggage, which included a
short sword, all three denied ownership. When the sekisho official pronounced the judgment that they would be refused passage and escorted
by a foot soldier to the border of the next village, Maki, exhibiting rather
bizarre behavior, fled out the Edo-bound gate pursued by a number of
sekisho guards and somehow managed to throw himself into Lake Ashi.
A group of guards got into a boat and rowed after him, but Maki
drowned. His body was removed from the lake and a physician called,
but he could not be revived. The sekisho officials were not sure what to
do with his body, because of their uncertainty over how to treat the case.
If they decided that it was simply a case of a man's drowning, the corpse
could be buried nearby without any further discussion. If, however, his
act was treated as sekisho smashing, then his body would have to be sent
to Edo for bakufu officials to decide the case. Unable to decide, an inquiry was sent to Edo. Meanwhile the corpse was packed in salt and put
in a temporary shelter. The bakufu, too, had great difficulty deciding
how to treat this case; but finally, ten months later, the word came to dispose of his corpse there, thereby putting an end to the case.[58]

In the case of Maki Chūzō we cannot be sure whether the officials
denied Maki passage because he seemed suspicious or because he seemed
insane, but the examples offered here reveal that sekisho officials took a
case-by-case approach with those individuals, samurai or otherwise, who
did not have permits. Taking this into consideration, the seemingly
contradictory evidence before us makes sense.

If we turn to bansho for a moment, in general, domains required that
their residents, including samurai, apply for exit permits and show them
at border checkpoints in order to leave the domain.[59] Regulations governing entry, however, varied from domain to domain. In Kaga and Toyama,
entry permits were never required: The traveler had merely to state his

name, place of origin, and, perhaps, his social status. Samurai were asked the identity of their overlord, in addition to their own name and rank. A notation of the information given, along with the date of passage, was recorded by a bansho official in a register.[60] Sometimes, however, "depending on the person"—evidence again of a case-by-case approach—someone could be held for two or three days for observation. If then judged not suspicious, he would be let through.[61] In the case of another domain, Tsuruoka, men did not need permits to enter, but women did.[62] Tosa required travel permits for all persons entering the domain: those caught without them were accompanied to the border by a bansho guard and, in one case, the guilty party was made to sign a statement saying that he would never return again.[63]

In Tosa and Awa travelers had to carry entry permits with them while in the domain. These permits were written up at border bansho upon entering the domain and were based on the information contained in the person's travel permit. The entry permit allowed one to travel only within the domain and was surrendered upon leaving at another border bansho.[64] Furukawa Koshōken showed his passport and received an entry permit (*yurushi kitte*) which gave his name, age, place of residence, and even listed the places he intended to visit in the domain (Satsuma).[65] A traveler on the Shikoku pilgrimage (*henro*) would return his permit when exiting from each domain he passed through, and pick up another when entering the next domain. While passing through Tosa from west to east, for instance, he would receive an entry permit at Kannoura and return it at Sukumo.[66]

Thus far we have only considered the general traveler passing through these physical barriers, but what about the local residents living nearby? How did the presence of sekisho and bansho affect their lives? In general, there appear to have been two different types of systems at work that governed the movements of local people through sekisho and bansho.

The first system did not require most local people to show travel permits to pass through for daily business. Women traveling for marriage or work as servants (*hōkōnin*) were, however, required to apply through normal channels for a travel permit, but all others were required to give only an oral report to pass through.[67] Exactly how wide an area of villages surrounding sekisho or bansho fell under this system varied according to place.

The permit requirement for outbound women appears to have affected the marriage patterns of commoners living around certain sekisho. Most marriage partners that Arai residents brought in from outside the town were from villages to the west of Arai (and the sekisho). A bride from east of the barrier would require a permit from a central issuing authority for the marriage ceremony and for every visit back to her parents. Even the post-station manager of Arai was discouraged by higher officials in 1781 from seeking the hand in marriage of the daughter of his counterpart at the next station to the east, Maisaka; consequently, one can imagine the difficulties facing a commoner trying to do the same.[68] As a result, there were few marriages between people from different sides of the sekisho. A sample covering the years 1784–1806 from a village located to the west of Usui sekisho reveals that only 18–20 percent of the marriages which took place involved partners from different sides of the sekisho.[69] About 80 percent of the temporary migration for labor undertaken by Arai residents was to the east, but most marriages were restricted to the west. Thus, we can see how sekisho affected the lives of commoners in different ways; there is, however, evidence that these effects were not so great at other sekisho.[70]

Other sekisho and bansho merely required local people to use wooden tags (known as *fuda, sakuba fuda,* or *yaki insatsu*) as permits. These tags were distributed to village headmen; and those villagers needing one for the day picked them up from the headman, returning them the same day.[71] Those traveling for a number of days, however, generally were required to apply for travel permits.[72]

In sum, then, with the exception of a few sekisho that checked permits both ways, permits were, for many people, necessary only when traveling in a direction away from Edo. It was nonetheless safer to have one. If a traveler aroused the suspicions of the guards for some reason, he might not be let through. Kaempfer, commenting that children took off on pilgrimage to Ise without permits, reflected that "the like attempt would be more difficult in other places, where a traveler would expose himself to no small trouble."[73] Not only might a traveler have difficulty passing through sekisho, but should he fall ill on the road, a permit could possibly save his life.

WOMEN AND TRAVEL PERMITS

Women were subject to many more travel restrictions than men were. Lord Redesdale, traveling with Ernest Satow in the closing years of the bakufu, noted this phenomenon and remarked, "This day we came to a place called Yanagose [Yanagase, in Omi province], where there was a curious institution, a sekisho, or barrier, which no woman might go through without a passport. Talk about women's rights!"[74] While his comment might seem ironic in light of the position of women in his contemporary England, Redesdale was correct that women were not treated equally: Not until 1867/7, with the relaxation of the alternate attendance system, were women treated the same as men according to bakufu travel statutes.[75]

As noted, women were denied passage for most of the Tokugawa era through seventeen sekisho so that traffic could be channeled onto a smaller number of routes where it could be monitored more easily. Some of them allowed domain women or local residents to pass, but we may say that in principle they were closed to female traffic. These sekisho restricted the routes available to women, and therefore—since women in Tokugawa Japan rarely traveled alone—to their male companions as well, directing that traffic onto major routes with middle- to large-scale sekisho, where it could be inspected more rigorously.

Not only was the application process for women to obtain sekisho transit permits highly regulated, but the permits themselves were required to contain detailed information. Ordinarily men did not carry transit permits, and even the passports they did carry did not contain the same sort of personal information as women's permits. According to bakufu regulations issued in 1661, the following information, if applicable, had to be included:[76]

1. Number of sedans [*norimono*] being used.
2. If a woman is the widow or sister of a person of high rank and has her head shaven [i.e., has taken religious vows],* this must be indicated by the term *zenni.*

---

*Shaving the head, or cutting one's hair, and taking holy orders did not necessarily mean that a woman was religiously inclined; rather, those acts marked the passage from an active to an inactive secular life.

3. If a commoner woman has a shaven head, this must be indicated by the term *ami*.

4. If a woman is an attendant of priests at Ise or Zenkō-ji or a maid-servant of a widow of high rank, or a *kumano bikuni*, this must be indicated by the term *bikuni*.[77]

5. If a woman's hair is cut, regardless of the length cut, it must be indicated by the term *kamikiri* [the hairstyle of widows, which meant that the length of a woman's usually long hair was cut and worn down at all times]. Also, if a woman has lost hair due to an illness, and it therefore appears cut, it must also be noted as *kamikiri*.

6. Women of any age wearing long-sleeved kimono [usually indicating an unmarried woman], must be indicated by the term *ko-onna* [lit., "small woman," generally referring to a young woman under fifteen or sixteen years of age, but for transit permits the term held for unmarried women over that age].[78]

7. Insanity

8. Wounds

9. Prisoners

10. Decapitated heads

11. Corpses

Although additional information further identifying an individual, such as hairstyle and marks or abscesses on the face, hands, feet, throat or breasts, were not required according to the orders from the Keeper of Edo Castle discussed above, such information was sometimes included, particularly in samurai women's permits. This rule must have been followed with some regularity, for an 1803 entry in the guard diaries kept at Hakone sekisho noted that it was no longer necessary to include this extra information, thus indicating that travel regulations affecting women simplified somewhat over time.[79]

Travelers could be denied passage at sekisho if there were irregularities with their travel documentation, and many of these problems occurred only with women's transit permits. Below are some representative examples of these irregularities.

The incorrect classification of women was one type of mistake found on permits. In such a case, for example, two women were listed on one transit permit simply as "two women," but when their inspection took place at Hakone, it was determined that one of them was, in fact, an "unmarried woman" (*ko-onna*) instead of the "married woman" (*dai-onna*) implied by listing them together. In this and a number of other cases at Hakone when the travel permit did not match the travelers carrying it, the women were turned away.[80] A notable example of this involved Inoue Tsūjo, a poet and the daughter of a Marugame domain samurai, who was denied passage through Arai sekisho in 1681. Her permit was not acceptable because it listed her as "woman" when it should have been "unmarried woman." The fact that she was unaware that her permit was technically invalid made no difference to the sekisho officials there.[81] There are other similar cases involving women traveling towards Edo (*iri-onna*): evidence that strict permit requirements went further than the bakufu's outbound women policy.[82]

Another mistake made on women's permits was the failure to list the fact that a woman had cut hair.[83] In one case a daimyo's maidservant was allowed to pass Hakone sekisho but was denied passage at Arai on the grounds that her cut hair was not listed on her transit permit. Hakone reported that they had inspected the woman; the official reply was that "it is not the case that she was not inspected at Hakone." Apparently, then, either Hakone decided to overlook the case, or the two sekisho had varying definitions of what constituted "cut hair."[84] Other cases at Hakone in which women with "cut hair" who were not listed as such on their permits but were allowed to pass suggest that in certain cases officials were willing to make exceptions. In one of these cases, the traveler's companion explained that a lot of the woman's hair had fallen out during an illness five years prior—in which case, of course, she still was officially required to have a permit listing her as having "cut hair."

Another common careless mistake was the incorrect listing of the number of travelers: for example, three people trying to pass with a permit for two.[85] Women heading west from Edo (*de-onna*) who gave birth just before passing through Hakone sekisho would be denied passage if the child was a girl (because the permit would list one person instead of two). If the child was a boy, however, the woman would be allowed to pass once she got her transit permit appended by the village elders at Hakone Yumoto.[86] Thus we have another example of the relative strictness with which women were treated in Tokugawa Japan. Moreover, Hakone lived up to its reputation as the strictest sekisho in the land, for Arai allowed women traveling west who gave birth to girls before reaching the area to pass with the same permit if there was a witness to the birth, such as an innkeeper.[87]

There were many other types of errors made on permits. For example, those addressed to more than one sekisho, or those addressed to "various sekisho" (*tokorodokoro gosekisho*) were not acceptable for transit permits, but were for passports.[88] Permits with incomplete information (e.g., a missing or incomplete date, the sekisho name omitted, or official's seal missing from the permit) or other erroneous information were also common.[89]

A number of defects or errors on permits could invalidate them. Such cases were not infrequent, but incomplete records do not allow us to say exactly how often they did occur. Apparently, they did occur often enough to be of concern to sekisho officials. A Hakone sekisho diary account from the beginning of the nineteenth century noted an increase in errors on transit permits issued by the Keeper of Edo Castle and recorded fifty-three cases in fifty-one years of permits with mistakes in dating.[90]

One example of how damaged permits were handled illustrates the decentralized nature of sekisho policy. The permit of a woman on the way to Ise in 1712 became wet when the pack horse carrying her belongings fell while she was crossing the Rokugō River at Kawasaki. The woman passed through Hakone without any problems, but was held up at Arai while inquiries were made to Hakone and even the Keeper of Edo Castle before she was let through, illustrating that the inspection of travelers could differ from sekisho to sekisho.[91] It also shows us that the traveler needed to take good care of his permit, or he might face delays and inconvenience in his travel or even be denied passage.

When a traveler was denied passage at a sekisho, usually that person would have to return to the place where the invalid permit was issued and either obtain a new one or a validating document explaining the error in the original permit. If traveling in a group, another member of the party could do so for the person with the invalid permit. If a woman heading down the Tōkaidō had an invalid permit, usually a male companion would return to obtain a new or validated document while the woman waited in Yumoto or Odawara. If the permit was obtained in Edo, applying for the change in permit could require up to two to three weeks.[92] This is, in fact, one of the few clues we have on how long it took to apply for a permit. Some commoners might have been able to secure another permit from a post-station inn—even though such permits were technically not acceptable—and avoid returning to the place where the permit was issued, but it is unclear how often this occurred.[93]

Unlike most sekisho officials, those at Arai sekisho treated women the same regardless of whether they were heading in a direction towards or away from Edo. A group of three women returning to the bakufu capital from a pilgrimage to Honganji in Kyoto were refused passage because their group transit permit failed to make note of the fact that one member of the group was unmarried. A male accompanying the party had to travel to Kyoto to the Shoshidai's office to get the permit corrected.[94] In theory—but only sometimes in practice—when women were refused passage at sekisho, the incident was reported to the bakufu Elders in Edo, who could then investigate the matter further if it appeared to be a breach of the hostage system.[95]

PASSING THROUGH THE BARRIERS

> If it's raining,
> Spend the night at Matsuida.
> If it's not,
> Go on to Sakamoto.[96]

The lyrics of this song relate the anxiety that travelers felt before passing through a major sekisho such as Usui. For the traveler on the Nakasendō, if it was raining, which made traveling more difficult and tiring, and he had yet to pass through the sekisho at Usui, then he was better off spending the night at Matsuida and proceeding on to Sakamoto (where Usui was located) the following day. Similarly, our happy-go-lucky travelers Kita and Yaji, after passing through Hakone sekisho without any problem, were so elated and relieved that they headed straight for a drinking establishment to celebrate.[97] Though they did not require much occasion to hold such celebrations, their sense of relief after passing through a sekisho was a feeling shared by other travelers.

Coming before government officials for an inspection of any sort can be a frightening experience, and from various travelers' accounts this was true at sekisho. At Hakone, which was reputed to be the strictest sekisho, Kiyokawa Hachirō, who was later to sail with Katsu Kaishū and others to America, remarked that "there is not a person alive whose hair does not stand on end out of fear when passing through Hakone for the first time."[98] Instructions to sekisho guards show that administrative authorities were aware of this fear; they were concerned that guards not intimidate travelers and check all of them fairly.[99] Orders to guards at Arai sekisho instructed them to be strict in their inspections, but not to scare or intimidate travelers, nor to accept "gifts" from them. Concern over bribery of guards was expressed at other sekisho and bansho as well, and as we shall see in the next chapter, this was for good reason.[100] If guards were uncertain how to handle a particular case, they were to notify Yoshida domain, the sekisho administrator, without delay and hold the traveler there until a decision was made.

Shortly before approaching Hakone, coming from Odawara, the Tokugawa traveler passed along a tree-lined road to Shinmachi, a small household settlement of teahouses, where he might stop for a brief rest before proceeding to the sekisho compound. At Hakone, the traveler, under normal circumstances, probably could be processed without delay; but at Arai a wait of uncertain duration was likely since westbound travelers on the Tōkaidō were ferried across together in boats from Maisaka. While Kita and Yaji were resting after making the crossing they noted that "a continual stream of people of all classes kept passing and repassing."[101]

Entering through the open east gate of Hakone sekisho, from which palisades extended on both sides, our west-bound traveler ordinarily would be flanked by two foot soldiers wielding staves (see Figure 5). Walking past them he would see an edict board to his right listing the regulations for passing through the sekisho, but he would already know its contents either from reading a travel guide, having one read to him— perhaps by a village official before setting out on his journey—or through word of mouth at post stations. Shortly after the edict board, the traveler would see a number of weapons displayed to impress with the authority of the institution those who were about to face the officials at the sekisho.[102] Similarly, at Usui, the traveler was made to walk up an

Figure 5 Passing through Hakone Sekisho. From *Tōkaidō gojūsantsugi*. Harvard University Art Museums, The Hofer Collection of the Arts of Asia.

incline and then ascend a number of steps in approaching the sekisho, thus forcing him to look up at the sekisho and the weapons on display there.[103]

In front of the main sekisho office the traveler would remove his hat and bow; from a kneeling position he would hand over his travel permit (see Figure 6). As the early nineteenth century travel handbook *Ryokō yōjin shū* advised, "The traveller should take good care of his travel permit. He should stop at a tea house and make sure that the permit is in place before proceeding on to the sekisho. It will not do to have to search for it [once before the sekisho office]."[104]

In the case of a commoner, the traveler would proceed to the lower guard house—not a separate building, but usually a separate room in the sekisho office—and present his permit to an official there. The official inspected the permit and compared the written document with the person before him. If the person did not look suspicious in any way, permission would be given to pass. The entire examination process for an adult male could be concluded very quickly. A male samurai, as we said, would approach the sekisho office and answer some questions as to his name, status, and destination before being allowed to pass through, as did Inoue Tsūjo's male companion at Arai.[105] If the officials were suspicious of a traveler, the inquiry would continue until a decision was made on how to deal with the person.

A commoner woman traveling on foot in the company of a man would proceed to the upper or lower guard house, depending on her rank. The official there would ask the identity of the woman and the man would respond. If they were traveling towards Edo and were being questioned at any sekisho besides Arai, then the inspection might end there.

At Arai, however, the woman's permit would be inspected—regardless of which direction she was traveling—in the following manner. The inspection would begin as noted above, with the male companion responding to an official's questions and handing the permit over to him. The woman would sit down on the wooden veranda in front of the sekisho office and the Inspector of Women would be summoned. At some sekisho like Mokugahashi and Usui, however, only samurai women were examined by the Inspector of Women; commoner women were pro-

Figure 6 Travelers' Permits Inspected at Arai. Hiroshige, *Tōkaidō gojūsantsugi.* Arai sekisho shiryōkan.

cessed by a male lower guard. During these physical examinations those travelers waiting to be processed were made to go outside the barrier gates, which were closed for the duration of the inspection.

The job of the Inspector, who was known variously as *hitomi onna, rōjo, aratame onna,* or *aratame oba,* was to physically check women to make sure that they matched up with the description given on the travel permits they carried. There were usually two Inspectors at sekisho that allowed non-local female traffic, and the positions were filled by either two of the wives or mothers of the sekisho's lower guard,[106] or, as was the case at Hakone, by women from a wealthy peasant family of long-established status.[107]

The Inspector would look at the woman's clothes to determine what type of kimono she was wearing; she would then check the woman's eyebrows and teeth (unmarried women did not usually shave their eyebrows or blacken their teeth) as well as her hair. As it was not always possible to determine a woman's hairstyle at a glance, female travelers were required to loosen their hair and allow the Inspector to comb through it. In at least two sekisho, Mokugahashi and Usui, however, commoner women would loosen their hair and have it examined by a male sekisho lower guard, instead of the Inspector of Women, whose responsibility was confined to samurai women only.[108] If there was any doubt as to the sex of the person, the breasts would also be examined. These physical examinations were routine up until 1867, when the alternate attendance system was suspended, eliminating the raison d'être behind the procedure.

While the physical examination was going on the travel permit itself was checked in a rather ritualized manner. The lower official who received it would hand it to a higher official without examining it first himself. The higher official would inspect the permit and then hand it back to the lower official, who would then examine it and return it once again to the higher official. Having briefed the document the first time, the higher official would now look more carefully at the name and seal of the permit issuer; in the case of a permit issued by a bakufu, daimyo, court or religious authority, he would check the seal on the permit against a copy of the seal contained in a register kept at the sekisho. All such issuing authorities were required to send a copy of their seal to every sekisho.[109] An up-to-date list of authorized issuers of women's permits, as noted earlier, was kept on a wooden board hung in the main sekisho office for the easy reference of the sekisho officials.

If the seal matched, then the officials would wait for the results of the physical examination. Once that was completed, the Inspector would report the result of the exam out loud to the officials: for example, if the woman had cut hair, she would call out, "She has cut hair" (*kamikiri de gozaimasu*). If the Inspector's report matched the classification listed on the woman's travel permit, the inspection was over, and permission was granted to pass. If the woman, for some reason, did not match up with her permit, she would have to submit to a second physical examination, this time by the reserve Inspector. If the results were the same, the woman would be inspected a third time, in the presence of a male sekisho official. This was the case with one woman traveling to Matsuzaka in Ise province who held a daimyo-issued permit. Two exams revealed that she had cut hair which was not listed on her permit. In such cases, passage was refused and the matter was reported to the bakufu Elders in Edo.[110] The traveler was then stranded until a corrected permit could be obtained.

Should any problem come up in the examination of a traveler, sekisho officials might consult a record kept of how other travelers with similar problems were treated. The *Hakone gosekisho nikki kakinuki*, to which frequent reference has been made, was in fact such a manual for sekisho officials. If there was no precedent for a case and officials were uncertain how to act, a letter of inquiry would be immediately dispatched by relay palanquin to the sekisho administrative authority and sometimes to Edo as well. A reply from Odawara authorities, for example, could be obtained the same day. Precedents were important, but once in a while a case was said to be "different" (often for unstated reasons) and an exception made.

Women traveling in palanquins (*kago*) or sedans (*norimono*) whose permits noted this fact were permitted to remain in their vehicles for the exam.[111] In such cases, checking procedures were similar to those discussed above: A guard would direct the vehicle to a spot in front of the sekisho office, where the Inspector of Women would carry out the physical exam with the traveler remaining in the vehicle. If the exam confirmed the information on the permit, the head official gave permission to pass. Negative results made a second examination by the reserve Inspector mandatory. If the second exam went exactly the same, however, the woman was made to get out of the vehicle and sit on the veranda of the sekisho office and be examined a third time in the presence of a male sekisho official.[112] Commoner women traveling in relay palanquins obtained from post stations or inns, or those riding on post station horses, were required to alight and sit on the sekisho veranda for inspection.

Most male commoners probably could pass through sekisho without much of an inspection, however, particularly when traveling towards Edo. In reading contemporary travel diaries, one is, in fact, struck by the lack of detailed information given regarding passage through sekisho and bansho. At Arai, Ōta Nanpo simply noted that he got out of the palanquin and passed through the sekisho.[113] Takagi Zensuke, a merchant from Satsuma, made six trips back and forth between Kyushu and Kamigata and hardly ever mentioned more than the fact that he handed over his permit when passing through bansho.[114] Many other travelers simply noted the existence of sekisho in their diaries.[115] Thus, for most male travelers, sekisho in themselves do not appear to have been a barrier to their mobility.

For samurai women traveling away from Edo (and both ways at Arai, Kega, and Yanagase), however, passing through sekisho could be a very disagreeable experience. Inoue Tsūjo, on her way home from Edo to Marugame in 1689, where she was an attendant to the Marugame daimyo's mother, was carried through the sekisho gate at Arai and waited for instructions. Her carriers were ordered to set the palanquin down near the sekisho office and the Inspector of Women was summoned to examine Inoue and her female attendant. She wrote that the Inspector examined her hair and other parts of her body "in a courteous manner," and reported the results of the examination to the sekisho officials, who granted her permission to pass. Even though Inoue felt that the examination had been "courteous," she was quite relieved when it was over. Once through the sekisho she put up her disheveled hair but did not stop to rest until they had reached Mishima, the next post station down the Tōkaidō.[116]

Another traveler, Shirabyōshi Masako, noted that while ordinary women could pass through the sekisho inspection "without being touched" (*isasaka no sawari mo naku*), samurai women had to undergo an ignoble inspection that "makes one break out in a sweat."[117] It was because of the unsettling experience these women might encounter at major sekisho such as Hakone, Usui, Arai, and Kiso Fukushima that they sometimes sought alternate routes. For this reason, two roads (one bypassing Arai and the other Usui) became known as Princess Roads (*Hime kaidō*). Although both roads had sekisho—Kega and Saimoku, respectively—their inspection of women was reputed to have been less severe.[118]

Daimyo wives, daughters, and female attendants could pass through sekisho without getting out of their vehicles. The vehicle would be put down in front of the sekisho office and the Inspector of Women would open the door and ask if there was any other person riding inside with the woman. Daimyo women did not undergo a physical examination at sekisho. Usually that examination was conducted the night before they were to pass through at the special daimyo inn (*honjin*) where they stayed. High-ranking women of the Court were also allowed the same privilege. Prior arrangements had to be made for the exam, however, by sending a travel itinerary to the sekisho before passing through, along with a written request for the special exam (*honjin aratame*).[119] At Kega, a sekisho official would come to the daimyo inn and check the travel permits. The innkeeper's wife or mother (daimyo inn operators frequently doubled as village headmen or elders of post stations) would examine the traveler in place of the sekisho Inspector of Women; in this way, she was treated as a sekisho official and was required to pledge an oath of responsibility.[120] Sometimes a daimyo wife's closest attendants would also be examined at the inn, but in other cases it was done at the sekisho itself.[121] Only a very few women, such as princesses, were ever exempt from inspections entirely.[122]

Not only was a lookout kept at sekisho for "outbound women," but also for young girls who might be disguised as boys. This was particularly true of young boys with forelocks (*maegami*), the common hairstyle of boys prior to passing through the rites of manhood. Young boys whose sex was in question were required to submit to a physical examination by the Inspector of Women. The same was also true of samurai, priests, monks, and yamabushi. With the exception of the three sekisho of Arai, Kega, and Yanagase, this occurred only when traveling away from Edo.[123] Regulations at Kiso Fukushima required that young boys under thirteen who appeared suspiciously like girls open the fronts of their kimonos for inspection; those over thirteen had to show the Inspector their chest, and if their sex was still ambiguous, open the front as well.[124]

The absurdity of the situation—that is, the necessity of maintaining a system of physical exams based on the notion that a potential daimyo rebellion could be prevented by stopping daimyo daughters disguised as boys from escaping from Edo—was captured by the woodblock artist Toyokuni in a print which satirically depicts a "dirty old woman" (the Inspector of Women), eyeglass in hand, examining the front of a young boy with the waist of his kimono open (see Figure 7).

Sekisho regulations required that travelers follow certain etiquette when passing through. Those samurai with the right of shogunal audience (*omemie*)—that is, housemen and up—were allowed to remain in their sedan when riding through sekisho. Those below were required to alight from their vehicles and walk through.[125] A number of contemporary foreign visitors to Tokugawa Japan such as Satow and Doeff were treated like daimyo in that they were granted the privilege of riding through sekisho in their sedans.[126]

All persons with the privilege of riding through sekisho were nonetheless required to open the door of their sedan—regardless of the direction they were traveling in—and greet the officials, usually with just a bow. Satow noted that a third party opened the door of his sedan "about half way" as he was carried past.[127] According to the records kept by a daimyo inn operator at Kega, however, opening the door served no real purpose, for it was only necessary to open it "a crack."[128] This requirement was, however, waived for a number of princesses.[129]

Although opening the door was perhaps a mere formality, there were a number of occasions when daimyo or other travelers were reluctant to comply. When the Owari daimyo passed through Hakone on his way up to Edo in 1751 with the door of his sedan closed, sekisho officials informed his attendants of the regulations, but still nothing was done. As the sedan continued moving through the sekisho one official there followed after it and repeated the regulations to the attendants, one of whom spoke to the daimyo, and the door was finally opened. Six years

Figure 7 Young Boy Being Examined at Arai. Hiroshige (top)/Toyokuni (bottom), *Sōhitsu gojūsantsugi.* Arai sekisho shiryōkan.

later, he did it again.[130] Such cases did not occur very often–there are records of only thirteen incidences at Hakone between 1696 and 1782– and there is no evidence that a hard line was taken against offenders. In some cases nothing was even said to the offending party.[131]

Likewise, all travelers, including daimyo, whether walking or riding, were required to remove their hats or head coverings when passing through sekisho. There were a number of cases of travelers refusing to do so, but with rare exception, no action was taken against high-ranking people. One such rare case of muscle-flexing involved the Tosa daimyo Yamauchi Yōdō, who neglected to remove his lacquered hat as he was carried through in a sedan. While no action was taken at the moment, over a month later the bakufu decided to punish him with seven days conciliary confinement.[132] People other than high-ranking samurai probably would not have dared disobey sekisho etiquette. The case of a foot soldier denied passage for refusing to remove his hat indicates that sekisho authorities were not as likely to be flexible with commoners in this matter.[133]

Passing through bansho did not appear to be quite the same unsettling or frightening experience that passing through sekisho could be for some travelers, but they, like sekisho, were stricter towards women. Regulations of internal bansho usually noted that women and certain commodity goods required travel permits, but men were rarely mentioned, except perhaps in general provisions that wounded or insane people needed permits.[134] Exactly how many women were physically examined at bansho, in addition to having their permits checked, is unclear; but women riding in sedans through at least one Kaga domain bansho were required to be examined–whatever that entailed–by an Inspector of Women there.[135]

Guards at bansho that were open to general traffic (some were closed to all but merchants) inspected travelers with varying degrees of strictness. Furukawa Koshōken noted, for example, that at Higo-guchi bansho of Satsuma domain (on the Satsuma-Higo border) travelers were checked, but that over the border at Fukuro bansho they "were not inspected very much."[136] In Hitoyoshi, or Sagara, domain (Higo), guards not only inspected travelers but were also required to accompany them to the next village.[137] Satsuma domain bansho required that travelers show that they had a certain amount of money (3 *bu* or 3/4 *ryō* gold–a large sum of money) known as *misekane,* or "show-me money," as a precaution that in the case of sickness or death they "would not become an expense to the domain."[138] Passage through bansho and sekisho was, we have noted, restricted to certain hours. Although the Tokugawa time system fluctuated, we can estimate closing time to be at 6 P.M. in the spring and fall, 7 P.M. in the summer, and 5 P.M. in the winter. Likewise, opening time would change from 6 A.M. in the spring and fall to 5 A.M. in the summer, and to 7 A.M. in the winter.

The four largest sekisho were particularly strict in prohibiting passage after closing time. At Hakone the watchtower bell was used to announce the opening and closing of the sekisho to traffic. Other sekisho, however, appeared to show some variation. At Nakagawa, a river sekisho on an important route for the transport of commodity goods into Edo, only boats heading away from Edo were prohibited night passage. Edo-bound boats were allowed through if the travel certificates of those on board were in order.[139] Here, apparently, commercial needs took precedence over others. Ōsasa sekisho in 1836 let people traveling to distant markets to buy food pass through after closing time due to a famine resulting from poor crops.[140]

The set of gates facing Edo (*tenka no mon,* or "the gates of the realm") were shut and locked at closing time, but the other set was usually left open later to allow checking station officials to come and go freely.[141] Once the gates were closed they were, according to regulation, "absolutely not to be opened."[142] Nevertheless, there were certain devices that are reputed to have been used to allow travelers to get through sekisho past closing time. If it seemed that a party of travelers would not make it to the sekisho in time, a strong-footed member could go on ahead and inform the sekisho officials that if the rest of the party did not make it through they would not be able to find lodging for the night. The advance man had to secure lodging and get the inn manager to act as a guarantor before the sekisho officials would allow the rest of the party to pass through after the formal closing time.[143]

Another device sometimes employed was that, if a traveler riding in a sedan was running late in getting to a sekisho, a transport worker could remove a door from the vehicle and run ahead with it through the one set of sekisho gates. Once a traveler was past the one set, while the other was still open, the sekisho could not close. By performing this feat, the worker could delay the closing of the gates long enough for the rest of the sedan—and travelers—to make it through.[144] It does not seem likely, however, that these devices were employed very often.

Once the gates were closed it was very difficult for travelers without special privileges to pass at night to get through. At Kobotoke a daimyo was on one occasion allowed passage after closing hours and tipped the officials for letting him do so.[145] In addition to certain bakufu officials, only the daimyo of the Three Houses, Echizen, and Kaga were normally allowed nighttime passage through sekisho.[146] Ordinary travelers, unless visibly ill, were not permitted through.[147] At Nanmoku sekisho local commoners were only allowed through "after careful inquiry, in cases where there were unavoidable circumstances."[148]

To regulate movement on Tokugawa roads the bakufu and the domains created permit systems whereby travelers, and especially women, were required to apply for and obtain written permission before setting out on any journey. Yet political authorities early in the Tokugawa period could not comprehend the implications of the tremendous social and economic changes taking place around them. In 1603, for example, surely no one in government could have imagined that the development of the official transport system and the onset of a period of peace and rapid economic growth would stimulate a surge of movement of people from all levels of society on the roadways; and that within a century, millions would be converging on the sacred Ise Shrine. As early as the mid-seventeenth century domain authorities were alarmed at the great number of their residents who left on pilgrimage without permission. The reaction of officials in domains like Aizu, who ordered that "there will be no more pilgrimage this year" reveals to us that they were totally unprepared for it, and unable to stop it.

Political authorities idealized a society where peasants remained fixed on the land, and thus they did not create a permit system meant to accommodate large numbers of travelers. The apparent result was a cumbersome system for obtaining permission to travel that they were never able to fully enforce. That the system was unwieldy is evident from contemporary complaints by both travelers and local government authorities, who at times proposed ways to make it function more efficiently. Though it is perhaps not readily apparent because their efforts were often reactive, government officials did attempt to create a system that would work.

Changing the requirement that commoner women in the city of Edo apply to the City Magistrate instead of the higher-ranking Keeper of Edo Castle is just one example of this effort to make the system work. Yet it was only when bakufu officials realized that the system, as it stood, could not accommodate the unexpectedly large numbers of women applying for permits, that modifications were made. And yet, even with that change, the system still could not fully accommodate the numbers of men and women wanting to travel. It appears that it was for this reason that the bakufu allowed religious institutions and landlords in urban areas, and religious institutions and village officials in rural areas, to issue permits for pilgrimages or trips to therapeutic hot springs. We say that government authorities "allowed" permit-issuing authority to devolve to a lower level because they almost never came out strongly against the practice. But why they failed to supervise or oversee the system leaves us puzzled. The one attempt to reverse the process made by the bakufu in the 1830s, requiring that all permits issued by village officials and religious institutions be co-authorized by intendants, seems like a shot in the dark to assume control over a process with which it had theretofore not seemed overly concerned. In the domains, too, there is evidence that officials tried to make their permit systems more realistic by simplifying application procedures. This was done to encourage commoners to apply for travel permits, rather than to leave home without them on *nukemairi*.

Both the bakufu and the domains were interested in controlling the movement of women. Bakufu edicts and decrees defined ideal roles for the four social groups and further divided each group into male and female categories, but only the female categories were singled out for specific attention; this is particularly evident with regard to regulations on travel and passage through sekisho. The reasons for the gendered nature of travel regulations clearly go beyond bakufu sekisho policy. This type of regulation appears to have been just a form of general population control in that, just as at Sakai bansho in Kaga, it was generally believed men would not abscond from the domain if they could not take their women with them.[149] Yet the fact that a number of domains went so far as to prohibit, in principle, women from traveling at all reveals that more than a paranoid fear of population loss was involved. As early as 1616, when the bakufu instructed sekisho officials at river crossings in Kantō to be vigilant against certain types of people, it lumped women together with the wounded and suspicious persons. Many domainal barriers operated under the same instructions.

Women did not often travel without male company and at sekisho the man acted, in effect, as the woman's sponsor in the checking procedures which took place there. The difference in the relative social positions of the sexes is perhaps best exemplified by the fact that there were no difficulties involved in procedures at Hakone for pregnant women giving birth to a male child before passing through the barrier, only in the case of a girl. Moreover, women's inferior status was firmly reflected in the lighter treatment they received under Tokugawa law in sekisho-related offenses. Changing inheritance patterns and superstitious beliefs were contributing factors, but Neo-Confucianism, which set forth the rule of a woman's subservience and obedience to parents, husband, and, when widowed, to a son, also reflected and reinforced the lower social position held by women. The greater social, legal and familial pressures that affected women led many to leave home without seeking the approval of the household or political authorities and travel on side roads, bypassing sekisho and bansho.

FIVE

The Benevolence of the Realm

Few institutions work exactly as designed; barriers and the permit system necessitated by them were no exception. Were this not the case, it would be difficult to account for the emergence of travel as recreation, the topic of the following chapter. For a variety of reasons, commoners had greater freedom of movement than a strict reading of government statutes would suggest. As suggested in the last chapter, this was in part because officials at sekisho and bansho often treated travelers case by case.

To explain further why the physical and institutional barriers to free mobility were not more effective, the present chapter will expand on the behavior of officials, or what might be called the "benevolence of the realm." The expression can be found in a number of travel diaries and is used here in several ways: First of all, at many barriers, both sekisho and bansho, there were small side roads that travelers could use to avoid inspection. Although use of them defeated the purpose of the barriers and permits, officials apparently either failed to discourage the practice consistently or actually gave it their tacit approval. In some cases the short-cuts were more than close to the barrier, they literally went through or over the palisade network; and travelers occasionally acknowledged in writing the benevolence that let them pass through such holes in the system. Sekisho officials could also show benevolence by allowing travelers to pass inspection with either no permits or defective permits, by passing through women in obvious disguise as men, and by interpreting the law to downgrade serious offenses.

The term "benevolence" can also have ironic overtones. Besides the negligence that allowed short-cuts to exist, it can refer to the way that government officials undermined the system to their own or the government's benefit. It was not in the interest of sekisho or bansho guards to impede the flow of traffic through overzealous application of the regulations. On the contrary, a backlog of traffic, with people lingering about waiting for new permits to arrive, would pose a more serious concern to the administrative authorities than the passage of people who posed no threat to civil peace.

The reach of government was limited—it could only go so far. Thus, the commoner traveler who was deemed suspicious or insane was simply refused passage through the barriers and escorted by foot soldiers to the border of the village before the barrier in the direction from which they came. So long as they committed no crime, there was no reason to do anything but send them along. In some cases, even when, technically, a crime was committed, it was easier to dispose of the problem by not treating it as such, rather than having to arrest the person and pursue legal proceedings.

Because the reach of government was limited it relied on self-regulation to a great extent. This phenomenon has been explained previously in terms of Five-Household Groups, the principle of group responsibility or accountability (*enza*), and the concept of "village autonomy"; but it has relevance for sekisho as well for, as noted, villagers in areas surrounding the barriers were drawn into a system of surveillance designed to uphold the integrity of the institution. The existence of many short-cuts around the barriers necessitated their active cooperation; otherwise the sekisho system would lose its meaning. While there is evidence that at times villagers could not resist the attraction of a monetary reward for their efforts in the apprehension of travelers bypassing barriers, there is also much to suggest that self-regulation was not terribly effective.

Government officials materially benefitted from the short-cutting. In a number of cases it is apparent that they were receiving kick-backs from privately run river-crossing operations which allowed travelers to avoid checking procedures at sekisho and domainal barriers. In other cases officials were in collusion with village officials or teahouse operators who helped "guide" the traveler through the barriers, or produced a permit that was sufficient for passage, in exchange for a fee.

Benevolence was also exhibited in the lenient treatment of pilgrims who set out from their domains without official permits. Domains issued laws aimed at trying to restrict flow of population, and currency, out of their borders; but it was extremely difficult to prohibit the act of pilgrimage. Although pilgrimage assumed a much more secular, recreational character during the Tokugawa period, it was still widely believed to be a religious act, hence the reluctance of political authorities to proscribe it. Furthermore, sekisho or bansho guards were reluctant to prevent legitimate pilgrims without permits from completing their ritual act because of its sacred nature and the fear of bringing harm unto themselves if they did so. Similarly, it was difficult for a househead or other person of authority to punish those in his care who left without his permission on pilgrimage.

FLEXIBILITY WITH DEFECTIVE PERMITS

Some of the discussion about permits in the previous chapter might give the reader the impression that officials were excessively zealous or petty in their requirements for transit permits and passage through sekisho. Their policies were, however, not rigidly enforced. Despite the existence of defective permits that could cause a detailed investigation, sekisho officials did not always pronounce such documents invalid. Case-by-case inspections allowed for great flexibility. Based on the evidence contained in the guard diaries kept at Hakone, there was a noticeable trend of increasing willingness to set new—and more permissive—precedents. Most of our evidence, however, is from the eighteenth century on and does not allow for comparison with much of the first century of Tokugawa rule, during which time sekisho were probably stricter.

Sekisho policy showed some flexibility in allowing the people not affected by any mistakes in group permits to pass. For example, if a group permit listed "ten women," but one of them had "cut hair," then only the one woman would be prevented from passing. Sometimes the group would continue on and the affected person would wait until an amended permit could be secured; in other cases, however, the whole group would wait together, retracing their steps to the nearest post station.[1]

Similarly, for men, if a group permit, usually a passport, did not list the total number in the group, only one would be allowed to pass. If the group contained more people than were listed on the permit, the extras were not allowed to pass; there was, however, flexibility the other way.[2]

While there were a number of cases in which transit permits with incorrect classifications of women were pronounced invalid, a new precedent was set in 1781 at Hakone, reputably the strictest sekisho. A group permit had been written up for "six married and four unmarried women," but in reality there proved to be four and six instead. After investigating the matter, the officials pronounced that, as long as the number of persons requesting passage through the sekisho matched the total number listed on the permit, passage was allowed.[3] Such flexibility regarding the breakdown of groups of women jointly listed on women's permits took away part of the raison d'être of the permit system, which was a strict accounting of the personal identity of travelers.

We also noted in the last chapter that a permit with the wrong sexagenary designation could be pronounced invalid, but in a number of cases travelers with such permits were allowed to pass through Hakone.[4] While there is no chronological trend apparent, the number of cases handled leniently suggests that sekisho officials were not rigid in dealing with travelers whose permits were not seriously defective.[5]

From all the evidence on defective permits it appears that sekisho allowed certain types of omissions but not errors. For example, permits that neglected to mention the name of the sekisho were allowed, whereas those with the wrong name (e.g., Kobotoke instead of Hakone) were not. This allowed for the occasional mistake but prevented people from using a permit issued for one sekisho at any other.[6] In some cases, such as missing dates or wrong numbers of travelers (as long as the number listed on the permit was in excess of the actual number), the responsible party or parties would have to write an explanatory note and hand it over to the sekisho officials. In other cases, however, passage was permitted without any such demand.[7]

In an undated document sekisho officials requested guidance from the Domain Elders of Owari domain, administrator of Kiso Fukushima, on how to deal with certain types of defective permits for women. The Elders replied that the sekisho officials should use their own discretion, but they also gave some suggestions about the type of remedial measures that might be taken to allow those with defective permits to pass through the barrier. For example, if someone listed as an "unmarried woman" came to the sekisho wearing a short-sleeved kimono, she would be told to change into a kimono with long sleeves. A woman in a similar case who did not have a long-sleeved kimono to change into was allowed to pass through after somehow affixing handtowels to her short sleeves to make them "long." Also, if a married woman came to the sekisho without the customary blackened teeth, then she might be told to blacken them if she wanted to pass. Or, if a woman's permit said that she had cut hair and that was not the case, she could perhaps cut a small piece of her hair and be allowed to pass. By these remedial measures women with irregular transit permits were able to complete their journeys without delay.[8] While no evidence that this occurred elsewhere has been found, it seems unlikely that only one sekisho would have taken such measures.

Although the trend was toward greater flexibility in terms of women's travel permits, we should not think that this was always the case. Sekisho like Hakone and Arai could be strict in applying regulations: for example, unmarried women with shaved eyebrows (another custom among married women) were at times sent back to their place of origin to obtain corrected permits.[9]

The application of Tokugawa law was at times unpredictable and random, but it could also be flexible, for it was a traditional principle in Japanese law that reason should prevail over custom and precedent. Sekisho authorities in large part applied the principle of "rule-by-man" by deciding individual cases on their own merit instead of simply applying precedents in a mechanical fashion. As explained by Hiramatsu Yoshirō, "It was a special feature of shogunal law that, while the letter of the regulations was preserved, in substance they were given different treatment. While the form of the law was retained, it was transformed in substance. The authority of the legislation was preserved, but it was made to harmonize with the 'tenor of the times' or the actual conditions of society."[10]

The same observation holds true for sekisho regulations. In taking the remedial measures outlined above, the form of the law was maintained, but its substance was radically transformed. This meant that the law was in place and could be applied as needed.

ENTERING THE BRUSH

Considerable benevolence was shown by officials to commoners caught trying to go through or around sekisho illegally. With the exception of the *rōnin* early in the seventeenth century who cut down a guard and ran through the barrier at Kiso Fukushima, there is no other case on record of people forcing a way through a sekisho. Nevertheless, some people did try to sneak or run through, although again the records tell of only one successful attempt. That man ran through the sekisho compound at Usui, not even bothering to try to gain permission to pass through legally, and never looked back. Foot soldiers were sent chasing after him, but he was never caught. The undated document detailing this incident said that it was the first time in the 200-year history of the sekisho that something like this had happened.[11] Less successful was a townswoman of about forty years of age who was told that she could not pass through at Hakone without a travel permit. Hearing this, she became violent and made a dash for the gate at the other end of the sekisho. Before reaching it, however, she was stopped at spear-point by some guards and escorted back to the border of the next village, where the waistcord tied around her to prevent any further rash behavior was removed.[12]

In another case, shortly after the sekisho opened for the day at Hakone, a man tried to sneak through the gate and was stopped by the guards. When questioned, he tried to run away, and had to be caught again and tied up. The man answered questions unintelligibly and appeared insane. He too was escorted back to the border of the neighboring village (always in the direction from which the person was coming), and released.[13]

A third case is very revealing of policy at Hakone in regards to people trying to pass through or by the sekisho illegally. At about 8 A.M. a townsman tried to pass through without a permit. He was refused passage and escorted to the border of the neighboring village. At 4 P.M. he returned to the sekisho and tried again, with the same results. Told that he absolutely could not pass without a travel permit, he said he would go and get one. Shortly thereafter he came back with the necessary document—

which he had apparently written himself—and was refused still a third time. The following day around dusk he tried to run through the sekisho, but this effort proved no more successful than his previous ones. There being no point in releasing him at the border again, he was tied up and a letter of inquiry sent to Odawara requesting instructions. The reply was that since the man "was not insane in the least bit," he should be released at the border of the neighboring village. Luckily, that was the last seen of him, or at least the last time he made an entry into the guard diaries.[14]

These cases are informative in that they show that sekisho policy at Hakone was not strict in prosecuting commoners who tried to go through the sekisho illegally. Rather than being arrested and sent to Odawara or Edo, they were all "turned back" to the border of the neighboring village. This is not to say, however, that commoners were permitted to disobey sekisho regulations. It is important to note that in the three cases cited above the parties involved were commoner men and that they were traveling to, not away, from Edo. Sekisho were concerned primarily with the movement of people—particularly women—out of Edo, contributing perhaps to the laxity with which other offenders were treated. Status was also a factor; while there are only two cases of samurai committing a sekisho-related offense, in both instances the samurai were made to suffer the death penalty. These cases, compared with those of commoners, emphasize the great distance that government maintained between status groups.

Some people tried to pass through sekisho illegally and others tried to go around them. *Yabuiri* (lit., "entering the brush") was the term used by officials at Hakone sekisho to describe travelers who accidentally strayed from the road. It is apparent, however, from some of the cases presented that the term was also applied to those who intentionally—and unsuccessfully—tried to go around sekisho. *Yabuiri* cases involved people either climbing over sekisho palisades or those found in the brush walking or hiding in the off-limits zone. Here, too, there are a considerable number of cases involving commoners, and one involving a samurai attendant (*chūgen*), who can only marginally be considered a samurai, yet the only penalty the offenders received was to be denied passage and escorted back to the next village neighboring Hakone. Like the persistent man in the case cited above, even though the samurai attendant had been refused passage at the sekisho twice before deciding to scale the palisade and enter the brush, his punishment was no different.[15] In many respects, it seems that the sekisho guards and commoner travelers were playing a game of cat-and-mouse. In this case, as in the others whose outcomes are known, the attendant was escorted to the border of the next village by two foot soldiers. There appears to be no case on record of a samurai committing the offense of entering the brush, but one suspects that if a samurai did commit such an offense, actual punishment would have been meted out.

Unlike sekisho smashing, entering the brush was apparently not considered a serious crime. Although it is not entirely clear exactly what defined sekisho smashing nor how it differed from entering the brush, there are a few clues which might allow us to distinguish the two crimes. For one, it appears from the incomplete information available that a number of those caught and crucified for sekisho smashing had committed a prior crime and were evading the sekisho to avoid arrest. A second clue is that in all cases of sekisho smashing the accused was not caught in the process of evading the sekisho—where it might be easier to overlook the act—but only days or weeks later. Some of the cases treated as entering the brush at Hakone appear indistinguishable from sekisho smashing except in this respect.[16] Certainly the benevolent treatment of commoners through the downgrading of a crime occurred elsewhere in Tokugawa society. For example, those who participated in urban riots (*uchikowashi*) technically were guilty of conspiracy (*totō*), but in the case of the Tenmei urban riots in Edo, with the exception of those thirty people who were perceived to be the ringleaders, the others arrested (close to a thousand) were released. This decision was justified on the basis that they had merely engaged in a quarrel or brawl (*kenka*), effectively absolving them of the crime.[17]

SHORT-CUTS AND CROSS-DRESSING

The absurdity of sekisho regulations concerning the physical inspection of young males was perhaps not lost on sekisho officials, who showed remarkable leniency in cases when young girls disguised as boys were caught. In one such case a man appearing like a masterless samurai, accompanied by a young boy of twelve or thirteen years of age and a girl of about ten, who was disguised as a boy, passed through Hakone sekisho in 1789 without any problem. Feeling a sense of relief in pulling off the disguise, the party stopped for a rest shortly thereafter. A transport worker who somehow realized what had happened tried to bribe the man, but the two could not come to terms. The worker then left to inform the sekisho officials, but a peasant who happened to walk by and overhear the discussion between the samurai and the transport worker approached the samurai and offered to have the young girl accompanying him exchange clothes with the samurai's disguised girl. After the change of clothes, the samurai's girl was dressed as a girl and the peasant's girl as a boy. The transport worker returned soon thereafter with a few sekisho officials, who checked the girl accompanying the samurai and declared that nothing was wrong. After the officials left, the girl and boy changed back into the clothes they were originally wearing. Apparently the peasant was a local man acting under orders from the sekisho; the entire deception was known and allowed to play through, perhaps to cover the guards' oversight. In the words of the author who related this incident, they "avoided the dangers of a tiger's den; they escaped inevitable death due to the benevolence of the sekisho officials."[18]

Although the identity of this presumably low-class samurai author is unknown, and we have no way of determining whether what he wrote was fact or fiction, a number of similar cases of the benevolence of government at sekisho indicate that as early as 1676 sekisho were beginning in some respects to transform the substance of the law while retaining its bare form. Three cases of disguised girls being caught at Kiso Fukushima, in 1676, 1788, and 1819, all resulted in lenient treatment. The guilty parties were refused passage through the sekisho and escorted away by sekisho guards.

In the first case, a group of three people dressed as *yamabushi* were denied passage when the two adults refused to allow the guards to inspect the young member in their party, who turned out to be a girl in disguise. After twice refusing the guards' request, the two men admitted their error and were escorted back to the previous station on the Kiso road. In the second case, a young girl of sixteen also tried to pass herself off as a male through her dress and by wearing the *maegami* hairstyle of a young man before attaining manhood. For her plan to deceive the guards (*gikei*) she was refused passage, but the three men travelers with her were not held back, as the girl said that they "had not guided her" (*fuannai to mōsu*), meaning that they had not put her up to the deception. In both this case and a third, the guards were even rewarded for catching the ruse—that is, rewarded for maintaining the form of the law.[19] That these cases were not just flukes is evident from a set of instructions sent to officials at Namiai sekisho (Shinano province) telling them simply to turn away—not arrest and hold—disguised girls.[20]

In a case with a different twist, however, a man named Tadasuke and a girl of twelve disguised as a boy were on their way to Zenkō-ji in Shinano on pilgrimage. The girl's hair was arranged in the style of a young man not yet passed through the rites of manhood. Something aroused the officials' suspicions and they questioned the man about the child's sex. The man replied that she was a boy, but a physical examination revealed the truth. Both parent and child were immediately jailed and a request sent to both Owari, the sekisho administrator for Fukushima, and Edo for instructions. A little over a month later the sentence was passed and carried out: Tadasuke was beheaded and the girl pardoned. Why this case resulted in such harsh treatment when it otherwise appears that sekisho officials were lenient in this kind of case probably lies in the fact that Tadasuke deliberately lied to the officials in an attempt to deceive them. Disguising a child, of course, was also a deception, but in this case the form of the law was not maintained. Perhaps had he apologized and confessed his error when the officials had detected the ploy, he might have received a lenient judgment. He denied that he was assisted by others in the attempt to deceive their way through the sekisho—sekisho officials were very concerned about conspiracy—just as those in the three lenient rulings had, but it did not help him.[21]

It was, of course, possible to go around many sekisho. There were inevitably small, local roads which could allow the informed traveler to bypass some sekisho—and the administrative authorities were in many cases aware of them. A bakufu survey of the road system in the Bunsei era in fact reveals a great concern with the problem of side roads because the use of these often more convenient routes was hurting business at the official post stations and because travelers were using side roads to bypass sekisho.[22] At Yagurasawa, for example, a guard home was built on a back road near the sekisho in the early nineteenth century in an attempt to close the road to all traffic. At Saimoku (Kōzuke), too, authorities were aware that there were a number of short-cuts around the sekisho. At one time, one such path was dug up, while at another a peasant guard was posted on the small road with instructions to allow only local traffic to pass through.[23] In 1822, the bakufu also heard of an illegal ferry-boat service's being operated by villagers near Kanamachi sekisho not only for their own use to and from the fields, but as a money-making scheme.[24] It was ordered closed, but whether any effective action was taken to do so is not known. In another instance, a late-Tokugawa traveler, Kiyokawa Hachirō, noted that it was no longer possible to use one particular route that bypassed Sekigawa sekisho in Echigo.[25] Presumably, the road had been closed down by the authorities.

Numerous travelers noted in their diaries the existence of what were referred to as "women's roads" (*onna no michi*), as in the case of a samurai from Matsuhiro domain on his way to Kusatsu hot springs (Kōzuke) who was traveling without permission; he, incidentally, was able to pass through the sekisho at Ōsasa without any problem.[26] The term *onna no michi* was used to signify a *nukemichi*, or side road, for women to take to evade a sekisho, as one merchant woman from Chikuzen on the Ise pilgrimage related when she wrote, "We arrived in the village of Tsumago. At the base of the bridge there is a road which women travelers can take which bypasses the sekisho at Fukushima."[27]

Bansho were no more immune to evasion by travelers than sekisho: Furukawa Koshōken, in the late-eighteenth century, noted that it was said that local Higo merchants all used side roads, evading border bansho, when traveling into Satsuma, generally perceived as tight-bordered.[28]

Although the bakufu and local administrative authorities made an effort to prevent travelers from bypassing sekisho, it is apparent that their actions were neither thorough nor whole-hearted. In 1825, at bakufu direction, sekisho authorities posted placards in villages bordering a side road that allowed travelers to bypass the barrier at Usui. The notice boards read, "Travelers and those transporting goods should be using the Nakasendō and not this road. If there are those who insist on doing so despite orders to the contrary, find out who they are and report them to the Magistrate of Road Affairs."[29] One can easily imagine that this type of prohibition, with no sanctions, had little effect. In a similar vein, Furukawa Koshōken wrote in the late eighteenth century of Kurihashi sekisho, just north of Edo on the Nikkō dōchū, "This barrier is under the administrative authority of Lord Ina Hanzoemon [the Kantō gundai]. The inspection of travelers is very rigorous here, but according to local people, because the area is very flat, there are many ways for women to evade the barrier (*nukemichi*) by taking roundabout paths for about five to seven miles. Is this due to the benevolence (*onjinsei*) of the realm?"[30]

Kurihashi, like other sekisho located in plains, was deprived of natural, geological barriers that would have made better surveillance possible—if that is what was wanted. Writing more than a half century after Furukawa, the rural samurai (*gōshi*) Kiyokawa Hachirō's experience evading Kurihashi sekisho with his mother only confirmed what Furukawa had heard: "Since women are not allowed to pass through the barrier at Kurihashi, if you leave the main road about two to three miles before Kurihashi and take the Tsukuba road, you will soon reach the Tone River, where there is a river-crossing place. A woman's passage costs one hundred copper coins. The price is high, but since this route allows one to avoid the barrier, there is nothing you can do about it (*shikata ga nai*)."[31]

According to what the daimyo of Hirado, Matsuura Seizan (1760–1841), heard, at Hakone travelers without permits were not allowed through the sekisho, but were instructed to use a mountain road instead. Apparently this road would take them to a domainal bansho of Odawara, through which they could pass with an easy-to-obtain permit written by an innkeeper. Far from censuring this apparent breach of law, Matsuura exclaimed that, "Even the prohibitions of the realm are examples of magnanimous government (*Sareba tenka no kin mo kandai no onsei omou beshi*)." He was also told that at Arai, travelers without permits who said that they were on pilgrimage to Akiha Shrine, located on the Honzaka road off the Tōkaidō, were given tacit permission to use a side road around the barrier (see Map 3). To this Matsuura proclaimed, "Isn't this yet more evidence of the benevolence of the realm! (*Kore mo mata kanjin no onkoto narazuya.*)"[32]

The fact that travelers were being steered to domainal bansho indicates that checking procedures there were less rigorous. The same was also true of branch sekisho in the bakufu system. According to one record from 1843, at Nanmoku sekisho (Kōzuke), only slightly more than one-half of the people who passed through the barriers there carried permits. Twenty-two out of ninety-five persons were able to pass simply with a verbal request.[33] Even at Hakone, according to the diary on an anonymous physician, those without permits were allowed passage if they pressed their request three times, apologizing for the oversight of not carrying travel documentation.[34]

There were holes in the bakufu's sekisho system in a very real sense of the word. For example, Kiyokawa Hachirō, in fulfilling a long-standing promise to take his mother on pilgrimage to Ise, had to pass through Sekigawa sekisho on the way to Zenkō-ji in 1855. Sekigawa, however, was closed to women not from the local area, as was the case at twenty of the fifty-three sekisho. "For this reason," he said, "if you are traveling in the company of a woman, no matter how early you arrive in Sekigawa, you are forced to spend the night there. The next morning you wake up early and sneak past the guard house." And that is exactly what they did. Kiyokawa, his mother, and a group of thirteen women with a single male escort staying at the same inn were led by an inn employee in the dark of the early morning to a dangerous road, which they followed until they came to a sekisho palisade, where they climbed through a break, crossed a bridge and entered the main road on the other side of the compound—a trip of about 1,000 feet. It was also necessary to do this when traveling in the other direction through Sekigawa. Kiyokawa accounted for the existence of this short-cut as "due to the benevolence of the realm (*Kore mata tenka no awaremi de aru*)." Moreover, in the hot season, he noted, women evaded the sekisho simply by crossing the river running behind it; but when the river ran high, that could not be done very easily.[35]

At Kega, the bannerman overlord gave tacit approval to the use of a side road around the sekisho by local farmers returning home after working late in the fields so that they would not have to cut their workdays short; but no doubt travelers make avail of the short-cut as well. Here it was necessary to take a road that passed behind a number of temples before going through a hole in the sekisho palisade to get around the barrier compound itself. The road was dubbed *inu kuguri michi* because the

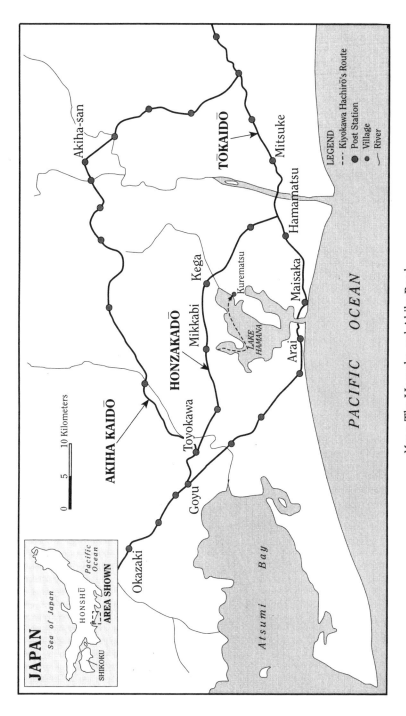

Map 3 The Honzaka and Akiha Roads

Within the map:

JAPAN

Sea of Japan

HONSHŪ

Pacific Ocean

AREA SHOWN

SHIKOKU

0 5 10 Kilometers

LEGEND

--- Kiyokawa Hachirō's Route
● Post Station
• Village
∿ River

Okazaki

Goyu

Toyokawa

AKIHA KAIDŌ

HONZAKADŌ

Mikkabi

Kega

Kurematsu

LAKE HAMANA

Arai

Maisaka

Hamamatsu

Mitsuke

TŌKAIDŌ

Akiha-san

Atsumi Bay

PACIFIC OCEAN

hole in the palisade was so small that only "a dog could crawl through."[36]

The bakufu and individual sekisho administrative authorities must have been aware of these "holes" in the sekisho system. It was common knowledge for instance that even at Hakone there were houses nearby where people "secretly" guided travelers heading west on the Tōkaidō around the sekisho (generally no permit was needed for those heading towards Edo).[37] Sekisho administrative authorities were aware of at least some of this short-cutting of the system and occasionally issued statements that local residents were not to guide travelers around sekisho,[38] but, judging from travel diaries from the second half of the Tokugawa period, these admonitions apparently had little effect.

Earlier in their travels, near Arai, heading east on the Tōkaidō, Kiyokawa and his party opted to take the "Princess road," the Honzaka dōri, in order to avoid the inspection at Arai. Unlike the situation at Hakone, at Arai, women travelers were inspected regardless of their direction. However, the Honzaka road had a sekisho at Kega, and this, too, had to be avoided by traveling overland as far as Mikkabi, north of Lake Hamana, about twenty kilometers from Arai (Map 3). Since Kega lay down the road, Kiyokawa and his party made arrangements when they arrived at Mikkabi in the afternoon to hire a boat to take them "stealthily" across the lake in the dead of night. When the boatman tried to overcharge Kiyokawa because he was traveling with a woman, a couple from Nagoya approached Kiyokawa and his mother and informed them that the price was too high. Kiyokawa responded to this attempted extortion by informing the boatman that they would go overland instead. Negotiations over the cost of their boat ride ensued, and a lower price was finally agreed upon. Having traveled extensively across the country before without female company, Kiyokawa was no doubt exasperated at the difficulties he had been put through on this journey with his mother: "When traveling with a woman, one is often put in impossible situations, and extreme care must be taken that one is not made a fool of."[39] As we saw earlier, when they had to pay a high fee for the river-crossing in evading Kurihashi sekisho, travelers with women were taken advantage of and charged high fees.

Shortly after midnight, with a light rain falling, Kiyokawa and his party, as well as some other passengers, quietly boarded a small, uncovered boat. The lake was extremely calm, and before long most of the passengers fell fast asleep. Arriving at the other side of the lake as dawn was breaking, the boatman announced, "We're in Kurematsu," and the other passengers went on their way. From Kurematsu, Kiyokawa thought to take a side road that ran directly to Mitsuke, where the Honzaka road meets the Tōkaidō. Finding the way confusing, however, he and his mother decided instead to take the longer (about fourteen kilometers) but more certain route to Hamamatsu (also on the Tōkaidō). Losing their way after going several kilometers on a deserted road, they stopped to ask directions at the home of an old man, who was presumably in the village support network. The man guided them a short way and before very long they were back on the Tōkaidō at Hamamatsu.[40]

A village headman and his wife, while on pilgrimage, were confronted by a number of local people while walking on a side road, after evading the sekisho at Sekigawa. Several of them told the travelers that they could not use the road; after apologizing, however, and hiring a guide for 100 *mon*, the pair continued on their way. They had been informed that ordinarily passage on this road was not a problem, but that many travelers had been using it to get to an exhibition of temple treasures (*ekō*) going on at Zenkō-ji. This illegal traffic was hurting business at Sekigawa and Nojiri, the post stations on either side of the sekisho that travelers bypassed. As a result, some officials from Nojiri apparently disabled or partially dismantled a bridge on the side road to stop the traffic, indicating that there were important economic reasons for travel restrictions. Of course, the fact that at least some travelers continued to use the road reinforces the point made earlier that local authorities were not very effective in channeling traffic to their specifications.[41]

Numerous other travelers had similar experiences bypassing barriers. For example, another couple, from Sekigahara, on pilgrimage to Zenkō-ji (in Shinano) and Tateyama (in Kaga), technically committed *sekisho yaburi* on two occasions. At Sekigawa, they were led through the dark by an inn guide to a spot in the palisade network, where they crawled through (perhaps using the same hole that Kiyokawa and his mother had used) to the other side, thereby bypassing the sekisho. They were led to do this because, as the wife noted in her travel diary, "women are not allowed to pass through the barrier." Later they were led around Ichifuri sekisho (Echigo) by a guide whom they paid sixty copper coins. Entering Kaga, they passed through a bansho with no trouble (no permits were required to enter Kaga); but on leaving the domain, they had to obtain (which basically meant purchase) an exit permit, which they were easily able to do at Kanazawa.[42] Even the village headman and his wife, cited earlier, who were traveling with four other women and one man, had been led by a paid guide to a crack in the palisade network at Sekigawa. They passed through this break, which the husband described as "slipping through the ends of a claw hammer," coming through on the other side of the sekisho, where they were led in the dark by torchlight along the ridge of some rice fields. Eventually, after passing in back of some dwellings, they came out into about the middle of the post station.[43] Yet a different group of four pilgrims, on their way to Ise, evaded no less than four sekisho, one of them twice, because the single female with them did not have a travel permit. They used hired guides on three occasions and took two short-cuts (*kakure michi*, or "hidden roads") on their own.[44]

These are just a sampling of a much larger number of travel accounts which indicate that stricter requirements at sekisho led those traveling with women to break the law by using alternative routes around the barriers; it also meant that they needed to have excellent knowledge of local conditions in order to make use of these routes. Commoners evaded sekisho, it seems, without great concern about possible punishment, implying that the authorities gave tacit approval of the short-cuts or that punishment was rarely exacted.

Domainal barriers were not immune to evasion either. The existence of a "woman's road" near Iida (Shinano) made it "a barrier in name only," according to Kiyokawa Hachirō.[45] Even close to the center of bakufu authority—at Nakagawa, a river bansho in Edo, east of Honjō—the writer Kobayashi Issa reported that evasion of the barrier was not difficult. In 1791 he was traveling with a small group of companions, which included two women, to Shimōsa province (Chiba). They requested safe passage, but the guards "glared fiercely" at the women, and refused, for as the notice board at that barrier read, "No woman, even a dead woman, may pass through here." While the guards would not disregard the law and allow them through, the sympathetic boatman instructed them how to go around the barrier by taking a short detour.[46] It is difficult to imagine that this activity went on without the knowledge of the officials at Nakagawa.

In some cases domainal officials acknowledged as much. For example, a circular issued by the Toyama City Magistrate to the City Elders in 1797 reported that "[s]ince ancient times in all provinces sekisho have been guarded, but recently there have been women illegally using secret roads or boats to sneak by during the day or night."[47] Kaga domain officials complained in 1814 that the numbers evading bansho had been "growing larger in recent years." The response of authorities was nonetheless passive: a statement was issued that the matter would be investigated thoroughly and that travelers should henceforth apply for the required permits.[48]

Punishments were threatened for evaders. Toyama authorities promised that women caught evading bansho "would be arrested and punished."[49] We have seen that while the bakufu at times executed criminals who evaded sekisho, the average commoner caught, who had not committed other crimes, did not meet harsh punishment, if any at all. Three people trying to go around the main sekisho at Usui in 1861 were apprehended as they inadvertently stumbled upon one of its branch sekisho. The officials there assembled and decided to call in the officials from the offenders' village. Once they arrived, the seriousness of the crime was carefully explained to them and then the offenders were released—an example again of the strong anti-legalistic bias in Tokugawa society.[50] Moral suasion was pursued, the letter of the law preserved, and life continued as usual.

While the evidence demonstrates that barriers were bypassed frequently, we can never know how many people did so successfully without ever being discovered, nor how many of the cases when watchtower guards at Hakone or other sekisho reported hearing noises in the brush but found no one were actually false alarms.[51] The number of people who evaded the sekisho, but did not leave written records of their experience, was probably great.

Sekisho like Arai relied on village support systems because the geographical features of the area left much opportunity for evading the barriers. The village support network was established in an attempt to patch up the perceived holes in the sekisho system, but from the evidence available it appears that it was not very effective.

The lakeside checking (*kaihen aratame*) system established at Arai drew some fifty villages into the support network; it was a weakly coercive system of cooperation that promised vague punishment for offenders and their villages, producing few tangible results. In this system, all villages in the network were required to sign a pledge to uphold bakufu law and sekisho regulations. That pledge included a promise not to provide travelers with illegal passage across the lake. Specifically, the article read:

> "It goes without saying that you absolutely should not transport by boat any woman or guns from this to any neighboring village, but the same applies for wounded persons, all travelers in general, containers, or anything at all suspicious. If you see anyone doing so, report it immediately, day or night, to the officials at the sekisho."[52]

The villages were also required to provide, on an irregular basis, census information which included data on the number of boats owned in each settlement. With more than 200 boats operating in the waters of Lake Hamana (1845) for fishing and the transport of travelers between Arai and Maisaka, it was no doubt extremely difficult to monitor compliance.[53] Sekisho officials went on inspection tours of the villages in the support network, at which time the pledges were signed and the census information handed over, but these occurred only about once every ten years and appear to have been a ritual largely devoid of meaning.[54] A similar system existed at Arai's branch sekisho, Kega; and there the number of villages in the support network increased steadily during the seventeenth century, from twenty-three (1627) to forty-one (1642) to forty-seven (1689) to sixty-eight (1694), until almost every village in the area was included. The growing scope of the system probably reflects the increased level of traffic on the Tōkaidō during that century. The increase in 1694 was a direct result of an incident during the previous year in which a local villager was caught taking a merchant across the lake.[55] Apparently the threat of sanctions was not sufficient to deter some villagers from earning extra money by transporting travelers in their private boats. Without the compliance of the people in the support network, the sekisho at Arai served little purpose.

GRAFT AND THE PURCHASE OF PERMITS

Permit-issuing authorities appear to have come under little supervision from above. A bakufu ordinance in 1711 stated that, "Recently the number of applications for women's travel permits has sharply increased," and instructed the Edo City Magistrate to be more careful in checking applicants' identities before issuing permits. It found officials too eager to issue permits to anyone who said that they were in a hurry. "From now on," they were ordered, "carefully check each person's identity, even if it takes two or three days."[56] There is no evidence, either, that the bakufu sought to curb or control the de-facto authority of temples to issue passports until the end of the Tokugawa period; but in at least one domain, Kaga, government authorities felt that temple officials were issuing the documents too freely, "in an arbitrary manner" (*katte ni*). Travelers in Kaga were notified that they must get the permission of village officials and the Magistrate of Rural Affairs in order to get a permit.[57] For a fee, a temple might issue permits to travelers who were not members of the parish. One such permit was issued to a man named Kawasaki Sukemon, who told the religious authorities that he was going to travel around the country praying for the salvation of his deceased parents.[58]

Domains also attempted to control travel by setting certain qualifications on applicants for permits, but their efforts met with only limited success. In the late Tokugawa period, during the Tenpō era (1830–1843), the bakufu tried in vain to outlaw permits issued by village officials, who were, according to one collection of documents, issuing the largest number of permits.[59] In other words, they tried in vain to assert control over a system about which they had theretofore shown little concern.

Many travelers applied for travel permits before starting out on a journey, but unknown numbers of them obtained their documentation on the road after already having begun their trip. These permits, sometimes called *tōchū tegata*, or "on-the-way permits," were obtained at stations near sekisho or at inns along the traveler's route. For example, almost 31 percent of a large body of travel permits collected from Usui sekisho were obtained in the two villages that lay on either side of the barrier, making the sekisho seem more like a local—and sanctioned—industry.[60] In two specific cases, a group of forty-five pilgrims from Chiba and another group of eleven merchants from Aizu, both heading for Ise, obtained their permits at inns while stopping in Edo.[61] Another example was Katsu Kokichi, who, setting out from Edo on his own in 1815 at the age of fourteen, was befriended by two townsmen also heading towards the Kamigata area. When the two learned that he did not have a travel permit for Hakone, they told him that they could get him one for 200 copper coins (*mon*). Though they were helpful to him in procuring a travel permit, the Tokugawa period adage not to befriend people when traveling rang true, for they robbed him of all his possessions, including his kimono, as he slept one night in a Hamamatsu inn.[62]

Sugae Masumi, a peripatetic scholar of National Learning (Kokugaku) who traveled extensively in northern Japan during the late eighteenth and early nineteenth centuries, did not seem to have any problem obtaining travel permits while on the road. At Ikari-ga-seki bansho in Tsugaru domain he was told that he could not pass without a travel permit and that he should go to Hirosaki, the domain capital, to get one; outside of bakufu territory, non-domain residents were, in theory, also required to obtain exit permits from the domain capital's City Magistrate. Since the day was late and Hirosaki far away, Sugae checked into an inn. Shortly thereafter he went to speak with the village headman, explained his situation, and convinced the official to issue him a permit. The following day Sugae passed through the bansho without incident. No mention is made of whether or not he paid money for the permit, but that would seem likely; for some collusion between the village headman and the bansho operators must have occurred in order for the bansho officials to have allowed Sugae to pass with only a permit issued by a village headman rather than by the Hirosaki's City Magistrate.[63]

On another occasion, after setting out on his journey, Sugae obtained a permit from a post station manager (*ton'ya*) for a sum of money, which he called *kakidai* (lit., "a fee for writing [a permit]"). The manager then led him to the sekisho, where Sugae "handed over the permit and passed through," implying that the sekisho officials and the transport operator were collaborating in their money-making scheme. Sugae noted, moreover, that it was the same at all sekisho.[64] While this was, no doubt, an overstatement, graft did seem to be commonplace in northern Japan and even at a number of bakufu sekisho: At Hakone and Goryō, for example, it was known that permits were for sale at one or more teahouses near the sekisho.[65] At Itaya bansho in Yonezawa domain, Kiyokawa Hachirō and his party found the gates unattended; the guard who finally detected their presence called them back and asked them their names and destination before granting them permits—without charge, which was unusual in the north. According to Kiyokawa, "Not the least bit of inconvenience was involved."[66]

Travel permits obtained indiscriminately while on one's journey defeated the primary purpose for which they were intended: that is, to provide a guarantee for the traveler's identity and behavior. Nevertheless, government authorities did not come out strongly against the practice. The only statement against it found to date is an 1832 entry in a diary kept by officials at Hakone sekisho; they noted that post station officials in Fujisawa were issuing many travel permits to non-resident travelers in defiance of the law. Unfortunately we are not told what, if anything, was done about it.[67] By not disallowing the use of "on-the-way" permits, which were in effect the same as counterfeit passports in Tudor and early Stuart England, the system became moot. These permits might be considered a "direct challenge to the state," but in Tokugawa Japan, the challenge was met with indifference.[68]

It is clear that in many parts of the country, particularly in the north, travelers without permits could obtain passage through domain barriers, and at least some bakufu sekisho, for a fee. In some cases the money went towards the purchase of a permit, while in others the fee charged was in effect a toll. In this respect, Tokugawa barriers resembled those of the Middle Ages.[69] In either case, however, it amounted to the same thing— the undermining of a control system.

The record of travelers paying money for passage through a barrier is quite extensive. For example, officials at one bansho in Toyama domain were reprimanded for letting a medicine peddlar through without a travel permit (according to the merchant, he was charged thirty-five *mon* to pass). The authorities were reminded that, "[t]he original intent of bansho is not (just) to collect taxes, but to do so in conjunction with checking travelers. . . . Those without permits are not to be allowed passage through the barrier."[70] Fujiwara Morohide (a stage name), an itinerant entertainer who wrote of his travels north of Edo (1828–1831), made a number of references to this phenomenon. In fact, in Dewa he noted that this was the case on all the roads he had traveled from Edo.[71] Muta Take-toshi, a samurai from Nabeshima domain in Kyushu who traveled around the country from 1853 to 1855 for training in swordsmanship, reported much the same. In Akita, he thought the fifty *mon* exit fee charged for the "upkeep of roads" particularly unreasonable.[72]

Sugae Masumi reported widely on this phenomenon. In Dewa, for example, he was traveling in piercing cold, snowy weather one day when he approached a bansho and had to make noises clearing his throat before an official pushed the gate open. "Who are you? At what inn are you plan-ning to stay?" the official asked. "If you don't have a place to stay, you'll need a permit to pass through."[73] For those without a permit, a night's stay in the area was the toll for passage through the barrier. Even in the closed society of Satsuma, at Nomabara bansho the traveler had the op-tion of going through the barrier if he had a permit, or around it by boat for a fee of 200 copper coins, payable to the bansho.[74] These sekisho and bansho amounted to toll barriers and, like their counterparts in the Dutch Republic or in seventeenth- and eighteenth-century England, they were "capable of imposing a considerable financial burden on the pedestrian."[75]

The experience of the couple on pilgrimage to Zenkō-ji mentioned ear-lier colorfully reveals that even sekisho guards were not beyond taking a bribe. Apparently, their information on local conditions was not as thor-ough as they would have liked, for the couple, just a few days away from home on the return leg of their journey, inadvertently stumbled upon the barrier at Yanagase. There, they tried to obtain permission to pass through, even though they did not have a permit; but they were refused. Their excuses for their failure to carry permits only caused the guards to glare at them, and deny them permission even more forcefully: "*Naran, naran to mōsu.*" Meeting this unexpected resistance, the couple retreated to the nearest teahouse, where they requested the assistance of the pro-prietor. They handed him fifty copper coins as a "fee for sweets," wrapped up discreetly in some kind of paper or cloth material, and were able to pass through the barrier without any difficulty. Exuberant, the wife later wrote a humorous ditty in her diary:

All it takes is money to pass through.
Fifty copper coins to gain the guard's understanding.[76]

Distant administrative authorities could repeatedly order sekisho officials and guards not to accept graft,[77] but as the evidence shows, these
orders were difficult to enforce in the field.

ATTEMPTS TO REGULATE PILGRIMAGE

Domains attempted to regulate travel for a number of reasons and in a
variety of ways. From the middle of the Tokugawa period on, regulations dealing with commoner travel were issued frequently and were inspired mainly by economics rather than a desire for totalitarian control.
As pilgrimage was the major reason for travel for the masses, most regulations were directed at that act itself. There were limits to what the
state could do to prohibit pilgrimage, which was widely accepted in society as a sacred act, and the evidence shows that the control measures instituted were generally ineffective.

Some of the ways domains sought to regulate pilgrimage were setting
certain economic qualifications for the issuance of travel permits, determining when and where travel was allowed, determining who was allowed
to travel, and establishing the length of time as well as the number of
times a person could travel. Not every domain used all of these methods,
but a number of them were common to many domains. In general we
will see that regulations, while not without some effect, were not able to
stem the irrepressible desire of the masses in Tokugawa Japan to travel.

Perhaps the most common restrictions on any long-distance travel
had to do with timing. Since travel during the agricultural season would
take a peasant away from the land, in theory decreasing the agricultural
output of a village, long-distance travel was generally restricted to the agricultural off-season, after taxes had been collected.[78] In Tsushima domain,
one had to include an oath that one's taxes were paid and that the proposed trip would not interfere with one's field work.[79]

It was also common for domains to set certain general economic qualifications before they would grant travel permits. For example, a person
could not be in debt or too poor to pay for the travel without resorting

to selling land or relying on alms received along the way. In Kaga domain, only those with "adequate wealth" and whose taxes were paid in full were granted permission to travel on pilgrimage.[80] In Ino domain (Kazusa), those with loans were denied permission to travel; and in Moriyama (Mutsu), the village headman had to guarantee that a person had no outstanding loans.[81] These requirements could be ignored, of course, as eleven peasants from Narita (Sagami) did after their application for a permit was declined due to their failure to pay the year's taxes in full.[82]

These economic requirements for travel were general conditions established by private domains and bakufu authorities. But, if we look closely at the requirements, they are not as strict as they appear, for they did not interfere with the flow of life. Not many responsible households would leave on an expensive journey with work to be done in the fields or with taxes unpaid. Consequently, these regulations seem to have been aimed more at commoners who would be more inclined to drop everything at a moment's notice to go on pilgrimage—servant personnel, temporary workers, and tenants. A Kaga regulation, for example, specifically prohibited tenants from going on pilgrimage during the weeding season.[83]

Early in the Tokugawa period pilgrimage retained much of the pure religious content it had in medieval Japan. But pilgrimage gradually developed as a form of recreation; pilgrims spent more time sightseeing on the way to and from the main pilgrimage site. As this happened, domains established regulations to try to curtail the length of travel. Limiting travel time, of course, decreased the amount of time a peasant would be away from his fields as well as the amount of money he would drain from the domain through travel expenditures.

Tosa domain, for example, limited the length of trips allowed its residents and those passing through on the Shikoku pilgrimage circuit. Tosa merchants traveling to the Kansai area to buy commodity goods were given a limit of eighty days, while a sixty-day limit was set on visits to hot springs in Bungo province in Kyushu, and a seven-to-fifteen day limit on merchants traveling to Uwajima in Iyo province.[84] Travelers on the Shikoku pilgrimage route who came from domains outside Tosa were handed an entry permit which listed the number of days they were given to complete the Tosa portion of their trip. The thirty-day limit to cover the

304-kilometer route from Matsuozaka to Kannoura was not a rigorous demand in an age when travelers commonly covered 40 kilometers a day.[85] Government authorities encouraged pilgrims to travel the course without delay and stick to the main roads.[86]

A number of other domains imposed time limits for various pilgrimage routes.[87] Domains in western Japan generally permitted relatively long periods of time for pilgrimage, which, judging by actual travel times, allowed extra time for sightseeing. In Mori domain (Bungo), for example, a ninety-day limit was set for pilgrimage to Ise, but the route could be easily completed in thirty to forty days. Fukuoka allowed twenty to thirty days over the time it actually took to make the trip to Ise. Likewise, even with a reduction from one-hundred days to sixty allowed for Tosa residents on the Shikoku pilgrimage (part of an economic reform movement of the late eighteenth century), contemporary records show that it could be done in thirty to forty days.[88]

In contrast, a number of eastern domains were strict with time limits, but gradually relaxed them. The Ise pilgrimage from Edo could be performed in approximately twenty-five days, so limits of thirty-three days for Miharu (Mutsu) and fifty for Shinjō (Dewa) did not allow much leeway. Nonetheless, the trend towards relaxation of strict time limits is apparent. For example, in 1728 Nambu domain increased a fifty-day limit for samurai to seventy days for ordinary samurai and ninety for those of high rank. Even Kaga increased its limits in 1764 from eighteen days to twenty-five (thirty-five for women), and then to fifty after the Meiji Restoration.[89] Still, Shinjō Tsunezō's analysis of seventy diaries from eastern Japan indicates that time restrictions were routinely exceeded by a fair margin.[90]

It is difficult to know to what we should attribute the fact that western domains were more generous than eastern ones. It could indicate a more lenient attitude in regulating the peasantry in Western Japan, or reflect the superior economic position of the populace in western domains. Time limits for eastern domains might have been gradually raised in an attempt to limit the length of trips of persons no longer obeying regulations. Or they could, instead, be seen as a reaction to better economic conditions. Nevertheless, the fact that punishment for abrogating time limits was rare lends support to the proposition that, with the generally improving economic conditions, Tokugawa commoners traveled more often and on longer journeys; and regulations tried to keep pace with that trend.

Theoretically, one of the most efficient ways for government authorities to limit travel outside the domain was to restrict the number of travel permits they were willing to issue. For example, in 1685, Okayama domain decided to allow only one person per village to go on pilgrimage to Konpira every year; and this was the quota that many other domains set as well.[91] Kurume domain (Chikugo) had the strictest policy of any domain not actually banning pilgrimage; in 1679, only one person per district was allowed to travel to Ise.[92] Registers kept at the Outer Shrine at Ise indicate, however, that this basic regulation was routinely flouted.[93]

Not only did domains limit the number of people allowed on pilgrimage, but some also restricted their sex and age. In Akita, for example, among peasants, only households over fifty and family members over thirty were eligible for permits. The eligibility for households and family members of townsman households was not as strict in most domains; this difference in attitude reflected the fact that peasants needed to be working the land in order to produce the taxes that fueled the Tokugawa state. Males over thirty were eligible, but women were completely prohibited from obtaining travel permits. Nabeoka domain (Hyūga) prohibited both males and females under seventeen from leaving the domain on pilgrimage.[94] In general, many domains were more lenient in allowing older women, who had given up their positions of responsibility within the household to travel.[95] Kaga prohibited townswomen that were "young" from going on pilgrimage to the Kansai area. Even the maidservants accompanying pilgrims there were required to be at least fifty years of age.[96]

Not as common as restrictions on time or the number of travelers were restrictions on the distance a pilgrim was allowed to travel. In 1816 Morioka domain officials declared, "In recent years many people have been going to the Kamigata [i.e., Kansai] area for sightseeing purposes when on pilgrimage. There are, however, many temples in the domain and therefore we will no longer grant applications for pilgrimage outside the domain."[97] In Morioka and other domains such as Saga, daimyo promoted pilgrimage within the domain in order to stem the tide of those leaving the domain for that purpose.[98]

To this end, copies of the Shikoku and Saikoku (Thirty-Three Kannon Temple) circuits, as well as other popular pilgrimage routes and sites, were made within individual domains. The Aizu daimyo, for example, built an Ise Shrine, a Kumano Shrine, and a Thirty-Three-Kannon Temple circuit right at home. A copy of the Saikoku or Western circuit was even created in the bakufu-controlled city of Osaka during the Genroku era.[99] Together with establishing these would-be diversions, daimyo also tried to convince the people that worshipping outside the domain would mean that the local kami, or deities, were being neglected.[100] The effects of these efforts to dissuade commoners from leaving the domain were, however, minimal.

Ever resourceful commoners found ways to work around restrictions imposed on them from above. In Chōshū, for example, there are cases where commoners granted travel permits for domainal "Shikoku pilgrimage" used their permits for the real thing. Or, using a tactic similar to one employed by English vagabonds in the sixteenth and seventeenth centuries, travelers would ask for permission to travel to a relatively close pilgrimage site, knowing that their application thus stood a better chance of being accepted, but once on the road traveled afar.[101] A group of Musashi peasants, for instance, received permission to travel on pilgrimage to Mount Fuji and once that was completed continued on to Shikoku.[102]

At least one domain limited the number of times a person could go on pilgrimage out of the domain or to a particular site. Kaga restricted travel to Hongan-ji in Kyoto to once in a lifetime. The reason authorities cited was the desire to stem the outflow of precious domain resources like gold and silver. Village headmen were warned to be on the lookout—and told that they would be held accountable—for peasants using other people's names in order to evade the restriction; apparently, some people were doing exactly that.[103]

This admonition to village headmen focuses attention on one important aspect of government controls on travel: That is, as in the case of the village support systems around some sekisho, the effectiveness of the permit-issuing system relied on the cooperation of people drawn into the state apparatus. The village headman acted as a quasi-government official, and the permit system relied on his cooperation. The Kaga example indicates, however, that they could not always be relied upon to enforce government's wishes. In Nihonmatsu domain in northern Japan, peasants appealed to their lord because of the "selfishness, egoism and lawlessness of the village officials"; and among the illegal activities they cited was the fact that some officials demanded payment before issuing permits for travel outside the village.[104] This indicates that village headmen, despite their positions of responsibility, were not above using their authority for private gain, even if it meant ignoring explicit orders from above. It was perhaps because village officials were an unreliable part of the control system for travel that the bakufu tried in 1830 to overstep them and require that travelers apply to a higher official, the intendants (*daikan*), for permits.[105] It appears that this order was ineffective, since village officials continued to issue permits after that date.

The best way to restrict the number of commoners leaving the domain on pilgrimage would have been simply to ban it altogether, without any provisions. A small number of domains tried this drastic and, no doubt, unpopular step, but often only briefly.[106] Most prohibitions occurred from the mid-Tokugawa on, particularly after the turn of the nineteenth century, when fiscal problems worsened for many domains.[107]

Akita domain's ban seems to have been in effect the longest. First enacted in 1756, it remained in effect after the designated three-year period had elapsed; not until 1764 was another three-year ban issued, this one lasting for six years. These bans of limited duration were routinely extended. In 1793 the prohibition was expanded to include any movement—not just pilgrimage—outside the domain. Nonetheless, peasant travel continued without permission, making the regulation a dead letter; and in 1806, the domain switched to other types of regulations, such as limiting the number of permits it would issue. These regulations remained in effect for approximately fifty years before the total ban was reinstated.[108] Despite these actions, however, we find evidence of disregard of the law. In 1784, five domain residents collapsed on the streets of Edo and were turned over to one of Akita's mansions in the city.[109] Furthermore, early in the nineteenth century authorities in Akita reported that "[m]any domain residents have been leaving on *nukemairi* [i.e., without travel permits] year after year, even though this has been repeatedly prohibited."[110]

It is impossible to know precisely why a total ban on pilgrimage was enacted in Akita, let alone why it was left in effect for so long when it was being routinely flouted; but economic considerations seem paramount. Many of the domains which banned pilgrimage lay at great distances from the major pilgrimage centers, suggesting that the economic drain of long-distance travel was a major consideration. In the case of Akita, the domain was hit by a great famine in 1755, the year before the ban was first enacted, and bad harvests continued thereafter, prompting the domain to prohibit the production of rice wine. The Tenmei Famine followed in 1783, during which time the domain population dwindled from about 320,000 to 270,000. In this context, the ban on pilgrimage, rather than being a draconian measure to control the movement of people, was more a common-sense relief measure at a time when the number of people able to go on pilgrimage was probably limited. Reasons given for bans in Yonezawa likewise were related to poor crops, drought, and inflation. A former daimyo of Yamagata praised Yonezawa's model policy, saying that "its scrupulous policy was responsible for enriching the domain and its people."[111]

That domains were reluctant to prohibit their residents from going on pilgrimage for fear of producing discontent among the masses is evident from the number of domains that made exceptions to blanket prohibitions or lifted the bans after a short period. Domains such as Ōmura and Kurume issued prohibitions on pilgrimage in principle, but allowed it in "unavoidable circumstances" or "when there is adequate reason." Clearly these terms allowed for loose interpretation. Saga, on the other hand, specifically exempted pilgrimage to Ise and Hiko-zan (Fukuoka) for a while, then removed Ise from the exemption, only to reinstate it later. Kishiwada (Izumi) made Ise and Kumano exceptions.[112] The twenty-two-year-old ban on pilgrimage in Yonezawa was removed in 1817, not on account of improving economic conditions, but apparently because of the displeasure of the people.[113] Daimyo were particularly leery of preventing people from worshipping at Ise; for in the words of Kaiho Seiryō, the late-Tokugawa political economist, such actions would cause the government to "lose the hearts of the people."[114]

The evidence shows that at least at certain times, particularly during the cyclical mass pilgrimages, or *okagemairi*, officials at bakufu and domainal barriers were not willing to try to stop pilgrims without travel permits from passing through. Kaempfer noted that children ran away from their parents and went on pilgrimage without the necessary permits; on their return, he said, the talisman they surely acquired would act as their passport.[115] Of such children 12,500 were let through Hakone during the pilgrimage season in 1651.[116] In 1705, the year of the first massive, spontaneous *okagemairi*-type pilgrimage, officials at Hakone sekisho recorded that 33,000 people passed through on the last day of the first month and noted that some of them had travel permits and others did not.[117] Granted that the figures may be inflated, there is no way that the permits of even a fraction of such a large group of people could be checked. According to one contemporary record, 1,000 men and women passed through Arai every day (over an unstated period of time) in 1830 without being checked for permits.[118] Elsewhere, in Tosa for example, late eighteenth-century bansho guards were ordered to stop allowing people in from other domains without passports and to stop granting them entry permits for use on the Shikoku pilgrimage circuit.[119]

The social acceptance of pilgrimage as a religious act as well as a rite of passage to adulthood could obviate the need for a permit, as the evidence on the Ise *okagemairi* demonstrates; and it could also protect many pilgrims from reprisals from those whose authority they had flouted by leaving without permission. A contemporary *senryū* relates much the same:

> Carrying both temple charm and lice on his back,
> the sake shop boy revealed the charm without a word.
> With that, why, there's no need to apologize.[120]

In other words, after completing the pilgrimage to Ise, during which time the shop boy probably did not bathe very often, the amulet he obtained at the shrine was all the proof and all the explanation he needed for having run off without permission. Having the amulet, he need not fear the reproach of his boss. Gifts brought back on the journey might smooth over an irate master, and apparently some, who might be afraid to lose good servants or workers, arranged a party on the worker's return.[121] The same social acceptance of the act of pilgrimage is reflected in a case in which two children of a samurai household left for Ise without permission. A retainer was sent after them, but was given a travel permit for himself should they refuse to turn back.[122]

Domain authorities also found it difficult to prohibit some pilgrimages because they were intimately connected with the agricultural work of the peasant class. Peasants traveling to Ise who bothered to pray at the shrine most often did so only at the Outer Shrine, whose kami, Toyouke, was associated with agriculture and the field plow. Similarly, at Ōyamasan in Sagami province, where the kami for water dwelled, farmers went there either to pray for rain for their crops or in thanksgiving for the plentiful rains already received. The religious talismans they received would then be hung in the fields.[123] Not many daimyo would dare prohibit pilgrimage that was so intimately tied up with agriculture.

The domains' reactions to the *okagemairi* of 1830, the largest of these cyclical events, with as many as an estimated five million participants, reveals the attitudes they assumed towards pilgrimage.[124] The *okagemairi* began towards the end of the third month of that year in Awa, where amulets were reported to have fallen from the sky, prompting groups of children to set out towards Ise. According to a record from Nara, more than 100,000 people passed through the city during two days (intercalary 3/3–3/4). In response to this early movement of people, a number of domains issued all sorts of documents to suppress it. For example, a small domain in Kawachi sent a proclamation to the villages in one of its districts that instructed, "Going on pilgrimage at the present time is a bad idea (*kokorochigai*), for it will interfere with your work in the fields." (p. 5) It went on to say that those who want to make a pilgrimage out of religious belief (*shinshin ni sōrōwaba*) should do so during the slack intervals in the rice cycle. Apparently the rice crop had not been very good in the previous year or so, and the villages had been receiving food aid from the government. Still, rather than ban the act of pilgrimage itself, which was difficult to do, the authorities encouraged its people to go during the slack season instead.

Other domains offered different reasons why commoners should not go to Ise. For example, the document sent to Ikeda, a *zaigōmachi* or rural market town north of Osaka that was under the authority of the Kyoto City Magistrate, read, "It is expressly forbidden to make a pilgrimage without the permission of your parents or master. . . . " (p. 6) In this and many other cases, political authorities targeted pilgrimage done without permission—*nukemairi*, not *okagemairi*. According to one contemporary, Kobayashi Kinnosuke, *okagemairi* meant making a pilgrimage without any money, relying on alms collected on the way, whereas *nukemairi* meant leaving home without the permission of political authorities and/or other persons of authority.[125]

An official notice issued by the Osaka City Magistrate was more explicit in that it offered a reason why *nukemairi* was prohibited: Pilgrims were, without discretion, simply dropping what they were doing and leaving home, neglecting to shut doors or put out fires. This posed a threat to civil peace (*amari hōgai ranzatsu*). Implied also was that those leaving on *nukemairi* were selfish, as the magistrate had heard reports of old people and infants being left behind unattended. Of course *nukemairi* not only posed a threat to civil peace but also caused great harm to the economy. One observer recorded that during an earlier, and smaller *okagemairi* in 1705, businesses in Osaka ground to a halt because so many apprentices had taken off to Ise.[126] In addition to the labor shortage, with so many people on the move, there were shortages of various goods and prices rose quickly.

Government, then, put forth a different message to those in rural and urban areas. To peasant farmers, it instructed that pilgrimage at this time would interfere with their work and hence hurt the agricultural economy. To those in urban areas, the message was that pilgrimage was a threat to civil peace.

The proclamations of some other domains add a different dimension to the prohibitions issued at the time of the *okagemairi* in 1830. Matsuyama, for example, instructed its people that going on *nukemairi* would cause one's parents or master great inconvenience (*meiwaku kakeru*), and that making the pilgrimage under these conditions would be an offense to the kami at Ise (lit., "they would find it unacceptable" [*kami wa nōju kore naku*] [p. 11]).

In 1830/9, by which time the *okagemairi* had largely run its course, one domain condemned the large-scale pilgrimage for the first time. An ordinance from Kami-Suwa (Shinano) stated, "Men and women have been making pilgrimages to Ise regardless of the fact that it is the busy season for agricultural work, giving the excuse that they are going on *okagemairi*. We have heard that large numbers of people have been doing so, and find this unpardonable (*furachi*)." (p. 11) It instructed those who wanted to make a pilgrimage out of "true belief" to apply for permission "without making a big fuss" (*sawagazaru yō*). (p. 12) The domain would then allow "one or two people (a year)" to make the pilgrimage in a "peaceful manner." (p. 12) The compliance and cooperation of local officials was sought: "You should understand this and explain it very carefully to the villagers and townspeople," they were instructed. (p. 12) Those who did not comply, it was threatened, would be censured.

The proclamation implies that *okagemairi* was not a peaceful activity; government officials, at least, found it disturbing. The document also reveals that, even in the face of a spontaneous, mass movement the domain tried to enforce the already unrealistic one or two person per village limit on pilgrimage and faulted local authorities who failed at the impossible task.

Some domains recognized the limits of their authority over the people, but still reminded them what they were supposed to be doing, as in the case of Matsuyama: "It is difficult to prevent devoted pilgrims from making a pilgrimage by force, but you must still get the permission of your parents and master before leaving." (p. 11) Rather than taking draconian measures to try to prevent pilgrims from traveling to Ise, a number of daimyo in Shikoku gave in to the wishes of their people and offered them alms in the form of free boat rides across the Inland Sea. Here, a sense of benevolence, as well as political acumen, compelled them to help the large numbers of pilgrims go on their way.

One of the main reasons why domains sought to regulate travel in general was clearly economic: travelers spending money outside the domain drained resources. One contemporary record stated that "except for merchants, all persons are prohibited from leaving the domain [Nambu] in order to prevent the outflow of money."[127] The same concern for the outflow of resources was expressed by numerous other domains, including Owari, Saga, Tosa and Chōshū.[128] As the daimyo of Himeji is reported to have said, "The people in this domain can go on pilgrimage as they see fit, so long as it does not interfere with their work in the rice fields."[129]

This concern for the outflow of funds must have existed early in the Tokugawa period as well, but as the numbers of people traveling grew and domain fiscal positions worsened, daimyo were prompted to take some sort of action to control travel. Many of the restrictions we have discussed appear in the historical record for the first time in the second half of the Tokugawa period, particularly after 1800.

Travel could be very expensive. Roughly speaking, a trip from Tōhoku to the Kinai area cost around 10 *ryō* and from the Kantō to the Kinai, about half of that.[130] But in addition to the actual travel costs for food, lodging, transport services, and entertainment, there were also standard expenses involved in the parties and gift-giving that would occur before and after pilgrimages.[131] Thus, travel could become a financial burden not only to the traveler but to his relatives and neighbors as well. One Edo-period traveler had to take out a loan in Kamakura before setting off down the Tōkaidō, and it was precisely for this reason that some domains issued regulations prohibiting people without adequate resources of their own from traveling on pilgrimage.[132] Similarly, our old friends Kita and Yaji from *Hizakurige* had to pawn some goods to raise their travel money.[133] Sometimes people went to extreme measures to raise the needed funds. According to one record, two brothers from Hachinohe domain (Aomori) set out on pilgrimage to Ise in 1688, but ran out of money along the way and were not able to collect any more as alms. The eldest brother, Saisaburō, sold his younger sibling, Tora, for two *bu* of gold and went on to Ise alone, promising to redeem him on the way back.[134] Many people ran out of funds while traveling, especially to Ise, but resorted to less extreme measures than Saisaburō, taking out loans in order to return home. Travel could thus set back some people even after they returned home—and a peasant who ruined himself financially hurt his domain's economy.

Related to this argument about the economic rationale for restrictions on travel is a hypothesis about the strict controls that Satsuma domain imposed on its people. Satsuma's state as a "closed country" (*sakoku*) within Tokugawa Japan's "closed country," where all who lived or traveled in the domain were required to carry wooden identification tags, is, of course, well known.[135] One contemporary account put Satsuma first in a list of the four strictest domains, followed by Hizen, Awa and Tosa.[136] According to Takagi Zensuke, who made six trips to Satsuma from the Kamigata area during the years 1828–1837: "As far as Higo, customs do not vary much from those in the Kamigata [Kinai] area, but in

Satsuma the situation is completely different: customs there seem, what shall I say, old-fashioned, or perhaps even like that of a foreign country."[137] Another contemporary account gives a number of reasons for Satsuma's closure: for example, to prevent the dispersion of domain population; to prevent the leaking out of domain secrets; to prevent prohibited religious groups, such as the *nenbutsu*, from contact with the outside; and to prevent unwanted outside religious influences from entering Satsuma.[138] Another reason we might suggest, however, for Satsuma's strict controls on travel—both in and out of the domain—is medical. The comments of Furukawa Koshōken during his trip to Kyushu in 1783 suggest that a fear of smallpox may have been a contributing cause for tight controls. In Ōmura domain, he noted, seven or eight out of ten people who contracted the disease during an epidemic died.[139] When a group from Satsuma went on pilgrimage to Ise they commonly did a "smallpox dance" to guard themselves against contracting the disease during their travels.[140] Apparently domain controls on travel were effective, for the names of Satsuma residents rarely appear in extant temple registers for the Shikoku pilgrimage.[141]

There was, however, one break in Satsuma's state of closure which reveals a different aspect to the relationship between pilgrimage and the domain economy. The daimyo Shimazu Shigehide loosened controls on the domain's borders as part of a policy to foster economic prosperity in Kagoshima. Merchants from other domains were encouraged to enter Satsuma, since it was held the gathering of many merchants made a castle-town prosperous. Even travel outside the domain, including pilgrimage to Ise, was allowed.[142] Furukawa Koshōken confirmed this, noting that "in contrast with the past, it is presently not very difficult to enter Satsuma." He found that it was possible to enter the domain without delay and that the bansho guards were not strict in questioning him.[143]

The historical record indicates that the various regulations restricting pilgrimage were widely flouted. Many travelers did not obtain permits to travel and engaged in *nukemairi*, either because of the difficulty involved in applying for travel permits, or because of domain restrictions and prohibitions on their issuance. The record of complaints against these travelers began around the middle of the seventeenth century and is quite extensive.[144] The authorities in Morioka reported, "Domain residents of all status groups with permits (*oyakiin*) for pilgrimage to Ise have been granted one-night's lodging in the domain mansion (*oyashiki*) in Edo. In recent years, however, there have been large numbers traveling without permission. Occasionally, some of these people come to the mansion. Up to this point they have been treated with benevolence and given food as well as lodging for the night, but from now on they are to be turned away from the gates." Apparently that proclamation did not have much effect, for five years later, in 1767, the message read, "It has been prohibited since 'ancient times' for women to travel to other domains, but we have heard that in recent years many have been going without permission to places such as Ise and Zenkō-ji. Moreover, there are even some who have stopped at the domain mansion in Edo. This is reprehensible."[145]

In Hiroshima, a notice sent by domain officials in 1853 to village officials related that a strict prohibition on pilgrimage to Ise, as well as on travel outside the domain in general, had been established; but "since the spring, we hear that large numbers have been leaving on pilgrimage."[146] A 1792 notice from Tsugaru domain related, "Despite the prohibitions, year after year people continue to go on pilgrimage to Ise. This is reprehensible. Henceforth we will enforce the law strictly."[147] According to the diary of one magistrate from this domain, peasants leaving on pilgrimage without permission were such a problem that in 1759 the penalty established for doing so was the same as for "sekisho smashing": death. Whether this was true and, if so, whether it was enforced is not known, but the latter seems unlikely.[148] In Nambu domain, officials reported that "in years past we ordered that it was prohibited for men and women to travel outside the domain, but we hear that in recent years they have been doing so."[149] The officials who issued that statement were right: Large numbers were traveling to Zenkō-ji and Ise.[150] Similarly, the fragmentary records from a temple on Kōya-san show that despite bans on pilgrimage, residents from Yonezawa were continuing to travel to the Kinai region.[151]

It is evident from a reading of domain regulations that, in the bakufu and many domain's gendered travel policies, women came under greater constraints than men. Many of the normal channels that men took to travel were more restrictive for women: Applying for travel permits was a more difficult and time-consuming process, particularly since many domainal regulations on travel, as well as sekisho inspection procedures, targeted women. This probably discouraged women from applying at all. According to the official records from Kasama castle town (Hitachi) during the years 1807–1846, more than 400 male townspeople applied for travel permits, while only eleven of their female counterparts did.[152] Also, village and urban confraternity groups (*kō*), which sent representatives to Ise or other pilgrimage sites every year, were usually open to households only, and therefore largely excluded women.

Political constraints on the full participation of women in travel were strengthened by social barriers. There was, for example, pressure exerted by husbands and extended family on women to stay within the confines of the politically and socially defined roles of wife and mother, leaving little room for travel. Neo-Confucianism and folk beliefs, particularly the notion of women as unclean, also subordinated women and thus further hindered their free movement. The notion that women were subservient and owed obedience to parents, husband, and when widowed, to son were spelled out in morals texts, like Kaibara Ekiken's *Onna Daigaku* (The Greater Learning for Women, 1672). This and other, similar, tracts reveal that women were viewed as inferior, dull-witted, and polluting. These attitudes were often echoed in society at large. They can be found, for example, in the doctor Yasumi Roan's travel guidebook, *Ryokō yōjin shū* (A Collection of Precautions for Travelers): He writes, "You should take certain precautions at river-crossings when traveling with women and children. Unlike men, women are timid creatures and sometimes are frightened when they look at the fast current of a wide river. Also at times they are afraid of the disorderly conduct of the river porters and may get light-headed or dizzy."[153] It was perhaps for this reason that the handbook given to all members of the Edo-based confraternity group Azuma-*kō* late in the Tokugawa period stated uncategorically, "Do not take women along when traveling."[154] Kaibara's text instructed that "women under the age of forty should not go to shrines, temples or other places where many people gather."[155] In another part of the book he wrote: "Sew kimono for your father- and mother-in-law, prepare the meals, obey your husband, sew cloth, sweep the floors, raise your children, wash away impurities, remain inside the home, and never leave it without permission."[156] A bakufu proclamation from 1649 was more forceful, stating that, "Women who go on pilgrimage, like women who drink a lot of tea, or who like going on outings, should be divorced."[157]

It bears noting here that while the interest in regulating the movement of women found in legal statutes and popular tracts such as Yasumi Roan's might be seen as evidence of male subordination of women, considered in the context of the time this interest may reflect a genuine concern for the safety of women and the maintenance of social order. These concerns are apparent in a regulation issued in Tottori domain which stated that, "Women are prohibited from walking outside at night; in unavoidable circumstances, however, they may do so if accompanied by a male, who should be carrying a lantern."[158]

Folk religious notions of women as unclean not only affected the allotment of women's duties, but the type of places she could travel to or visit: for example, the climbing of sacred mountains central to the mountain cult, or the Fuji cult, was long forbidden to women.[159] The same was true of many temples: the traveler Shirabyōshi Masako came upon a placard at Mishima Shrine, near Odawara, which barred her entry. It said simply, "Women may not enter."[160]

With bakufu and domainal laws echoing the tone of the texts mentioned above, women wanting to travel faced considerable roadblocks, which led many to relieve the greater social pressures they came under by ignoring all legal procedures for traveling: in other words, to fail to carry permits and travel on side roads, bypassing barriers. In many instances, the permission of the househead or employers was also not obtained.

There are several interesting cases of this type of travel (*nukemairi*), or "French leave-taking," in Kiyokawa Hachirō's diary, *Saiyūsō*, which reveal the capacity of the household to influence, if not control, female behavior. A little more than a week out of his hometown in Shōnai domain, Kiyokawa's party, which included his mother, a servant, and, for a short time, his aunt, spent a few nights at an inn in Sendai. The innkeeper's wife intended to see them off as far as Kameda, about five miles down the road, but decided instead to join them on their pilgrimage to Zenkō-ji in Shinano, leaving her son behind. Her husband, who also worked as a city official, was away on business at this time. The woman sent her servant back to inform the household of her intentions, and Kiyokawa himself wrote a letter of explanation to the husband. A few days later a manservant sent from the wife's maternal household caught them all by surprise. He carried a letter from the woman's old mother which expressed her concern about the long trip (about ten days round-trip) and the impropriety of leaving home without permission while her husband was away. The innkeeper's wife was indignant and remained determined to go on. Nevertheless, she felt that she could not rudely shake off the messenger, since he was sent by her mother. The wife argued, "I understand that even though I am on a pilgrimage there is good reason for people to be upset with me because I left home without permission. However, the trip will not take many days, so please ask them to manage without me until I return." But the faithful servant declined to return home alone. The woman became exasperated since the man refused to leave her side; and, finally, she gave up. In tears at having to go home, she said, "Since it is my mother's wish, it is unavoidable. Still, to have come this far and have to return is truly regrettable."[161]

Kiyokawa's mother and aunt had also left for Ise on *nukemairi*. After eight days on the road, the aunt, who had been reluctant to join them in the first place, became increasingly worried about leaving home in that manner. In this case, too, family members (the aunt's brothers) sent someone to bring her back. Kiyokawa tried to assure his aunt that her affairs would be looked after by her siblings. Nonetheless, because of fear that the family (*honke*) would get terribly upset, she turned back. The very next day a letter came from Kiyokawa's father telling him that everything was fine at his aunt's household, for her not to worry, and that she should by all means continue her journey. The father said that, "Her relatives might complain for a while, but in the final analysis no one could deny that it was a good thing for her to make a pilgrimage to Ise." Kiyokawa thought her cowardly for returning, but conceded that "since she is a woman, it is not unreasonable that she is concerned about things at home."[162] While these cases are only from one diary, they suggest the types of pressures brought to bear upon women, even those on pilgrimage, during which social norms of behavior were ordinarily suspended. Since it was so much more difficult for women than for men to travel, the experience must have been particularly meaningful for the large numbers of women able to overcome these social and political forces.

One of the reasons why peasants did leave on pilgrimage without per-

mission in such large numbers was that government authorities did not—
or did not want to—come out strongly enough against pilgrimage outside domain borders to sufficiently discourage people from leaving their
domains. Common, perhaps, was the reaction of officials in Kaga domain, who issued a declaration stating that "[p]ilgrims to Ise are to follow
the time limit recorded in their travel permits and return without fail on
time. If they do not, the matter will surely be investigated."[163] Tsuyama
domain promised that residents traveling to other domains without permission "would be called back."[164] Punishment against offenders was
rare and amounted to tacit approval.[165]

Rather than come out against pilgrimage with strong measures and
enforced punishments, government authorities were content to issue and
re-issue prohibitions which were hortatory in nature and thereby functioned more as sumptuary legislation. For example, a notice sent to all
Hiroshima domain villages in 1819 said, "We have heard that there are people traveling outside the domain who have not been carrying passports.
This is a grave mistake." Assuming the role of a benevolent elder, it went
on to warn that those who insisted on traveling without a permit might
not be able to find lodging, and should they fall ill or encounter misfor-
tune, help would not be easily forthcoming.[166]

The bakufu never told commoners that they could not travel afar. It
was content, rather, to use moral suasion to try to reduce the number of
commoners on the road. A magistrate's ordinance from Shinano (1701)
stated that pilgrimage "is of no value (*muyō*), but that in unavoidable circumstances people [who must travel] should come to the magistrate's
office and apply for a permit."[167] Around the end of the seventeenth century, the exclamation that "pilgrimage is of no value" appeared as a stock
phrase in many Five-Household Group ledgers across the country; but
disapproval of pilgrimage by bakufu authorities was never expressed in a
more oppressive form to the people.[168]

The sekisho system, along with permit procedures, were effective in
that they, to a certain extent, limited mobility by making travel inconvenient and, at times, difficult. An assessment of all our evidence, however,
makes clear the fact that bakufu sekisho and domainal bansho were not
true barriers to travel. These procedures did not affect all travelers: Some
were not required to carry permits, and others without permits were

often allowed through sekisho. Officials frequently bent the rules for travelers with defective permits, and sometimes downgraded travel offenses to avoid having to prosecute commoners. Some travelers evaded sekisho by going around the barriers, bypassing them by traveling on minor roads; if caught, they were rarely punished. Thus sekisho inadvertently promoted the development of roads not on the Gokaidō. Other travelers, even at least one village headman, were led through breaks in the sekisho palisade network.

Institutions like the sekisho system are difficult to dismantle, even when they no longer serve their original purpose. The system assumes a life of its own, and procedures that were once useful seem absurd. Strict sekisho regulations may have been enforced early in the Tokugawa period, but by the middle of the eighteenth century, as Ernest Satow remarked, the sekisho had become "curious relics of a past full of suspicion."[169] The "feudal form" of Tokugawa government and its administration, which, according to Rutherford Alcock, was based on "the most elaborate form of espionage ever attempted,"[170] remained in place; but the substance of the law changed considerably. The physical and legal barriers erected by the state were insufficient to thwart commoners' desire to travel; although the government continued to keep these barriers in place, they gave their tacit and sometimes explicit approval to travelers who circumvented them. The active willingness of travelers to evade the barriers, along with some cooperation from political authorities, allowed travel to develop as recreation; the following chapter will examine more closely some of the causes and characteristics of that phenomenon.

SIX

Travel as Recreation

The recreational character of travel in the Tokugawa period is in part evident from the "great numbers of people" who used the roads. Kaempfer explained that this was "owing partly to the Country's being extreamly populous, partly to the frequent journies, which the natives undertake, oftner than perhaps any other nation, either willingly and out of their free choice, or because they are necessitated to it."[1] Kaempfer was not alone in finding the number of people on the road remarkable. Even earlier, at the beginning of the seventeenth century, foreigners such as Rodrigo de Vivero y Velasco wrote of the traveler "always seeing people coming and going." John Saris also found the road "exceedingly traveled, full of people."[2] In the closing years of the bakufu, foreigners continued to be impressed by the crowds. Alcock, for instance, remarked that "the traffic seems to be great," and "the whole road is a scene of constant traffic."[3]

As Kaempfer noted, people moving from place to place on business contributed to the bustle on the roads, but an even more remarkable feature of life on Tokugawa roads was the number of people traveling for recreational purposes.[4] The recreational character of their trips is indicated in part by the increasing length of trips taken and the number of stops made at shrines and temples, famous places (*meisho*), and historical sites (*kyūseki*). For example, a pilgrim whose ultimate destination might be Ise would stop at a number of places along the way; in fact, Ise became less of a destination and more like just one attraction of the journey. On the way home a different route was commonly selected to allow travelers to take in new sights. The return leg of the journey probably would not be direct either, since many attractions lay off the main roads. More stops meant longer trips: fifty to seventy days on the road became commonplace, but journeys as long as two-and-a-half to three months were not unusual among confraternity (*kō*) members and the wealthy; some of them remained on the road for as long as four to six months.

The substantial amount of movement on Tokugawa roads was partially the result of the unified rule brought about by the collective efforts of Oda Nobunaga, Toyotomi Hideyoshi and Tokugawa Ieyasu. The strong arms of the early Tokugawa shoguns made the peace more than a temporary respite between battles. Japan experienced much social dislocation and uncertainty in the first decades of the Edo era, but as the reality of the peace set in, the great energies of the people were unleashed. Just how rapid and fundamental the changes in the early modern order were is evident from the fact that in 1658 Asai Ryōi could write about sending "a cherished child on a journey" to gain experience "in all matters."[5]

With the newfound harmony of the times, the natural industry of the people could be directed towards constructive labors. The economy took off on an extended period of growth and the population increased rapidly; thus a greater number of people traveled to castle towns and other major urban centers. The requirements of alternate attendance likewise stimulated tremendous economic changes of national significance which were felt in the domains and all along the routes the daimyo traveled to and from Edo. Taking control of the country's central arteries, the Tokugawa established a well developed system of overland communications; and the daimyo followed their lead with similar efforts in the domains. All of these changes contributed to the rise of travel and its emergence as a form of recreation among the masses—a national pastime.

While difficult to pinpoint exactly, we can trace the emergence of travel as recreation from the late seventeenth century, roughly the same time as in England.[6] By this time government authorities were taken aback by the number of people traveling on the roads, many without official permission, and began issuing a steady stream of prohibitions against their actions. Furthermore, by the beginning of the nineteenth century a veritable "travel boom" was taking place, with a more secular form of pilgrimage being the principal objective of most wayfarers. This boom can be seen as nothing less than the creation of a "culture of movement." Long before then, however, travel had already become a form of recreation, or *yusan tabi* (lit., "pleasure-seeking travel"), an escape from the rigid patterns governing day-to-day living, a time when, as Jippensha Ikku said, one could flee from the "bill collectors at the end of the month." Traveling, to him, meant "cleaning one's life of care."[7]

Improving economic conditions, the proliferation of religious confraternities, and the practice of alms-giving meant that a wider spectrum of the population could engage in travel. Not only did more people travel, but they traveled far from home—for the first time in Japanese history. In an age when healthy persons could routinely cover forty kilometers a day on foot, on good roads, the Tokugawa person could expand the geographic scope of his life to an extent that may be difficult to comprehend for those who have become accustomed to our modern, automobile culture. The 487-kilometer trip from Kyoto to Edo, for example, generally required only twelve to fourteen days.[8] From Edo, points in Kyushu were only a thirty- to forty-day walk away. By traveling far from home, the geographic scope of people's lives expanded; in doing so they were able to "gain experiences in all manner of things," to become directly exposed to local culture, and to engage in social intercourse with people from all parts of the country, thereby creating a common body of shared knowledge and experience that is necessary for the emergence of a sense of nationhood.

THE DEVELOPMENT OF A TRAVEL INDUSTRY

At the beginning of the nineteenth century, Jippensha Ikku wrote, "The highways seem like the hair of the head. Not a single hair is disturbed—a sign of the glorious times in which we live, when the reputation of our warlike heroes survives only in the pictures of the cock-crowing Adzuma; when our bows and swords—even those made of wood—are hung up as an offering to the god of the thousand swift-brandishing weapons."[9] Even earlier, in 1720, Tanaka Kyūgu remarked, "The road is like the comfort of one's home. All that can be observed on the road is due to the virtue of our government. From here, as far as the distant mountains and solitary valleys, the 'illness' of theft has been gradually eliminated in recent years."[10] Both authors were clearly impressed by the Tokugawa peace and the order that it seemed to bring to the land. In the merchant writer Saikaku's words, Japan had become a "well-governed land where the sword remains forever sheathed and peace reigns eternal."[11] Warfare was over, and even the danger from highwaymen and pirates that threatened travelers in earlier times is nowhere evident in Tokugawa travel diaries. The only fear that any Tokugawa wayfarer seems to have expressed was that of wolves.[12] This is not to say that highway crime no longer existed,[13] but rather that the possibility of incurring physical harm or violent death on the road does not appear to have restrained Tokugawa travelers. Gangs did, on occasion, create difficulties for government officials,[14] yet considering the lack of gendarmerie plying the roads, social order there seems remarkable.

The traveler did have to be on the lookout for porters who might try to extort money or merchants who charged "ignorant tourists" exorbitant prices.[15] Even one carrying two swords (samurai) had to be careful not to be cheated in a place where he was not known. Far from his native Shōnai, Kiyokawa Hachirō ordered a drink of sugared water on a summer's afternoon, forgetting to ask the price beforehand. When it came time to pay the bill he was charged twenty *mon* per person. He attributed the high price to the fact that they "looked like they were from another province, just travelers passing through, so the proprietor could do as he pleased with them." In resignation, Kiyokawa shrugged his shoulders, saying that it was "unavoidable since it was after the fact" (i.e., that it was his fault for not asking the price before ordering).[16]

The basic framework for the transport infrastructure was built, as outlined in Chapter One, during the first four decades of the seventeenth century and afforded the traveler generally good road conditions on which to make his journey; with trips overseas closed to the Japanese, domestic travel was encouraged by these advances. The *Tōkaidō meishoki* reveals the wide variety of travel and travel-related services that were already available by the mid seventeenth century—evidence of the commercialization of travel in Japan, which is "one of the incontestable signs of growing affluence in a society."[17] For example, while most commoners had previously walked from station to station on the Gokaidō, for the first time in

Japanese history, they had the opportunity to ride. Moreover, it was possible for many to ride by bargaining for a cheaper fare on empty horses being led by post horse workers back to their station of origin; the same was true of palanquins as well. The rider did not control the horse's bridle; he merely sat back in the saddle while the footman led the horse. If a traveler's load was too heavy, he could hire a porter or a pack horse to carry it. It was even possible for those with money to spare to have baggage forwarded to an intermediate point or final destination. For example, Kiyokawa Hachirō forwarded excess baggage on a number of occasions during his journey, and had gifts, including 150 plates of Bizen-ware and an unspecified amount of porcelain (*seto mono*), tea cups and rice bowls with his family emblem on them, sent to distant locations.[18]

In France, "the rich and mighty took the mail coach,"[19] but in contemporary Japan they rode in the much-maligned palanquin. Townsend Harris expressed a common complaint against the vehicles, saying that they were "made after the model of iron cages said to have been invented by Cardinal Balve, in the reign of Louis XI of France. They are so low that you cannot stand upright in them, and so short that you cannot lie down at full length."[20] There were many different types of palanquins, but there were essentially two major classifications: *norimono*, which were enclosed palanquins with doors; and *kago*, a "sort of half box, half platform, swinging from a pole" used by the lower classes. Major Henry Knollys (1886) found them "the most clumsy, heavy, and uncomfortable means of transport which could be devised, but allowed that "they are comfortable enough to the natives, because they have been accustomed from infancy to sit on the ground with their feet tucked under them."[21]

There were no prohibitions issued against commoners riding in palanquins on the roads, although such edicts did exist for inner-city movement from the mid-seventeenth century on.[22] Travelers to Edo were instructed to get out of their vehicles after they reached the last station before the city—Shinagawa, Senjū, Itabashi, Takaidō, or Nakagawa, depending on which road they were using.[23] Similarly, although commoners were not legally permitted to ride horses until 1871, there was no prohibition against their doing so when traveling on the Gokaidō.[24]

If the traveler needed anything between stations en route to his destination—a snack or a new pair of straw sandals, perhaps—the "numberless small retail-merchants and children of country people, who run about from morning to night" could provide it for a few copper coins. There is nothing which travelers wore out as fast as sandals and therefore there was nothing "more commonly exposed to sale in all the towns and villages."[25] According to Thunberg, old worn-out pairs were found lying "every where by the side of the roads, especially near rivulets, where travelers, on changing their shoes, have an opportunity at the same time of washing their feet."[26] In the post stations Griffis found "little variation in the shops all over the country" with regard to staple articles of sale, such as paper umbrellas, rush hats, bamboo-work, matting for coats, flint, steel and tinder, sulphur splints for matches, oiled paper coats, grass cloaks, paper, and wooden clogs.[27]

Many of these items were also for sale in roadside villages between stations. A high volume of traffic on the travel routes increased the demand for travel and travel-related services between post towns, leading to the establishment of designated rest facilities (*tateba*) where the weary traveler could stop for a few minutes to enjoy a cup of tea and some rice cakes or sweets. Late in the Tokugawa period (1843), there were four such places between Shinagawa and Kawasaki, two between Hodogaya and Totsuka, and five over the difficult stretch of road separating Odawara and Hakone.[28] No transport services were officially permitted there; but as we saw in Chapter Two, rest facility owners did not adhere to this prohibition. They threatened the economic viability of the post stations as early as the beginning of the eighteenth century by providing services and offering lodging to travelers. Not to be outdone, some inns sent women to the rest stations closest to their post stop to drum up business.[29]

Rising productivity, coupled with the declining ability of the ruling class to tax away surpluses in the eighteenth and nineteenth centuries, left peasants with more disposable income. While economic growth was uneven, varying from region to region and often from village to village, a generally rising standard of living allowed greater opportunity to pursue recreational activities, foremost of which was travel. Surpluses gave many peasants cash to pay for straw sandals, food, lodging, or any other costs incurred while traveling.

The widespread practice of purchasing souvenirs and other gifts was an indispensable part of the experience of travel and evidence of the commercialization of travel and the economy in general. For example, in almost all travel accounts of visits to hot springs, one finds a discussion of the gifts the traveler bought or thought of buying for people back home. Also, since long-distance pilgrimage to Ise may have been a once-in-a-lifetime experience for many travelers, they often came back loaded down with gifts. The large number of souvenir dealers at Ise caught Saikaku's attention, leading him to remark that, "Souvenir dealers, making their livings by selling their whistles, sea-shell spoons, and edible seaweed, are as countless as the grains of sand on the seashore."[30] In one contemporary travel account, a pilgrim from Tosa who went to Ise spent four times as much money on gifts as he did on travel-related expenses. Among the items he purchased were Uji tea, inkstone covers from Arima, ink brushes (forty of them), pipes, combs, and fans.[31] Another traveler, a merchant from Chigasaki, near Kanagawa, returned home with forty-five charms from Ise, fifty-one *furoshiki* (square cloths used for tying up and carrying goods), writing brushes, geta, sweets, lacquer bowls, sake cups, and other goods. He, like many other travelers, had an eye to purchase gifts which would not overburden his load too much.[32]

Many of these gifts were for people back home who expected something in exchange for the send-off present (*senbetsu*)—usually cash—bestowed upon the traveler before his departure. In the case of the traveler from Chigasaki, he (or they, as he was probably part of a group) received gifts from fifty-eight percent of the households in the village, and six households from outside the village. In return, the merchant brought back gifts for a total of seventy people, including seven family members, ten shop workers, and fifty-three members of his and neighboring villages.[33] Many people no doubt found the exchange of gifts troublesome, prompting some to avoid the ritual by leaving home without informing neighbors or political authorities (*nukemairi*), as did Kiyokawa Hichirō and his traveling companions. Adding to the obligation to bring back presents was the custom of villagers giving "sympathy" gifts (*omimai mono*) to the households whose members were away on pilgrimage.

Among the gifts given to travelers before departure were a variety of foods, such as rice, tofu, and dried fish. The food was not meant to be taken along on the journey, but to be consumed by the travelers and those villagers remaining behind in a send-off feast. Upon their return to the village, another feast was held, at which time the travelers' presents were dispersed; these welcoming-home parties are only rarely noted at the end of travel diaries, which are essentially accounts of actual traveling rather than activities at home before and after one's trip.

Very early in the Tokugawa period, Hayashi Razan's travel diary mentions the various souvenirs available to travelers at the different post stations along the Tōkaidō.[34] Each station had its own "famous product" (*meibutsu*), whether it be a natural product, like pounded rice cakes (*Abegawa mochi*), a cultural product (Narumi tie-dyed cloth, Nishijin silk, Bizen pottery, religious charms or talismans [*oharai*]), or wood-block prints (*ukiyoe* or *nishiki-e*). *Ukiyoe*, which originated in the Kansai area but became associated with Edo by the end of the eighteenth century, were a special gift. According to the travel guidebook *Tōkaidō meisho zue* (Famous Places of the Tōkaidō), they were the "best gift." In his comic *Ukiyo-buro* (The Floating World Bathhouse; 1809–1822), Shikitei Sanba quotes some children in Edo as saying, "We always take Toyokuni prints as presents when we go to Kansai."[35] The satirical prints of Ōtsu (*Ōtsu-e*), which are noted or depicted in Saikaku's writings, Hiroshige's Tōkaidō series, and in various *meisho-zue*, also made fine presents.

Travel expenses, including souvenirs and gifts purchased, were paid for in cash. In the medieval period currency was usually of low value, so that a long journey required many heavy coins;[36] in the Tokugawa era, however, when currency came into widespread use for the first time, gold and silver coins were minted which "could be conveniently carried on a journey," significantly lightening a traveler's load.[37] Copper coins were used for small purchases and could be obtained, as needed, through an exchange for gold and silver that was performed at post stations. Thunberg, for example, changed a gold coin for a string of copper coins that were "strung on a ribbon by means of a square hole made in the middle" for convenience, and from time to time gave one or two to the mendicant nuns that followed his palanquin.[38]

The entrances to post stations were lined with eating and drinking establishments. Approaching them, the weary traveler was assaulted by the shrill voices of the *tome-onna*: women with painted faces employed by teahouses and inns whose job was quite similar to the barker of today. Many travelers found them annoying. To Ōta Nanpo (1749–1823), a low-ranking samurai with a talent for comic writing, their cries "sounded like the chirping of a hundred, or even a thousand birds."[39] Sometimes, when the competition was rough or the traveler recalcitrant, they might leave their doorways and forcibly drag prospective patrons into their establishments, a scene which Jippensha Ikku graphically recreated in his literary work of genius, *Hizakurige:*

> Teahouse girl trying to get a postboy (with his customer) to stop:
> "Stop here," said the girl, seizing hold of one of them.
> "Here, here!" said the traveler. "You'll twist my arm off."
> "That won't matter," said the girl. "Stop here."
> "Don't be a fool," said the traveler. "If I lost my arm how should I be able to eat?"
> "That would be all the better for us," said the girl.
> "Don't be troublesome. Let go," said the man. He broke loose from the girl and went on.[40]

The bakufu prohibited the luring of travelers into inns (*yado hiki*) but obviously not to much avail. At one station, Kusatsu on the Tōkaidō, the competition between inns for customers was so fierce that an agreement had to be made in 1819 to divide the women into two groups, one offering lodging to Edo-bound travelers and the other for those headed towards Kyoto. The inns also agreed to send only one person each to solicit customers.[41] The range of amenities that the inns offered is revealed in this example of another *tome-onna,* who recited them in an effort to convince a traveler to stop for the night:

> If you're going to stop, here's the place. Stop here, stop here! The rooms are cheap; we'll put you up. We have luxury suites and modest apartments, whatever you're looking for, whatever you like. The dishes are clean, the mats in the rooms were changed this summer. The bedding is good, the sake is good, the tea is the best. Stop just for the cost of your firewood. The bath has its own boiler, there's plenty of hot water; dip a little from the soaking-tub and test it yourself, wash away the dust of the journey. Will you be leaving at the crack of dawn or at seven? If you need some diversion in bed, we have what you want, whether a blushing girl or an experienced woman. She'll rub your legs and massage your back, she'll offer you a pipe with a lighted bowl, she'll bowl you over, she'll send shivers down your spine.[42]

In deciding at which inn to stop for the night the traveler had quite a selection, and to a certain extent the type of lodging he would choose was determined by the amount of cash he had. For daimyo, there was no choice—officially, at least. They were required to stay at one of the inns specially designated for their use, but they tended to avoid them later in the Tokugawa period because of the expense involved. Foreign dignitaries, court nobles, and officials of religious institutions would likewise stay there, but if all were filled, provisions could be made at some local temple. Bushi other than daimyo could also lodge at the *honjin* or their auxiliary inns, the *waki-honjin*, if they were not all occupied by the entourage of a daimyo from another domain. One traveler (1692) found that these inns:

> are like other well built houses, only one story high, or if there be two stories, the second is low and good for little else but stowage. The Inns are not broader in front, than other houses, but considerably deep . . . with a Tsuboo, that is, a small pleasure garden behind, enclosed with a neat, white wall. The front hath only lattice windows, which are kept open all day long, as are also the folding-skreens, and moveable partitions, which divide the several apartments, unless there be some man of quality with his retinue at that time lodged there. This lays open to travelers, as they go along, a very agreeable perspective view across the whole house into the garden behind.[43]

Daimyo inns were off-limits to commoners, but when not full, their auxiliary inns were free to take them in, giving the *waki-honjin* an additional source of income which helps account for their greater economic resilience in the face of the loss of daimyo business.

The widespread availability of affordable lodging during the Tokugawa period stimulated the masses to travel more frequently. Commoners not on a shoestring budget would most likely head for a *hatagoya*, often a two-story building, where they could expect a full range of services. (See Figure 8.) At these inns they could expect to pay 100–300 *mon*, depending on the quality of the establishment and the road it was on—the Tōkaidō generally being the most expensive. Most places, however, seem to have been in the range of 130–200 *mon*. These prices given for a night's lodging are based on actual costs recorded in travel diaries during the eighteenth and the beginning of the nineteenth century, before the rapid infla-

Figure 8 A Full-service Inn at Ishibe. Hiroshige, *Gojūsantsugi meisho zue*. Spencer Museum of Art, The University of Kansas (William Bridges Thayer Memorial).

tion of the bakumatsu years. The fee did not necessarily entitle the traveler to a private room, as it was common to share rooms with complete strangers. In Akasaka, a small post station on the Tōkaidō, over one-half of the 160 households on the roadfront in 1733 were full-service inns and, as was common elsewhere, were generally concentrated in the center of town, around the *honjin*. These inns provided an important source of labor for the surrounding area.[44] With an average (1843) of fifty-five full-service inns per station on the Tōkaidō, thirty-nine on the Nikkō dōchū, and twenty-seven on the Nakasendō and Ōshū dōchū, one can well understand the reason for the fierce competition between the *tome-onna*. Seven stations on the Tōkaidō had more than ninety inns each; two castle towns, Okazaki and Kuwana, had over 100 each; and one station, Atsuta (Miya), boasted as many as 248. The latter two stations were great collection points for travelers because of the twelve-kilometer boat trip that was necessary between them; Atsuta also offered direct boat service to Ise and this accounts for the extraordinary number of inns there.

There is still debate as to when full-service inns first went into widespread operation, but from some contemporary accounts they appear to have been common on the Tōkaidō early in the Tokugawa period.[45] Guests were offered breakfast and supper, but no lunch: Since leisurely sightseeing was not officially condoned, and travelers were limited in principle to one night's lodging at a particular inn, it was expected that they would purchase lunch either while sightseeing or at a teahouse down the road.[46] The operation of the tour guide business is not entirely clear; but it is apparent that in many places travelers could arrange to hire guides at their inn (see Figure 9), especially in tourist havens such as Edo, Kyoto, Osaka and Nara, as well as at major pilgrimage sites.[47] In Edo, full-day or just night tours of the city were available. For those who could not afford a tour guide, or just wanted to strike out on their own, an inn operator in Bakurō-chō distributed to his customers a single sheet guide, which he had published, to the "famous places" (*meisho*) of Edo.[48]

Even with the emergence of full-service inns for the masses in the Edo period, a less-expensive form of lodging was widely available to commoners. *Kichin-yado* (lit., "firewood inns") were "no-frills" lodges, almost always with just a single story, that did not at first provide meals: the traveler was required to carry his food around with him and cook it himself.

名どころを
さしを都礼
案内者
圖會
そらうを
そく
うつし画
湘夕

Figure 9 Tour Guide at Seta Pointing Out Scene Captured in Travel Book. *Shūi miyako meisho zue* (1787). Historiographical Institute, Tokyo University.

His staple was instant rice (*hoshii*)—rice boiled and then parched to prevent spoilage, which was later reconstituted with hot water provided at the inn. Consequently, lodging fees were assessed on the basis of the amount of firewood used. Other types of food, mostly dried products and pickles, would likely be carried to add some variety to the diet. From fairly early on, however, these lower-class inns offered rice for sale, but still required guests to do their own cooking. Guests were then assessed two fees, one for rice and another for firewood. With rates as low as three *mon* per person in 1614 and only thirty-five in 1711, one can well understand how the attraction and widespread availability of these establishments stimulated travel. *Kichin-yado* never were replaced by *hatagoya*—they continued to exist, even on the Tōkaidō, down through the bakumatsu years.[49]

The inns (and teahouses) offered more than a place to rest: Tanaka Kyūgu understood the economic significance of serving girls/prostitutes when he remarked that "those stations with them prosper, those without them fall into decay."[50] Saikaku, perhaps unknowingly, put it another way when he said that "Okazaki has a long bridge [meaning the Yahagi] and Akasaka has the women."[51]

Still, some travelers were simply after rest when they laid their heads down for the night; and to accommodate these travelers, lodging organizations of regional scope emerged in the early nineteenth century, such as the Naniwa-kō, with its headquarters in Osaka; the Santo-kō; the Three Cities Federation, with its head branches in Edo, Osaka and Kyoto; and the Edo-based Azuma-kō.[52] Establishments belonging to these organizations offered the weary traveler the guarantee that his sleep would not be disturbed by the nocturnal goings-on of inn harlots and guests in adjoining rooms, separated from his by only a paper or cloth-covered door. Moreover, these organizations acted almost like the modern AAA, with identification cum credit cards that entitled users to lodge at any member inn without paying money, and provided a source of information on travel-related matters. Travelers could determine which establishment they might want to stop at by consulting a detailed directory of member businesses or by searching for the federation's logo hung out in front of the inns. Kiyokawa and his party stayed at member inns on at least two occasions, in Osaka and Miyajima. In Osaka, where he stayed at the Naniwa-kō head branch, he obtained information on which boat companies were reputable for his party's upcoming voyage to Miyajima, Iwakuni, and back.[53]

Travelers leaving home could do so with some comfort, knowing that if they were stricken ill, they would not be left to die, alone and unaided, by the roadside. This was true in part because the Tokugawa Japanese, like their modern counterparts, preferred to travel in groups; in fact, the expression *"tabi wa michizure"* ("travel calls for a companion") dates from the Edo period.[54] Members of one confraternity group, which had to pledge to follow a set of rules drawn up before departure, were offered assistance in the following circumstances: "If a member injures his foot and must ride a horse, the confraternity will pay half his expenses," or "If a member runs out of money, the group will lend him some, but it must be paid back immediately upon returning home."[55] Traveling in a group was the rule, and it offered the individual companionship as well as protection in time of injury or illness.

The guest registers of Seishinbō, a temple inn at Zenkō-ji, confirm this. The register for 1865 indicates that the lodge gave shelter to 1,001 people during that year and of this total, only 17 were single travelers. As illustrated below, the majority of guests there traveled in groups of 2 to 10 people:

Persons in Group	Number of Groups
1	17
2	51
3	45
4	35
5	25
6	17
7	6
8	8
9	7
10	8

Groups of more than 10 people were rare at Seishinbō that year; there were only two groups with 11 people, one each with 12, 13, 14, and 19 people, and three groups with 17 people.[56]

In addition to the personal assistance that might be offered by companions, there were also institutional mechanisms to aid travelers. Both the bakufu and the domains required that a local doctor be dispatched immediately to treat a stricken traveler. If the person was too ill to move or had incurred a disabling physical injury, such as a broken leg or ankle, and was unable to continue his journey under his own power, then there were two possible ways of dealing with the problem. If the traveler was in such a condition that he could be transported by relay-palanquin, then he was sent home—at local expense. Otherwise it was required that the village or locality where he was stricken pay for his medical, food, and lodging costs while recuperating. In such cases notification was to be sent by messenger to the traveler's next of kin.[57]

One resident of Kōfu (Kai), Seimon, and his wife were on a long trip of more than two months during the spring of 1773 when he suddenly became ill at a small village called Numa, located between Fujii and Hitoichi post stations on the Sanyōdō route, near Okayama castle town. Unable to walk, he was given medical treatment and made to rest, but after four days there was still no improvement, and he asked to be sent home. A personal statement explaining his circumstances and a copy of his travel permit were sent to the local Rural Magistrate, who then issued a document authorizing his transportation back to Kōfu, with his food, lodging, and carriage on the way to be provided at local expense.[58]

Sick and disabled travelers had to be dealt with. Although a traveler in need might occasionally be turned away, particularly if he did not have a travel permit, many received humanitarian assistance. The regional breakdown of travelers that fell ill in Numa village in 1717 indicate the wide range of travel in the early modern period: Kantō, 4; Kinki, 36; Chūgoku, 26; Kyushu, 13; Shikoku, 10; Hokuriku, 4; unknown, 1. Of 36 sick or disabled travelers it dealt with during the year, only 2 died, 3 were able to walk away after a four-day recuperative period, and the remaining 31 had difficulty walking and had to be relayed to the next village after one night's rest. In addition to the 36 that were held overnight, 58 disabled travelers were relayed through the village during the day over that year.[59]

In cases where the medical treatment given stricken travelers did not work at all and the patient died, the body was to be given a temporary burial while notification was sent to next of kin. Even if the deceased had not been traveling alone, most likely the cremated remains would stay at the original burial site, since to transport it back home would have involved prohibitive costs to the deceased's family or relatives.[60]

Travel was stimulated by the great amounts of published information. The details of travel on the major roads were well-known through word of mouth, temple schoolhouse textbooks, and the vast body of travel literature that developed from early in the Edo period, as well as through the medium of wood-block prints, which reached new heights of popularity in the nineteenth century. Added to this were the parlor games called *dōchū sugoroku* (journey *sugoroku*), which were a popular pastime for both children and adults; the game boards were made of paper, came in different sizes, and although the Tōkaidō was the most popular, other roads were common as well. Even when feasting, one might find himself staring at representations of the Tōkaidō on sake cups or on food platters. Through a variety of mediums it was possible to "travel the fifty-three stages of the Edo Road [i.e., the Tōkaidō] without leaving your home."[61]

Early in the Tokugawa period the highway became the stage for the comedy of picaresque heroes—most commonly a pair—in search of their fortunes. Karasumaru Mitsuhiro's *Chikusai monogatari*, the prototype for this genre, was published during the Kan'ei era (1624–1643), and clearly inspired the first popular guidebook of the period, Asai Ryōi's *Tōkaidō meishoki* (1658–1660). *Tōkaidō meishoki* was primarily a guidebook—the travelers merely provided a "comic sound track for the more factual travelogue with its accounts of shrines, temples, famous local products, peculiar provincial customs, and prosaic mileage data."[62] Both books belong to the literary genre known as *kanazōshi;* by being written in the kana syllabary, with a minimum of Chinese characters, they were able to reach a wide audience.

This sort of armchair travel guide or travelogue, which became common during the Genroku era, was too bulky to have been taken along on any actual journey. For that purpose there were stripped down, pocket-sized travel guides, or *dōchūki*. Booksellers' shops, according to Ernest Satow, abounded in "printed itineraries which furnish the minutest possible information about inns, roads, distances, ferries, temples, productions, and other particulars which the tourist requires."[63] These guides first became available in the 1650s and were published in considerable numbers by the early eighteenth century. About the same time travel maps of all kinds began to be published, the first and most famous of which was Hishikawa Moronobu's *Tōkaidō bunken ezu* (1690), a work that went through multiple editions.[64] As in England, in the early nineteenth century the number of personal travel accounts written in Japan simply exploded.[65]

Maps were not usually drawn to scale, but afforded "every geographical detail that can be of any real service."[66] Kaempfer noticed that instead of a road book many travelers carried fans upon their journeys which had the roads printed upon them, telling "how many miles they are to travel, what inns they are to go to, and what price victuals are at."[67] Similarly, single-sheet maps were printed using the wood-block technique for Hakone, Nikkō, Narita, Kamakura, Enoshima, Arima and other tourist attractions.

Illustrated guidebooks (*meisho zue*) were also published in great numbers beginning in the late eighteenth century. One example of this genre was the guide that covered a specific road, such as the *Tōkaidō meisho zue* (1797), without doubt the most famous of the lot. Another type was concerned with pilgrimage sites or circuits, such as the *Zenkō-ji meisho zue*, *Ise sangū meisho zue*, and *Konpira sankei meisho zue*. Still other types dealt with provinces or groups of provinces.[68] These guidebooks, which made wonderful souvenirs, were of great use to travel writers, who used them as encyclopedias of sorts to fill in the gaps of their own accounts. Sometimes even the language of the guidebooks, in only slightly disguised form, found its way into individual accounts—the opening line of Shimazaki Tōson's *Yoake Mae* (Before the Dawn) about the Kiso region being a notable example.

The various forms of the culture of movement built upon one another and were mutually reinforcing: Literature and artistic media greatly influenced one another and increased the popularity of travel. *Tōkaidō meisho zue*, for example, was a clear influence on Jippensha Ikku's *Hizakurige*. Ikku in turn stimulated the wood-block artist Andō Hiroshige's efforts, as the characters Yaji and Kita seem to appear in a number of his first and most famous series of Tōkaidō prints (Hoeidō, 1833). The *Hizakurige* figures also show up in *sugoroku*.[69] The success of Ikku's work likewise inspired Hokusai to publish his first Tōkaidō series (1806), but unlike Hiroshige, he did not bother to actually make a trip down the road himself; his prints express more of an interest in people than in the landscape setting of a particular locality, as Hiroshige's did.[70]

The guides and travelogues told those planning a trip what day to start out and what to bring along; they even contained health tips for the journey, such as ointment to keep one's feet "from getting sore for thousands of miles."[71] While travel diaries were often written with the needs of future travelers in mind, and contained implicit advice for those about to make the same trip, Yasumi Roan's *Ryokō yōjin shū* (A Collection of Precautions for Travelers; 1810) was, however, the first and only work as far as is known whose explicit purpose was to provide travelers with extensive counsel. It offers advice on practically all aspects of travel. For example, it instructs one how to: avoid motion sickness when riding in a palanquin, treat worn leg muscles, pass through a sekisho, prevent theft at inns (*makura sagashi*), and ward off wolves and other wild animals.[72] It is impossible to know, of course, how many people read it or had it read to them. But the fact that it was printed from wood-blocks (and not by hand), that other authors repeated Yasumi's advice, and that copies of the book exist today in fair numbers, suggests that the work probably enjoyed a wide circulation.

Two of the items that *Ryokō yōjin shū* says the traveler must carry with him are an empty notebook and a portable ink and brush case (*yatate*). In some travel diaries, financial information made up the bulk of the text; in other cases travelers kept a separate expense log in addition to a more narrative diary. For group travel, it is likely that a representative maintained the record for his entire party. Those diaries that rose above the level of an expense log contained information on the activities of the traveler or travelers as well as notes about the famous places, historical monuments, shrines and temples visited, and perhaps even some original poetry.

It is apparent that many women traveled but that, in comparison with men, relatively few left travel diaries of their own. For this reason Toyokuni II's wood-block print of a women with travel diary in hand and ink brush in her mouth (see Figure 10) is extraordinary. Only recently have historians and specialists in women's studies begun to collect and publish these accounts in a systematic manner. At present we are aware of slightly

more then 150 travel diaries brushed by women;[73] it appears that no one
has attempted to count the number written by men, but these exist in the
thousands, if not tens of thousands. Of the 150 diaries written by women,
four-fifths were written after 1780, which supports other evidence about
the spread of literacy as well as the development of Japan's first travel
boom from the late eighteenth century.

THE SECULARIZATION OF PILGRIMAGE

Kaempfer remarked that the Japanese "are very much addicted to Pilgrimage."[74] The intimate relationship between pilgrimage and travel is readily
apparent from a quick perusal of a number of travel diaries, many of
which are no more than an expense log and list of shrines, temples and
famous places visited. Similarly, the amount of space devoted to these religious institutions in the *Tōkaidō meisho zue* and other travel guides is an
indication of the extent to which travel and pilgrimage were synonymous.

Pilgrimage, in its basic form, is a religious act; and this religious element was perhaps the most evident during the medieval period. During
the early modern era, the religious element appears to have remained
strongest in the Shikoku Eighty-eight Temple and Saikoku Thirty-three
Temple circuits. Ascetics and itinerant monks and priests, such as an
anonymous Ji-sect priest who left an extensive travel diary,[75] continued
to wander around the country in the Tokugawa period in their quest for
religious salvation.

It is also important to note the continuing link between religion and
travel, not only in terms of travelers' motivations, which are difficult to
assess, but also in terms of temples as cultural centers that attracted both
pilgrims and tourists to exhibitions of temple treasures. Exhibitions of
these treasures on site rather than as a traveling show drew commoners
to major temples such as Zenkō-ji, where they could not only view the
religious artifacts but also enjoy the food stands and circus-like shows
(*misemono*) put on by performers within the temple precincts.[76]

While no one should discount the religious component of the act for
many people, pilgrimage during the Tokugawa period appears to have
undergone a process of secularization whereby it became little more than
sightseeing. In the words of one authority, it became "seventy percent rec-

Figure 10 Woman Keeping a Travel Diary at Arai. Toyokuni II (1777–1835). Arai sekisho shiryōkan.

reation and thirty percent faith."[77] Our purpose here is not to debate the
relative percentage of these two components; it is merely to discuss this
secular element. For example, in reading the *Illustrated Guide to the
Famous Places of the Thirty-three Stations of Saikoku* (*Saikoku sanjūsanka-
sho meisho zue*, 1848), James Foard has observed that "the pleasures of the
trip have come to the fore, and we seem to have crossed the threshold to
tourism." The illustrated text takes the reader only to the eighth station
on the circuit, but requires ten volumes to do so.[78] One diary kept by a
member of a confraternity group of twenty individuals making a leisurely pilgrimage reads like an "Eater's Guide to the Ise Pilgrimage," noting the restaurants the group ate at, the more than one hundred types of
food products tasted during the two-month-long trip, the inns stayed at,
the various local speciality products seen or purchased, and the "famous
places" (*meisho*) visited.[79]

   As travel became increasingly recreational in nature,[80] many types of
travelers could be considered, at least secondarily, tourists: For example,
students on study-trips; merchants traveling on business;[81] Confucian
scholars commuting between Edo, Kyoto, and their domainal castle
town;[82] and even village officials traveling to Edo to present petitions lin-
gered in the city to take in the sights (*monomi yusan*, or sightseeing). Pilgrims and visitors to hot springs were even more apt to travel for pleasure
(*yusan tabi*, or recreational travel).[83] But the concept of tourism suggests
that "culturally sanctioned reasons or goals exist for leaving home to
travel."[84] In contemporary Britain, for example, people eager for a holiday liked to have a sound moral excuse to free themselves from a sense
of guilt for enjoying themselves. Thus, holiday travel and the development of settlements devoted to leisure in the eighteenth century, such as
the spa towns at Bath, Tunbridge Wells, and Scarborough, were linked to
health. It was only toward the end of that century that people began to
accept in a frank manner the idea of a "holiday for a holiday's sake"; and
in Japan not really until after the Second World War.[85] Certainly, the
Tokugawa government did not recognize the concept of tourism: The
only culturally or politically sanctioned reasons for travel were pilgrimage and convalescence at hot springs; but the expressions *yusan tabi* and
monomi yusan imply the emergence of travel as pure recreation. This
world of play was, of course, encouraged by the popular theater.[86]

Both pilgrimage and travel to hot springs were not, however, without utilitarian or religious elements or both; to argue otherwise would be to deny the fact that some travelers went to shrines and temples in order to accumulate grace, to perform a vow, to give thanks to the divinities for blessings bestowed, and that some commoners sought cures for their ailments at hot springs.[87] Saikaku, in fact, criticizes the utilitarian nature of the act of pilgrimage among merchants, finding them money-hungry, seeking only gain in this world rather than salvation in the next.[88] These forms of travel do, however, qualify as tourism because most pilgrims and visitors to hot springs also engaged in sight-seeing.[89]

Government did not recognize the concept of tourism. Domain authorities in particular explicitly discouraged frivolous travel. In Kaga (1708), for example, residents in rural areas were told that, "Sightseeing or the making of pilgrimages to temples in Kanazawa is of no worth (*muyō*). The same is all the more true for long-distance travel."[90] Kaga and other domains were more tolerant, however, of pilgrimage to Ise, and thus for many people the trip there, whether officially sanctioned or not, became an excuse to travel. Still, government officials were aware of the fact that at least some of those leaving the domain were, in the words of a proclamation from Kaga, "not truly performing a pilgrimage" (*shinjitsu no sangū ni te mo kore naku*).[91] Elsewhere, the authorities in Aizu Wakamatsu complained in 1745 that, "No matter how much we issue edicts to the contrary, great numbers set out from our domain every spring under the pretext of making a pilgrimage to Ise, but instead use the trip as an occasion for sightseeing."[92]

In recreational travel, one authority tells us, "the intent and meaning of the religious voyage is secularized; it loses its deeper, spiritual content. Though the tourist may find his experiences on the trip 'interesting,' they are not personally significant. He does not have a deep commitment to travel as a means of self-realization or self-expansion."[93] After traveling all the way to Ise, some "pilgrims" did not even bother to pray at the Inner Shrine. In one of Saikaku's works, in which a peasant girl working in Osaka as a servant leaves with three others for Ise, he informs us that, "None of the group had any real interest in the pilgrimage itself. At Ise they failed to visit the Inner Shrine or the sacred beach at which homage is paid to the Sun, shopping only at the Outer Shrine for a few minutes and purchasing as their only souvenirs a purification broach and some seaweed."[94] As a humorous lyric of the day related, a "pilgrimage to Ise means just stopping by the shrine for a moment" (*Ise sangū daijingū e mo issun yori*). In other words, Ise was a brief stop where one prayed at the Outer Shrine and obtained the obligatory *oharai*, "an indulgence box," tied under the brim of the hat before the forehead which acted like a travel permit for those who left home without one.[95] Like modern tourists, it appears that Tokugawa travelers could be more concerned with such "on-site markers" as placards, plans, and appropriate souvenirs than with the sites themselves, "as though they were checking off a list of having truly visited the approved sights by the mere recognition of the markers."[96]

While the ostensible purpose of many travelers like Kiyokawa Hachirō was a pilgrimage to Ise (his travel diary begins, "The day to set out on pilgrimage to Ise had finally arrived"), he was in no special hurry to get there, taking a very leisurely thirty-eight days to make the trip. Once the obligatory stop at the shrine was completed, many travelers headed for the temple-front town (*monzen machi*) of Ise known as Furuichi, where many teahouses, brothels and play houses were concentrated.[97] Kiyokawa noted that here were "the most interesting brothels in the land." For those not seeking carnal pleasure, taking in a performance of *Ise ondo*, a type of dance that, Kiyokawa reported, could not be seen in the three metropolises, was a "must";[98] kabuki and kyōgen were among the other types of entertainment available there. After the pilgrimage was completed, he and his party continued on their journey for five more months, visiting most of the major tourist sites in the land. For Tokugawa travelers, the pleasures of the trip, the local delicacies, the entertainments, and the prostitutes made the trip as much as the actual pilgrimage did.

A trip to a hot springs resort was often included in the itinerary of pilgrims who were not in a hurry to get home; for example, a merchant from Tosa, after making a pilgrimage to Ise, stopped at the hot springs in Kusatsu, then visited Mt. Hiei and Kyoto before taking the waters at Arima; from Osaka, he returned by boat to Tosa.[99] Of course, others made special trips to hot springs. A late-seventeenth century account even noted that the therapeutic value of the spas was giving some women an excuse to get away from husband and home: "Recently the numbers of women who abandon their husbands at home under the pretext of going to hot-springs for therapy and spend money on pleasure-seeking travel (*yusan tabi*) has been great."[100]

So many accounts of trips to hot springs begin with an explanation of the journey in terms of curing a particular health problem that one suspects that in many cases it was little more than a literary device. Nevertheless, the curative powers of Arima (part of Kobe city today), near Osaka, were so well regarded that even daimyo and other samurai were granted permission to visit it.[101] As the travel handbook *Ryokō yōjin shū* informed its readers, hot springs "are not only for those seeking to improve their health, but also for pilgrims and pleasure-seekers." Trips to hot springs, it said, were popular among all segments of the population.[102]

Just like pilgrims, those taking the waters always brought gifts back home with them. A late Tokugawa foreign visitor to Japan observed that at Miyanoshita, one of the "seven hot springs" of Hakone, camphor-wood boxes, marquetry and toys of different sorts, very pretty and tasteful, were available "which the bathers take home as keepsakes to their families." Noting the similarity with a resort in his native England, he remarked: "It is a most fashionable watering-place, a sort of Japanese Tunbridge Wells."[103]

The fact that about one-fifth of *Ryokō yōjin shū* is devoted to a province-by-province listing and account of hot springs is a reflection of their popularity. Although not an exhaustive list, it includes 292 places in forty provinces. Some of the more popular waters were at Arima, Atami and Hakone Yumoto in the Kantō region; and Kusatsu and Ikaho, in Kōzuke. Arima, which was known for its female bath attendants and prostitute-courtesans, had as many as 1,000 households late in the Tokugawa period, and according to one traveler, had been the most popular hot springs in Japan since the turn of the nineteenth century.[104] Lodging records from Kusatsu dating from the early nineteenth century inform us that the annual number of visitors there ranged from 9,245 to 13,155.[105]

In addition to stops at hot springs resorts, pilgrims' itineraries nearly always included stays in major urban centers, such as Edo, Osaka, Kyoto, Nagoya, and Nara, where cultural events, like the theater, were a main attraction.[106] A full one-third of Kiyokawa Hachirō's trip around Japan was spent in them; the longest stay, twenty-six days, was in Edo. Many travelers who included a few days in the bakufu capital in their itineraries tended to follow set courses in their sightseeing; their trips invariably included stops at Yoshiwara, Asakusa, and Daimyō koji, the latter being where the mansions of the most powerful lords were located.[107]

THE MAJOR PILGRIMAGE SITES

Ise Shrine was the foremost Japanese pilgrimage site. In Saikaku's words, "Surely there is no shrine as dear to us as the holy Ise Shrine."[108] It is difficult to provide concrete figures, but based on contemporary accounts, it has been estimated that for the first half of the nineteenth century as many as 400,000 to 500,000 pilgrims were drawn to Ise in busy years and 200,000 to 240,000 in slow ones.[109] Perhaps it was because of the extraordinarily large number of pilgrims to Ise that a special saddle holding three persons instead of the usual two was used on post horses plying the Ise road.[110] No doubt the number of pilgrims varied as a result of economic fluctuations, which are reflected in local records of participation. Kibita village (Harima), for example, was responsible for as many as forty-five pilgrims in good years and as few as two in bad.

Ise was, as Kaempfer indicated, extremely popular among the residents of the Kantō and Ōshū areas. Figures from before the Genroku period are not available, but it is apparent that the Ise faith, while known in Kyushu and the north, was not widespread there. For peripheral areas farthest from Ise such as Kyushu and Tōhoku, pilgrimage to Ise, even late in the Tokugawa period, was truly a "once-in-a-lifetime" goal; yet in the nearby Kinai and Tōkai regions, househeads might go as many as four or five times.[111]

A major reason for the popularity of the Ise pilgrimage was the network of religious confraternities (*kō*) created by Ise priests (*oshi*). By the mid-nineteenth century their efforts extended the catchment area of the pilgrimage to all areas of Japan, with the exception of the Tōhoku area. The priests traveled to their parishes at least once prior to the pilgrimage season in late winter or early spring and distributed religious charms, souvenirs, or small gifts such as tea, fans, or face powder (*oshiroi*), a speciality product of Ise. In Ise the priest arranged for lodging, sometimes hosted his guests at elaborate banquets, and led his parishioners to the shrine.[112]

The popularity of this pilgrimage peaked in the early eighteenth century, along with the number of priests at the Outer Shrine, which totaled 615 in 1724.[113] Religious confraternities provided perhaps the greatest opportunity for travel. While Ise groups (Ise-*kō*) could be found across most of the country, groups for Zenkō-ji, Fuji-san and other places had a more local, regional distribution. Some Ise confraternity groups sent members—generally only househeads—on pilgrimage on rotation once a year, while others sent their members from once a month to once every three or five years; according to the records of a village in Nambu domain, more than one member from each household made the trip to Ise between the years 1800–1839, with as few as four and as many as thirty-six going in a particular year.[114] During some years the entire confraternity membership might make the trip, and on one journey there were as many as a hundred persons.[115]

Confraternity groups from different villages often banded together, probably for companionship and reasons of safety, and traveled as a larger group. For example, fifty-one people from twenty villages in Aizu district made the pilgrimage to Ise together, with stops along the way at Nikkō, Kyoto, and Zenkō-ji.[116] At the pilgrimage site these individuals from different villages sometimes pooled their money to donate a stone lantern to the shrine or temple.[117] While individual confraternity groups did not usually cross village boundaries, these informal associations of groups from different villages expanded the social worlds of individuals, helping to break down local isolation.

Most *kō* were open to men only, but it was possible for non-members, including women, to travel with a particular group on pilgrimage.[118] Moreover, from about the middle of the Tokugawa period, women's confraternities began to form (and some still exist today). According to one mid-eighteenth century account, "all-women groups of twenty to thirty members can travel to Ise without any harm befalling them. Truly, this is due to the divine protection of the Ise Shrine."[119]

Large-scale pilgrimages to Ise, drawing people from all parts of the country, took place three times during the Edo period: in 1705, 1771, and 1830. These *okagemairi* were different from regular pilgrimages in that they were frenzied, spontaneous events, touched off by the rumor of falling amulets; and they occurred at roughly sixty-year intervals. No doubt the *oshi* played a role in encouraging the "spontaneity" of the events. As noted in the previous chapter, *okagemairi* did not take people's work schedules at all into account.[120] Unlike routine pilgrimage, which usually took place during the lax winter months, before the spring planting season, *okagemairi* usually took place during the busy late spring and early summer months, making the pilgrimage a true escape from life. These cyclical events attracted large numbers of women of all ages, children, and indentured servants—segments of the population that found it the most difficult to get official permission to travel.[121]

Urban centers played a dominant role in these pilgrimages, although the trips did not necessarily begin there. For example, the last major *okagemairi*, in 1830, began in rural Shikoku before spreading to urban settlements in the Kinai. The *okagemairi* of 1705 began in the Kinai region and drew large numbers from Kyoto and Osaka;[122] the total number of pilgrims was said to be 3.62 million, with as many as 220,000 to 230,000 pouring into Ise on a single day over a fifty-day period. At Hakone, as mentioned earlier, a staggering 33,000 pilgrims were counted passing through the sekisho on a single day, the last day of the first month, in 1705.[123] The following *okagemairi* of 1771 began in the Uji area as women and children abruptly left their work in the tea fields and headed for Ise. The movement soon spread to all areas of the country except for the northeast and southern Kyushu. Although participation was estimated at around 2 million, at least one scholar believes that it was probably as large as the 1705 event.[124] The largest mass pilgrimage, and the most richly documented, was the last one, which began in Awa in 1830. Although its geographic scope was more restricted—the pilgrimage had little impact on Kantō, Tōhoku, and Kyushu—according to contemporary accounts, as many as 5 million are said to have participated.[125]

Second after Ise in popularity was the Saikoku or Western pilgrimage, a circuit of thirty-three Kannon temples spread out over thirteen provinces, twelve of which were in the Kinai, but were largely concentrated in Kyoto and Nara. (See Map 4.) Beginning in Kii province near present-day Wakayama, the circuit "curved back inland through Nara, and then, in its very middle, contained several stations in and around the capital. From there it went in a generally western direction as far as Himeji on the Inland Sea, before going nearly straight north to the Japan Sea, where it turned west and then north to its conclusion in Gifu prefecture."[126] A round trip from Edo with no side trips was a journey of about 2,000 kilometers. Like the Ise pilgrimage, the Western circuit had its origins in the history of a much earlier day, the late Heian period, but both could reach the height of their popularity only once commoners were able to participate in large numbers during the Edo period. According to Kaempfer, pilgrims on this circuit "commonly travel two or three together, singing a miserable Quanwon [Kannon]-song from house to house, and sometimes playing upon a fiddle or upon a Guitar, as vagabond beggars do in Germany: However they do not importune travelers for their charity. They have the names of such Quanwon Temples, as they have not yet visited, writ upon a small board hanging about their neck in proper order."[127]

According to a study of votive cards pilgrims left at temples, the Western circuit experienced three high points of popularity, the first occurring during the turn of the seventeenth century, and the other two around the mid to late eighteenth century and the beginning of the nineteenth. The pilgrimage was a well-entrenched tradition in the Kinai area, but during its first period of popularity the Kantō produced the largest number of pilgrims. Later in the eighteenth century, with the exception of Musashi province, the numbers dropped considerably due to the development of regional pilgrimage routes there.[128]

The third major pilgrimage was the Shikoku *henro*, a clockwise, circular route of eighty-eight Buddhist temples beginning in Awa province, passing through Tosa and Iyo, before finishing up in Sanuki 1,200 kilometers later. Its origins lie in the Kamakura period and were founded on the belief that Kōbō Daishi (774–835) had completed the same route when returning to Shikoku after his conversion to Buddhism. While the Ise pilgrimage peaked in popularity in the early eighteenth century, the Shikoku circuit did not begin to attract a large number of travelers until the economic surge of the Genroku period (1688–1703). No doubt Shikoku's inaccessibility and the generally poor conditions of transport on the island contributed to its slow start.[129]

The Shikoku circuit always drew the largest number of pilgrims from Shikoku and central Japan, especially those on the Inland Sea side, but in 1689, authorities in Nagoya were reporting that, "In recent years men and

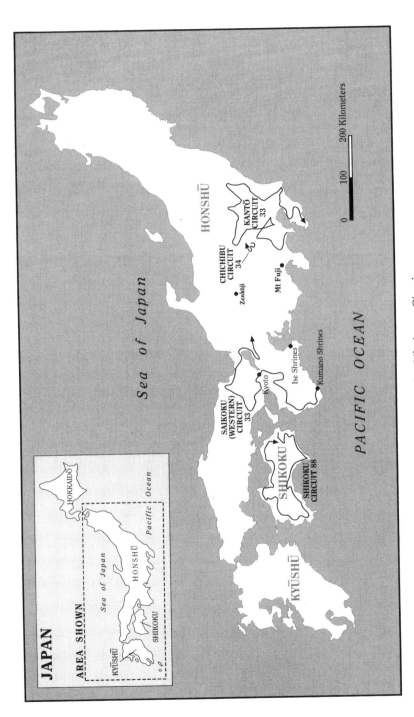

Map 4 The Major Pilgrimage Circuits

women from the castle town have been traveling on pilgrimage to the Western or Shikoku circuits, and their numbers continue to grow every year. We hear that for the past two years particularly large numbers have gone. From now on apply to the proper city officials for permission to travel."[130]

The number of people traveling this circuit decreased in areas farther east, and was quite low in the north. It was a long trip for easterners just to get to Shikoku; therefore, those who did come were most likely to perform the Shikoku circuit, or part of it, in conjunction with the Western circuit or the Ise pilgrimage. Tosa's records from 1764 indicate that 200 to 300 people from outside the domain were passing through daily during a six-month period, meaning a total of 30,000 to 40,000 pilgrims for the half-year. Estimating annual figures based on this data is, of course, hazardous because of the seasonal nature of pilgrimage; for example, another source puts the annual number of pilgrims in the area of 10,000 to 20,000.[131] From evidence of the growth in the number of pilgrims' lodges and alms-giving groups formed, one authority believes that the Shikoku *henro* did not reach its peak of popularity until the beginning of the nineteenth century.[132] Unlike the Ise pilgrimage, where group travel was the norm, pilgrims on the Shikoku route tended to go alone. This factor, together with the relative lack of brothels along the route, imbued the pilgrimage with more of a religious flavor than the others.

Although not officially part of the Shikoku circuit, most travelers on that pilgrimage stopped at Konpira-san* as well; for easterners this stop probably marked the western boundary of their travels.[133] As a shrine new to the Edo period, Konpira could not draw on tradition to attract pilgrims, and consequently, like the Shikoku circuit itself, did not become popular until the middle of the Tokugawa period. The main deity enshrined there was associated with ocean navigation; thus, it is believed that the rapid dispersion of the faith was due to the proselytizing efforts of fishermen and water transport merchants with the opening of the eastern and western sea routes in the late seventeenth century. By the beginning of the nineteenth century it was one of the most popular pilgrimage sites

---

*Kotohira is the name of the shrine on Konpira-san, but the names for the shrine and the mountain it sits on have become synonymous with one another.

in the nation. In Kiyokawa's words, "With the exception of Ise, the only shrines or temples that can rival Konpira are Asakusa and Zenkō-ji."[134]

Konpira was, however, able to attract a large number of pilgrims who did not then go on to the Shikoku circuit. Part of the reason for this was its extremely favorable location in terms of transportation. Positioned right on the sea lane for any traffic coming from central or western Japan, Konpira became a standard part of the itinerary for pilgrims headed from there to Kyoto or Ise. From three ports located near present-day Kurashiki in Okayama it was a short boat ride of just a few hours, and from Osaka about three days to Marugame, the entrepôt for Konpira. The pilgrimage had a tremendous economic impact not only on Marugame but on the entire Inland Sea area across the stretch of sea from Konpira.[135]

Another important regional pilgrimage center was Zenkō-ji, which was described by Kiyokawa as the "most bustling place in Shinano."[136] While that in itself may not be saying very much, a side trip off the main road to Zenkō-ji was a standard feature on the itinerary of pilgrims to Ise from the north and east, who usually returned home via the Nakasendō. Pilgrimage there was not limited to easterners, however, as the faith, popular since medieval times in the Kinai, drew many westerners and reached as far north as Nambu (Rikuchū). For many, Zenkō-ji, combined with stops in Edo and at Mount Fuji, provided an attractive travel package which would take them far from home and the familiar tourist and pilgrimage sites there.[137]

One did not necessarily have to travel great distances to go on pilgrimage, as a number of important regional centers developed in the second half of the Tokugawa period, mostly in the east. The most popular of these were Mount Fuji, Ōyama, and the Chichibu Kannon-temple circuit. Pilgrimage to Ōyama, in fact, was often combined with a stop at Enoshima or the hot springs of Hakone, and the Chichibu circuit. It was also the custom for pilgrims to Mount Fuji to stop at Ōyama on their return; failing to do so was said to have been tantamount to not completing one's pilgrimage in full (*katamairi*)—an unpropitious act.[138] Confraternity groups existed for both Ōyama and Fuji, helping spread their popularity throughout the Kantō and its perimeter provinces.[139] Replicas of the Saikoku and Shikoku circuits were also developed in the east and north and provided those not able to travel afar with a form of recreation closer to home. Although these regional centers played an important part in early modern pilgrimage, we have very few contemporary records with which to detail that role. The reason for this lies largely with the fact that people tended to keep diaries only when on long trips away from home. Thus, most of the records we have are for the Ise pilgrimage and were not written by people from the Kinai region.[140]

SOCIAL PARTICIPANTS

In ancient times it was the court aristocracy who went on pilgrimage. The medieval era saw the emergence of warriors and wealthy farmers as pilgrims. It was even possible for some less wealthy peasants from the Kinai region to travel to Kumano and Ise because of their close physical proximity. In the early modern period, however, pilgrimage was a social act performed by a wide range of social classes, but it was clearly dominated by commoners and not warriors. The pattern set in the Kinai area during the medieval years spread to almost the entire country as more and more peasants, with improving economic and travel conditions, particularly from the Genroku period on, were able to participate. Long-distance pilgrimage became the hallmark of the early modern period.

The association of pilgrimage with commoners was so strong that, when in the last years of the Tokugawa period, Sir Rutherford Alcock informed some officials of his desire to make a pilgrimage to Mount Fuji, he was told that it was "not consistent with the dignity of a Daimio, or even an officer of any rank, to make the pilgrimage—perhaps because too many of the greasy mob must unavoidably come in close contact with them."[141] Women traveled in far greater numbers than ever before; some even traveled in groups without male chaperons. The poor, too, were able to participate because of the popularization of the custom of almsgiving.

Men and women from samurai households played but a minor role in pilgrimage of the Tokugawa period. Daimyo travel was constrained, as they were required to obtain permission from the bakufu for any movement out of Edo or their domains; they also needed permission to deviate from their established course on the alternate attendance in order to make a pilgrimage.[142] Recreational travel for domainal retainers was strictly regulated and many domains—Kurume, Yanagawa, Wakayama, and Matsushiro, to name a few—banned it outright, at least for certain periods of time. In Nakatsu domain (Bungo), admittedly not an exciting place from Fukuzawa Yukichi's description of it, records show that only 40 samurai—or about one a year—applied to leave the domain during the years 1716–1750. Since it was difficult for a samurai to get permission for private travel, pilgrimage was often combined with official business, and this is indicated by the records of samurai sent on domainal business for Yanagawa (Chikugo) over the years 1781–1860. Incomplete records provide evidence that Konpira, with 39 samurai visitors, and Ise, with 28, were the most popular places, but the majority of bushi probably never had the opportunity for this kind of travel. A number of samurai belonged to the Sanuki parish of an Ise priest named Kurida, but those that went on pilgrimage were few indeed: only one out of the 134 pilgrims from the parish made the trip to Ise in 1772; two years later, only 3 out of a total of 179 people went.[143]

In addition to the political constraints on their mobility, samurai travel was also limited by a lack of finances. Fukuzawa, traveling from Nakatsu to Osaka, did not, unlike the other, presumably commoner passengers on board, have the money to make a pilgrimage to Konpira, even though the boat brought them close by.[144] Such was the economic plight of the lower samurai. With the exception of daimyo transfers, women from samurai households rarely traveled. For example, records from Usui sekisho reveal that only 204 had passed through the barriers there in 1790.[145]

Male commoners made up the bulk of the participants in regular, that is, non-_okagemairi,_ pilgrimage (see Figure 11). Confraternity members were usually househeads; and therefore the increase in the number of independent households in the Tokugawa period increased the pool of people most likely to go on pilgrimages.[146] The important role of urban dwellers in _okagemairi_ has already been noted; merchants, in particular, played a strong supporting part. Travel, in fact, appears to have been a hobby for many of them. For example, merchants from Sakai and the Lake Biwa area were famous for their extensive and frequent recreational travel, one Sakai businessman making no less than thirty-three trips to Ise.[147]

Figure 11 Group of Country Bumpkins Sightseeing in Edo. Hiroshige, *Tōkaidō gojūsantsugi saiken ezu.* Kanagawa Prefectural Library.

Not only did a larger number of househeads engage in pilgrimage in the Tokugawa period, but a wider spectrum of society was able to participate through the inclusion of women, children, and the poor. Because of the social and institutional controls directed at limiting their physical mobility, most women left home without obtaining permission from the proper government authorities. Even a woman belonging to a rural samurai household, like Kiyokawa Hachirō's mother, told everyone she would be making a pilgrimage to a nearby temple; but she actually intended to travel for an extended period of time to Ise and beyond.[148] Penalties, as we have seen, were not severe, if imposed at all, since there was a general social attitude that making a pilgrimage, particularly to Ise, was a virtuous act.

Only a small percentage of the pilgrims who went to Ise during non-*okagemairi* years were women. Representative are the records of one Ise priest from Sanuki for scattered years during the period 1782–1859; they indicate that women comprised only 3 to 7.6 percent of the pilgrims from his parish.[149] As noted earlier, women were sometimes included in mostly male confraternity groups; and, although not a widespread phenomenon, women's confraternity groups for the pilgrimage to Ise, Fuji-san, and probably for Zenkō-ji, existed during the Tokugawa period.

Women did, however, play an important role in pilgrimage to the Western and Shikoku circuits, as well as to Zenkō-ji. The records of a village head in Sanuki province, for example, indicate that, during the first three decades of the nineteenth century, almost equal numbers of men and women from his settlement traveled on the Shikoku circuit. In fact, for almost half that period, women outnumbered men.[150] The lodging records kept at Seishinbō, a temple inn at Zenkō-ji, reveal that a startling 48 percent of the guests over the years 1848–1871 were female.[151] Not only did a greater percentage of women go to Zenkō-ji—most of them from surrounding provinces—but evidence shows that they sometimes eschewed male companionship and traveled by themselves in groups, or else with just a single male. Lodging records from Seishinbō from the year 1857 indicate that 149 men traveled in 55 all-male groups, 99 women traveled in 25 all-female groups, and 301 people were in mixed groups. Of the people in the mixed groups, however, 89 were in 19 groups with only one male each. One cannot help but wonder whether all these women climbed through the same hole in the palisade at Sekigawa sekisho as did Kiyokawa's mother.

Women were attracted to the Shikoku route as well; for women from Tokushima domain, making a pilgrimage to the eighty-eight religious sites in the circuit was an important rite of passage before marriage.[152] They were also attracted to Shikoku in part because of the institutionalized system of alms-giving (*settai, segyō,* or *hoshi*) in place there. Almsgivers believed that they would benefit spiritually or materially or both through their generosity and that pilgrims could be disguised divinities; in the case of the Shikoku *henro*, many believed that any pilgrim could be the reincarnation of Kōbō Daishi himself. Pilgrims on both the Ise pilgrimage and the Shikoku circuit were offered free food, lodging, transport services, and money. Some might even return home with a profit, as was the case for a number of pilgrims after a trip to Ise in 1767, a non-*okagemairi* year.[153]

The poor were also able to participate in pilgrimage because of alms-giving. One record from Awa stated that 90 out of 100 on the Shikoku pilgrimage were poor townsmen and peasants, particularly from Ōshū and Kyushu.[154] There were so many of them on the Ise pilgrimage that multitudes were: "obliged to pass whole nights, lying in the open fields, expos'd to all the injuries of wind and weather, some for want of rooms in inns . . . others out of poverty."[155] Not surprisingly, dead people lying along the road were, at times, a common sight. Women leaving home without the permission of both the proper government authorities and their husbands would not likely have had any money and thus relied on alms-giving to make it to their destination and back.

Children also left home without permission: *Okagemairi* drew large numbers of children, such as the six-year-old mentioned in the Introduction who defied his parents by joining up with his friends headed for Ise in 1830. The official records of a small domain in northeast Japan, Hachinohe, are full of accounts of children traveling.[156] Ernest Satow wrote of meeting small children on the road. He saw "two little boys of twelve and fourteen years of age, who, having begged their way as pilgrims all the way from Yedo to the sacred temples of Ise and of Konpira in Sanuki, were now on their way home, carrying slung across their backs huge packages of temple charms done up in oiled paper."[157] Kiyokawa met a

number of unaccompanied children on the Tōkaidō at Hata, near
Hakone, without even a coin in their pockets. Taking pity on them, he
put them up for a night at an inn.[158] The sekisho there at Hakone recorded in a much earlier year (1651) that 12,500 children passed through
its gates (during an unspecified period of time), so apparently their numbers were great at times.[159] Children were thus an important part of the
wide spectrum of society that was able to engage in travel for the first
time in the Tokugawa period.

Conclusion

This book has employed travel and transport as a lens through which to view state and society in the Edo period. In its formative period, the Tokugawa bakufu created a national system of transportation, one which drew wide praise from European travelers, who compared conditions in Japan favorably with those back home. Political forces shaped the contours of that system, making it less efficient than it might have been, but nonetheless it functioned adequately, meeting most of the needs of the time.

Economic forces shaped the contours of the transport system as well: restrictions on the use of side roads, short-cuts and the use of water routes were imposed in order to maintain the financial health of the bakufu's monopoly system by directing traffic onto the main roads. The cost of reconstructing bridges destroyed by raging waters led, in certain instances, to the decision to institute a river-crossing service rather than to rebuild the structure. Likewise, the decision to maintain river-fording operations rather than to institute ferry-boat crossings was usually dictated by the desire to save jobs that would have been eliminated by the more labor-saving method.

These political and economic influences on the transport system, together with the frequent reliance on ferry crossings rather than bridges and the scarcity of carts on the Gokaidō, might give the false impression that the Tokugawa system was retarded in development and symptomatic of a regressive government; but, in fact, we have seen that conscious restrictions on the use of carts kept road conditions good and avoided traffic tie-ups. The reliance on ferry crossings, furthermore, had parallels elsewhere, as it was the norm, not the exception, in early modern Europe.

To maintain its centralized transport network, the Tokugawa employed a number of financial strategies, some of them quite inventive and others misguided, and were forced to turn to a system of corvée labor, or *sukegō,* when the volume of official traffic grew so large that it exceeded the ability of the post stations to handle it alone. This form of taxation, which was the closest that the Tokugawa bakufu came to instituting a national system, became a source of conflict of economic interests between the state, represented by the post stations, and assisting villages. It also caused tension and conflict between villages, who, acting as corporations, tried to minimize the economic costs to themselves and pass them on to others. Furthermore, common concerns of assisting villages servicing the same station or stations linked the villages into regional economic units that transcended local village boundaries.

The *sukegō* levy affected a growing number of villages, transforming the system and eliciting a variety of economic responses that are indicative of the complex patterns of life in this agrarian society. A repertoire of contention was developed by assisting villages against the *sukegō* levy, including passive resistance, remonstrance, and formal petitioning to the Magistrate of Road Affairs, as well as violent protest. While violent outbursts were the most conspicuous forms of contention, they were infrequent, and distract us from the more significant, continuous pattern of signalling, negotiation, and struggle between assisting villages and post station authorities. This process of give-and-take demonstrates the limits of the state's ability to exercise authority at the local level.

The Tokugawa bakufu, limited in its resources and aims, had been able with great effort to impose a political settlement on a country that had been engaged in civil war for more than a century. In the chaos of the early seventeenth century, strict controls on movement seemed called for; and the chief mechanism by which the state attempted to regulate it was the system of sekisho and the permits that were often required to pass through them.

The bakufu relied on the fudai daimyo to administer most of the sekisho, and by default gave these local officials great flexibility to interpret directives issued by the center. Some individual sekisho administrators also tried to draw in neighboring villages as arms of the state to prevent evasion of the system, but the local population was not always very cooperative. There was little incentive to enforce laws created by distant and largely unseen political figures. Sympathy and common sense seemed to dictate that travel not be made more difficult for individuals than it already was by insisting on enforcing these laws. The historical record has revealed many examples of travelers who were aided by local residents, or sekisho officials, in their efforts to go around or through the holes in the barrier networks. Likewise, village headmen, who were the central link between the state and the village, could not always be counted on to support the state, as they were known to undercut the control system by issuing travel permits too freely, and, as we saw in one case, even going so far as to commit *sekisho yaburi* by evading sekisho.

Our examination of travel regulations and their effect on society has also revealed the limits of the state's ability to impose its will. Permit systems devised early in the period were created by government officials who could not possibly have foreseen that the climate of peace and economic growth would unleash the great energies of the people in the form of increased travel. Also, with the onset of the "great peace" there was no need for the state to try to exercise the wide range of power over people's lives to which it once laid claim. (The same was true, of course, of the bakufu and its relations with the domains.) Official procedures for travel were therefore never significantly amended to take into account the substantial physical mobility that characterized society from the late seventeenth century on. Troublesome procedures for obtaining permits only encouraged evasion of the system, particularly for women, who had to overcome considerable political and social controls in order to travel.

While travel restrictions were extensive in volume, they were not as strict as they appear at face value; moreover, the restrictions applied by government officials were largely inspired by economic concerns rather than a desire for totalitarian control. The widespread practice of *nuke-mairi*, the variety of ingenious ways in which resourceful commoners circumvented restrictions, and the volume of complaints by government officials against the numbers of people flouting the law clearly indicate that travel regulations served much the same function as sumptuary legislation—and were equally ineffective. The legal and physical walls constructed by the state to control travel were only marginally effective: they were not able to stem the tide of commoners wanting to travel.

That those controls were ineffective is partly due to the fact that the system was so weakly coercive. The state exhorted the people not to engage in "useless travel," but realized that it was relatively powerless to stop them. Fear of punishment was not an effective deterrent to travelers. While bounty systems were established in some places, offering rewards to people who caught travelers evading sekisho, they do not appear to have attracted much interest. Tokugawa justice certainly could be draconian at times, but it was more lenient with ordinary travelers who broke the law. The application of regulations at sekisho was much more flexible than suggested by statute, as offenses were often downgraded to avoid prosecuting commoners. This flexibility has been explained by one scholar of Japanese law "as a preference of the regime for moral rather than legal controls; law was said to be a second-best method, to be used only as a last resort."[1] Similarly, pilgrims who fled from their homes and domains without permission on *nukemairi* rarely faced punishment (unless they did something illegal that was later discovered).

Thus it is important for us to recognize not only the interventions of the state but also its abstentions. The development of passports (in contrast with sekisho transit permits) and *tōchū tegata*, permits that could be obtained en route, were tantamount to abstentions. They represent a de facto devolution of authority to issue written permission to travel, and thus reveal the unintrusive nature of the state: This state did not try to oppose the growing social forces which in effect demanded an easing of travel restrictions.

While the Gokaidō network gave priority usage to officials designated by the bakufu, the creation of a well-integrated transport network had the unintended effect of stimulating the development of travel as recreation. This was because recreational travel, or tourism, "requires a population with the money and the leisure to travel, an adequate means of transportation, and the conditions of reasonable safety and comfort at the places people go to visit. It also demands a body of images and descriptions of those places—a mythology of unusual things to see—to excite people's imaginations and induce them to travel."[2] All of this was in place for Tokugawa Japan by the late eighteenth or early nineteenth century. The transport infrastructure in its fullest form included firewood and full-service inns, restaurants, teahouses, travel guide services, and souvenir shops. These all developed to meet the needs of a growing number of travelers.

During the Tokugawa period travel was not restricted to an aristocratic class, as it had been in earlier times. Growth and commercialization of the economy, the proliferation of confraternity groups, and the practice of alms-giving were some of the factors responsible for the spread of pilgrimage and recreational travel across a broad spectrum of society. Despite their lower social position, commoners, in fact, found it easier, for economic and other reasons, to engage in recreational travel than samurai.

By the early nineteenth century travel had developed into what seems like a national obsession. The evidence for this can be found in the development of a culture of travel, the physical manifestations of which were produced in large numbers in an attempt to keep up with an insatiable demand. Travel guidebooks, personal travel accounts, wood-block prints, travel game boards, maps, and school textbooks did much to excite the popular imagination, induce people to set out on the road, and remind many of the experience once they had returned to the comfort of home.

The development of travel as recreation in the early modern period was of course part of a wider phenomenon: the popularization of culture. This phenomenon is evident in other areas of Tokugawa life as well, such as literature, scholarship, and the arts.[3] The diffusion of popular culture was promoted by numerous factors, only a few of which can be mentioned here. The bakufu's domains, spread out as they were in forty-seven of the sixty-eight provinces of Japan, certainly worked against parochialism. Major urban centers such as Edo, Osaka, Kyoto, Sakai, and Nagasaki were strategic points where people from all over Japan met and exchanged ideas. Furthermore, although not the subject of the present study, the political system of alternate attendance (*sankin kōtai*) played a key role in promoting the diffusion of culture in a variety of patterns.[4]

Pilgrimage and recreational travel, and the well developed transport infrastructure that made them possible, played an important part in the emergence and diffusion of Edo-period popular culture. Customs and material culture—local speciality goods as diverse as porcelain or ceramic

ware, Abe River mochi, and Edo prints; rice seed; kabuki librettos and
costumes; as well as other clothing—were carried as baggage when travelers departed on and returned from their journeys.[5] Short stays in the
major urban centers were an important component of the travel experience, and surely influenced the lifestyles and mindsets of participants.

Through travel, individuals could break free from the constraints
which might otherwise have tied them to their localities. While the
range of geographic mobility was limited in this era by technological and
economic factors, the known boundaries of personal experience, both
individual and collective, widened greatly. Irokawa Daikichi's study of
early Meiji cultural figures shows their remarkably wide geographic distribution throughout the country, the result of the constant stirring of
the cultural melting pot in Tokugawa Japan permitted by travel.[6]

Once on the road, the Tokugawa man or woman could make the
acquaintance of people from across political boundaries, as the following
anecdote from Jippensha Ikku's *Tōkaidō Hizakurige* relates: Sharing the
boatride down the Yodo River from Fushimi to Osaka with Yaji and Kita
were men from Kyoto, Osaka, Nagasaki, and Echigo. During the bore-
dom of the overnight trip they were able to exchange local culture, the
Echigo and Nagasaki men singing songs from their home provinces. Yaji
and Kita, too, were called on to entertain the other passengers, and Yaji
attempted to imitate a famous Edo actor. The Kyoto man, who had lived
in Edo for a number of years, realized that Yaji's imitation was poor and
exposed his prank to the others. The Osaka man, displaying a knowledge
of Edo culture, successfully imitated the actor.[7] In a similar, non-fictional
account, Fukuzawa Yukichi, traveling from Shimonoseki to Osaka in
1854, shared a boat "with all kinds of travelers—a foolish-looking son of
a rich man; a bald-headed grandsire; some geisha, gay and richly dressed,
and other women of questionable reputation; farmers; priests; rich and
poor: all sorts, crowded together in the narrow boat, drinking, gambling,
clamoring over any nonsensical matter."[8] By traveling, the people of
Tokugawa Japan expanded their knowledge of the world in which they
lived. Or, as Jippensha Ikku said, the "Edo man can make acquaintance
with the Satsuma sweet potato."[9]

The Japanese, in other words, were coming to know themselves and
their land more fully. Through social intercourse between people from

diverse localities, the exchange of ideas and popular culture could take place, building the solid foundation which was necessary for the formation of a national identity in the years after the arrival of the black ships.

Appendices
Notes
List of Works Cited
Index

Appendix 1
Overview of Tōkaidō Post Stations (1843)

	Population	Households	Daimyo Inns	Commoner Inns
Shinagawa	6,890	1,561	3	93
Kawasaki (r)	2,433	541	2	72
Kanagawa (r)	5,793	1,341	2	58
Hodogaya	2,928	558	4	67
Totsuka	2,906	613	5	75
Fujisawa	4,089	913	2	45
Hiratsuka	2,114	443	2	54
Ōiso	3,056	676	3	66
Odawara (c/r)	5,404	1,542	8	95
Hakone	844	197	6	36
Mishima	4,048	1,025	5	74
Numazu (c)	5,346	1,234	4	55
Hara	1,939	398	1	16
Yoshiwara (r)	2,832	653	5	60
Kambara (c)	2,480	509	2	32
Yui	713	160	2	32
Okitsu	1,668	316	4	32
Ejiri	6,498	1,340	5	50
Fuchū (c)	14,071	3,673	4	34
Mariko	795	211	3	24
Okabe	2,322	487	4	27
Fujieda	4,425	1,061	2	37
Shimada (r)	6,727	1,461	3	48
Kanaya (r)	4,271	1,004	4	51
Nissaka	750	168	2	33
Kakegawa (c)	3,443	960	2	30

	Population	Households	Daimyo Inns	Commoner Inns
Fukuroi	843	195	3	50
Mitsuke	3,935	1,029	3	56
Hamamatsu (c)	5,964	1,622	6	94
Maisaka	2,475	541	3	28
Arai	3,474	797	3	26
Shirasuka	2,704	613	2	27
Futagawa	1,468	328	2	38
Yoshida (c)	5,277	1,293	3	65
Goyu	1,298	316	2	62
Akasaka	1,304	349	4	62
Fujikawa	1,213	302	2	36
Okazaki (c)	6,494	1,565	6	112
Chirifu	1,620	292	2	35
Narumi	3,643	847	3	68
Atsuta (c)	10,342	2,924	3	248
Kuwana (c)	8,848	2,544	6	120
Yokkaichi	7,114	1,811	3	98
Ishiyakushi	991	241	3	15
Shōno	855	211	2	15
Kameyama (c)	1,549	567	2	21
Seki	1,942	632	4	42
Sakanoshita	564	153	4	48
Tsuchiyama	1,505	351	2	44
Mizuguchi (c)	2,692	692	2	41
Ishibe	1,606	458	2	32
Kusatsu (c)	2,351	586	4	72
Ōtsu	14,892	3,650	3	71
Fushimi (c)	24,227	6,245	6	39
Yodo (c)	2,847	836	0	16
Hirakata	1,549	378	1	69
Moriguchi	764	177	1	27

Source: Kodama, *Shukueki*, pp. 177–187.

Note: c = castle town; r = river crossing station

Appendix 2
Sekisho Travel Permits

Sekisho Transit Permit no. 1

Four women, among them one with cut hair [*kamikiri*], and one who is not married, will be traveling from Kyoto to Edo. Please grant them safe passage through the sekisho. The four women are the mother of actor Takeshima Kōemon, his wife, daughter, and a maidservant. The City Elders from Taka-segawa Tennō-chō and their Group of Five Households [*goningumi*] are their guarantors. 1706/10/11

[From] Nakane Setsu no kami and Andō Suruga no kami [Kyoto City
    Magistrates]
[To] Imagiri [i.e., Arai] sekisho Inspector of Women

Sekisho Transit Permit no. 2

[Front side:]
Hayakawa Rokurōbei, retainer of Matsudaira Aki no kami, will be traveling to Edo accompanying his wife and children. I respectfully request that the women be granted a transit permit for four females.

[From] Fujimura Hachirōhei, oru-
    sui [Keeper of the castle] for
    Matsudaira Aki no kami
[To] Suo no kamisama [Kyōto
    shoshidai]

[Back side:]
Grant these four women safe passage on the roadways. 1653/2/17

[From] Suo no kami
[To] Inspector of Women from
    Kyoto to Edo

Passport

Genjirō, a peasant from Moro Village in the Saku District of Shinano Province, wishes to make a pilgrimage to various shrines and temples. He is accompanied by one child. It is therefore requested that they be granted safe passage through all sekisho. Furthermore, it is respectfully requested that in case of sickness or death the appropriate village or city officials send notice here and that they be cared for with benevolence according to the customs of the local area.

1782/11/19

Shinano Province, Saku District, Moro
Village headmen
Sadaemon
Goemon

[To] All officials of sekisho, towns, and villages

Sources: *Arai chōshi shiryō hen*, vol. 8, no. 54, p. 185; Ibid., no. 10, p. 129; *Nagano kenshi kinsei shiryō hen*, vol. 2, pt. 2, p. 199.

Notes

The following abbreviations are used:

HGNK   *Hakone gosekisho nikki kakinuki*
KKSS   *Kinsei kōtsū shiryō shū*
NSSS   *Nihon shomin seikatsu shiryō shūsei*
THSS   *Tōkaidō Hakone shuku, sekisho shiryō shū*

INTRODUCTION

1. Theda Skocpol, "Bringing the State Back In: Strategies of Analysis in Current Research," in Peter Evans, Dietrich Rueschemeyer, and Theda Skocpol, eds., *Bringing the State Back In*, p. 7.
2. Alfred Stepan, *The State and Society: Peru in Comparative Perspective*, as quoted in Theda Skocpol, "Bringing the State Back In: Strategies of Analysis in Current Research," p. 7.
3. William G. Staples, *Castles of Our Conscience: Social Control and the American State, 1800–1985*, pp. 6–7.
4. Gordon L. Clark and Michael Dear, *State Apparatus: Structures and Language of Legitimacy*, p. 36.
5. For two essays which take different views on the strength of the early modern Japanese state relative to its contemporary European counterparts, see Mary Elizabeth Berry, "Public Peace and Private Attainment: The Goals and Conduct of Power in Early Modern Japan," in *Journal of Japanese Studies*, vol. 12, no. 2, pp. 237–271 (Summer 1986) and James W. White, "State Growth and Popular Protest in Tokugawa Japan," in Ibid., vol. 14, no. 1, pp. 1–25 (Winter 1988).

    Philip C. Brown reviews this debate in the introduction to his *Central Authority and Local Autonomy in the Formation of Early Modern Japan: The Case of Kaga Domain*, especially pp. 10–12, and then in the body of his monograph offers a fresh, local perspective that will no doubt rekindle the debate on the relative strength of bakufu and domain authority in the political order. Brown, White, and this author prefer the term "Tokugawa state" rather than *bakuhan* (lit., "bakufu and domains") state, the latter of which has been widely used by Western scholars. Brown's study of Kaga domain history explores the tension between nominal authority and state capability, and finds that the state's reach exceeded its grasp—a conclusion which this monograph reaches as well. Rejecting the dichotomy of a strong or weak state, he argues that the Tokugawa version lay somewhere in the middle ground, calling it a "flamboyant state." (pp. 232–233) Many thanks to Professor Brown for sharing his work with me while it was in the page proof stage.

6. Evans, Rueschemeyer, Skocpol, eds., *Bringing the State Back In,* pp. iii–vii.
7. John A. Meyer, "Notes towards a Working Definition of Social Control in Historical Analysis," in Stanley Cohen and Andrew Scull, eds., *Social Control and the State,* p. 24.
8. Joel S. Migdal, *Strong Societies and Weak States: State-Society Relations and State Capabilities in the Third World,* p. 22.
9. Miyazaki Katsunori, "Osso daihyōsha no tabi," in Kōtsū shi kenkyū kai, ed., *Nihon kinsei kōtsū shi ronshū,* pp. 303–328.
10. "Ukiyo no arisama," in *NSSS,* vol. 11, *Sesō* pt. 1, Tanigawa Ken'ichi, ed., p. 85.
11. Kiyokawa Hachirō, *Saiyūsō,* pp. 5–6.
12. Dan Fenno Henderson, *Village "Contracts" in Tokugawa Japan,* p. 7.
13. Dan Fenno Henderson, "The Evolution of Tokugawa Law," in John W. Hall and Marius B. Jansen, eds., *Studies in the Institutional History of Early Modern Japan,* p. 228.
14. Yujirō Hayami and Saburō Yamada, "Technological Progress in Agriculture," in Lawrence Klein and Kazushi Ohkawa, eds., *Economic Growth: The Japanese Experience Since the Meiji Era,* pp. 143–144.
15. E.g., R. B. Hall, "The Road in Old Japan," in *Studies in the History of Culture,* p. 154. William H. Coaldrake, in an excellent article on post station architecture, maintains that "unauthorized travelers . . . faced the penalty of execution for traveling without official permits." "Unno: Edo Period Post Town of the Central Alps," *Asian Art,* vol. 5, no. 2, p. 17 (Spring 1992).
16. Richard Rubinger, *Private Academies of Tokugawa Japan,* p. 19.
17. Gabriel Ogundeji Ogunremi, *Counting the Camels: The Economics of Transportation in Pre-industrial Nigeria,* p. 4.
18. E.g., W. H. Boulton, *The Pageant of Transport Through the Ages;* H. T. Dyos and D. H. Aldcroft, *British Transport: An Economic Survey from the Seventeenth Century through the Twentieth.*

19. Michael Robbins, "The Progress of Transport History," *Journal of Transport History*, Third Series, vol. 12, no. 1, p. 85 (March 1991).

20. Hayami Akira, "Labor Migration in a Pre-industrial Society: A Study Tracing the Life Histories of the Inhabitants of a Village," *Keio Economic Studies*, vol. 10, no. 2, p. 5 (1973). Also noteworthy are Susan Hanley's study of migration in Okayama, "Migration and Economic Change in Okayama during the Tokugawa Period," *Keio Economic Studies*, vol. 10, no. 2, pp. 19–36 (1973), and W. Mark Fruin's dissertation, "Labor Migration in Nineteenth Century Japan: A Study Based on Echizen Han."

21. On medieval travel diaries, see Herbert Plutschow and Hideichi Fukuda, *Four Japanese Travel Diaries of the Middle Ages* and Marumo Takeshige, *Chūsei no tabibitotachi.* Also, Donald Keene introduces a number of medieval diaries, some of which may be considered travel diaries, in his *Travelers of a Hundred Ages*, pp. 93–260.

22. Charles H. Cooley, "The Theory of Transportation," *Sociological Theory and Social Research*, p. 40. While published long ago (1894), Cooley's theoretical essay still stands alone.

23. The key contribution of transport to economic development has long been acknowledged. Adam Smith's *The Wealth of Nations* is the seminal work in the field.

24. E.g., Thomas C. Smith, "Farm Family By-employments in Pre-industrial Japan," *Journal of Economic History*, vol. 29, no. 4, pp. 687–715 (1969).

25. See Kawana Noboru, *Kinsei Nihon suiun shi no kenkyū* for a recent and highly accessible history of sea and river transport in early modern Japan.

26. This is in sharp contrast with the situation in the Low Countries in early modern Europe. According to Jan de Vries, the chief function of the elaborate canal system created in the Dutch Republic was not the movement of freight. The canal network, from the middle of the seventeenth to the beginning of the nineteenth century, with its passenger-carrying barges pulled by horses (*trekschuit*), was "almost exclusively dedicated to the movement of people." Jan de Vries, *Barges and Capitalism: Passenger Transportation in the Dutch Economy*, p. 9.

27. William Naff, "Introduction," in his translation of Shimazaki Tōson, *Before the Dawn*, p. 7.

28. John W. Hall, "Rule by Status in Tokugawa Japan," *Journal of Japanese Studies*, vol. 1, no. 1, p. 39 (Autumn 1974).

29. E.g., Isabella L. Bird, *Unbeaten Tracks in Japan;* Major Henry Knollys, *Sketches of Life in Japan;* Leon Descharmes, "Itinerary of a Journey from

Yedo to Kusatsu With Notes Upon the Waters of Kusatsu," *Transactions of the Asiatic Society of Japan,* First Series, vol. 2, pp. 25–54 (1874).

30. Englebert Kaempfer, *History of Japan, Together With a Description of the Kingdom of Siam, 1690–1692,* vol. 2, p. 330.

31. Shinjō Tsunezō, *Sengoku jidai no kōtsū.*

32. Reinhard Bendix, *Kings or People: Power and the Mandate to Rule,* p. 440. Bendix has calculated that in contrast with the long period of peace Japan experienced, France was at war for 115 years during the years 1600–1850; Great Britain, 125; Spain, 160.5; Austria, 129.5; Prussia, 97; and Russia, 147.5.

33. Asai Ryōi, *Tōkaidō meishoki,* vol. 1, p. 3.

34. Susan Hanley and Kozo Yamamura, *Economic and Demographic Change in Tokugawa Japan, 1600–1868,* pp. 24–27.

35. This term is an adaptation of Nishiyama Matsunosuke's *"kōdō bunka."* He discusses it in a number of his works; e.g., "Edo bunka to chihō bunka," *Iwanami kōza Nihon rekishi,* vol. 15, *Kinsei* no. 3, pp. 183–186. Recently, the term has become widely used. See, for example, Takeuchi Makoto, ed., *Bunka no taishūka,* pp. 30–37.

36. Jippensha Ikku, *Hizakurige or Shanks' Mare,* Thomas Satchell, trans., p. 237.

37. Kaempfer, vol. 2, p. 330.

38. Fujitani Yoshio, *'Okagemairi' to 'eejanaika,'* pp. 78, 89–90. He is citing a contemporary account, "Bunsei shin'iki," which states that according to a bakufu census, 4,862,080 people crossed the Miyagawa River to Ise during the high season for pilgrimage. Added to this figure must be an undetermined number of travelers from the Tōkai region who went directly to Ise by boat. The accuracy of the figure is highly suspect, of course, but it indicates that the *okagemairi* of 1830 was of extraordinary, unprecedented proportions.

1. THE ARMS AND LEGS OF THE REALM

1. Tanaka Kyūgu, "Minkan shōyo," in Takimoto Seiichi, ed., *Nihon keizai taiten,* vol. 5, p. 67.

2. E.g., Harold Bolitho, *Treasures Among Men: The Fudai Daimyo in Tokugawa Japan,* pp. 7–19.

3. *KKSS,* vol. 8, no. 33, pp. 14–20. The sengoku daimyo Go-Hōjō, for example, maintained three post horses at each station for official use in peacetime and increased the number to ten during wartime mobilization. Aida Nirō, *Chūsei no sekisho,* pp. 422–428.

4. The concept of the Gokaidō as a system did not emerge immediately in the first years of the Edo period. The establishment of a Magistrate of

Road Affairs in 1659 (as explained in the text below), with jurisdiction over the routes in what would later be called the Gokaidō, indicates that the concept was evolving, but the term was not recognized in legal documents until 1687. The names and Chinese characters to be used for the individual roads in the system were fixed, according to Arai Hakuseki's suggestion, in 1716. Maruyama Yasunari, ed., *Jōhō to kōtsū*, vol. 6 of *Nihon no kinsei*, pp. 206–207.

5. *KKSS*, vol. 8, no. 31, p. 13. The order was given in 1601.
6. Ibid., no. 35, p. 21 and no. 70, p. 38. For the instructions to the station (Mitake), see Ibid., no. 44, pp. 24–25.

   In order to foil potential abusers of the system, the shogunate sent all stations a sample document with which they could check the authenticity of those presented by travelers. Ibid., no. 32, p. 14.
7. Watanabe Kazutoshi, "Edo bakufu rikujō kōtsū seisaku no hatten," in Kodama Kōta, ed., *Nihon kinsei kōtsū shi kenkyū*, p. 7.
8. For Hakone, *KKSS*, vol. 8, no. 140, pp. 82–83; for Totsuka, Ibid., no. 73–no. 74, pp. 40–41; for Kawasaki, Ibid., no. 149, pp. 89–90.
9. *KKSS*, vol. 8, no. 140, p. 82.
10. *Kanagawa ken shi shiryō hen*, vol. 9, *Kinsei* 6, Kanagawa ken kikaku chōsabu ken shi henshū shitsu, ed., no. 77, pp. 125–126.
11. Ibid., no. 75, p. 124.
12. Ibid., no. 77, pp. 125–126 and no. 79, p. 126.
13. On Ōtsu-e, see Watanabe Morimichi, "Ōtsu-e no haitachi to denpa," in Ōishi Shinsaburō, ed., *Edo no chihō bunka*, vol. 1.
14. Most post-station managers were people of local power and usually of warrior lineage. Many also served concurrently as village headmen and/or operators of *honjin* inns. Tanji Kenzō, "Kinsei shukueki ton'yasei no kakuritsu katei," *Nihon rekishi*, vol. 220, pp. 42–59 (1966).
15. *KKSS*, vol. 9, no. 667, pp. 125–126; *Kanagawa ken shi shiryō hen*, vol. 9, *Kinsei* 6, no. 74, p. 120.
16. The *honjin* and *waki-honjin* were the largest and most impressive buildings in the post towns. They were also the only buildings allowed to have gatehouses marking their entrances. Coaldrake, pp. 19–30.
17. Kodama Kōta, *Shukueki*, pp. 177–187. All population figures in this discussion of types of post stations are, unless otherwise noted, from 1843.
18. Haga Noboru, *Shukubamachi*, p. 216. In comparison, only one out of eight wards in Kōfu assumed the function of post station. In castle towns these wards were usually referred to as *tenma-chō* ("post-horse wards"). Tsuchida Ryōichi, "Kōshū dōchū no shukubamachi," p. 547.
19. Fujimoto Toshiharu has analyzied post-station function in terms of the number of inns, both those for official travelers (*honjin*) and those for commoners (*hatagoya*), compared to the total number of households.

"Economic," multi-functional, stations (e.g., Okazaki, Ejiri) had a low number of inns in relation to total household number. "Political" stations (e.g., Hakone and Sakanoshita), were singular in function, having been created as official transport centers, and conversely had a high number of inns. Most stations, however, lay somewhere between these two types and provided links with both "economic" stations and rural marketing centers (*zaigōmachi*). The number of inns per station was considerably higher for Nakasendō post stations, indicating that transport-related functions were paramount on that road. See his *Kinsei toshi no chiiki kōzō: Sono rekishi chirigakuteki kenkyū,* pp. 44–47.

20. Philipp Franz von Seibold, *Edo sanpu kikō,* Saitō Makoto, trans., p. 220.
21. *KKSS,* vol. 8, no. 33, pp. 14–20. For example, Hodogaya was granted about 167 square meters per post horse maintained at the station; Yokkaichi, 283; but Fujieda, only 99.
22. Ibid., no. 178, p. 114. These exemptions, in their expanded form, amounted to an average of 44,433 sq. meters per station on the Tōkaidō, 16,775 meters on the Nakasendō, 30,386 on the Nikkō dōchū, 50,802 on the Ōshū dōchū, and 3,297 on the Kōshū dōchū. Averages were calculated by Watanabe Kazutoshi, *Kaidō to sekisho: Arai sekisho no rekishi,* p. 26. Figures for individual stations can be found in *KKSS,* vol. 10, pp. 56–61.
23. *KKSS,* vol. 10, pp. 225–227.
24. *KKSS,* vol. 8, no. 163, pp. 100–101.
    As was the case for land tax exemptions, the amount varied from station to station. Stipends for both station managers and the messenger relay service were paid by local intendants out of collected tax rice. Ibid., nos. 164–165, pp. 101–102. A record of stipends for all Gokaidō stations can be found in *KKSS,* vols. 4 and 5.
25. *The Cambridge History of Europe,* vol. 2, *Trade and Industry in the Middle Ages,* M. M. Postan and E. E. Rich, eds., p. 322.
26. Fernand Braudel, *The Perspective of the World: Civilization and Capitalism,* vol. 2, *The Wheels of Commerce,* p. 349.
27. *KKSS,* vol. 8, no. 233, pp. 156–157 and no. 344, pp. 242–243. When passing through Kyoto, Osaka, or Edo, however, travelers were required to continue on to the next station without stopping at the city's relay station. Ibid., no. 431, pp. 318–319.
28. Ibid., no. 273, pp. 187–188.
29. Ibid., no. 95, pp. 53–54.
30. Ibid., no. 199, pp. 125–126.
31. E.g., Dr. Willis, who was in Japan during the closing years of the Tokugawa and the early years of the new Meiji government, complained, "I wanted to send a pack horse up to Edo [from Yokohama] with luggage

some twenty-two miles, but I found it necessitated four different relays owing to certain rules and regulations of traffic along the high road." Hugh Cortazzi, ed., *Dr. Willis in Japan, 1862–77: British Medical Pioneer*, pp. 70–71.

32. *KKSS*, vol. 8, no. 47, pp. 25–26 and no. 125, pp. 74–75.
33. Ibid., no. 562, pp. 29–30. In theory it was prohibited to skip a station; yet, at least in the early Tokugawa period, some exceptions were allowed in emergency situations or when there was an extreme shortage of horses. Ibid., no. 233, pp. 156–157. Other exceptions were also allowed at a small number of post stations: E.g., although separate stations on the Tōkaidō, Goyu and Akasaka were only separated by a distance of less than two kilometers and therefore, for relay purposes, were treated as one station.
34. Ibid., no. 145, pp. 86–87; *Tottori ken shi*, vol. 4, *Kinsei shakai keizai*, pp. 423–424.
35. *KKSS*, vol. 8, no. 98, pp. 54–55.
36. Ibid., no. 503, p. 397; *KKSS*, vol. 10, pp. 61–64.
37. *KKSS*, vol. 1, pp. 324–331.
38. *KKSS*, vol. 10, p. 141.
39. *KKSS*, vol. 8, nos. 47–55, pp. 25–31.
40. Tamura Eitarō, *Edo jidai no kōtsū*, p. 17. Transport costs for all Gokaidō stations in 1711 and 1843 can be found in Kodama, *Shukueki*, pp. 177–230.
41. *KKSS*, vol. 8, no. 252, pp. 172–173 and no. 173, pp. 187–188.
42. Phyllis Deane, *The First Industrial Revolution*, p. 79. The load limit for horses transporting official goods was initially set at 30 *kan* (112.5 kg.) and 40 *kan* (150 kg.) for those carrying commoner goods, but both were fixed at 40 *kan* in 1616 and remained constant for the rest of the Tokugawa period. *KKSS*, vol. 8, no. 47, pp. 25–26 and no. 125, pp. 74–75.
43. *KKSS*, vol. 8, no. 459, pp. 356–357.
44. For example, a frontage of 6 *ken* (10.8 m.) in the middle of the station, which was considered the best location for business, was assessed a higher rate of taxation than a household with the same frontage farther away from the center. Kodama, *Shukueki*, p. 35.
45. Kodama Kōta, *Kinsei shukueki seido no kenkyū*, pp. 209–210.
46. *KKSS*, vol. 8, no. 169 (1635), p. 106; no. 222 (1653), p. 148; no. 397 (1701), pp. 291–292; no. 450 (1712), pp. 346–347; no. 494 (1721), pp. 391–392.
47. The breakdown of the number of daimyo using the various roads in 1822 was Tōkaidō, 146; Ōshū dōchū, 37; Nakasendō, 30; Mito-Sakuradō, 23; Nikkō dōchū, 4; Kōshū dōchū, 3; Iwatsukidō, 1; Nerima dōri, 1. The other twenty-five daimyo were retained in Edo and were therefore exempt. *KKSS*, vol. 10, pp. 106–116.
48. Conrad Totman, *Tokugawa Ieyasu: Shogun*, pp. 93–94.

49. *KKSS*, vol. 8, no. 167, pp. 103–105.

50. Ibid., no. 152, p. 91.

51. *KKSS*, vol. 10, p. 171.

52. *KKSS*, vol. 8, no. 179, p. 115.

53. Sir Rutherford Alcock, *The Capital of the Tycoon: A Narrative of a Three Years' Residence in Japan*, vol. 1, p. 455.

54. *The Cambridge Economic History of Europe*, vol. 6, *The Industrial Revolution and After*, M. M. Postan and H. J. Habakkuk, eds., pp. 217–218; Gilbert Sigaux, *History of Tourism*, p. 54. The toll-gates on the turnpikes frequently were the cause of mob violence. William Albert, "Popular Opposition to Turnpike Trusts in Early Eighteenth Century England," *Journal of Transport History*, Third Series, vol. 5, pp. 1–17 (1979) and Roger Hart, *English Life in the Eighteenth Century*, p. 51.

55. Alcock, vol. 1, p. 455.

56. *KKSS*, vol. 8, no. 138, p. 81.

57. "Goeki benran," in *KKSS*, vol. 10, pp. 32–45. The exact figures are 53.8 percent for bakufu and 46.2 percent for private lands.

58. *KKSS*, vol. 8, no. 91, pp. 50–51 and no. 383, pp. 279–280.

59. *Yamaguchi ken shiryō, Kinsei hen, Hōsei*, pt. 1, no. 23, p. 21.

60. Kaempfer, vol. 2, p. 317.

61. Alcock, vol. 2, p. 80.

62. *KKSS*, vol. 8, no. 240, p. 164.

63. Ibid., no. 390, p. 286. A list of the officials who served as Magistrates of Road Affairs can be found in *KKSS*, vol. 10, pp. 1–2 or pp. 233–234.

64. *Nihon kōtsū shiryō shūsei*, vol. 2, *Eki kanroku*, Hibata sekkō, ed., no. 5, pp. 101–106; *KKSS*, vol. 8, no. 198, p. 125.

65. *KKSS*, vol. 8, no. 471, pp. 371–372.

66. Inoue Tsūjo, "Kika nikki," in *Inoue Tsūjo zenshū*, Inoue Tsūjo zenshū shūtei iinkai, ed., p. 64.

67. Imai Kingo, "Shomin no michi," in Yamada Munemutsu et al., eds., *Michi no bunka*, pp. 142–148. For the Hachioji force, see Murakami Tadashi, *Edo bakufu no sennin dōshin shiryō*, pp. 3–5.

68. Suminokura Ryōi, under shogunal orders, was responsible for developing this route which brought the Fuji River to the deep mountains of Kai. Kimura Motoi, "Bakuhan seika no seikatsu no tenkai," in Morisue Yoshiaki, Hōgetsu Keido, and Kimura Motoi, eds., *Taikei Nihon shi sōsho*, vol. 16, *Seikatsu shi* pt. 2, p. 173.

69. Both roads in contemporary times were frequently referred to as "kaidō" instead of "dōchū," but a bakufu ordinance in 1716 which fixed the names of each of the Gokaidō stated that these two roads must be referred to as "dōchū" because they did not run through provinces bordering the sea or ocean. *KKSS*, vol. 8, no. 469, pp. 369–370.

70. The eight branch roads: 1) the Minoji, which ran from Miya to Tarui, connecting the Nakasendō and Tōkaidō; 2) the Mito-Sakuradō, from Senjū, the post station on the northern outskirts of Edo, to Sakura castle town; 3) the Nikkō onaridō, a road reserved for the shogun's use when traveling on pilgrimage to Nikkō, which ran parallel to the Nikkō dōchū from Edo before intersecting with that road at Satte; 4) the Reiheishidō, the road used by the Imperial envoys to Nikkō Tōshō-gū, linking the Nakasendō and Nikkō dōchū via the Mibu dōri; 5) the Mibu dōri, connecting the Nikkō dōchū with the Reiheishidō; 6) the Yamazaki dōri, from Nishinomiya to Fushimi; 7) the Honzaka dōri, a branch road on the Tōkaidō running from Mitsuke to Goyu; and 8) the Sayaji, another branch road on the Tōkaidō which allowed travelers to detour around the main road.

71. On the Hokkoku kaidō and its important role in the transport of mineral wealth from Sado, see Watanabe Kei'ichi, "Edo jidai ni okeru Hokkoku kaidō no tokusei," *Shinano*, vol. 18, no. 1, pp. 69–85 (1949).

72. For a detailed study of roads and post stations in Kyushu, see Maruyama Yasunari, "Kyūshū ni okeru kaidō to shukueki," in Kodama Kōta koki kinen kai, ed., *Kinsei Nihon kōtsū shi*, pp. 97–142.

73. Jippensha, *Hizakurige or Shanks' Mare*, p. 128.

74. Tachibana Nankei, *Tōzai yūki*, vol. 1, pp. 50–53. Apparently this remained true in the early Meiji years as well. Shintarō Kikuchi, the protagonist in Tokutomi Kenjiro's historical novel *Footprints in the Snow*, after experiencing a storm when traveling from Shikoku to Honshu in 1883, remarked: "How should I make the rest of the journey? Going by boat saved your feet all right, but suppose you had to face more of those storms—no, it was overland for me, whatever the hardships." Tokugawa travelers, it seems, largely shared these sentiments. Kenjiro Tokutomi, *Footprints in the Snow*, Kenneth Strong, trans., p. 150.

75. Kaempfer, vol. 2, p. 290.

76. Ihara Saikaku, *Tales of Samurai Honor*, Ann Callahan, trans., p. 45.

77. *KKSS*, vol. 2, p. 145.

78. Kaempfer, vol. 2, p. 290.

79. *KKSS*, vol. 10, no. 149, p. 146.

80. This discussion of road widths is, unless otherwise indicated, based on *KKSS*, vols. 4–6.

81. For most of the Nakasendō the average range was about 2–3 *ken* (1 *ken* = 1.82 m.), except for both ends of the road, where averages were 3–4, and the Kiso kaidō section, where it was only 1–2. The Nikkō dōchū, on the other hand, compared favorably with the Tōkaidō, and in fact, many stretches of road from Edo to Utsunomiya ranged between 4–6 *ken*. The fifth of the Gokaidō's main roads, the Kōshū dōchū, was quite wide—

4–6 *ken*–as far as Hino (the station after Fuchū), after which it narrowed to 2–3 *ken* for most of the way to Shimo Suwa. Gokaidō branch roads tended to be on a par with major roads in private domains, usually about 2–3 *ken*. *Kenshōbo*, vol. 4, Yamamoto Takeshi, ed., no. 2, p. 5; *Okayama ken shi*, vol. 7, *Kinsei 2*, Okayama ken shi hensan iinkai, ed., p. 502.

82. James L. McClain, *Kanazawa: A Seventeenth Century Castle Town*, p. 48.
83. *Okayama ken shi*, vol. 7, *Kinsei 2*, p. 502.
84. *Tochigi ken shi tsūshi hen*, vol. 4, *Kinsei 1*, pp. 591–594.
85. *Okayama ken shi*, vol. 7, *Kinsei 2*, p. 500.
86. Joseph Jones, *The Politics of Transport in Twentieth-Century France*, p. 6.
87. Bendix, p. 433.
88. Joseph Jones explains that enthusiasm was lacking at the local level because improving roads would only "serve to make the tax collector and the recruiting sargeant less remote." Jones, pp. 6–7. See also Eugen Weber, *Peasants into Frenchmen: The Modernization of Rural France, 1870–1914*, pt. 1, for a discussion of the French isolationist mentality.
89. *Cambridge Economic History*, vol. 6, p. 217.
90. Luke Shepherd Roberts makes this point about the export-driven nature of domainal economies with regard to Tosa domain in his 1991 Princeton doctoral dissertation, "The Merchant Origins of National Prosperity Thought in Eighteenth Century Tosa."
91. Weber, on p. 196, describes the French highway system in the nineteenth century as "lacking a supporting network of secondary thoroughfares . . . only a skeleton."
92. *Tokugawa kinrei kō*, vol. 1, Hōsei shi gakkai, ed., p. 94.
93. See, for example, *KKSS*, vol. 9, no. 541, p. 7 for the order to repair road, bridges, and dilapidated houses on the routes traveled by the 1747 mission. Orders were also given to repair the streets in and around Edo. On the use of foreign embassies and bakufu legitimacy, see Ronald P. Toby, *State and Diplomacy in Early Modern Japan*, pp. 67–76.
94. *KKSS*, vol. 8, no. 135, pp. 80–81 and no. 548, pp. 11–12.
95. E.g., Alcock, vol. 1, p. 457 and Cortazzi, p. 127. Cf. John Black, who recorded that, "The old Dutch writers described the road long ago, and it was even in their day, precisely as it was in ours." John Black, *Young Japan: Yokohama and Yedo, 1859–79*, pp. 164–165.
96. Charles Peter Thunberg, *Travels in Europe, Africa, and Asia*, vol. 3, p. 107.
97. Christopher I. Savage, *An Economic History of Transport*, pp. 12–13.
98. By most accounts, Daniel Defoe, who traveled around England from 1724 to 1726, gave an overly optimistic portrait of the turnpikes. See his Appendix to vol. 2 of *A Tour Through the Whole Island of Great Britain*, pp. 429–444.

99. Braudel, vol. 1, p. 428. For a brief discussion of the various advances made in road-building in the first half of the nineteenth century, see A. H. Stamp, *A Social and Economic History of England from 1700 to 1970*, pp. 60–62.

100. Michael Cooper, comp., *They Came to Japan: An Anthology of European Reports on Japan, 1543–1640*, p. 283. Saris also noted that the roadbed "was laid deep with gravel and covered with sand," but I have found no other documentation to substantiate this.

101. Olof Eriksson Willman, "Nihon ryokōki," in Murakawa Kengo and Ozaki Yoshi, trans., *Serisu Nihon tokōki: Viruman Nihon taizaiki*, p. 56.

102. Aimé Humbert, *Anbēru bakumatsu Nihon ezu*, Takahashi Hōtarō, trans., vol. 1, p. 260. Humbert was in Japan during 1863–64.

103. Kaempfer, vol. 2, p. 293.

104. Townsend Harris, *The Complete Journal of Townsend Harris*, p. 427.

105. Alcock, vol. 2, p. 146; Kaempfer, vol. 3, pp. 107–114.

106. Watanabe Kazutoshi, "Tōkaidō no kinsei shi teki igi," *Aichi daigaku bungaku ronsō*, vol. 86, pp. 8–12 (1987).

107. See, for example, Sin Yu-han, *Kaiyū roku*, Kang Chaeon, trans., pp. 222 and Harris, p. 414. William Griffis was one of the few to record comments to the contrary. He wrote, "The Hakone Mountains are ascended and enjoyed. The path is one long aisle under mossy monarch pines, through superb scenery." William Elliot Griffis, *The Mikado's Empire*, vol. 2, p. 547.

108. Ōta Shokusanjin, "Jinjutsu kikōshō," supplement in Sugiura Minpei, *Ōta Shokusanjin*, p. 192; *Zufu Nihon kaisō roku: Fuisseru sanpu kikō*, p. 35.

109. Inoue, "Kika nikki," p. 66.

110. See, for example, Kiyokawa Hachirō's comments when traveling near Sekigawa. Kiyokawa, p. 39.

111. *KKSS*, vol. 9, no. 844, p. 346. The three stretches of road near Hakone were first paved with stone in 1680; they were 164, 7663, and 2195 meters in length, respectively. Previous to this, they were paved with bamboo. *KKSS*, vol. 8, no. 319, pp. 227–228. The stone-paved road that modern-day travelers may hike over today dates from the major reconstruction project completed in 1862 for the shogun Iemochi's trip to Kyoto. *KKSS*, vol. 9, no. 844, p. 346.

112. Ōwada Kōichi and Itō Jun, "Hakone kyūkaidō," *Kōtsū shi kenkyū*, vol. 20, pp. 66–67 (1988).

113. Watanabe Kazutoshi, "Tōkaidō no kinseishiteki igi," pp. 12–13.

114. *KKSS*, vol. 8, no. 103, pp. 58–59.

115. Kaempfer, vol. 2, p. 293.

116. *KKSS*, vol. 4, pp. 623–631. Responsibility for maintaining the ten kilometers of road on the Tōkaidō between Yoshida and Goyu, for exam-

ple, was divided among more than seventy villages: some were located along the road, but others were further away. The largest section assigned was just over one kilometer and the shortest, under four meters. For one village, located at a distance of almost fourteen kilometers from the Tōkaidō, the assignment to clean about 600 meters of road was a particular burden.

117. There are nine mountain passes on the route, six of them roughly 1,000 meters in height. Griffis, vol. 1, p. 267. Shimazaki Tōson describes the Kiso area quite graphically in his *Yoake mae*, vol. 1, pt. 1, p. 5.

118. Muta Takatoshi, "Shokoku kaireki nichi roku," in Noma Mitsunobu et al., eds., *Zuihitsu hyakkaen*, vol. 13, pp. 360–361.

119. Kiyokawa, p. 42.

120. Furukawa Koshōken, *Tōyū zakki*, p. 6.

121. Alcock, vol. 2, p. 81.

122. Griffis, vol. 2, p. 545.

123. Kaempfer, vol. 2, p. 293. Roadside trees were first planted during the Nara period. The practice subsequently fell into disuse, before being revived by the sengoku daimyo late in the Warring States period. Maruyama Yasunari, "Kinsei no rikujō kōtsū," in Kodama Kōta and Toyoda Takeshi, eds., *Kōtsū shi*, p. 115.

124. Furukawa, *Tōyū zakki*, p. 5.

125. Griffis, vol. 2, p. 545.

126. The bakufu dispatched officials in 1803 to survey the Gokaidō for the purpose of making road maps. *KKSS*, vol. 9, no. 655, pp. 115–116. The maps were known as *Gokaidō sono hoka bunken mitori nobe ezu* and are being reproduced and published by the Tōkyō bijutsu in 130 volumes as *Gokaidō sono hoka bunken mitori nobe ezu* (Kodama Kōta, ed.). The Tōkaidō series, for example, runs 24 volumes.

The shogunate seems to have expended considerable effort in maintaining the trees, as the Magistrate of Road Affairs regularly issued orders to replant old, dying trees and replace them with seedlings. Inspectors must have been sent out to investigate local conditions because the orders made note of areas where tree maintenance was lacking. Vines which entwined and sometimes killed the trees, as well as roots which protruded from the road surface, were to be removed. From travel accounts the road surface appears to have been clear of roots and vines, but apparently, at least by the late Tokugawa period, it was not always economically possible to replace all old trees. Whatever maintenance work was performed was done per order of the overlord of the area, whether daimyo or bakufu intendant. In either case, as the Gokaidō was bakufu territory, no repairs could be made on private initiative alone. *KKSS*, vol. 10, pp. 13–14, 265; *KKSS*, vol. 9, no. 658, p. 118 and no. 617, pp. 80–89.

Roadside trees from the Tokugawa period still remain today in many parts of Japan, and those near Nikkō are particularly famous. The trees lining the 8.5 kilometer route between Nikkō and Imaichi, which can be viewed from the comfort of the train from Utsunomiya to Nikkō, are well preserved and give a good sense of what Tokugawa roads must have been like.

127. E.g., *Etchū shiryō*, vol. 2, pp. 92–93 (Kaga domain), *Yamaguchi ken shiryō*, pt. 1, no. 10, p. 69 (Chōshū).

128. Kaempfer, vol. 2, pp. 290–291.

129. Ibid. The orders to build these *rizuka* ("*ri* mounds") was first given in 1604. They were nine meters in diameter (and of an unregulated height), and were topped with a tree, usually a huckleberry or Chinese nettle. *KKSS*, vol. 8, nos. 79–80, p. 42.

130. Esther Moir, *The Discovery of Britain: The English Tourist, 1540 to 1840*, pp. 8–9.

131. Yamamoto Mitsumasa, "Kinsei no shiteki dōro shisetsu: dōhyō ni tsuite," *Kōtsū shi kenkyū*, vol. 20, pp. 67–68 (1988).

132. This conclusion is based on observations made after looking at several volumes of *Gokaidō sono hoka bunken mitori nobe ezu*.

133. *KKSS*, vol. 10, p. 18. In an unusual case, a bakufu intendant authorized a petition (the identity of the filer is unknown) to build stone lanterns along a difficult stretch of mountain road (a branch road) between Ōtsu and Kyoto in 1795. The document granting the permission stated that there was a precedent for granting such a request in Tōtōmi province along a road leading to Akiha Shrine.

134. J. Crofts, *Packhorse, Waggon and Post: Land Carriage and Communications under the Tudors and Stuarts*, p. 17.

135. Thunberg, vol. 3, p. 107. For a history of wheeled vehicles in pre-industrial Japan, see Kobayashi Shigeru, "Nissha," in Nagahara Keiji, et al., eds., *Kōza Nihon gijutsu no shakai shi*, vol. 8, *Kōtsū, unyū*, pp. 296–312.

136. E.g., Toyoda Takeshi, *A History of Pre-Meiji Commerce*, p. 52 gives the classic argument: "Because there were many mountain roads and the roads themselves were narrow, carts or wagons for freight transport were little used outside Edo and Osaka."

137. Seymour Dunbar, *A History of Travel in America*, vol. 1, pp. 194, 200–201.

138. Tōkyō to komonjokan, ed., *Edo no ushi*, pp. 21–30; Kumai Tamotsu, "Edo no ushi kasegi," *Kokuritsu rekishi minzoku hakubutsukan kenkyū hōkoku*, vol. 14, pp. 124–137 (1987); *KKSS*, vol. 8, no. 382, p. 279. The operators were required to provide horses for official transport needs and thus relied on wages earned from non-official transport. The number of

carts continued to increase for the rest of the Tokugawa period and by 1860 there were about 3,500.

139. *KKSS*, vol. 8, no. 382, p. 279 and no. 395, p. 289.

140. Ibid., vol. 9, no. 716, pp. 192–193.

141. Griffis, vol. 2, p. 322.

142. *KKSS*, vol. 8, no. 382, p. 279; no. 420, pp. 310–311; no. 498, pp. 393–394; no. 515, pp. 411–412; Ibid., vol. 9, no. 556, pp. 21–22.

143. Ibid., vol. 8, no. 468, pp. 368–369.

144. On carts and bridges, see Ibid., no. 493, pp. 390–391; Ibid., vol. 9, no. 642, pp. 109–110; Ibid., no. 668, p. 127. On public health concerns, see Ibid., no. 716, pp. 192–193.

145. Ibid., vol. 8, no. 112, pp. 63–64.

146. Thunberg, vol. 3, p. 134.

147. Sir Ernest Satow, *A Diplomat in Japan: An Inner History of the Meiji Restoration*, p. 209. The tramway was constructed with rutted rocks to guide the wheels. The road itself was divided into two halves, one side for ox-drawn carts and the other for human and post-horse traffic. Nihon gakushiin Nihon kagakushi kankō kai, ed., *Meiji mae Nihon doboku shi*, p. 238.

148. *KKSS*, vol. 9, no. 798, pp. 297–298.

149. Ibid., vol. 8, no. 798, pp. 297–298.

150. Ibid., vol. 9, no. 843, p. 345.

151. The first quote is from Edwin L. Neville, "The Development of Transportation in Japan: A Case Study of Okayama han, 1600–1868," p. 21 and the second from Patricia J. Graham, "The Political and Economic Importance of the Tōkaidō," in Stephen Addiss, ed., *Tōkaidō: Adventures on the Road in Old Japan*, p. 11.

152. Seymour Broadbridge, "Economic and Social Trends in Tokugawa Japan," *Modern Asian Studies*, vol. 8, no. 3, pp. 349–350 (1974).

153. The breakdown is: Tōkaidō (7), Nakasendō (7), Ōshū dōchū (6), Kōshū dōchū (2), Nikkō dōchū (4), Sayaji (2), Minoji (3), Honzaka dōri (2), Mito Sakuradō (3), Nikko reiheishidō (4), and Mibu dōri (1). Yamamoto Mitsumasa, "Watashibune," in Kodama Kōta et al., eds., *Edo jidai no kōtsū to tabi*, p. 94.

154. Kaempfer, vol. 2, p. 294. For a similar comment, see Alcock, vol. 2, p. 407.

155. Takechi Mitsuaki, *Ōigawa monogatari*, pp. 350–351. The *ren* of *rendai* means lotus blossom and thus alludes to the Buddhist heaven. *Ren*, therefore lies in juxtaposition with *jigoku*, or "hell," and the play on words suggests alternative meanings.

156. Philipp Franz von Siebold, *Manners and Customs of the Japanese in the Nineteenth Century*, Saitō Makoto, trans., p. 77.

157. Sin, p. 161. The force of the river could be so strong during the spring and summer months that even with the boatmen "rowing with all their might" the boat would bring the travelers "obliquely to the opposite shore." Kaempfer, vol. 3, pp. 154–155.
158. Thunberg, vol. 3, pp. 154–155.
159. Kaempfer, vol. 3, p. 54.
160. *KKSS*, vol. 8, no. 333, pp. 235–236.
161. From *Chikusai monogatari*, as quoted in Lawrence Bresler, "The Origins of Popular Travel and Travel Literature in Japan," p. 273.
162. Inoue, "Kika nikki," pp. 78–79. Similarly, at the Fuji River, Kaempfer forded the first stream and was ferried across the second. Kaempfer, vol. 3, p. 54.
163. Alcock, vol. 1, p. 48.
164. Ibid., p. 407.
165. Quoted in Takechi, p. 352.
166. Kaempfer, vol. 2, pp. 295–296.
167. This discussion of bridges is, unless otherwise noted, based on *KKSS*, vols. 4–6. To be exact, the Yahagi was 156 *ken* (284 meters) long.
168. For example, between Kawasaki and Kanagawa stations, there were twenty-three stone bridges, one wooden bridge (the Tsurumi Bridge), and two earthen bridges. More typical perhaps was the stretch of road between Fujisawa and Hiratsuka, with five stone, three wooden, and eight earthen bridges. *KKSS*, vol. 4, pp. 20–35, 56–73.
169. Shaku Keijun, *Jippō anyū reki zakki*, p. 189. The Rokugō River refers to the lower reaches of the Tama River; the upper portion was referred to as the Taba River.
170. Griffis, vol. 1, p. 360. He said of the Rokugō, "The Japanese have used this river for centuries, and have never yet built a bridge."
171. Murakami Tadashi, "Rokugō no watashi," in Kodama Kōta et al., eds., *Edo jidai no kōtsū to tabi*, pp. 104–105. Large bridges such as the Yahagi, Yoshida and Seta were repaired at bakufu expense, but most others were at local cost. *KKSS*, vol. 8, no. 102, pp. 57–58 and no. 124, pp. 73–74. Some villages illegally charged travelers a "bridge-crossing fee" to help recoup a portion of the costs. *KKSS*, vol. 10, no. 100, p. 130.
172. *KKSS*, vol. 8, no. 101, p. 57.
173. For the first three years the ferry was under direct bakufu administration, but thereafter management alternated between Shinagawa and Kawasaki stations before passing in 1709, upon the request of the Kawasaki station manager, Tanaka Kyūgu, permanently into the hands of Kawasaki. *Kawasaki shi shi*, p. 119.

The income potential provided by river crossings led post stations like Shinagawa and Kawasaki to compete over them. For the dispute over control of the Yanase river crossing, see Igarashi Tomio, "Kinsei watashibune no sonzai keitai: Nakasendō Yanase watashibune o jirei to shite," *Shinano*, vol. 22, no. 5, pp. 17–28 (1970).

174. Murakami, "Rokugō," p. 107.
175. Weber, p. 119.
176. Asai Ryōi, vol. 1, p. 212.
177. Asai Naohira, *Ōigawa to sono shūhen*, pp. 20–21. Other proponents of this line of argument include Tamura, p. 230 and Ōyama Shikitarō, *Kinsei kōtsū keizai shi ron*, p. 196. Maruyama Yasunari reviews the scholarly debate over bridges in his article, "Kinsei no watashiba ni kansuru jakkan no mondai," in Toyoda Takeshi kyōju kanreki kinen kai, ed., *Nihon kinsei shi no chihōteki tenkai*, pp. 227–256. Maruyama himself (Ibid., pp. 243–244) believes that military/political factors were paramount, but that economic considerations were also important.
178. *KKSS*, vol. 8, no. 155, p.94.
179. Quoted in Asai Naohira, pp. 235–236.
180. During the years 1746 to 1809, about 326 porters were employed; early in the nineteenth century, that figure rose to over 400 and by bakumatsu times had swollen to about 650. *Shimada shi shi*, vol. 2, Shimada shi hensan iinkai, ed., pp. 202–204.
181. Being carried across the Ōi River, for example, cost from 24–100 *mon* (1710), depending on the depth of the water, while in contrast, a ride across the Rokugō or Tenryū rivers was only 10–12. *Goeki benran*, no. 13, pp. 64–66.
    Although centrally directed, the Gokaidō system was not uniform in all aspects. Regulations at all water crossings were not the same: e.g., samurai could cross at no cost at some rivers, but had to pay at others. *KKSS*, vol. 10, pt. 3, no. 175, pp. 162–163.

2. The Social Organization of the Gokaidō Network

1. Maruyama Yasunari, *Kinsei shukueki no kisoteki kenkyū*, vol. 1, p. 649.
2. E.g., Stephen Vlastos, *Peasant Protests and Uprisings in Tokugawa Japan;* Anne Walthall, *Social Protest and Popular Culture in Eighteenth-Century Japan.*
3. One study which focuses entirely on violent uprisings or revolts (*hōki*) and thus distorts the nature of peasant protest is Herbert P. Bix's *Peasant Protest in Japan, 1590–1884.*
4. William Jones Chambliss, *Chiaraijima Village: Land Tenure, Taxation, and Local Trade, 1818–1884* and Neil Waters, *Japan's Local Pragmatists: The Transition from Bakumatsu to Meiji in the Kawasaki Region* are exceptions, and each briefly discusses assisting villages.

5. Other forms of corvée labor include castle construction and repair as well as the repair of roads and irrigation works.
6. *Hamamatsu shi shi shiryō hen,* vol. 1, Hamamatsu shiyakusho, ed., p. 526.
7. *Kanagawa ken shi shiryō hen,* vol. 9, *Kinsei 6,* no. 28, pp. 194–195.
8. *Gifu ken shi shiryō hen, Kinsei,* vol. 7, no. 47, pp. 188–189.
9. Harasawa Bun'ya, "Annaka shukueki to sukegō to no kankei," *Nihon no rekishi,* vol. 128, pp. 33–36 (1959).
10. *Hamamatsu shi shi shiryō hen,* vol. 1, pp. 521–527.
11. *KKSS,* vol. 9, no. 696, pp. 177–178.
12. *Nakasendō kōtsū shiryō shū,* vol. 1, Hatano Tominobu, ed., no. 11, p. 19.
13. Most specialists agree that no coercive element was involved. Maruyama Yasunari, *Kinsei shukueki,* vol. 1, pp. 527–537; Watanabe Nobuo, "Kaidō to suiun," *Iwanami kōza Nihon rekishi,* vol. 10, *Kinsei 2,* pp. 308–311; Kodama Kōta's statement can be found in *Shinagawa ku shi tsūshi hen,* pt. 1, Shinagawa ku, ed., pp. 642–644. Another author calls it a "semi-compulsory system." Fujisawa Hiroshi, "Sukegō no sōsetsu katei to sonzai keitai," *Shigaku zasshi,* vols. 77–79, pp. 191–192 (1960).
14. *KKSS,* vol. 8, no. 174, p. 100. The decree is referred to as the "*sukeumarei.*"
15. Ibid., no. 175, pp. 111–113; *Gifu ken shi shiryō hen, Kinsei,* vol. 7, no. 87, p. 398.
16. Tanaka Kyūgu, p. 308. (1 *koku* = 4.96 bushels.)
   Tanaka was later appointed to the position of bakufu intendant (*daikan*) after having successfully directed the completion of riparian works on the Arakawa and Sakata rivers. His rise in position was just one notable example of the shogun Yoshimune's program to promote the use of local men of talent in government.
17. *KKSS,* vol. 8, no. 175, pp. 111–113.
18. *Gifu ken shi shiryō hen, Kinsei,* vol. 7, no. 87, p. 398.
19. Hirakawa Hajime, "Sukegō seido no seiritsu to tenkai," in *Hōsei shiron,* vol. 4, pp. 16–37 (1976); Fujisawa, pp. 196–198.
20. See, for example, Fujisawa, pp. 188–189 and Hirakawa Hajime, "Sukegō seido no kakuritsu katei," in Kodama Kōta, ed., *Nihon kinsei kōtsū shi kenkyū,* pp. 38–41. Fujisawa, however, calls horses obtained from villages prior to 1637 *aitai sukegō,* or "*sukegō* obtained through negotiation," and those requisitioned from villages after that date, "*shitei sukegō,*" or "designated *sukegō,*" to indicate the transition to a compulsory system. Maruyama Yasunari, *Kinsei shukueki,* vol. 1, pp. 527–537, and Watanabe Nobuo, "Kaidō to suiun," pp. 308–311, agree. However, Kodama and Fukai believe that only Fujisawa's *shitei sukegō* are truly *sukegō;* they see the lack of compulsion involved in obtaining horses prior to 1637 as invalidating his *aitai sukegō* classification. Kodama, in *Shinagawa ku shi*

tsūshi hen, pt. 1, pp. 624–644; Fukai Jinzō, "Sukegō no seiritsu to sono sonzai keitai," *Bunka*, vol. 42, nos. 1–2, p. 2 (1978).

The *aitai* classification basically treats those villages designated by the bakufu and those not designated, but performing the same service, as the same. Maruyama and Watanabe, instead, both speak of a *sukeuma* system, based on the 1637 *sukeuma* order, as an earlier form of *sukegō*. On the basis of the Nakatsugawa document, Hirakawa denies the existence of such a system because of the evidence that villagers as well as horses were being requisitioned for transport corvée labor.

21. *KKSS*, vol. 8, nos. 375–377, pp. 270–275 and no. 379, pp. 276–277.
22. An example of the census taken for Hodogaya post station is found in *KKSS*, vol. 3, no. 362, pp. 260–263.
23. Hayashi Miwako, "Kinsei zenki no sukegō yaku futan," *Yokohama kaikō shiryōkan kiyō*, vol. 2, pp. 35–36 (1984). Copies of *sukegō* registers are found in *Tochigi ken shi shiryō hen, Kinsei*, vol. 1, Tochigi ken shi shiryō hensan iinkai, eds., nos. 6–19, pp. 681–699.

   Technically the *sukegō* tax was determined on the basis of a village's *sukegōdaka* (lit., "*sukegō* yield"), a figure expressed in *koku* which represented a certain percentage of a village's total assessed yield. A number of variables, such as the distance of the village from the post station and local conditions, were taken into consideration when fixing the numerical value. The *sukegōdaka* for fifty-one assisting villages of Odawara post station ranged from 14.3 percent–96.2 percent of their respective *kokudaka*. Usami Misako, "Odawara shuku ni okeru sukegō futan," *Hōsei shigaku*, vol. 36, no. 1, p. 30 (1984).
24. Hirakawa, pp. 52–57.
25. Akimoto Norio, "Ryōshu kenryoku to shuku, sukegō," *Shakai keizaishigaku*, vol. 27, no. 1, pp. 44–45 (1967).
26. Hirakawa, pp. 59 and Akimoto, p. 45.
27. Tanaka Tomojirō, *Tōkaidō Enshū Mitsuke shuku*, pp. 222–228.
28. Ōwada Kōichi, "Bunkaki Odawara shuku ni okeru sukegō funsō ni tsuite," *Hōsei shigaku*, vol. 33, pp. 34–35 (1981).
29. *Tochigi ken shi shiryō hen, Kinsei*, vol. 1, no. 5, pp. 680–681.
30. *KKSS*, vol. 8, no. 375, pp. 270–272; *Kanagawa ken shi shiryō hen*, vol. 9, *Kinsei* 6, no. 141, pp. 224–226.
31. On the Nakasendō the average was 8,936 *koku;* on the Kōshū dōchū, 3,543; and on the Ōshū dōchū, 7,566. *Goeki benran*, vol. 1, no. 31, pp. 117–132.

   The figures for the Nakasendō, however, are misleading because some post stations there shared assisting villages. The averages given do not take into consideration those post stations without assisting villages: three on the Tōkaidō, one on the Nakasendō, and five on the Nikkō dōchū. Figures have been rounded off to the nearest *koku*.

32. *KKSS*, vol. 10, p. 64.

33. *KKSS*, vol. 8, no. 510, pp. 404–407.

34. Watanabe Nobuo, "Kaidō to suiun," p. 312 and Maruyama Yasunari, *Kinsei shukueki*, vol. 1, pp. 534–544.

35. *KKSS*, vol. 10, pp. 171–172.

36. Maruyama Yasunari, *Kinsei shukueki*, vol. 1, p. 594. See Ibid., pp. 539–666 for a discussion of the various types of assisting villages.

37. On *tōbun sukegō*, see Usami Misako, "Bakumatsu ni okeru sukegō futan no tenkai," *Hōsei shigaku*, vol. 42, no. 1 (1990).

38. *Chigasaki shi shi*, vol. 4, *Tsūshi hen*, Chigasaki shi shi, ed., p. 262.

39. *Kanagawa ken shi shiryō hen*, vol. 9, *Kinsei 6*, no. 123, pp. 200–201.

40. *Tochigi ken shi shiryō hen, Kinsei*, vol. 2, pp. 413–418. Shogunal pilgrimages to Nikkō took place nineteen times during the Tokugawa period; sixteen of them were prior to Yoshimune's journey in 1728, when 228,306 porters and 325,940 horses were needed to meet the transport needs of the 133,000 people in the massive pilgrimage. Representatives were sent in years in which the shogun was not able to make the journey personally. Ibaraki kenritsu hakubutsukan, ed., *Nikkō sankei no michi*, pp. 63–64.

41. Kodama, *Kinsei shukueki*, pp. 235.

42. *KKSS*, vol. 10, pp. 106–116.

43. Kodama, *Kinsei shukueki*, p. 235.

44. *Yokohama shi shi*, vol. 1, Yokoyama shi shi, ed., pp. 654–655.

45. Maruyama Yasunari, *Kinsei shukueki*, vol. 1, p. 648. Figures for other assisting villages confirm the general trend. Nagata, an assisting village for Hodogaya, was taxed at the high rate of 375–500 horses per 100 *koku* during 1661–1724. Similarly, the tax rate for the assisting villages servicing Kawasaki post station on the Tōkaidō rose from 50 porters in 1725 to 300–400 in 1785. The rate also increased rapidly for Tarui post station's villages (from 7 porters and 13 horses in 1731 to 100 porters and 57 horses in 1748, adjusting to a level of 35 porters and 62 horses in 1761). Neil Waters, "Local Leadership in the Kawasaki Region from Bakumatsu to Meiji," *Journal of Japanese Studies*, vol. 7, no. 1, pp. 53–84 (Winter 1981).

46. *KKSS*, vol. 9, no. 901, p. 389.

47. Kodama, *Shukueki*, p. 42.

48. Yamamoto Hirofumi, "Boshin ki no gunji yusō to sukegō saihensei: shukueki sei shūmatsu no ichi kenkyū," pp. 248–249. For example, Kusatsu station, located at the fork of the Nakasendō and Tōkaidō, saw 20,841 men and 247 horses pass through its village limits on their way north, all belonging to the Imperial forces. Lodging and transport fees were not

always paid in advance, as they should have been. One-third of the fees owed Kusatsu were to be paid at a later date, but in fact never were received. The Boshin War was fought during a period of spiralling inflation, and this only made the economic burden worse, and assisting villages bore the brunt of it. (Ibid., pp. 255–256.)

49. *KKSS*, vol. 9, no. 879, p. 379.

50. Ibid., no. 885, p. 381.

51. See Ōyama, pp. 226–237, for information on the system at the Imagiri crossing at Lake Hamana in Suruga province.

52. Tamura, pp. 75–78. There was considerable variation from village to village in the number of males aged 15–60 as a percentage of the total population of the village. For Honjō's assisting villages, the range was 4–33 percent.

53. *KKSS*, vol. 9, no. 684, pp. 141–142.

54. Kodama, *Kinsei shukueki*, pp. 227–228; Maruyama Yasunari, *Kinsei shukueki*, vol. 1, pp. 607–610.

55. In 1725 Hanejima yielded an estimated 240 *koku*. Using this fact and the common estimate that a household comprised five persons on average during the late Tokugawa period, we can estimate that Hanejima contained approximately 48 households at that time.

56. *Fujisawa shi shi*, vol. 2, *Shiryō hen*, no. 6, pp. 711–716.

57. *KKSS*, vol. 8, no. 495, p. 392.

58. Possibly referring to this situation, the historian George Sansom has misinterpreted *sukegō* corvée labor as being a service "without pay." George Sansom, *A History of Japan, 1615–1867*, pp. 99–100.

59. Anzai Kazutoshi, "Shinagawa shuku ni okeru sukegō kayaku," *Hōsei shigaku*, vol. 17, pp. 84–86 (1965).

60. *Fujisawa shi shi*, vol. 2. *Shiryō hen*, no. 6, pp. 74–76.

61. For a summary of taxation in the Tokugawa period, see Chambliss, pp. 47–61.

62. Kodama, *Shukueki*, pp. 111–112; Nakami Hideo, "Sukegō yaku to mura zaisei," *Rekishi kyōiku*, vol. 4, no. 12, pp. 49–55 (1956).

63. Kodama, *Shukueki*, p. 112.

64. *KKSS*, vol. 8, no. 175, pp. 111–113; *KKSS*, vol. 10, pp. 253–254. The three levies in question were: (1) *gotenma yaku iriyōmai*, a tax of 0.6% per 100 *koku* of estimated yield, to pay post-station officials' salaries and to cover the general expenses at the station; (2) *okuramae iriyōmai*, a tax of 250 copper coins per 100 *koku* that was stored at the bakufu's rice warehouse at Asakusa; and (3) *rokushaku kyūmai*, a tax of 0.2% per 100 *koku* for Edo Castle's kitchen. Kodama Kōta, *Kinsei nōmin seikatsu shi*, p. 55.

65. Conrad D. Totman, *Politics in the Tokugawa Bakufu, 1600–1843*, p. 62.

This is the standardized view in the English-language literature on Tokugawa Japan and not just Totman's.

66. *Tochigi ken shi tsūshi hen,* vol. 5, *Kinsei* 2, pp. 495–500.

67. Arai Hakuseki, *Oritaku shiba no ki,* pp. 152–154; Fukai Jinzō, "Yoshimune seiken ni okeru shukueki, sukegō seisaku," *Nihonshi kenkyū,* vol. 272, p. 28. See also Kate Wildman Nakai's work on Arai Hakuseki, *Shogunal Politics: Arai Hakuseki and the Premises of Tokugawa Rule.*

68. *Shinagawa ku shi tsūshi hen,* pt. 1, pp. 653–654.

69. *Gifu ken shi shiryō hen, Kinsei,* vol. 7, no. 90 (supplement), pp. 435–444; *Fujisawa shi shi,* vol. 2, *Shiryō hen,* no. 27, pp. 827–830.

70. Maruyama Yasunari, *Kinsei shukueki,* vol. 1, pp. 648–649.

71. Yazawa Yōshi, "Bakumatsuki ni okeru sukegō ninsoku yaku ni tsuite," pp. 83–88; Usami, "Odawara," p. 53.

72. *Kanagawa ken shi shiryō hen,* vol. 9, *Kinsei* 6, no. 115, pp. 181–182.

73. *Kanagawa ken shi tsūshi hen,* vol. 3, *Kinsei* 2, p. 945.

74. *Tochigi ken shi tsūshi hen,* vol. 5, *Kinsei* 2, p. 521.

75. *Shinpen Saitama ken shi shiryō hen,* vol. 15, *Kinsei* 6, no. 105, pp. 450–455.

76. Kodama, *Shukueki,* pp. 153–154.

77. Watanabe Nobuo, *Kaidō,* pp. 115–116.

78. Crofts, p. 58.

79. Ibid., p. 68.

80. Yamamoto Mitsumasa, "Tōkaidō ni okeru jimba chinsen ni tsuite," *Hōsei shigaku,* vol. 21, p. 91 (1969).

81. *KKSS,* vol. 8, no. 169, p. 106 (1635); no. 222, p. 148 (1653); no. 397, pp. 291–292 (1701); no. 450, pp. 346–347 (1712); and *KKSS,* vol. 9, no. 650, pp. 113–114.

82. For attempts to limit official traffic, see, for example, *KKSS,* vol. 8, no. 494, pp. 391–392 and no. 504, pp. 400–401. Through his Shōtoku Reform, Arai Hakuseki was able to reduce the number of free official travelers, beginning from 1711; but after he fell from power a few years later, the number returned to its former level. Arai Hakuseki, p. 154.

83. Kaempfer, vol. 2, p. 331.

84. Furukawa, *Tōyū zakki,* p. 7. He noted that despite economy measures the retinue of the Sendai daimyo was far greater than any of those of the large, province-holding daimyo he had ever seen before and numbered in the "thousands."

85. *KKSS,* vol. 10, p. 164; *KKSS,* vol. 9, no. 729, p. 213. On the imperial envoy, see Igarashi Tomio, *Nikkō reiheishi kaidō.* The envoy first traveled to Nikkō upon the completion of the shrine in 1617, and from 1646 he made the trip every year for the festival celebrating Ieyasu's death anniversary on 4/14.

86. Kodama, *Shukueki,* pp. 74–75.

87. *KKSS*, vol. 1, pp. 117–126.
88. Tanaka Kyūgu, pp. 243–244.
89. *KKSS*, vol. 8, no. 343, p. 241.
90. Ibid., vol. 1, p. 433.
91. Ibid., vol. 8, no. 447, pp. 344–345.
92. Ibid., no. 448, pp. 345–346; Ibid., vol. 9, nos. 788–789, pp. 289–290.
93. Ibid., no. 689, pp. 148–150.
94. Ibid., no. 815, pp. 319–320 and no. 643, p. 110.
95. Ibid., vol. 10, pp. 274–276; Ibid., vol. 9, nos. 607–609, pp. 73–80. For an account of the misuse of the placard system, particularly by the Mito daimyo, see Kodama Kōta, "Efu no fusei shiyō ni tsuite," *Kōtsū shi kenkyū*, vol. 8, pp. 80–90 (1982).
96. "Naniwa kō teishuku chō," in Imai Kingo, ed., *Ryokō yōjin shū*, p. 169.
97. *KKSS*, vol. 9, no. 873, pp. 372–373.
98. *Kanagawa ken shi shiryō hen*, vol. 9, *Kinsei* 6, no. 8, p. 8; *KKSS*, vol. 8, no. 451, pp. 347–348.
99. Harasawa Bun'ya, "Edo jidai ni okeru shukueki to wakimichi ōkan to no kankei," *Nihon rekishi*, vol. 119, no. 5, pp. 59–60 (1958).
100. Furushima Toshio, *Furushima Toshio chosaku shū*, vol. 4, *Shinshū chūma no kenkyū*, especially pp. 40–68. From a reading of *Shinshū Shiojiri Akabane ke Genroku ōjōya nikki* the trains of horses appear, however, to have been more subject to accidents, although this is, at least in part, on account of the mountain roads and not a result of the horses themselves.
101. Kodama Kōta, "Edo jidai no shukueki seido" (pt. 2), *Nihon rekishi*, vol. 96, p. 38 (1956).
102. Hirasawa Kiyoto, *Hyakushō ikki no tenkai*, 127–128.
103. Nakai Nobuhiko, "Edo jidai chūki ni okeru rikujō kōtsū no ichi danmen," *Shigaku*, vol. 34, no. 1, pp. 29–37 (1961); Harasawa, "Annaka," pp. 33–36.
104. Weber, pp. 195–220.
105. Many examples of prohibitions against the use of side roads can be found in *KKSS*, vol. 1, pp. 587–625. Post stations on side roads were authorized only in 1872 by the Meiji government. Ibid., vol. 9, no. 900, pp. 388–389.
106. Ibid., vol. 1, pp. 605–606.
107. Ibid., p. 593.
108. *Kanagawa ken shi shiryō hen*, vol. 9, *Kinsei* 6, no. 214, p. 314.
109. *KKSS*, vol. 9, no. 582, pp. 48–49.
110. *Kanagawa ken shi shiryō hen*, vol. 9, *Kinsei* 6, no. 745, p. 227 and no. 750, p. 231; *KKSS*, vol. 1, p. 590.
111. Ibid., p. 590.
112. The normal depth at the river-crossing place on the Ōi River was 2.5

shaku (75.8 cm.). If the water level rose above 3.5 *shaku* (1.06 m.), travelers on horses could not be taken across; above 4.5 *shaku* (1.36m.), the river was closed to all traffic. The river was opened for service again for horseback traffic when the waters receded to 3 *shaku* (91 cm.) and 4 *shaku* (1.2 m.) for human traffic. Ibid., vol. 10, p. 64. Once a flooded river was opened to traffic, post-station messengers were the first allowed across. *Nihon kōtsū shiryō shūsei*, vol. 2, *Eki kanroku*, Hibata Sekko, ed., no. 15, pp. 30–32.

113. *KKSS*, vol. 10, p. 16; Ibid., vol. 9, no. 696, pp. 174–176.
114. *Shimada shi shi*, vol. 2, pp. 224–226.
115. Kiyokawa, p. 49.
116. *Kanagawa ken shi shiryō hen*, vol. 9, *Kinsei 6*, no. 89, pp. 131–132; *KKSS*, vol. 8, no. 464, p. 365; Ibid., vol. 9, no. 571, pp. 37–38; no. 644, pp. 123–124; no. 694, pp. 173–174.
117. *Fujisawa shi shi*, vol. 2, *Shiryō hen*, no. 19, pp. 803–804.
118. *Kanagawa ken shi shiryō hen*, vol. 9, *Kinsei 6*, no. 62, pp. 101–104; *KKSS*, vol. 9, no. 270, p. 199 and no. 762, pp. 248–251.
119. For a full-length treatment of daimyo inns, see Ōshima Nobujirō, *Honjin no kenkyū*.
120. Kodama, *Shukueki*, p. 106.
121. Ibid., p. 162.
122. Watanabe Kazutoshi, "Tōkaidō Arai shuku ni okeru shukueki zaisei no ichi danmen," *Kōtsū shi kenkyū*, vol. 8, pp. 56–78 (1982). A bakufu audit of Arai post station's ledgers—itself of questionable accuracy—showed a surplus rather than a serious deficit as the station had claimed in its petition for a subsidy.
123. See, for example, *KKSS*, vol. 10, pp. 46, 118; *KKSS*, vol. 8, no. 305, pp. 214–216.
124. *KKSS*, vol. 5, p. 210.
125. Ibid., vols. 1–2, are a compilation of documents dealing primarily with bakufu efforts to reform the official transport system in the early nineteenth century.
126. Etatsu Yoshiyuki, "Shukueki josei kashitsukekin ni tsuite," *Chihō shi kenkyū*, vol. 62–63, pp. 33–44 (1963).
127. *KKSS*, vol. 8, no. 243, pp. 166–167.
128. Ibid., no. 290, pp. 201–203.
129. Ibid., vol. 9, no. 724, pp. 204–205 and no. 768, pp. 258–260.
130. Ibid., no. 794, pp. 293–294.
131. Tanaka Kyūgu, p. 358.
132. Usami, "Tōkaidō shukueki ni okeru meshimori onna no sonzai keitai," in Kinsei josei shi kenkyū kai, ed., *Ronshū kinsei josei shi*, pp. 360–361.

133. *Arai chō shi shiryō hen*, vol. 8, pp. 20–21. The base rates, known as the Shōtoku rates, are listed in *KKSS*, vol. 10, pp. 179–206.

134. *KKSS*, vol. 9, no. 774, pp. 226–227.

135. *Kanagawa ken shi shiryō hen*, vol. 9, *Kinsei* 6, no. 164, p. 275 and no. 119, pp. 195–196; *Nakasendō Kumagaya eki*, no. 25, pp. 83–84.

136. *Kanagawa ken shi shiryō hen*, vol. 9, *Kinsei* 6, no. 71, pp. 115–116; *Kanagawa ken shi tsūshi hen*, vol. 3, *Kinsei* 2, p. 945.

137. Anzai, pp. 82–83.

138. See, for example, *KKSS*, vol. 8, no. 509 (1725), pp. 403–404; Ibid., vol. 9, no. 696 (1821), pp. 177–178.

139. Ibid., no. 581, pp. 47–48.

140. See Ibid., vols. 5–6 for other Gokaidō roads.

141. Ōwada, "Bunka ki Odawara," pp. 30–32; *KKSS*, vol. 9, no. 558, pp. 22–26 and no. 586, pp. 51–54.

142. *Shinpen Saitama ken shi shiryō hen*, vol. 15, *Kinsei* 6, no. 97, pp. 437–438; *KKSS*, vol. 9, no. 589, pp. 55–57.

143. Ibid., vol. 8, no. 495, p. 392; Ibid., vol. 9, no. 555, pp. 19–21.

144. Ibid., vol. 8, no. 174, p. 110; Ibid., vol. 9, no. 555, pp. 19–21.

145. *KKSS*, vol. 8, no. 237, pp. 161–163 and no. 551, pp. 19–21.

146. *Shinagawa ku shi shiryō hen*, no. 199, p. 349.

147. *KKSS*, vol. 9, no. 551, pp. 19–21; see also Ibid., no. 785, pp. 284–286.

148. *Shinpen Saitama ken shi shiryō hen*, vol. 15, *Kinsei* 6, p. 25.

149. *KKSS*, vol. 8, no. 405, pp. 296–298.

150. Arai Hakuseki, p. 152.

151. *KKSS*, vol. 8, no. 443, pp. 326–327.

152. Overseers were appointed for assisting villages servicing Odawara in 1728, Ochiai and Nakatsugawa in 1787 and Shinagawa in 1746. *KKSS*, vol. 8, no. 514, pp. 409–411; *KKSS*, vol. 9, no. 601, pp. 68–71; and *Shinagawa ku shi tsūshi hen*, pt. 1, p. 661.

153. Walthall, *Social Protest*, pp. 104, 119.

154. *KKSS*, vol. 9, no. 88, pp. 383–389.

155. Ibid., vol. 10, pp. 51–52.

156. Kodama, *Kinsei shukueki*, p. 334.

157. Charles Tilly, *The Contentious French*, p. 397.

158. *KKSS*, vol. 9, no. 555, pp. 19–21; no. 558, pp. 22–26; no. 785, pp. 284–286.

159. *Gifu ken shi shiryō hen, Kinsei*, vol. 7, no. 97–98, pp. 464–467.

160. Ibid.

161. *Nakasendō Kumagaya eki, josukegō kokon shushi kakidome*, Ibaraki kenritsu Urawa toshokan, ed., no. 4, pp. 30–32.

162. Maruyama Yasunari, *Kinsei shukueki*, vol. 1, pp. 665–675. Disputes over the amount of wages paid to assisting villages were frequent. See, for example, *Shinpen Saitama ken shi shiryō hen*, vol. 5, *Kinsei* 6, no. 98,

pp. 438–440 and no. 101, pp. 443–435; *Nakasendō Kumagaya,* no. 13, pp. 43–44 and no. 15, p. 46.

163. Maruyama Yasunari, *Kinsei shukueki,* vol. 1, pp. 649–651.

164. *Shinagawa ku shi shiryō hen,* no. 194, p. 344.

165. Ōyama, pp. 191–192.

166. According to Neil Waters, the links between villages created by irrigation systems and corvée labor obligations led to a growing, regional identification. See his *Japan's Local Pragmatists* for further discussion on the topic.

167. *Shinpen Saitama ken shi shiryō hen,* vol. 15, *Kinsei 6,* no. 73, pp. 377–380 and *Gifu ken shi shiryō hen, Kinsei 7,* no. 90, pp. 431–435.

168. Nishigori Gohei, "Tōbu nikki," in *Nihon toshi seikatsu shiryō shūsei,* vol. 2: *Santo hen,* Harada Tomohiko, ed., p. 691.

169. *KKSS,* vol. 9, no. 560, pp. 27–28 and no. 813, pp. 316–317.

170. Nishigori, p. 699. According to Nishigori, he and the two officials who accompanied him "danced for joy" after leaving the Magistrate of Road Affairs Office, where they had been told of the acceptance of their petition. No doubt the success of their mission encouraged them to stay in Edo and celebrate. They made certain to stop by their lord's upper residence (*kami yashiki*) to thank the officials who had assisted them with their petition for tax relief.

171. *Tochigi ken shi shiryō hen, Kinsei,* vol. 1, no. 21, pp. 701–703.

172. *Tochigi ken shi tsūshi hen,* vol. 5, *Kinsei 2,* pp. 510–511.

173. Maruyama Yasunari, *Kinsei shukueki,* vol. 1, pp. 510–511.

174. Tanaka Tomojirō, pp. 203–221.

175. *KKSS,* vol. 9, no. 879–880, p. 379.

176. *Nakasendō kōtsū shiryō shū,* vol. 1, no. 98, p. 214; *Shinpen Saitama ken shi shiryō hen,* vol. 15, *Kinsei 6,* no. 83, pp. 411–413.

177. See, for example, *KKSS,* vol. 9, no. 560, pp. 27–28.

178. Chambliss, pp. 58–59.

179. *Kanagawa ken shi shiryō hen,* vol. 9, *Kinsei 6,* no. 113, pp. 178–179; *Hiratsuka shi shi,* vol. 4, *Shiryō hen kinsei 3,* no. 21, pp. 122–123. Conrad Totman has pointed out that the amount of riparian maintenance work increased appreciably by the middle of the Tokugawa period because of ecological mismanagement, mainly erosion caused by deforestation and land overuse. This work, unlike corvée labor earlier in the period, which increased current production, "served only to sustain existing levels of social production and capital." Conrad Totman, "Tokugawa Peasants: Win, Lose, or Draw," *Monumenta Nipponica,* vol. 41, no. 4, p. 466 (Winter 1986).

180. *Shinpen Saitama ken shi shiryō hen,* vol. 15, *Kinsei 6,* no. 70, pp. 361–363 and no. 73, pp. 380–381.

181. Akimoto, pp. 52–55.
182. Aoki Kōji, *Hyakushō ikki no nenjiteki kenkyū,* pp. 3–260.
183. *Shinpen Saitama ken shi shiryō hen,* vol. 11, *Kinsei 2,* no. 2, pp. 111–121; no. 5, p. 156; and no. 8, p. 208. Anne Walthall correctly states that in my "Post Station and Assisting Villages: Corvée Labor and Peasant Contention," p. 411, I failed to note the bakufu's effort to change the status of the supplemental assisting villages as a factor in the uprising. While I did overstress the importance of the announcement of the new impost for the procession to Nikkō, which is a matter of some debate, she, in turn, failed to note that on the same page I do mention the ad hoc tax for the Korean mission of 1764 in accounting for the mounting tensions which led to the violent outburst. Anne Walthall, ed. and trans., *Peasant Uprisings in Japan,* p. 249 n. 3. Walthall skillfully translates and analyzes an account of this uprising entitled "A Thousand Spears at Kitsunezuka" in chapter 3.
184. Ibid., pp. 21–23.
185. Yokoyama Toshio, *Hyakushō ikki to gimin denshō,* pp. 106–108.
186. "Mashi sukegō sōdōki," ch. 1, quoted in Kitazawa Fumitake, *Meiwa no dai-ikki,* p. 8.
187. *Shinpen Saitama ken shi shiryō hen,* vol. 11, *Kinsei 2,* pp. 215–223 and Maruyama Yasunari, *Kinsei shukueki,* vol. 1, pp. 174–192.
188. Yokoyama, pp. 101–113.
189. The *Kodansha Encyclopedia of Japan,* vol. 7, under the heading of *sukegō,* incorrectly states that peasants "frequently rose up in rebellion" against the *sukegō* tax (p. 265). Protest against the transport corvée labor tax has been associated with twenty-one uprisings over a period of more than one hundred years. This is not a very significant number, especially when one considers that there were a total of 1,858 peasant disturbances over approximately the same time period, 1751–1867. Aoki, pp. 36–37.
190. An edict issued in 1769 permitted domain authorities to dispatch troops to neighboring domains to put down uprisings, and authorized the use of firearms, which had previously been forbidden. Vlastos, p. 65.
191. Maruyama Yasunari, *Kinsei shukueki,* vol. 1, pp. 657–658.
192. *Kanagawa ken shi shiryō hen,* vol. 9, *Kinsei 6,* no. 115, pp. 181–182 and no. 127, pp. 206–207.
193. See James C. Scott, *Weapons of the Weak: Everyday Forms of Peasant Resistance.*

3. A Curious Institution

1. A.B.F.M. Redesdale, *Memories,* vol. 2, p. 406.
2. Kaempfer, vol. 3, pp. 44–45.

3. Siebold, *Manners*, p. 77.
4. Ogyū Sorai, *Seidan*, p. 43.
5. The seminal work in this field is Aida Nirō's *Chūsei no sekisho.* For a general, English-language survey of the history of sekisho, see Curtis Alexander Manchester, Ph.D. dissertation, "The Development and Distribution of Sekisho in Japan." Richard Louis Edmonds discusses the use of barriers to delimit a border between settled parts of the country and the frontier in *Northern Frontiers of Qing China and Tokugawa Japan.*
6. Tokuda Ken'ichi, *Chūsei ni okeru suiun no hattatsu*, p. 32. The two sekisho at the port of Hyōgo, administered by Tōdaiji and Kōfukuji temples respectively, were perhaps the top income earners, taking in as much as 1000 *kan* (1 *kan* = 3.75 kg.) of silver a year.
7. Ōshima Nobujirō, *Sekisho: sono rekishi to jittai*, pp. 52–65.
8. For example, Ieyasu built barriers at Yagurasawa in 1590, at Yamashina in 1600, and at Yodo in 1615. Watanabe Kazutoshi, "Kinsei sekisho no shokeitai," *Hōsei shigaku*, vol. 23, pp. 17–19 (1973); Watanabe Kazutoshi, "Edo bakufu rikujō kōtsū seisaku no hatten," in Kodama Kōta, ed., *Nihon kinsei kōtsū shi kenkyū*, p. 30; *KKSS*, vol. 8, no. 109, p. 62.
9. The date in which Arai was established has been a point of contention among scholars. Futagawa Yoshifumi claims that it was established in 1600, before the Battle of Sekigahara, because it lends support to his theory that sekisho were established solely for political surveillance. According to Futagawa, Arai was needed to prevent the escape of hostages that Maeda Toshinaga and a few other daimyo had sent to Ieyasu as a sign of loyalty prior to that important battle. (Futagawa Yoshifumi, "Tōkaidō no sekisho," *Nihon rekishi*, vol. 295, pp. 41–43 (1972).) Watanabe Kazutoshi also accepts the 1600 date, but for different reasons. He maintains that Arai was established around the time of Sekigahara, either before the conflict for military reasons, or shortly thereafter to monitor traffic and restrict the movement of warriors from the losing side. (Watanabe Kazutoshi, *Kaidō to sekisho*, pp. 50–52.) Many other scholars, however, accept the 1601 date, interpreting the establishment of Arai as part of the same effort responsible for organizing the Tōkaidō post-station network. They contend, as do I, that if the purpose of sekisho was to prevent hostages from escaping from Edo and Sunpu Castles, there was no need to go to distant provinces to establish checking stations. A more effective means would simply have been to intensify the guard at the two castles. (Kondō Tsuneji, *Tōkaidō Arai sekisho no kenkyū*, pp. 20–21 and Maruyama Yasunari, "Kinsei sekisho oyobi bansho no kenkyū," *Kyūshū bunka shi kenkyū kiyō*, vol. 19, p. 7 (1974), are two examples.)
10. Igarashi Tomio, *Kinsei sekisho no kisoteki kenkyū*, pp. 59–81.

11. Two standard works in Japanese are Fujino Tamotsu, *Shintei bakuhan taisei shi no kenkyū,* and Kitajima Masamoto, *Edo bakufu no kenryōku kōzō;* in English, see Bolitho, pp. 7–19, for a concise summary.

12. *Tokugawa kinrei kō,* vol. 1, p. 93.

13. See Gilbert Rozman, "Edo's Importance in the Changing Tokugawa Society," *Journal of Japanese Studies,* vol. 1, no. 1 (Autumn 1974) and McClain's *Kanazawa* for two studies on early modern Japan's urbanization.

14. *Tōkyō hyakunen shi,* vol. 1, pp. 679–682; McClain, p. 60.

15. The bakufu heard reports of many crimes on the Tōkaidō and dispatched Inspectors to investigate the situation in 1635/10. *Tokugawa jikki,* vol. 42, p. 691.

16. McClain, pp. 66–67.

17. See Itō Toshiichi, *Edo no machi kado,* for a detailed study of the system of gates in the city of Edo.

18. *Nagoya shi shi, Seiji hen,* vol. 2, pp. 261–267. For Edo, see Maruyama Yasunari, "Kinsei sekisho" (pt. 2), p. 447.

19. Kuroita Mototsugu, *Edo jidai shi,* vol. 1, pp. 308–312. George Sansom, *A History of Japan 1615–1867,* p. 32, puts the number of *rōnin* as high as 500,000. Daimyo transferred to the fiefs of attaindered lords usually expelled at least the top retainers of the former leader. The Yamauchi, for example, expelled the senior retainers of the Chōsokabe daimyo when they were transferred to Tosa and treated the rustic farmer-soldiers there, known as *ichiryō gusoku,* as farmers. Marius B. Jansen, "Tosa in the Seventeenth Century," in John W. Hall and Marius B. Jansen, eds., *Studies in the Institutional History of Early Modern Japan,* p. 117.

20. Ordinance quoted in *Tokugawa jikki,* vol. 1, pp. 327–332.

21. *KKSS,* vol. 8, no. 122, pp. 72–73. The sixteen river crossings were: Shirai, Goryō, Kawada, Koga, Kurihashi, Sekijuku, Kanzaki, Matsudo, Ōwatari, Kawamata, Bōsen, Shichiri-ga-watashi, Fukawa, Obigawa, Ichikawa, and Ippongi. Of these sixteen, seven would remain sekisho for the remainder of the Tokugawa period. Of the remaining nine, however, some continued to function as non-official sekisho until the mid-eighteenth century. Maruyama Yasunari, "Kinsei sekisho," pp. 6, 9.

22. *KKSS,* vol. 8, no. 122, pp. 72–73; *Gyōda shi shi,* vol. 2, Gyōda shi shi hensan iinkai, ed., p. 426.

23. After sending inspectors all over the Kantō to investigate sekisho and bansho in 1631, the bakufu planned to close down unnecessary side roads as well as dig ditches and build fences between sekisho in the region; there is, however, no evidence available at this time that it was at all successful in doing so. Watanabe Kazutoshi, "Sekisho, kuchidome

bansho no kinō to unei," in Maruyama Yasunari, ed., *Jōhō to kōtsū,* vol. 6 of *Nihon no kinsei,* p. 234.

24. *KKSS,* vol. 8, nos. 352–353, pp. 250–252 and no. 360, p. 259.

25. The figure 53 as the total number in the mature sekisho system is based on the document "Shokoku gosekisho oboegaki," issued by the bakufu in 1745. *KKSS,* vol. 10, pp. 67–70. Other contemporary sources give the total at anywhere between 16 and 57. Igarashi Tomio, *Kinsei sekisho seido no kenkyu,* pp. 52–53 and Watanabe Kazutoshi, "Futatabi Edo bakufu no sekisho ni tsuite," *Nihon rekishi,* vol. 334, p. 15 (1976).

The province-by-province breakdown of the fifty-three is as follows: Kōzuke (14), Musashi (9), Sagami (8), Shinano (7), Echigo (5), Tōtōtmi (3), Kai (3), Ōmi (3), and Shimōsa (1).

26. Futagawa, "Echigo no sekisho," *Shinano,* vol. 22, no. 8, pp. 23–24 (1969).

27. Murakami Tadashi, ed., *Edo bakufu sennin dōshin shiryō,* pp. 3–5.

28. Watanabe Kazutoshi, *Kaidō to sekisho,* pp. 73–74.

29. *Matsuida chō shi,* Matsuida chō shi hensan iinkai, ed., p. 461.

30. Satow, p. 226.

31. *KKSS,* vol. 8, no. 223, pp. 149–150.

32. Kaempfer, vol. 3, pp. 59–60.

33. Strictly speaking, Kurihashi sekisho (of Bōsen-Kurihashi), Matsudo (of Kanamachi-Matsudo) and Ichikawa (of Koiwa-Ichikawa) are all in Shimōsa, but because their main sekisho are located in Musashi, the three sekisho pairs are counted as being in Musashi province. The same rule holds for Kawamata (of Shingō-Kawamata) in Kōzuke.

34. *KKSS,* vol. 8, no. 289, pp. 200–201.

35. See Aida Nirō, *Odawara gassen,* pp. 59–62 for details of the battle as it centered around the Hakone area.

36. Nakamura Shizuo, "Hakone sekisho tatemono kankei shiryō ni tsuite," *Hakone sekisho tayori,* vol. 6, p. 2 (1984). The jail cell measured 2.3 x 1.5 x 2.8 meters and was clearly not meant to hold large numbers of people. *THSS,* Hakone sekisho kenkyū kai, ed., vol. 2, p. 106.

37. Kaempfer noted when passing through Arai that it was "open without either walls or ditches." Kaempfer, vol. 3, p. 125. The exception was Kega. Established in 1620 on the Honzaka dōri as an auxiliary barrier for Arai, the sekisho was surrounded by a moat 776 meters in length, which could be crossed with the proper permit at only two places. As the only example, it is safe to say that Kega's moat was a lingering remnant of the medieval sekisho as stronghold. Ōyama, p. 244.

38. The palisade network at Hakone stretched out over 609 meters. The length at its branch sekisho were as follows: at Nebukawa, 259; Kawamura, 372; Sengokugahara, 239; and Tanimura, 161. *KKSS,* vol. 8, no. 347, pp. 244–248.

39. Nakamura Shizuo and Iwasaki Munezumi, "Hakone sekisho tōmi ban-sho to Hakone kanetsukidō ni tsuite," *Hakone sekisho tayori*, vol. 5, pp. 3–4 (1982). For Usui, see *Gunma ken shi shiryō hen*, vol. 9, *Kinsei 1*, no. 269, pp. 644–653. For Kariyado, see Ibid., vol. 11, *Kinsei 3*, no. 442, p. 693.

40. Records of this exist for 1770, 1803, and 1833. For the 1770 order, see *HGNK*, Hakone komonjo o manabu kai, ed., vol. 1, p. 110.

41. Watanabe Kazutoshi, "Edo bakufu no sekisho seido no kakuritsu to kinō," *Nihon rekishi*, vol. 39, p. 35 (1974).

42. Ibid., p. 37.

43. Futagawa, "Tōkaidō no sekisho," p. 56.

44. *Gunma ken shi shiryō hen*, vol. 10, *Kinsei 2*, no. 269, pp. 652–653.

45. Igarashi, *Kinsei sekisho seido*, pp. 153–158.

46. Futagawa, "Kōzuke no sekisho," *Shinano*, vol. 22, no. 12, p. 42 (1970).

47. Igarashi, *Kinsei sekisho seido*, pp. 170–171. For Ōsasa, see *Gunma ken shi shiryō hen*, vol. 11, *Kinsei 3*, no. 404, p. 751.

48. Igarashi, *Kinsei sekisho seido*, p. 152.

49. *HGNK*, vol. 3, p. 21; Ibid., vol. 1, pp. 224–225.

50. *HGNK*, vol. 2, pp. 157–167; Ibid., vol. 3, p. 312; and *THSS*, vol. 1, p. 219.

51. Yataka Kōjirō, *Kiso Fukushima sekisho*, pp. 448.

52. *Kanagawa ken shi shiryō hen*, vol. 9, *Kinsei 6*, pp. 228–229.

53. *Tokugawa jikki*, vol. 42, p. 524.

54. Fifty-five men (fifteen domain samurai and forty foot soldiers) were in the force at Hakone; at Nebukawa, twenty-five men; and sixteen each for Yagurasawa, Sengokugahara, and Kawamura. *THSS*, vol. 2, pp. 406–407.

55. *Kanagawa ken shi tsūshi hen*, vol. 2, *Kinsei 1*, p. 260.

In the case of Arai, it was administered until 1702 by a bakufu official who manned the sekisho with his own retainers. In an emergency there-fore, he would have had to call upon the bakufu for reinforcements. After 1702, when administration of the sekisho was turned over to Yoshida, reinforcements would have been sent from that domain's castle town, located at a distance of sixteen kilometers, or a walk of almost four hours.

56. In addition to Hakone, there is evidence that reserve systems were also established at its branch sekisho, and at Ōsasa as well, but they were probably employed at a number of other places as well. At Ōsasa, which was administered by a bakufu intendant whose headquarters were located quite some distance away, fifty guns were assigned to com-moners living in twelve villages in the surrounding area. *Gunma ken shiryō shū*, vol. 5, *Nikki hen 1*, Yamada Takemoro and Hagiwara Susumu, eds., no. 38, pp. 186–187.

57. Michael Mann, "The Autonomous Power of the State: Its Origins, Mechanisms and Results," as quoted in Migdal, pp. 22–23.

58. *Kanagawa ken shi shiryō hen,* vol. 9, *Kinsei* 6, pp. 355–358 and *THSS,* vol. 2, pp. 16, 407.

59. *HGNK,* vol. 2, pp. 145–149.

60. *THSS,* vol. 2, pp. 111–114 and 79–91.

61. Bolitho, p. 245. Like many domains, Odawara had inter-domainal factions which opposed or supported the Imperial side; the opposition faction organized following the transfer of the sekisho and did cause a skirmish there, but no battle took place with Imperial and bakufu forces on opposite sides of the sekisho. Maruyama Yasunari, "Kinsei sekisho oyobi bansho," p. 57.

62. Watanabe Kazutoshi, "Kinsei sekisho no chihōteki tenkai," *Aichi daigaku bungaku ronsō,* vol. 74, p. 44 (1984).

63. *KKSS,* vol. 8, no. 150, p. 90. See Ibid., no. 170, p. 106 for the contents of the edict board as it read at Goryō sekisho. Only sekisho classified as "very important" (*omoki*), with the notable exception of Kiso Fukushima, were given edict boards to post. Igarashi, *Kinsei sekisho seido,* p. 271.

64. *KKSS,* vol. 8, no. 288, p. 200 and no. 283, p. 197.

65. For example, Tokugawa Ieyasu's second son, Hideyasu, traveling from Echizen to Edo to pay his respects to his father the shogun in 1603, was angered when the guards at Usui sekisho questioned his retainers about the weapons being transported in the retinue. *Tokugawa jikki,* vol. 38, p. 95.

66. *KKSS,* vol. 8, no. 159, pp. 97–98.

67. The bakufu changed the wording or the content or both of the notice boards posted at sekisho eight times, from 1625 to 1711. The two major revisions were in 1667, when the inspection of guns was added, and 1711. Watanabe Kazutoshi, *Kaidō to sekisho,* p. 89.

68. *KKSS,* vol. 8, no. 433, pp. 319–320.

69. Dan Fenno Henderson distinguishes between "notices" (*tatsu*) and "proclamations" (*ofuregaki*) in his "The Evolution of Tokugawa Law," pp. 228–229.

70. *KKSS,* vol. 8, no. 433, pp. 319–320.

71. Ibid., no. 233, pp. 149–150 and no. 217, p. 146.

72. Ibid., no. 289, pp. 200–201.

73. *THSS,* vol. 2, pp. 6–20.

74. In Sagami, only local people could pass through Kawamura, Tanimura, Sengokughara, Yagurasawa, Nenzaka, and Aonohara, thereby forcing all but local traffic through Hakone, on the Tōkaidō, and Nebukawa, on the coastal Atamidō. Both sekisho, like the five on major arteries in

Musashi, strictly required women to obtain permits from the Keeper of Edo Castle. In Kōzuke, only local women were allowed to pass through seven of the fourteen sekisho, channeling non-local traffic to the Nakasendō, Nikkō reiheishidō, Shinshūdō, Mikuni kaidō, and Kusatsudō, where again women were required to hold permits from the Keeper of Edo Castle. Almost all sekisho where only local women were permitted were classified by the bakufu as "less important."

75. *THSS*, vol. 2, pp. 6–20.

76. Permits for guns were obtained from different sources depending on the number being transported: ten or more guns called for a permit from the bakufu Elders, but less than that number required a permit from the Odawara daimyo. Regulations were less strict on bows. No permit was demanded for up to nine bows, but ten or more again required a permit from the Elders. A permit from the Elders was imperative, however, for even one cannon at sekisho that permitted the passage of weapons.

77. *KKSS*, vol. 8, no. 289, pp. 200–201. Similarly, an edict board at Nakagawa sekisho in Musashi, where river traffic near Edo was monitored, read: "Any container large enough to conceal a person in it must be examined before being allowed to pass through. Small containers need not be examined." Ibid., no. 351, p. 250.

78. Kaempfer, vol. 3, p. 123; Ōta Shokusanjin, "Jinjutsu kikō," in Sugiura, p. 123.

79. Miyazaki Katsunori, p. 309.

80. The following discussion of the inspection of arms at sekisho is, unless otherwise noted, based on *THSS*, vol. 2, pp. 6–20.

81. Igarashi, *Kinsei sekisho seido*, p. 614.

82. The seven sekisho in Kōzuke that permitted only local traffic did not allow the passage of any type of weapon. Six out of the seven sekisho that did allow weapons required a permit from the bakufu Elders—in order to keep strict surveillance on the northern outer lords. The same was true of the sekisho on the Musashi-Kōzuke border, Shingō-Kawamata, and three on the Musashi-Shimōsa border: Bōsen-Kurihashi, Kanamachi-Matsudo, and Koiwa-Ishikawa. At Sarugakyō (Kōzuke) and the three sekisho on the Musashi-Shimōsa border mentioned above, permits from the Elders for guns were required not only when traveling towards Edo, but also when leaving the city, again indicating the bakufu's concern with the northern daimyo. At another two in Musashi, Kobotoke and Shingō-Kawamata, the same permit was required if the number of guns or weapons being transported was great.

83. *THSS*, vol. 2, p. 7.

84. *HGNK*, vol. 3, pp. 184–185 and Ibid., vol. 1, pp. 23–25, 195.

85. Ibid., vol. 3, pp. 184–185.
86. See, for example, the case involving a retainer named Endō Shōha in Ibid., vol. 1, pp. 140–145.
87. Ibid., p. 3.
88. Ibid., vol. 3, pp. 190–191.
89. Ibid., vol. 1, p. 155.
90. Ibid., vol. 2, p. 136.
91. Ibid., vol. 3, pp. 174–175, 169 and Ibid., vol. 2, p. 11.
92. Ibid., vol. 1, p. 89.
93. Ibid., vol. 3, p. 247.
94. Ibid., vol. 2, pp. 145–149.
95. Fragmentary records do not allow us to know exactly how many cases occurred, but there were at least six cases at Hakone, with two resulting in crucifixion; at least seven at Odo; two at Sengokugahara; three at Arai; ten at Usui; and one each at Yagurasawa, Nanmoku, and Kobotoke.

   In a rather sensational case—and the only one discovered to date involving samurai—retainers of the bakufu's Nagasaki magistrate smuggled prostitutes and other women back with them to Edo, avoiding detection at the sekisho on the Tōkaidō, but were caught after the fact. More than twenty people were involved, and both retainers received the death sentence. (Watanabe Kazutoshi, *Kaidō to sekisho*, pp. 111–113. For Hakone, see Katō Toshiyuki, "Sekisho yaburi no shin monjo," Hakone sekisho tayori, vol. 6, p. 5 (1984); *Kanagawa ken shi shiryō hen*, vol. 4, *Kinsei* 1, p. 227; Ibid., vol. 9, *Kinsei* 6, pp. 394–398; and *THSS*, vol. 2, p. 94. For Sengokugahara, see Ibid., pp. 418–421. For Usui, see Futagawa, "Kōzuke no sekisho," p. 32; Igarashi, *Kinsei sekisho seido*, pp. 401–403; "Usui sekimori nikki," in *Gunma ken shiryō shū*, Gunma ken bunka jigyō shinkō kai, ed., vol. 5, *Nikki hen*, no. 1, pp. 94–98. For Ōdo, *Gunma ken shi shiryō hen*, vol. 11, *Kinsei* 3, no. 435, pp. 684–688. For Kobotoke, see "Kōshū kaidō Kobotoke tōge sekiban nikki," in *Nihon nōmin shiryō shusui*, Ono Takeo, ed., vol. 6, pp. 81–93.)

   One reason why sekisho records are so fragmented is that after the Meiji Restoration the head guards at individual sekisho customarily divided up the official records amongst themselves. While this perhaps increased the chance of some surviving, because of natural disasters and human negligence or indifference, we are often left with only a partial picture of the institution.
96. Servitude as applied to women was called *yakko kei*. Women were put in a place of detention, where they were "forced to work with rice straw or employed in chopping firewood or in civil engineering projects." Hiramatsu Yoshirō, "History of Penal Institutions: Japan," *Law in*

Japan, vol. 6, p. 18 (1973). Often, however, the actual sentences imposed on women were even lighter than the statutes called for. According to Nagano Hiroko, there are many examples of women who went around sekisho in the company of men (i.e., were led by men around the sekisho in the eyes of the political authorities) that were let off with only an official reproof. Nagano Hiroko, "Bakuhan hō to josei," in Josei shi sōgō kenkyū kai, ed., *Nihon josei shi,* vol. 3, *Kinsei,* p. 173. This informative article surveys the treatment of women under bakufu and domainal law.

97. Futagawa Yoshifumi, "Edo bakufu hō to saiban kara mita sekisho no honshitsu," *Nihon rekishi,* vol. 271, p. 63 (1970).
98. *Gunma ken shi shiryō hen,* vol. 11, no. 435, pp. 684–687.
99. Futagawa, "Edo bakufu hō," pp. 60–61.
100. *Arai chō shi shiryō hen,* vol. 8, no. 3, pp. 36–38; Watanabe Kazutoshi, "Imagiri sekisho ni okeru kaihen aratame seido," *Aichi daigaku bungaku ronsō,* vol. 92 (1990).
101. Sugae Masumi and Takagi Zensuke are two examples of Tokugawa travelers who used either *sekisho* (or other similar words such as *sekiya*) or *bansho,* regardless of whether they were referring to a bakufu sekisho or domain bansho. Sugae Masumi, *Sugae Masumi yūranki,* vol. 4, pp. 37, 73, 87, 153, 167–168; Takagi Zensuke, "Satsuyō yukikaeri kiji," *NSSS,* vol. 2, p. 641.
102. Toyama and Kaga domains each referred to two of their bansho as sekisho. These sekisho were assigned greater importance and hence were staffed with foot soldiers (*ashigaru*), whereas bansho were staffed solely with peasants. *Toyama ken shi tsūshi hen,* Toyama ken, ed., vol. 4, *Kinsei* 2, pp. 368–371. The same was true in Awa domain. *Tokushima ken shi,* Tokushima ken shi hensan iinkai, ed., vol. 4, pp. 45–47.
103. *Sakai sekisho shi,* Sakai sekisho shi hensan iinkai, ed., pp. 43–55.
104. *Bansho* sometimes refers to bakufu sekisho, but as noted earlier, the two were clearly defined in legal terms regarding the punishment offenders met. At least one sekisho, Shirai, in Kōzuke, referred to itself at one point as a bansho, further adding to the indiscriminate use of the two terms. *Gunma ken shi shiryō hen,* vol. 9, *Kinsei* 1, pp. 492–493, 787–788.
105. Furukawa, p. 97. Ikari-no-seki is on Hirosaki's border with Akita domain.
106. *Toyama ken shi tsūshi hen,* vol. 4, *Kinsei* 2, pp. 373–376 (a diagram of the bansho can be found on p. 373) and *Sakai sekisho shi,* pp. 87–100.
107. Nishi Inotani bansho, also in Kaga, consisted of one building that doubled as living quarters for the guards, with a modest seventy-five meters of palisades. *Toyama ken shi tsūshi hen,* vol. 4, *Kinsei* 2, pp. 375–376. Two bansho in Niigata measured 4 x 6 meters and 6 x 7 meters, respec-

tively. Other bansho in Kaga, such as Mizusu and Okunoyama, appear to have been little more than a wooden gate straddling the road. *Niigata ken shi shiryō hen,* Niigata ken, ed., vol. 7, *Kinsei* 2, no. 197, pp. 692–694 and no. 208, pp. 701–703.

108. A map showing the distribution of road bansho in Tosa domain can be found in *Yamauchi ke shiryō,* vol. 1: *Daiichidai Kazutoyo kōki,* final page insert. See Maruyama Yasunari, *Nihon kinsei kōtsū shi no kenkyū,* pp. 132–171 for a study of road bansho in Tosa.

109. In Sendai, for example, eighteen of its thirty-odd bansho, most of which were in place by 1643, were located on its borders with Dewa and Nambu. (*Iwate ken shi,* Iwate ken, ed., vol. 4, *Kinsei* 2, pp. 1,058–1,067 and Matanabe Nobuo, ed., *Miyagi no kenkyū,* vol. 5, *Kinsei* 3, p. 358.) In Nambu itself as well, approximately two-thirds of the domain's twenty-six bansho were positioned on its borders (*Iwate ken shi,* vol. 5, *Kinsei* 2, pp. 1,203–1,205.) Satsuma domain placed nine bansho on its borders and twelve inland. Kai, bakufu-controlled territory, surrounded on all sides by other domains, placed almost all of its bansho on its borders: eleven on the border with Shinano; two with Musashi; and eight with Suruga. Only three bansho were distributed inland. (For Satsuma, see *Kagoshima ken shi,* Kagoshima ken, ed., vol. 2, pp. 557–558; for Kai, see Murakami Tadashi, "Kai ni okeru kuchidome bansho no seiritsu," *Shinano,* vol. 16, no. 1, pp. 45–53 (1964).) Seven of the eight bansho in Kaga and Toyama in the late eighteenth century lay near the border with Takayama domain (Echigo province) border. (*Toyama ken shi tsūshi hen,* vol. 4, *Kinsei* 2, pp. 368–371.)

110. Watanabe Nobuo, ed., *Miyagi no kenkyū,* vol. 5, *Kinsei* 3, pp. 358–362.

111. *Etchū shiryō,* vol. 3, p. 210 and *Sakai sekisho shi,* pp. 1–4.

112. Mamiya Hisako, *Tosa han no sanson kōzō,* p. 120.

113. *Iwate ken shi,* vol. 5, *Kinsei* 2, pp. 1,203–1,205.

114. Hirao Michio, *Tosa han nōgyō keizai shi,* pp. 4–5.

115. *Yamauchi ke shiryō,* vol. 3: *Dainidai Tadayoshi kōki,* pp. 38–39. For a detailed study of run-away peasants in Tosa, see Ishiodori Kazuo, "Tosa han shoki no 'hashirimono' taisaku ni tsuite," in Yamamoto Takeshi, ed., *Tosa shi no shomondai,* pp. 127–141.

116. For Tosa, *Kenshōbo,* vol. 4, pp. 3–5; for Kumamoto, see *Kumamoto ken shiryō, Kinsei,* vol. 3, p. 447.

117. *Kaga han shiryō,* vol. 1, p. 837.

118. Ibid., vol. 2, pp. 406–407 (1615), pp. 747–748 (1635), pp. 839–840 (1637); Ibid., vol. 3, p. 789 (1659) and p. 392 (1674). For a summary of the reforms, see Tanaka Yoshio, *Kaga hyakumangoku,* pp. 64–69.

119. *Toyama ken shi tsūshi hen,* vol. 4, *Kinsei* 2, pp. 381–382.

120. A Tosa ordinance from 1628 prohibited service personnel (*hōkōnin*),

townsmen, and peasants from passing through bansho without travel permits. *Kenshōbo,* vol. 4, no. 122, p. 93. Similarly, a Kumamoto edict stated that "Men and women without travel permits are not to be allowed out of the domain." *Kumamoto ken shiryō, Kinsei,* vol. 3, p. 449.

121. *Kenshōbo,* vol. 4, nos. 1–2, pp. 3–5 and no. 57, pp. 45–46; *Tokushima ken shi,* vol. 4, pp. 44–48; *Iwate ken shi,* vol. 5, *Kinsei* 2, pp. 1,258–1,260.

122. *Kumamoto ken shiryō, Kinsei,* vol. 3, p. 448.

123. *Shinpen Saitama ken shi shiryō hen,* vol. 15, *Kinsei* 6, nos. 161–162, pp. 631–634; no. 165, pp. 646–648.

124. *Nagano ken shi kinsei shiryō hen,* Nagano ken shi kankō kai, ed., vol. 7, pt. 3, p. 27.

125. *Toyama ken shi tsūshi hen,* vol. 4, *Kinsei* no. 2, pp. 80, 375.

126. In Tosa, for example, bansho numbers increased from thirty-six (1688–1703) to eighty-six (1781–1788). Hirao Michio, *Kinsei shakai shikō,* pp. 153–163. But in Tottori domain, bansho decreased from thirteen, early in the seventeenth century, to seven by the turn of the next century. During the turbulent final decades of the Tokugawa period, however, they increased in number again. *Tottori ken shi,* vol. 4, *Kinsei shakai keizai,* pp. 461–462; *Tottori han shi,* Tottori ken, ed., vol. 3, pp. 223–233. Poor documentation, unfortunately, does not allow for any nationwide generalizations about bansho numbers and changing function.

127. Yamamoto Mitsumasa, ed., *Kinsei Aizu shi no kenkyū,* vol. 1, pp. 198–199.

128. See, for example, *Toyama ken shi shiryō hen,* vol. 5, nos. 921–923, pp. 1,239–1,245 for records of tax income collected at Nishi Inotani bansho.

129. Controlled goods varied from domain to domain, but in Tosa, for example, twenty-three items (such as paper, tobacco, cloth, lacquer, bamboo, and coal) were prohibited from export and three (sake, tobacco, and rice) from import. (*Kenshōbo,* vol. 4, no. 18, p. 15 and nos. 4–5, pp. 5–7. See also *Iwate ken shi,* vol. 5, *Kinsei* 2, no. 5, pp. 1,265–1,268 for a similar list from Nambu domain. Eight items were prohibited from export without a special permit in Aizu domain. *Fukushima ken shi,* vol. 10, *ge, Kinsei shiryō hen* 4, no. 24, pp. 826–827 and Yamamoto Mitsumasa, *Kinsei Aizu shi,* p. 201. For Kaga, see *Kaga han shiryō,* vol. 4, p. 323.)

The primary role of bansho in Kurume domain was to prevent the export of grains, as reflected in the name, *kokudome* ("grain-stopping"), given bansho there. (*Kurume shi shi,* vol. 2, pp. 885–887.) Goods restricted from export required special authorization from domainal authorities to be transported through a bansho. (*Fukushima ken shi,* vol. 10, *ge, Kinsei shiryō hen* 4, no. 24, pp. 826–827.)

4. PERMITS AND PASSAGES

1. Jippensha, *Hizakurige or Shanks' Mare*, p. 48. The original can be found in Jippensha Ikku, *Tōkaidō Hizakurige*, pp. 78–79.
2. Hayami Akira, "Thank You Francisco Xavier: An Essay in the Use of Micro-Data for Historical Demography of Tokugawa Japan," *Keio Economic Studies*, vol. 13, p. 75 (1976).
3. A. L. Beier, *Masterless Men: The Vagrancy Problem in England 1560–1640*. Documentation for China is difficult to obtain. In the T'ang period, at least, there was some sort of permit and barrier system. Edwin O. Reischauer, *Ennin's Travels in T'ang China*, pp. 138–139. The missionary and historian Mendoza related some (second-hand) information on the situation in the mid-sixteenth century: "No man can go from one province to another without taking a license of the governor; and he who is found without one is punished." Quoted in the introduction by R. H. Major to Gonzalez de Mendoza, *The Historie of the Great and Mightie Kingdom of China and the Situation Thereof*, vol. 1, p. xxxix. Ogyū Sorai briefly notes the existence of barriers and permits in different periods of Chinese history. Ogyū Sorai, *Seidan*, pp. 42–43. In eighteenth-century France, where mobility was common, passports were "very irregularly taken out." Olwen H. Hufton, *The Poor of Eighteenth Century France, 1750–1789*, p. 69.
4. Watanabe Kazutoshi's introduction and annotated comments in *Arai chō shi shiryō hen*, vol. 8, is a rare exception, but even this study is limited in scope to women's permits collected at one sekisho.
5. Kodama Kōta and Toyoda Takeshi, eds., *Kōtsū shi*.
6. Jippensha, *Tōkaidō Hizakurige*, p. 52. Although Thomas Satchell translated *tegata* as "permits," as in the passage opening this chapter, and I have used the plural here as well, it is not clear from the text whether they received one or two permits, since more than one person could be listed on a permit. See *Kōchi ken shi, Kinsei shiryō hen*, pp. 878–882, for some examples.
7. *Kanagawa ken shi shiryō hen*, vol. 9, *Kinsei 6*, p. 362.
8. *Hanpōshū*, vol. 1: *Okayama han*, pp. 639, 641; *Toyama ken shi shiryō hen*, vol. 4, *Kinsei 2*, p. 379.
9. *THSS*, vol. 2, pp. 6–20.
10. *KKSS*, vol. 8, pp. 167–168.
11. *Arai chō shi shiryō hen*, vol. 8, no. 11, p. 130.
12. Ibid., pp. 31–32.
13. Watanabe Kazutoshi, *Kaidō to sekisho*, p. 101.
14. *Okayama ken shi*, vol. 25, *Tsuyama han monjo*, pp. 710–712.
15. *Hiroshima ken shi tsūshi hen*, vol. 4, *Kinsei*, pp. 705–706.

16. *Ichinomiya shi shi shiryō hen,* vol. 8, no. 3,751, p. 518.
17. *Gifu ken shi shiryō hen, Kinsei,* vol. 7, no. 115, p. 504. The outcome of the petition is unknown.
18. See Tanaka Yoshio, p. 69, for a convenient introduction to the ten-village group system.
19. *Toyama ken shi tsūshi hen,* vol. 4, *Kinsei* 2, pp. 376–381.
20. *Kaga han shiryō,* vol. 5, pp. 57–59.
21. "Zenkō-ji Tateyama sankei tabi nikki," in *Gifu ken shi shiryō hen, Kinsei,* Gifu ken, ed., vol. 7, no. 131, p. 544.
22. *Hanpōshū,* vol. 1: *Okayama han,* p. 639 and *Kumamoto ken shiryō,* vol. 3, p. 477.
23. *Arai chō shi shiryō hen,* vol. 8, no. 11, p. 130; no. 14, p. 135; no. 30, p. 158.
24. The application for a travel permit and the permit itself could take two forms. In the first case the applicant presented a written request to the issuer, who then endorsed it on the reverse side with his seal, signature, the date, and a statement such as: "Please grant the person(s) listed on the back of this document safe passage through the sekisho." A permit prepared in this manner was called a "reverse-side transit permit" (*ura tegata*). In the second case, the applicant presented the written request and the issuer wrote up the permit on a separate piece of paper, hence the appellation "separate paper transit permit" (*bessho tegata*). In this case the application—the front side—only established the identity of the applicant; technically, therefore, only the back side of the document was the permit. Historically there was a progression from the first to the second method of writing permits. Although the first method was the standard for most of the seventeenth century, the second was also occasionally used. From the eighteenth century on, the second, separate paper method became the predominant form, although some permits issued to commoners nevertheless continued to follow the first form throughout the Tokugawa period. Samurai permits, however, were always written using the separate paper method. Igarashi, *Kinsei sekisho seido no kenkyū,* pp. 69–73.
25. Despite the more or less basic form permits followed, there were some minor differences according to issuer in the type of signature or seal used, the way of addressing the permit, the type of paper used, and the way in which the paper was folded. Yataka, pp. 85–89.
   Many of the extant Tokugawa travel permits lack information on the purpose of travel and sometimes the destination as well. In the case of travel permits for pilgrimage, at least, the function of travel could be left out, as it was apparent in most cases from the destination—pilgrimage sites and the location of hot spring resorts being widely known.
26. *THSS,* vol. 1, p. 228.

27. In the case of a daimyo transfer to a new domain, a single travel permit could be used for hundreds of people. In such cases the guards tabulated the numbers going through the sekisho with an abacus and relayed the information to the head officials to ensure that no one unaccounted for sneaked through. There were, however, some restrictions on the numbers of travelers that could be listed on one permit for commoner women, as a reply to an inquiry to the bakufu Keeper of Edo Castle stated that more than one permit was necessary for a group in excess of ten women. *Kanagawa ken shi shiryō hen,* vol. 9, *Kinsei* 6, no. 242, p. 367.

28. *THSS,* vol. 2, p. 1.

29. *Okayama ken shi,* vol. 25, *Tsuyama han monjo,* p. 986–989; *Hiroshima ken shi, kinsei shiryō hen,* vol. 4, no. 1,343, pp. 236–238.

30. *Gunma ken shi shiryō hen,* vol. 2, *Kinsei* 2, no. 268, p. 643; *Gunma ken shiryō shū,* vol. 5, *Nikki* pt. 1, pp. 118–119, 127. See also *THSS,* vol. 2, p. 16 for further discussion of transfer permits.

31. *HGNK,* vol. 1, p. 96. Used permits were stored at sekisho for a number of years–three in the case of Hakone–possibly for the future reference of the guard officials. After the designated time period elapsed, the valuable paper was used at the sekisho according to need.

32. *Shinpen Saitama ken shi shiryō hen,* vol. 15, *Kinsei* 6, no. 166, p. 656 and *HGNK,* vol. 3, pp. 60–61.

33. *Kenshōbo,* vol. 4, no. 62, p. 48.

34. *Yataka,* p. 226.

35. Igarashi, *Kinsei sekisho no kisoteki kenkyū,* pp. 590–593.

36. R. K. Hall, p. 154.

37. Aimé Humbert, p. 255.

38. *THSS,* vol. 2, pp. 72–77, 101–105; *HGNK,* vol. 3, pp. 318–320.

39. *HGNK,* vol. 2, p. 104.

40. Ibid., vol. 1, pp. 33, 109–110; Ibid., vol. 2, p. 11; see also *Shinpen Saitama ken shi shiryō hen,* vol. 15, *Kinsei* 6, no. 164, pp. 644–645.

41. *Arai chō shi shiryō hen,* vol. 8, nos. 53–55, pp. 184–186.

42. *Nagano ken shi kinsei shiryō hen,* vol. 4, pt. 3, p. 691.

43. For Yanagase, see *Shiga ken shi,* vol. 5: *Sangyō shiryō,* pp. 435–436. For Kega, *Hosoe chō shi shiryō hen,* vol. 1, pp. 93 and 113. Many examples for Arai can be found in *Arai chō shi shiryō hen,* vol. 8.

44. *HGNK,* vol. 3, p. 241.

45. *Gyōda shi shi,* vol. 2, p. 423.

46. *Gunma ken shi shiryō hen,* vol. 9, no. 490, pp. 783–787.

47. Kaempfer, vol. 3, p. 60.

48. *HGNK,* vol. 1, p. 143; *THSS,* vol. 2, p. 103.

49. Miyazaki Katsunori, pp. 309, 320–321.

50. Nagakubo Sekisui, "Nagasaki kōeki nikki," in Yanagida Kunio, ed., *Kikō bunshū*, p. 233.

51. Ōta Nanpo, "Kaigen kikō," in *Ōta Nanpo shū*, p. 342.

52. *HGNK*, vol. 1, pp. 140–145.

53. Ibid., pp. 1–2.

54. Ibid., pp. 111–126; Ibid., vol. 2, p. 172; Ibid., vol. 3, pp. 186–187, 191.

55. Katsu Kokichi, "Musui dokugen," in his *Musui dokugen, hoka,* Katsube Mitake, ed., pp. 54–55.

56. Takayama Hikokurō, "Jōkyō ryochū nikki," in *Takayama Hikokurō zenshū,* Takayama Hikokurō sensei itoku kenshō kai, ed., vol. 2, p. 126.

57. Takayama Hikokurō, "Hokkō nikki," in ibid., p. 346.

58. *HGNK*, vol. 1, pp. 111–126.

59. *Iwate ken shi,* vol. 5, *Kinsei* 2, pp. 1,261–1,264 for Nambu domain; *Kenshōbo,* vol. 4, no. 6, p. 8 for Tosa; *Yamagata ken shi shiryō hen,* vol. 6, pt. 2, pp. 251–253 for Tsuruoka domain; for Kumamoto, *Kumamoto ken shiryō,* vol. 3, p. 447; for Okayama, *Hanpōshū,* vol. 1, *Okayama han,* no. 1,651, p. 639. For Tsuruoka, see also Sugae Masumi, "Tsugaru no oku," in *Sugae Masumi yūranki,* vol. 3, p. 111.

60. *Toyama ken shi tsūshi hen,* vol. 4, pp. 376–381; *Toyama ken shi shiryō hen,* vol. 5, no. 968, pp. 1,276–1,278.

61. *Toyama ken shi shiryō hen,* vol. 4, *Kinsei* 3, no. 658, p. 819; *Kaga han shiryō,* vol. 4, pp. 599–600.

62. *Yamagata ken shi shiryō hen,* vol. 6, pt. 2, pp. 251–253.

63. Mitani ke monjo, no. 795. The man was from Awa.

64. *Kenshōbo,* vol. 4, no. 6, pp. 8–9; *Tokushima ken shi,* vol. 4, pp. 49–52.

65. Furukawa Koshōken, "Saiyū zakki," in *NSSS,* vol. 3, p. 355.

66. *Kenshōbo,* vol. 4, nos. 21–22, pp. 17–19.

67. *Gunma ken shi shiryō hen,* vol. 9, no. 489, pp. 779–783, 787–788; *Nagano ken shi kinsei shiryō hen,* vol. 2, pt. 2, no. 1,069, p. 868.

68. Watanabe Kazutoshi, "Shukubamachi jūmin no seikatsu," *Aichi daigaku sōgō kyōdo kenkyū kiyō,* vol. 30, pp. 125–126 (1985).

69. *Matsuida chō shi,* pp. 517–520.

70. *Sarugakyō sekisho shiryō,* Harazawa Yuranosuke, ed., pp. 222–320, for instance, contains many examples of marriages to women who had to pass through the checking station. The permits here were granted by village officials, not centrally-designated issuers.

71. *Nagano ken shi kinsei shiryō hen,* vol. 4, pt. 3, no. 2,279, p. 928; Nakamura Shin'ichi, ed., *Takada hansei shi kenkyū,* vol. 1, pp. 11 and 143; *Toyama ken shi shiryō hen,* vol. 5, no. 910, pp. 1,230–1,231.

72. *Arai chō shi shiryō hen,* vol. 8, no. 5, pp. 123–124; *Yamagata ken shi shiryō hen,* vol. 6, pt. 2, pp. 251–253.

73. Kaempfer, vol. 2, p. 37.
74. Redesdale, vol. 2, p. 406.
75. *KKSS*, vol. 9, no. 853, p. 365.
76. The list is based on information contained in *HGNK*, vol. 2, p. 50 and *KKSS*, vol. 8, no. 247, p. 169.
77. *Bikuni* were members of an order of religious nuns, affiliated with nunneries at Kamakura and Kyoto, who were often seen on Tokugawa roads. Kaempfer found the traveling nuns the "handsomest girls" he saw in Japan and noted that they often used their beauty by offering sexual favors to solicit contributions, a percentage of which was given to the religious establishment with which they were affiliated. Kaempfer, vol. 2, p. 340.
78. *HGNK*, vol. 1, p. 39.
79. Ibid., vol. 2, pp. 94–95.
80. Ibid., vol. 3, pp. 133–134, 147, 149–150; *THSS*, vol. 1, pp. 28–34.
81. Inoue Tsūjo, "Tōkai kikō," in *Inoue Tsūjo zenshū*, Inoue Tsūjo zenshū shūtei iinkai, ed., p. 47. Inoue did eventually marry, in 1689, at the age of 29.
82. Another example can be found in *Arai chō shi shiryō hen*, vol. 8, no. 48, p. 36.
83. Ibid., pp. 31–36, 113–116.
84. *HGNK*, vol. 3, pp. 166, 169.
85. Ibid., p. 45.
86. *THSS*, vol. 2, p. 7.
87. Ibid., vol. 2, p. 7.
88. *HGNK*, vol. 1, p. 102 and *THSS*, vol. 1, p. 21.
89. *HGNK*, vol. 2, pp. 12, 135; Ibid., vol. 3, pp. 74–75.
90. Ibid., vol. 3, pp. 100–102.
91. Kondō, *Tōkaidō Arai sekisho*, pp. 137–138.
92. See *HGNK*, vol. 3, pp. 30–36 for some actual cases.
93. One case of a pilgrim doing this is recorded in "Konpira sankei dōchū nikki," Yamamoto Mitsumasa, ann., *Kokuritsu rekishi minzoku hakubutsukan kenkyū hōkoku*, vol. 4, p. 82 (March 1984).
94. *Arai chō shi shiryō hen*, vol. 6, no. 48, p. 36.
95. *HGNK*, vol. 3, pp. 30–31.
96. Quoted in Igarashi, *Kinsei sekisho seido no kenkyū*, p. 65.
97. Jippensha, *Hizakurige or Shanks' Mare*, pp. 98–99.
98. Kiyokawa, p. 182.
99. An example of the set of instructions sent to Hakone from Odawara read:

(1) Enforce regulations as written on the sekisho edict board and in official notices sent to the sekisho. The checking of travelers of both sexes should be done with diligence.

(2) The checking of women travelers should be done without obstructing the flow of traffic.

(3) Do not be rude to bakufu housemen or daimyo; pay attention to show correct manners. . . .

(4) Do not be rude to travelers or commit any excessive behavior while checking them. Sekisho guards, the Inspector of Women, as well as those below the rank of foot soldier, should exhibit good manners.

THSS, vol. 1, p. 219.

100. *Shiga ken shi*, vol. 5, pp. 435–436 and *Yamagata ken shi shiryō hen*, vol. 6, pt. 2, p. 251. The instructions to Arai guards are quoted in Igarashi, *Kinsei sekisho seido*, p. 528.

101. Jippensha, *Hizakurige or Shanks' Mare*, p. 131.

102. Shirabyōshi Masako, "Kōshidō no ki," in Yanagida Kunio, ed., *Zoku kikō bunshū*, p. 214. The Englishman Mitford, too, found the weapons intimidating. Hugh Cortazzi, *Victorians in Japan: In and Around the Treaty Ports*, p. 218.

103. *Matsuida chō shi*, pp. 462–464.

104. Yasumi Roan, *Ryokō yōjin shū*, folio 62.

105. Inoue, "Kika nikki," p. 79.

106. Kondō, *Tōkaidō Arai sekisho*, p. 128.

107. *THSS*, vol. 1, pp. 3–4.

108. Regulations are quoted in Igarashi, *Kinsei sekisho seido*, p. 544.

109. *THSS*, vol. 1, pp. 7–8; *Kanagawa ken shi shiryō hen*, vol. 9, *Kinsei 6*, p. 363.

110. *HGNK*, vol. 3, pp. 30–31.

111. Igarashi, *Kinsei sekisho seido*, pp. 523–533, 541.

112. Ibid., vol. 2, p. 95.

113. Ōta, p. 361.

114. Takagi, pp. 615, 617, 624, 637, 639, 671, 678.

115. E.g., Takayama Hikokurō, "Tenmei gekō," in *Takayama Hikokurō zenshū*, Takayama Hikokurō sensei itoku kenshō kai, ed., vol. 2, pp. 305–309 and "Konpira sankei dōchū nikki," p. 57.

116. Inoue, "Kika nikki," pp. 67–68.

117. Shirabyōshi, p. 467.

118. Igarashi, *Kinsei sekisho seido*, p. 534. On the Princess Road in Tōtōmi province, see Kamiya Masashi, *Hime kaidō*.

119. Igarashi, *Kinsei sekisho seido*, p. 560.

120. *Hosoe chō shi shiryō hen*, vol. 1, pp. 339–340; Kondō, *Tōkaidō Arai sekisho*, p. 147.

121. *Hosoe chō shi shiryō hen*, vol. 1, pp. 59, 93, 97.

122. Igarashi, *Kinsei sekisho seido,* pp. 552–558.

123. *THSS,* vol. 3, p. 73.

124. Regulations quoted in Igarashi, *Kinsei sekisho seido,* p. 544.

125. *Shinpen Saitama ken shi shiryō hen,* vol. 15, no. 164, pp. 635–636; *KKSS,* vol. 9, no. 605, pp. 72–73.

126. See Satow, p. 216; see also Hendrik Doeff in *Zufu Nihon kaisō roku; Fuisseru sanpu kikō,* trans. Saitō Abe, p. 162.

127. Satow, p. 216.

128. *Hosoe chō shi shiryō hen,* vol. 1, p. 336.

129. *HGNK,* vol. 2, pp. 126–127.

130. Ibid., vol. 1, p. 73.

131. Ibid., vol. 3, pp. 192–193.

132. Futagawa, "Kōzuke," pp. 37–38.

133. *HGNK,* vol. 1, p. 2.

134. *Nagano ken shi shiryō hen,* vol. 7, pt. 3, p. 27; *Yamagata ken shi shiryō hen,* vol. 18, *Kinsei* 1, no. 123, p. 714.

135. *Kaga han shiryō,* vol. 4, pp. 176–177.

136. Furukawa, "Saiyū zakki," pp. 364–366.

137. Ibid., p. 367.

138. Ibid., p. 355.

139. *KKSS,* vol. 8, no. 289, pp. 200–201.

140. *Gunma ken shi shiryō hen,* vol. 11, *Kinsei* 3, no. 455, pp. 716–718.

141. *Usui gun shi,* pp. 345–348.

142. *Gunma ken shi shiryō hen,* vol. 10, *Kinsei* 2, no. 2,269, p. 647.

143. Kodama and Toyoda, *Kōtsū shi,* pp. 225–226.

144. Ōshima Nobujirō, *Sekisho: sono rekishi to jittai,* p. 94.

145. *Nihon nōmin shiryō shusui,* Ono Takeo, ed., vol. 6, pp. 81–82.

146. Yoshioka Sakutarō, "Usui sekisho gaisetsu," in *Shinano,* vol. 16, no. 1, p. 66.

147. Yataka, p. 407; *Sakai sekisho shi,* p. 35.

148. *Gunma ken shi shiryō hen,* vol. 9, *Kinsei* 1, p. 784.

149. Mizushima Shigeru, "Etchū sekisho no tsūkō aratame" (pt. 1), *Toyama shidan,* vol. 38, p. 32 (1967); Amino Yoshihiko et al., "Rekishi to minzokugaku," *Rettō no bunka shi,* vol. 3, p. 4 (1986).

5. The Benevolence of the Realm

1. *HGNK,* vol. 1, p. 136. The document dates from 1775.

2. *Nagano ken shi, Kinsei shiryō hen,* vol. 6, p. 540.

3. *HGNK,* vol. 3, pp. 45–54.

4. Ibid., vol. 2, pp. 133–135, 207–213; Ibid., vol. 3, pp. 170–172; *THSS,* vol. 1, pp. 220–221.

5. Likewise, travelers carrying permits with missing, erroneous, or unreadable Chinese characters were treated fairly leniently. Some of these permits not pronounced invalid, for example, had a Chinese character missing in the person's name or county of residence. A diary account from Hakone in 1803 noted that permits with the following defects were still valid: wrong county in traveler's address, scribbling on the permit, mistaken characters, no sexegenary cyclical sign, and wetness. Incomplete dates were also permitted. *HGNK*, vol. 2, pp. 95–96, 133–135, 207–213; Ibid., vol. 3, pp. 91, 116–117.

6. Ibid., pp. 207–213; *THSS*, vol. 1, pp. 18–19.

7. *HGNK*, vol. 3, pp. 91–93.

8. Igarashi, *Kinsei sekisho seido*, p. 540; Yataka, pp. 277–278.

9. *HGNK*, vol. 3, p. 168.

10. Hiramatsu Yoshirō, "Tokugawa Law," *Law in Japan*, vol. 14, p. 43 (1981). These comments refer specifically to bakufu law but can be applied as well to the application of bakufu law—as interpreted by individual sekisho administrative authorities—at sekisho. See also Dan Fenno Henderson, *Conciliation and Japanese Law: Tokugawa and Modern*, pp. 58–59.

11. Document quoted in Igarashi, *Kinsei sekisho seido*, p. 401.

12. *HGNK*, vol. 2, p. 136.

13. Ibid.

14. Ibid., vol. 1, p. 143.

15. Ibid., vol. 3, pp. 220–221; Ibid., vol. 1, p. 107.

16. For example, four men and two women who crossed through the mountains in 1840, bypassing Sengokugahara, were arrested three days later, about twelve miles down the Tōkaidō. The four men were crucified shortly thereafter. *THSS*, vol. 2, pp. 418–421.

17. Takeuchi Makoto, "Edo ni okeru hō to minshu," p. 2.

18. "Baiō zuihitsu," in *Nihon zuihitsu taisei*, Second Series, vol. 11, Nihon zuihitsu taisei henshūbu, ed., pp. 68–69. Siebold heard a similar story and recounted it in his *Manners and Customs*, pp. 79–80.

19. See Yataka, pp. 459–461 for the three cases.

20. *Nagano ken shi, Kinsei shiryō hen*, vol. 4, pt. 3, p. 688. The document dates from 1742.

21. Document quoted in Ibid., pp. 452–456.

22. *KKSS*, vol. 1, pp. 587–625.

23. For Yagurasawa, see *THSS*, vol. 2, p. 18; for Saimoku, see *Gunma ken shi shiryō hen*, vol. 9, *Kinsei 1*, no. 486, p. 777.

24. *KKSS*, vol. 1, p. 588.

25. Kiyokawa, p. 39.

26. "Jōshū Kusatsu dōhō," in *Gunma ken shi shiryō shū*, vol. 6, *Nikki hen 2*,

p. 77. Kiyokawa Hachirō (*Saiyūsō*) used this term on numerous occasions as well.

27. Oda Takuo, "Azuma nikki," (1841), quoted in Shiba Keiko, "Kinsei josei no tabi nikki kara: tabi suru joseitachi no sugata o otte," *Kōtsū shi kenkyū*, no. 27, p. 35 (1991).
28. Furukawa, "Saiyū zakki," p. 365.
29. *KKSS*, vol. 1, p. 606.
30. Furukawa, *Tōyū zakki*, p. 4.
31. Kiyokawa, p. 210.
32. Matsuura Seizan, *Kashiyawa: zoku hen*, vol. 4, pp. 108–109. He began writing his opus in 1822 upon his retirement.
33. "Nanmoku sekisho ōrai aratame nikki," as quoted in *Gunma ken shi tsūshi hen*, vol. 6, *Kinsei* 3, p. 255. The record covers the period 1843/4/12–1843/4/22.
34. The unnamed physician was from the Isezaki area. The diary, "Ise sangū nikki," dates from 1850. *Gunma ken shi tsūshi hen*, vol. 6, *Kinsei* 3, p. 259.
35. Kiyokawa, p. 40.
36. Kamiya, pp. 63–64.
37. Kiyokawa, p. 40.
38. See for example, "Kateyama ke monjo," in *Gunma ken shi shiryō shū*, vol. 5, *Nikki hen* 1, no. 9, pp. 168–169 and no. 21, p. 175; "Kōshū kaidō Kobotoke tōge sekiban nikki," p. 91.
39. Kiyokawa, pp. 173–175.
40. Ibid.
41. Kobayashi Kuzufuru, "Gochi mode," in Yaba Katsuyuki, ed., *Edo jidai no Shinano kikō shū*, pp. 227–228.
42. "Zenkō-ji, Tateyama sankei tabi nikki," pp. 544–545.
43. Kobayashi Kuzufuru, pp. 227–228. The headman's wife, Kimi, hurt her foot in the process and had to be transported to the next post station by palanquin.
44. The author of the travel guide, which dates from 1862, was a townsman. The identities of his companions, other than the fact that one was a woman, are not known. Fukai Jinzō gives the itinerary of these travelers in his "Sekisho yaburi to onna tabi," p. 23.
45. Kiyokawa, p. 50.
46. Issa's experience is recounted in his "Kansei sannen kikō," in Maruyama Kazuhiko and Kobayashi Keiichirō, eds., *Issa shū*, pp. 409–431. The article from the noticeboard at Nakagawa is quoted in Kumai Tamotsu, "Nakagawa no kensa to kinmu," in Tsuda Hideo, ed., *Kinsei kokka to Meiji ishin*, p. 166.
47. *Toyama ken shi shiryō hen*, vol. 5, no. 947, pp. 1,261–1,262.
48. *Kaga han shiryō*, vol. 5, p. 371.

49. *Tōyama ken shi shiryō hen,* vol. 5, no. 947, pp. 1,261–1,262.

50. "Usui sekimori nikki," pp. 94–98.

51. *HGNK,* vol. 1, pp. 140, 220–221, 224–225.

52. *Arai chō shi, bekkan: sekisho shiryō,* pp. 368–372.

53. Ibid., pp. 377–378.

54. Watanabe Kazutoshi, "Imagiri," pp. 45–52.

55. Ibid., pp. 49–50.

56. *Ofuregaki Kanpō shūsei,* Ishii Ryōsuke and Takayanagi Shinzō, eds., pp. 73–74.

57. *Hanpōshū,* vol. 6, *Zoku Kanazawa han,* pp. 421–422. The document dates from 1818.

58. Igarashi, *Kinsei sekisho no kisoteki kenkyū,* p. 517.

59. According to one set of records from Usui sekisho, village officials issued 203 permits, in contrast to 80 by daimyo and their officials, and 70 by shrine and temple authorities. Igarashi Tomio, "Kinsei sekisho tegata no kenkyū," pp. 81–82. The ordinance which instructed all village officials in bakufu territory to forward permit applications to Rural Magistrates for approval can be found in *Arai chō shi shiryō hen,* vol. 6, p. 984.

60. 570 out of the 1795 permits were thus obtained. *Matsuida chō shi,* pp. 496–510.

61. "Ise sangū dōchū nikkichō," in *Nagayama shi shiryō shū,* quoted in Yamamoto Mitsumasa, "Tabi nikki ni miru kinsei no tabi ni tsuite," *Kōtsū shi kenkyū,* vol. 13, p. 82 (1985); "Ise sangū dōchūki," in *NSSS,* vol. 20, p. 500.

62. Katsu, "Musui dokugen," p. 167.

63. Sugae, "Sotogahama kaze," in *Sugae Masumi yūranki,* vol. 1, p. 167.

64. Ibid., p. 107. See also Sugae's "Akita no karine," in *NSSS,* vol. 3, p. 660 for another example. In Sendai and Akita, non-domain residents were charged a small fee upon entering the domain. For Sendai, see *Miyagi ken shi,* vol. 5, pp. 511–514. For Akita, see Muta, vol. 13, p. 278.

65. Asakawa Masasaburō, "Tabi no kozukaisen ni tsuite," *Shinano,* vol. 3, no. 5, p. 45 (1951). One traveler paid 32 copper coins for his permit.

66. Kiyokawa, p. 226.

67. *HGNK,* vol. 3, p. 5.

68. Beier, pp. 142–144.

69. E.g., Fujiwara Morohide, "Fude makase," in *NSSS,* vol. 3, p. 662.

70. *Tōyama ken shi shiryō hen,* vol. 5, no. 943, p. 1258.

71. Fujiwara, pp. 660–662.

72. Muta, pp. 278–280.

73. Sugae, "Yuki no michi noku yuki Idewaji," in *Sugae Masumi yūranki,* vol. 4, pp. 44–48.

74. Takagi, p. 653.

75. de Vries, p. 82. On English tolls, see Eric Pawson, *Transport and the Econ-*

omy: The Turnpike Roads of Eighteenth Century Britain, pp. 202–216; Moir, p. 8.

76. The Japanese reads: *Arigataya tōren toko ni zeni shidai / sekimori-san no kokoro gojū ka*. "Zenkō-ji, Tateyama sankei tabi nikki," p. 546.
77. E.g., *Shiga ken shi*, vol. 5, pp. 435–436; *Yamagata ken shi shiryō hen*, vol. 6, p. 251.
78. *Hanpōshū*, vol. 1, *Okayama han*, no. 1,666, p. 641 and no. 1,671, p. 643; for Aizu, see Shinjō, *Shaji sankei*, pp. 797–798; for Kaga, *Hanpōshū*, vol. 4, *Kanazawa han*, no. 198, pp. 634–636.
79. Shinjō, *Shaji sankei*, p. 797.
80. *Hanpōshū*, vol. 4, *Kanazawa han*, no. 198, pp. 634–636.
81. Shinjō, *Shaji sankei*, p. 797.
82. *Kanagawa ken shi shiryō hen*, vol. 5, *Kinsei 2*, no. 179, p. 607.
83. Ibid., pp. 790–798.
84. *Kenshōbo*, vol. 4, no. 53, pp. 44–45.
85. Ibid., no. 50, pp. 41–42.
86. Ibid., no. 22, p. 19.
87. E.g., Morioka domain (*Hanpōshū*, vol. 9, *Morioka han* pt. 1, no. 2,007, p. 920), Kaga (*Kaga han shiryō*, vol. 4, p. 392 and *Etchū shiryō*, vol. 2, p. 624).
88. Shinjō, *Shaji sankei*, pp. 817–818.
89. Ibid., pp. 819–820.
90. Ibid., pp. 821–835.
91. For Okayama, *Hanpōshū*, vol. 1, *Okayama han*, no. 1,564, p. 639–640; Shinjō, *Shaji sankei*, p. 822.
92. *Hanpōshū*, vol. 11, *Kurume han*, no. 309, 125 and no. 1,753, p. 603.
93. Shinjō Tsunezō, *Shaji to kōtsū*, pp. 133–134.
94. Shinjō, *Shaji sankei*, p. 800.
95. For example, after surrendering her authority to her daughter-in-law, the mother of the "snow country" writer Suzuki Bokushi made various pilgrimages in the Edo area (to Chichibu, Enoshima, Kamakura, Nikkō), and at the age of seventy-two completed her seventh trip to Zenkō-ji. Anne Walthall, "The Life Cycle of Farm Women," in Gail Lee Bernstein, ed., *Recreating Japanese Women*, p. 66.
96. *Kaga han shiryō*, vol. 11, p. 437.
97. *Hanpōshū*, vol. 9, *Morioka han* pt. 1, no. 2,007, p. 920.
98. Furukawa, "Saiyū zakki," p. 377.
99. Nishiyama Matsunosuke, *Kinsei fūzoku to shakai*, vol. 5 of his *Nishiyama Matsunosuke chosaku shū*, p. 410.
100. Shinjō, *Shaji sankei*, pp. 794–795.
101. English vagabonds had "passports made by justices stating distant desti-

nations," which enabled them to travel extensively across the country. Beier, p. 79.

102. Shinjō, *Shaji sankei*, pp. 813–814.

103. Document quoted in Wakabayashi Kisaburō, *Kaga han nōsei shi kenkyū*, pt.2, p. 837.

104. Walthall, *Social Protest*, p. 100.

105. *Arai chō shi shiryō hen*, vol. 6, p. 984.

106. The following is a partial list of domains banning pilgrimage: Satsuma (in 1611), Aizu (temporary ban in 1652), Saga (1776), Akita (1758–1868, except for 1804–1848), Yonezawa (1789), Chōshū (1823), Nambu (1813), Hiroshima (1849), Shōno (1853, for three years), Shimabara (1861–1863), Nakatsu (1828). Shinjō, *Shaji sankei*, p. 829; *Hanpōshū*, vol. 9, *Morioka han* pt. 1, no. 2,007, p. 920; *Hiroshima ken shi, Kinsei shiryō hen*, vol. 4, no. 1,862, p. 679.

107. Shinjō, *Shaji sankei*, p. 830.

108. Ibid., p. 833.

109. *Akita han machi fure shū*, vol. 1, no. 413, pp. 269–270.

110. Ibid., vol. 2, no. 1,428, p. 362.

111. Shinjō, *Shaji sankei*, pp. 833–836. The quotation can be found on pp. 835–836.

112. Ibid., pp. 827–828.

113. Ibid., pp. 841–842.

114. Kaiho Seiryō, *Keikodan*, as quoted in Ibid., p. 827.

115. Kaempfer, vol. 2, p. 37. In medieval Europe, badges or talismans obtained on pilgrimage were "used to prove that the wearer was entitled, as a pilgrim, to exemption from tolls and taxes." Jonathan Sumption, *Pilgrimage: An Image of Medieval Religion*, pp. 173–175.

116. *Kanagawa ken shi shiryō hen*, vol. 4, *Kinsei* 1, no. 355, p. 894.

117. *THSS*, vol. 2, p. 95.

118. "Bunsei jūsan toradoshi Ise okagemairi jitsuroku kagami," in Jingū shichō, ed., *Daijingū sōsho*, vol. 10, *Jingū sanpaiki taisei*, p. 541.

119. *Kenshōbo*, vol. 4, no. 49, pp. 39–40.

120. Nomura Katsu, *Ise no furuichi are kore*, p. 41. The Japanese text reads: *Oharai to shirami o goyō seotte kuru / mugon ni te oharai o dasu taru hiroi / oharai de wabigoto o sumu taru hiroi.* Another word for *oharai* is *ofuda*.

121. Winston B. Davis, "Pilgrimage and World Renewal: A Study of Religion and Social Values in Tokugawa Japan," (pt. 2), *History of Religions*, vol. 23, no. 3, p. 214 (February 1984).

122. *Hachinohe shi shi shiryō hen, Kinsei*, vol. 3, p. 4.

123. Kodama et al., *Edo jidai no kōtsū to tabi*, p. 29.

124. This account of the 1830 *okagemairi*, unless otherwise noted, is based on

Kawai Kenji, "Okagemairi e no ryōshu shihai no taiō, *Chihō shi kenkyū,* vol. 224, pp. 1–24 (1990).

125. Cited in Kawai, p. 7.

126. *Nagoya sōsho zoku hen,* vol. 11, *Ōmurō chūki,* vol. 3, pp. 40–41. The observer was the Nagoya Magistrate of the Castle Tatami Mats; the diary entry is from 1705/intercalary 4/20.

127. "Fūdo zakki," in *Nihon nōmin shiryō shusui,* vol. 2, Ono Takeo, ed., p. 72.

128. For Owari, see *Ichinomiya shi shi shiryō hen,* vol. 8, no. 2,944, p. 209; for the others, Shinjō, *Shaji sankei,* pp. 791–792.

129. "Ukiyo no arisama," p. 335.

130. Shinjō, *Shaji sankei,* pp. 790–791.

131. See for example, "Ise sangū nikki," in *Ise dōchūki shiryō,* pp. 175–176 for a description of a post-pilgrimage party.

132. Fujiwara, p. 597.

133. Jippensha, *Hizakurige or Shanks' Mare,* p. 52.

134. Not surprisingly, Saisaburō did not keep his word and two years later Tora ran away, only to be apprehended at a domain barrier. *Hachinohe shi shi shiryō hen, Kinsei,* vol. 1, p. 207.

135. See Torao Haraguchi and Robert K. Sakai, *The Status System and Social Organization of Satsuma: A Translation of the Shumon Tefuda Aratame Jomoku.*

136. Ōmi Katada, "Saiban nikki," in *Nihon toshi seikatsu shiryō shūsei,* vol. 7, *Minatomachi* pt. 1, Harada Tomohiko, ed., p. 335. The author noted that "it is said that Tosa people do not travel to other domains."

137. Takagi, p. 610.

138. "Fūdo zakki," pp. 69–70.

139. Furukawa, "Saiyū zakki," pp. 378–379.

140. Kodama et al., "Edo jidai no kōtsū to tabi," p. 28.

141. Shinjō, *Shaji sankei,* p. 831.

142. The break in the isolation apparently did not last long, as Shigehide stepped down for his son in 1787, who then reversed his policies. Shigehide reasserted power shortly thereafter, purging his son in 1808, and installed a more tractable replacement, but whether or not his open door policy was continued is uncertain. With the oncoming turmoil of the bakumatsu years, however, it seems unlikely. *Kagoshima ken shiryō kyūki zatsuroku tsuiroku,* Kagoshima ken ishin shiryō hensanjo, ed., vol. 6, no. 909, p. 328 and Kanbashi Norimasa, *Shimazu Shigehide,* pp. 73–74.

143. Furukawa, "Saiyū zakki," p. 355.

144. According to Shinjō Tsunezō they first were issued during the Kanbun era (1661–72) in a handful of domains like Sendai, Kaga, Mōri, and Tsugaru, and spread all over. Shinjō Tsunezō, "Kinsei no Ise sangū," pp.

42–43. A steady stream of prohibitions on *nukemairi* was issued from the turn of the eighteenth century in Hachinohe, a small branch domain of Morioka. See *Hachinohe shi shi shiryō hen, Kinsei,* Hachinohe shi hensan iinkai, ed., vols. 3–9.

145. Both quotations are from *Hanpōshū,* vol. 9, Morioka pt. 1, no. 585, pp. 265–266.

146. *Hiroshima ken shi, Kinsei shiryō hen,* vol. 4, no. 1,862, p. 679.

147. *Hirosaki shi shi, Hansei hen,* Hirosaki shi shi hensan iinkai, ed., pp. 651–652.

148. Ibid.

149. *Hanpōshū,* vol. 9, Morioka han pt. 1, no. 844, pp. 359–360.

150. Shinjō, *Shaji sankei,* p. 802.

151. Ibid., p. 838.

152. Hayashi Reiko, "Kasama jōkamachi ni okeru josei zō," in Kinsei josei shi kenkyū kai, ed., *Edo jidai no joseitachi,* pp. 223–224, 227. This does not mean, of course, that only eleven townswomen traveled legally. Permits were probably not needed for day trips, particularly if no sekisho would be encountered.

153. Constantine N. Vaporis, "Caveat Viator: Advice to Travelers in the Edo Period," *Monumenta Nipponica,* vol. 44, no. 4, p. 475 (Winter 1989).

154. Quoted in Ono Masao, *Gokaidō fūzoku shi,* vol. 1, p. 99.

155. Quoted in Shiba Keiko, "Kinsei josei to tabi," p. 31.

156. Kaibara Ekiken, "Onna daigaku hoseki," quoted in Shiba, "Tabi nikki kara mita kinsei josei no ikkōsatsu," p. 149.

157. The quote is from the "Keian ofuregaki," quoted in Shinjō, *Shaji sankei,* pp. 801–802.

158. Quoted in Nagano, pp. 173.

159. Miyata Noboru, "Josei to minkan shinkō," in Josei shi sōgō kenkyū kai, ed., *Nihon josei shi,* vol. 3, *Kinsei,* pp. 242–246. For a study of pollution in Japanese society, see Emiko Namihara, "Pollution in the Folk Belief System," *Current Anthropology,* vol. 28, no. 4, pp. S65–S74 (August–October 1987).

160. Shirabyōshi, p. 215.

161. Kiyokawa, pp. 20–35.

162. Ibid., pp. 17–19.

163. *Kaga han shiryō,* vol. 4, pp. 392–393.

164. *Okayama ken shi,* vol. 25, *Tsuyama han monjo,* p. 700.

165. Ibid., p. 700. In Okayama in the mid-eighteenth century the penalty on the books for those who went on *nukemairi* were as follows: for men, twenty days banishment; for boys up to thirteen or fourteen, ten days; for women, fifteen days; and for girls up to thirteen or fourteen years of age, seven days. *Hanpōshū,* vol. 1, Okayama han, p. 642. It is not clear to

what extent these regulations might have been applied. Records from Hachinohe domain in the early nineteenth century show that two peasants were formally pardoned for making the pilgrimage to Ise without permission (*Hachinohe shi shi shiryō hen, Kinsei,* vol. 6, pp. 259, 550), whereas a low-level member of the samurai status group (probably a *komono* or attendant) had his rice-stipend reduced in 1711 as punishment for doing the same. Ibid., vol. 3, p. 334. According to Shinjō, *Shaji sankei,* p. 808, punishments were imposed early on but gradually became formalized.

166. *Hiroshima ken shi, Kinsei shiryō hen,* vol. 4, no. 1,335, pp. 228–229.
167. *Gunma ken shi shiryō hen,* vol. 11, *Kinsei* 3, p. 16.
168. Shinjō, *Shaji sankei,* pp. 793–794.
169. Satow, p. 247.
170. Alcock, vol. 2, p. 250.

6. TRAVEL AS RECREATION

1. Kaempfer, vol. 2, p. 330.
2. Cooper, pp. 282–283.
3. Alcock, vol. 3, pp. 456–458. John Black, too, found the volume of traffic remarkable. He noted that "the crowds on portions of the road [the Tōkaidō] were as great as in the most crowded thoroughfares of London." Black, p. 164.

The question of quantifying the volume of traffic is a difficult one. Post stations maintained records of official traffic (in terms of post horses and porters used) but these only give us an index to the general volume of traffic, and only for official travelers and baggage. Post stations kept no records of commoner traffic. The figures presented for individual stations in Chapter Two, e.g., 60,471 porters and 25,050 post horses used at Hodogaya in 1834, do not tell us how many official travelers passed through the station during that year because horses were used for baggage as well as people, and many people walked rather than rode. In theory, travel permits would provide an index for commoner traffic, but because of the nature of the checking station system, records were dispersed among sekisho administrators and the bakufu, and many have been divided up or lost since then, making a general study of them difficult at best. Of course, even if we had complete records they would only give us a general picture of the volume of commoner traffic for, as evidence from contemporary travel diaries and the chorus of complaints of government officials shows, many people did not bother to obtain the proper documentation when traveling.

4. Ōmi merchants traveled frequently on business, but were also known

for actively engaging in recreational travel. On Ōmi merchants, see Eigashira Tsuneji, *Ōmi shōnin: Nakai ke no kenkyū* and Shima Takeshi, *Ōmi shōnin monogatari.*

5. Asai Ryōi, vol. 1, pp. 3–4.

6. J. H. Plumb writes that, "Large scale travel for the pleasure of traveling or in order to broaden the mind was a development of the eighteenth century." *Georgian Delights*, p. 128. According to Ian Ousby, "tourism" developed in England between the mid-eighteenth and mid-nineteenth centuries. *The Englishman's England. Taste, Travel and the Rise of Tourism*, p. 9. Ousby's interesting study examines the growth of domestic tourism in England, concentrating on four types of attractions: 1) literary shrines or places connected with writers, 2) country homes, 3) ancient monuments and medieval ruins, and 4) natural landscapes.

7. Jippensha, *Tōkaidō Hizakurige*, pp. 237, 323.

8. While sightseeing in the Kinai area, Kiyokawa Hachirō, his attendant, and his mother together traveled 55 kilometers a day off the main Gokaidō roads. Stopping many places along the way, the Edo-to-Kyoto trip took them fourteen days. (Kiyokawa, p. 70.) On his return from Nagasaki in 1853, a bakufu official named Kawaji Toshiakira hastened home, covering 59–63 kilometers of road a day on a number of occasions. (Kawaji Toshiakira, "Nagasaki nikki," in Kawaji Toshiakira, *Nagasaki nikki, Shimoda nikki*, pp. 1–134.) In contrast, Yaji and Kita moved along at a leisurely pace of about 36 kilometers per day. The bakufu's "super express" messenger service could travel the 487 kilometers between Edo and Kyoto in the mid-eighteenth century in under three days; the "limited express" required four days; and the "regular service" took five. (*KKSS*, vol. 9, no. 565, p. 31.)

9. Jippensha, *Tōkaidō Hizakurige*, p. 23.

10. Tanaka Kyūgu, p. 240.

11. Ihara Saikaku, *Tales of Samurai Honor*, p. 145.

12. A short distance from Tsuchiyama on the Tōkaidō, the late-Tokugawa loyalist Kiyokawa Hachirō noted that, "In this area there are many wolves, and it is reported that they attack people at night." Kiyokawa, p. 165. Hideyoshi made great efforts to rid the waters, particularly the Inland Sea, of pirates. For a discussion of mountain bandits and pirates in the medieval period, see Shinjō, *Sengoku jidai no kōtsū*, pp. 222–233.

13. See Teruko Craig's translation of "Musui dokugen," *Musui's Story: The Autobiography of a Tokugawa Samurai*, for a contemporary account which describes the darker side of Tokugawa life, including some examples of highway crime, through the eyes of an unemployed Tokugawa vassal. His story often seems self-glorifying, and was no doubt embellished with fictive elements.

14. *Nakasendō kōtsū shiryō shū*, vol. 2, pp. 23–24; *KKSS*, vol. 8, no. 368, p. 267.
15. *KKSS*, vol. 9, no. 577, pp. 45–46 and no. 607, pp. 73–76.
16. Kiyokawa, p. 107.
17. Neil McKendrik, John Brewer, and J. H. Plumb, *The Birth of a Consumer Society. The Commercialization of Eighteenth-Century England*, p. 265. The quote refers to leisure in general, but can be applied fairly to the specific case of tourism or touristic travel.
18. Kiyokawa sent the 150 small plates of Bizen ware from Imbe to Osaka and the porcelain from Owari home to Shōnai. Kiyokawa, pp. 55, 87, 159, 170. According to one authority, tourism had some impact on the nature of Bizen pottery, as the plates were made smaller to transport more easily. Conversation with Noritake Kanzaki, Ōsaka minzoku hakubutsukan, March 1991.
19. Braudel, vol. 2, p. 320.
20. Harris, p. 413.
21. Knollys, pp. 83–84. Alcock described *kago* as being "made of light wicker-work, and consist[ing] of a bottom, back, and front, in the shape of a truncated "V," or a "U" with the sides pulled out. Into the bottom the Japanese place a cotton quilt." Alcock, vol. 2, p. 97.
22. See *KKSS*, vol. 8, no. 358, p. 258 for one example.
23. *KKSS*, vol. 8, no. 324, p. 321.
24. *KKSS*, vol. 9, no. 896, p. 388.
25. Kaempfer, vol. 2, p. 345.
26. Thunberg, vol. 3, p. 152. From a reading of travel diaries its appears that a pair of sandals generally lasted one or two days of routine wear. One pilgrim to Ise from Edo, for example, wore out twelve pairs in eighteen days, or two pairs every three days. They cost him an average of 15 *mon* a piece. "Ise sangū oboe," in *Ise dōchūki shiryō*, pp. 1–41.
27. Griffis, vol. 2, pp. 356–357.
28. *KKSS*, vol. 4.
29. Jippensha, *Tōkaidō Hizakurige*, pp. 119, 199–200.
30. Ihara Saikaku, *The Japanese Storehouse: Or the Millionaires' Gospel Modernised*, p. 89.
31. Hiroe Kiyoshi, *Kinsei Tosa no shūkyō*, pp. 162–163. This account is based on a travel diary by Uga Zenji, "O-Ise gosankei nikki," from 1757.
32. *Chigasaki shi shi*, vol. 4, pp. 364–365.
33. Ibid.
34. Hayashi Razan, "Heishin kikō," in Yanagida Kunio, ed., *Zoku kikō bunshū*, pp. 279–306.
35. Tatsurō Akai, "The Common People and Painting," in Ōishi Shinsaburō and Chie Nakane, eds., *Tokugawa Japan*, pp. 183–188. The quote is on pp. 187–188.

36. Shinjō Tsunezō, *Shomin to tabi no rekishi*, pp. 58–60.
37. Ogyū Sorai, quoted in J. R. McEwan, *The Political Writings of Ogyū Sorai*, p. 103.
38. Thunberg, vol. 3, pp. 145–146. Post stations played an important role in bakufu fiscal policy: when the bakufu reissued coins it sent the new currency to the Gokaidō post stations in order to spread it throughout the country more rapidly. Watanabe Kazutoshi, "Shukubamachi jūmin no seikatsu," p. 5.
39. Ōta Nanpo, p. 365.
40. Jippensha, *Tōkaidō Hizakurige*, pp. 29–30.
41. *Kusatsu shi shi*, vol. 2, p. 333. At Nakatsugawa (Nakasendō) an agreement was made that inn women at the edge of town would take turns soliciting customers. *Gifu ken shi shiryō hen, Kinsei*, vol. 7, no. 121, pp. 516–517.
42. Chikamatsu Monzaemon, "Yosaka from Tamba," in Donald Keene, ed., *Major Plays of Chikamatsu*, pp. 103–104.
43. Kaempfer, vol. 2, pp. 317–318.
44. Kondō Tsuneji, "Kinsei no hatagoya to sono hōkōnin: Tōkaidō Akasaka no baai," in Aichi daigaku sōgō kyōdo kenkyūjo, ed., *Kinsei no kōtsū to chihō bunka*, pp. 88–91. Like honjin, full-service inns in Akasaka and elsewhere had a short frontage (about fifteen meters or less) and a considerable depth (up to about forty-seven meters). The largest inn had eighteen rooms, the smallest, five, but the average was about twelve. Eight percent of these rooms had four to six tatami mats, 20 percent had eight mats, 22 percent had ten mats, 13 percent had twelve mats, and 7 percent had sixteen to twenty-four mats. Over 64 percent of the eighty-three inns in operation in 1773 maintained more than one service person, providing employment in that year to seventy-six males and 109 females.
45. Kodama Kōta, *Shukuba to kaidō: Gokaidō nyūmon*, pp. 26–27.
46. *KKSS*, vol. 8, no. 306, pp. 216–217.
47. See, for example, "Konpira sankei dōchū nikki," pp. 61, 77–80; Muta, pp. 258, 274, 288, 311–312, 357; and Kiyokawa, p. 98.
48. Takeuchi Makoto, ed., *Bunka no taishūka*, pp. 21, 48–49. The night tour cost 130 *mon*, the full-day version 250 *mon* (1839). The full-day tour thus cost about the same as one night's lodging in a full-service inn.
49. Kankō kiga kenkyū shochō, ed., *Tabi to shuku: Nihon ryōkan shi*, p. 115.
50. Tanaka kyūgu, p. 242.
51. Ihara Saikaku, *Hitome tamaboko*, p. 116.
52. Haga, pp. 197–199; Nishiyama, "Edo bunka to chihō bunka," p. 202.
53. Kiyokawa p. 82. Hiroshige depicts an inn that was part of the Naniwa organization in his Hōeido series print of Totsuka.
54. The custom may have been encouraged by the general mistrust of the

lone traveler. Many inns simply refused to lodge them: from an innkeeper's's perspective, lodging the single traveler was a calculated risk, for if the person caused any incidents while in the post town, or should happen to fall ill or even die, the innkeeper was held liable. Bakufu policy towards single travelers was inconsistent, at once prohibiting stations from denying them lodging, while at the same time punishing stations heavily when a traveler caused some trouble. In those cases post station officials were assessed responsibility because they lodged a single traveler. It was a no-win situation: inns were to lodge the lone traveler for the night "if there was nothing suspicious" about him, but were still held accountable. (*KKSS*, vol. 8, no. 209, pp. 136–137; no. 315, pp. 223–224; no. 356, p. 257; no. 761, pp. 247–248.) When Sugae Masumi and Fukuzawa Yukichi traveled alone they both had the experience of being refused lodging by innkeepers. (Fukuzawa Yukichi, *The Autobiography of Fukuzawa Yukichi*, p. 29; Sugae, vol. 3, p. 118).

55. Quoted in Sakurai Kunio, "Kinsei ni nokeru Tōhoku chihō kara no tabi," *Komazawa shigaku*, vol. 34, pp. 168–169 (1986).

56. Kobayashi Keiichirō, "Kinsei makki no Zenkō-ji sankeisha ni tsuite," p. 780.

57. *KKSS*, vol. 9, no. 570, pp. 36–37; *KKSS*, vol. 10, pp. 95, 127; *Okayama ken shi*, vol. 25, *Tsuyama han monjo*, p. 625. It was required that the bakufu be sent written notification when a traveler collapsed or was otherwise incapacitated while traveling on the Gokaidō. Outside the Gokaidō, daimyo had similar requirements. The reports to the bakufu described the traveler, his possessions and physical condition. See, for example, *Shizuoka ken shi shiryō hen*, vol. 13, *Kinsei 5*, Shizuoka ken, ed., no. 719, pp. 1,123–1,125 and no. 726, pp. 1,130–1,132.

58. Naitō Jirō, "Bakuhan ki shomin ryokō to sono hogo," *Nihon rekishi*, vol. 175, pp. 17–25 (1957).

59. Ibid., pp. 27–28. The temples in Fukuoka domain were ordered by domain authorities to take care of stricken travelers and comfort the souls of those who died, lest entire villages become haunted by their hungry spirits. Arne Kallard and Jon Pederson, "Famine and Population in Fukuoka Domain During the Tokugawa Period," *Journal of Japanese Studies*, vol. 10, no. 1, pp. 37–38 (1984).

60. *Gifu ken shi shiryō hen kinsei*, vol. 7, no. 116, pp. 504–505; *Kanagawa ken shi shiryō hen*, vol. 9, *Kinsei 6*, no. 10, pp. 10–11.

Two townsmen from Aizu Wakamatsu were returning home from a pilgrimage to the Western and Shikoku circuits in 1694 when one of them, Kakuemon, died at Seba station (Shinshū) on the Nakasendō. His companion, Shihei, arranged for his burial at a local temple. Later Kakuemon's brother made a trip all the way to Seba to thank the temple and village officials, and even gave sake to the station porters (who probably had transported his brother to Seba). *Shinshū Shiojiri Akabane ke Genroku ōjōya nikki,* no. 336, p. 202.

61. The quote is from Chikamatsu, "Yosaku From Tamba," pp. 94–95. The mention of *dōchū sugoroku* in this play is perhaps the earliest. The earliest appearance of the travel game board in a work of art may be in wood-block artist Harunobu's "Evening Snow on Matsuchi Hill" (1769), in his Fanciful Eight Views of Edo (*Fūryū Edo Hakkei*) series. The print is reproduced in Jack Hillier, *Suzuki Harunobu: An Exhibition of His Colour-Prints and Illustrated Books on the Occasion of the Bicentenary of His Death in 1770,* p. 200. For a study on *sugoroku,* see Takahashi Junji, *Nihon-e sugoroku shūsei.* A fine collection of board games can be found in the Charles Nelson Spinks Collection, American University.

62. Charles Nelson Spinks, "The Tōkaidō in Popular Literature and Art," *Transactions of the Asiatic Society of Japan,* Third Series, vol. 3, p. 12 (1954).

63. Satow, p. 204.

64. Yamamoto Mitsumasa, "Tabi nikki ni miru kinsei no tabi ni tsuite," p. 73.

65. According to Ian Ousby, English guidebooks "became one of the popular staples of late eighteenth century publishing." He quotes a contemporary, John Byng, who wrote that "tour writing is the very rage of the times." Ian Ousby, *The Englishman's England: Taste, Travel and the Rise of Tourism,* p. 12. The large number of early nineteenth century diaries in Japan may be at least partially due to the better survival of more recent materials, but it would be difficult to deny that there was a rapid increase in their numbers.

66. Satow, p. 204.

67. Kaempfer, vol. 2, p. 287.

68. Many of the *meisho zue* have been conveniently included in the printed series *Nihon meisho fūzoku ezu,* edited by Ikeda Yasaburō, Noma Kō-shin, and Minakami Tsutomu. For a recent article on them, see Mark H. Sandler, "The Traveler's Way: Illustrated Guidebooks of Edo Japan," *Asian Art,* vol. 5, no. 2 (Spring 1992).

69. E.g., in Ikeda Eisen's Tōkaidō *sugoroku* (ca. 1804–1817?). Charles Nelson Spinks Collection, American University.

70. For more on Andō Hiroshige, see Yamaguchi Keizaburō, *Hiroshige.*

71. Jippensha, *Tōkaidō Hizakurige,* p. 23.

72. See Yasumi, *Ryokō yōjin shū.* A printed version with some minor textual differences can be found in Imai Kingo, ed., *Ryokō yōjin shū.* The points cited can be found on pp. 469–483 in my translation and commentary on Yasumi's work: Vaporis, "Caveat Viator," pp. 461–483. In that piece

I translate the list of sixty precautions that make up the core of the book as well as other key sections.

73. See Shiba Keiko, "Kinsei josei," pp. 31–51, and "Tabi nikki kara mita kinsei josei no ikkōsatsu," in Kinsei josei shi kenkyū kai, ed., *Edo jidai no joseitachi*, pp. 147–184, for a preliminary discussion of women's travel diaries as well as an annotated list of those discovered thus far. While literary rates for women were much lower than men's, it may also be the case that women's diaries were not judged as worthy of preservation as men's, and thus fewer remain today. Maeda Yoshi discusses the travel diaries of several exceptional women in his "Tabi nikki no josei," in Enchi Fumiko, ed., *Nikki ni tsuzuru aikan*, pp. 207–244.

Two-thirds of the women's travel diaries found to date were written by commoners and one-third by members of the samurai status group. The large number written by samurai is not surprising given the high degree of literacy among that social group, but perhaps gives the mistaken impression that they traveled frequently. While samurai women no doubt achieved higher rates of literacy compared with those from the other social groups, their physical mobility was much more constrained. Shiba, "Kinsei josei," p. 51.

74. Kaempfer, vol. 2, p. 35.

75. See Tamamuro Fumio, ed., *Yūkō nichikan*, vols. 1–3 for an account of his travels, from Kagoshima in the south, to Akita in the north, over the years 1711–1728.

76. Kobayashi Keiichirō, *Zenkō-ji-san*, pp. 144–154. There were fourteen such exhibitions at Zenkō-ji during the years 1745–1865. The temple treasures also toured the large urban centers a number of times and thus probably attracted viewers to visit the temple as well in order to see more.

77. Shinjō, *Shomin to tabi*, p. 73.

78. James Foard, "The Boundaries of Compassion: Buddhist and National Tradition in Japanese Pilgrimage," *Journal of Asian Studies*, vol. 41, no. 2, p. 238 (1982).

79. "Ise sangū kondate dōchūki," in *NSSS*, vol. 20, pp. 599–622. The diary dates from 1848.

80. For works on travel and leisure, see Erik Cohen, "Who Is a Tourist? A Conceptual Clarification," *The Sociological Review*, vol. 22, no. 4, p. 530 (1974) and Dennison Nash, *Tourism in Pre-Industrial Societies*, p. 4.

81. Merchants, many of whom traveled widely as a hobby, often fulfilled partial touristic roles in mixing business with pleasure. For the account of a Hino merchant who traveled around in northern Japan paying courtesy calls on, and giving gifts to, the best customers of his family's branch store in Sendai, see "Nakai Genzaemon Mitsuoki tabi nikki," in

Nihon toshi seikatsu shiryō shūsei, Harada Tomohiko, ed., vol. 8, *Shuku-bamachi hen,* pp. 737–782. Also in the same volume is an account of the extensive travels of a Sendai rice merchant from Osaka to his home town: See "Masuya Heiuemon Sendai gekkō nikki," in Ibid., pp. 720–736.

82. Kaibara Ekiken (1630–1714), a Confucian scholar from Fukuoka do-main, was an inveterate traveler, making his way to Edo twelve times, Kyoto twenty-four times, and Nagasaki five times: See Ekiken kai hen-san, vol. 7.

83. Erik Cohen, "A Phenomenology of Tourist Experiences," *Sociology,* vol. 13, no. 2, p. 182 (May 1979). See Kanzaki Noritake, *Monomi yusan to Nihonjin* for a popular work on sightseeing from the Edo period to today.

84. See Valene L. Smith's Introduction to Valene Smith, ed., *Hosts and Guests: The Anthropology of Tourism,* p. 15.

85. McKendrick, Brewer, and Plumb, pp. 283–285; Plumb, pp. 14–15.

86. H. D. Harootunian, "Late Tokugawa Culture and Thought," in Marius B. Jansen, ed., *The Cambridge History of Japan,* vol. 5, *The Nineteenth Century,* p. 215. On the concept of "play" in Tokugawa society, see Nishiyama, *Kinsei fūzoku to shakai,* pp. 291–318. For the same in relation to villager society in particular, see Tsukamoto Manabu, "Murabito no asobi to tabi," in Nihon sonraku shi kōza henshū iinkai, ed., *Nihon son-raku shi kōza,* vol. 7, *Seikatsu 2, Kinsei,* pp. 238–251.

87. Accounts of hot springs resorts often listed the putative curative powers of specific waters, e.g., "Hakone onsen michi no ki" (1763), Mitsui Col-lection, University of California, Berkeley.

88. Ihara, *The Japanese Family Storehouse,* p. 14.

About the greedy merchants, Ihara wrote: "Through the spring haze shrouding the hills men and women, rich and poor, were making their way on pilgrimage to the shrine of Kannon at Mizuma temple in Izumi province. None went in search of enlightenment. The road they trod together was the road of greed. . . . their prayers were mere requests for wealth, varying only in the quantity each considered his due." (p. 14)

Furthermore, some temples were commonly associated with a cer-tain curative or ameliorative power which attracted a particular constit-uency; e.g., Enoshima Benten attracted the blind (as depicted in a number of Hiroshige prints of Fujisawa) as well as those involved in arts and crafts.

89. I deal with the question of the applicability of the term "tourism" to Tokugawa Japan at greater length in my "The Early Modern Origins of Japanese Tourism," forthcoming in *Senri Ethnological Studies* (1994).

90. *Hanpōshū*, vol. 6, *Zoku Kanagawa hen,* quoted in Shinjō, *Shaji sankei no shakai keizaishiteki kenkyū,* p. 725.
91. *Kaga han shiryō,* vol. 5, p. 366. The document dates from 1696.
92. *Aizu han kasei jikki,* vol. 8, pp. 611–612.
93. Erik Cohen, "A Phenomenology of Tourist Experiences," p. 184.
94. Ihara Saikaku, *Five Women Who Loved Love,* p. 97.
95. Kaempfer, vol. 2, p. 37 and vol. 3, p. 34.
96. Nelson Graburn, *To Pray, Pay, and Play: The Cultural Structure of Japanese Domestic Tourism,* p. 46.
97. On Furuichi, see Nomura.
98. Kiyokawa, pp. 61–64.
99. Hiroe, p. 157.
100. "Kyōkun manbyō kaishun" (1771), quoted in Shinjō, *Shaji sankei,* p. 724.
101. *Arima onsen shiryō,* Kazahaya Jun, ed., vol. 2, contains numerous accounts and examples of daimyo and domain retainers requesting permission to visit Arima. Included is the request of a samurai from Bizen who was wounded at the Battle of Shimabara (1638) and requested permission to make "three rounds" of the hot springs there. (p. 20) Also, see Hara Masaoki, "Tamakushige futatsu ideyu michi no ki," in Itasaka Yōko, ed., *Edo onsen kikō,* for an account of a trip to Atami and Miyanoshita, near Hakone, by a Numada domain samurai stationed in Edo. Despite complaining of long-term head and eye aches, he walked to Atami in just three days. On the return trip to Edo, he stopped at Enoshima temple (perhaps because of his eye problem) and Kamakura. Illness was a pretext used by both commoners and samurai when they wanted a break from routine life to travel and enjoy themselves.
102. Yasumi, folio 78.
103. Mitford, quoted in Cortazzi, *Victorians in Japan,* p. 213. For travel accounts of hot springs in England, see for example, Christopher Morris, ed., *The Journeys of Celia Fiennes,* Daniel Defoe's famous *Tour of the Whole Island of Great Britain,* and Ruth Michaelis-Jena and Willy Merson, eds., *A Lady Travels: Journeys in England and Scotland From the Diaries of Johanna Schopenhauer.*
104. Kiyokawa, pp. 148–151. Numerous artists captured Arima's beautiful women in wood-block prints. A number of examples are included in *Arima onsen shiryō,* vol. 2, pp. 329–332, 471.
   Wood-block printed poems written by Arima courtesans were among the gifts taken back to Aki by a Tosa domain retainer on his return-trip from Edo on the alternate attendance. "Arima nyūtō miyage-e nado," Gotō Family Documents no. 930, 1730, Aki City Library, Aki City, Kōchi prefecture.
105. *Gunma ken shi tsūshi hen,* vol. 6, *Kinsei 3,* p. 248.

106. These sojourns in the major cities were important for the transplanting of urban culture to peripheral areas. Some villagers, for example, brought back from Osaka clothing or scripts to use for their local kabuki performances. Moriya Takeshi, *Mura shibai: Kinsei bunka no susuno kara,* pp. 208–209.

107. Yamamoto Mitsumasa. "Shokokujin ni totte no Edo: Shaji sankeisha o chūshin to shite," pp. 335–355.

108. Ihara Saikaku, *Some Final Words of Advice,* Peter Nosco, trans., p. 168.

109. Shinjō, *Shomin to tabi,* pp. 110, 141–143.

110. The saddle was called *sanbō kōjin,* which refers to the three faces that the kitchen deity, *kōjin,* was said to have.

111. Shinjō, *Shomin to tabi,* pp. 85–86.

112. "Ise sangū shoshinsho," in Koike Masatane, ed., *Edo no ehon: shoki kusazōshi shūsei,* vol. 1, gives a good account of the activities performed by the *oshi.* It describes the elaborate meals that some priests served their parishioners. For a secondary account on *oshi,* see Onishi Gen'ichi, *Sangū no konjaku,* pp. 123–162.

113. Some figures for other years are 391 (1671), 400 (1677), 509 (1766), 357 (1792), 395 (1836), 487 (1870). Shinjō, *Shaji sankei,* pp. 758–776.

114. Takeuchi Makoto, ed., *Bunka no taishūka,* pp. 47–48.

115. A group of about a hundred pilgrims from Hatori village in Kanagawa spent two months on a pilgrimage to Ise. *Kanagawa ken no rekishi,* p. 131. On religious confraternities, see Sakurai Tokutarō, *Kōshūdan no kenkyū;* Akada Mitsui, "Kō to ohenro," in Kimura Motoi, ed., *Edo to chihō bunka,* vol. 2, pp. 229–250; Iwashina Koichirō, *Fuji-kō no rekishi.*

116. After returning home many confraternity groups erected stone lanterns in thanks for having completed the pilgrimage safely. These towers were often placed on roads leading up to temples or at crossroads in villages. One such tower was recently seen by the author along a canal at Kurashiki, near Okayama. The lantern, dating from 1791, was donated by a confraternity group from Kurashiki upon completion of a pilgrimage to Konpira-san.

117. This became evident to me after a study of stone lanterns which line the pathway up the almost 800 steps to the main shrine building at Konpirasan. Most of the lanterns donated there, however, are from individual confraternity groups. The place of origin of the donors is usually chiseled into these devotional lanterns; even a cursory examination of the lanterns reveals the national appeal of Konpira-san.

118. See, for example, "Ise sangū kondate dōchūki," pp. 599–622.

119. "Ise sangū shoshinsho," p. 145. On women's *kō,* see Miyata, pp. 235–246. In that chapter he discusses women's groups for pilgrimage to Mount Fuji, which was normally off-limits to women.

120. The parish records of one Ise priest from Sanuki for the mid-Tokugawa through the early Meiji years indicate that 70 to 80 percent of the travelers completed their pilgrimage during the first three months of the year. The remaining numbers, as expected, were scattered over the other nine months. Many pilgrims headed for Ise during non-*okagemairi* years commonly set out on the road early in the first month, soon after New Year's activities were completed. (Shinjō, *Shomin to tabi,* pp. 145-146.)

The records from Sanuki, furthermore, reveal that the late sixth and seventh months—the period after weeding and before harvesting—were also a time when peasants could escape from the fields to travel. This period seems to have been particularly favored in the north, where heavy winter snows made even local traffic difficult during the early months of the year. This period of respite from field work was, because of winter snows, the only time when commoners could climb mountains associated with religious deities such as Mount Fuji, the "Three Mountains" (Dewa sanzan), Mount Takayama (Etchū), and Mount Shirayama (Kaga). (Ibid.) The break was not long, however, and limited the distance one could travel. Once back in the fields, farmers were kept busy through at least part of the eleventh month. Thus, commoner and official patterns of movement assumed different and largely non-overlapping cycles.

121. Smaller-scale *okagemairi* occurred in 1650, 1718, 1723, 1730, 1748, 1755, 1803, and 1855. Fujitani, pp. 35-36 and Davis, p. 100.

122. *Nagoya sōsho, Zoku hen,* vol. 11, *Ōmurō chūki,* no. 3, pp. 40-41.

123. *THSS,* vol. 2, p. 95.

124. Davis, p. 100 and Fujitani, pp. 58-59.

125. Fujitani, pp. 78, 89-90. The most famous account of the 1830 event is "Ukiyo no arisama," written by a doctor from Osaka. The Hirado daimyo, Matsuura Seizan, recorded a number of the stories about the event circulating at the time in his *Kashiyawa: zoku hen,* vol. 4, pp. 80-93.

126. Foard, pp. 231-256.

127. Kaempfer, vol. 2, p. 339

128. Maeda Takeshi, *Junrei no shakaigaku: Saikoku junrei to Shikoku henro,* pp. 72-80, 131-137.

129. Lack of ferry-boat crossings and road markers, as well as poor lodging facilities, are some of the complaints expressed in a Shikoku pilgrimage diary from the mid-seventeenth century. From the middle of the next century, with improving conditions, the number of days required to complete the circuit decreased from 91-120 to 40-50. Shinjō, *Shaji sankei,* pp. 1,024-1,025.

130. *Nagoya sōsho,* vol. 3, *Hōsei hen* 2, Nagoya shi kyōiku iinkai, ed., p. 402.

131. Shinjō, *Shaji sankei,* p. 1042.

132. Maeda Takeshi, p. 113.

133. Shinjō, *Shaji sankei*, p. 941; Kiyokawa, p. 104.

134. Kiyokawa, pp. 91–93. He also noted that "a constant stream of boats cross over from the mainland" to Marugame in Shikoku. (p. 91.)

135. Marugame was a bustling port town that grew from 300–400 households (1653) to 2,000 at its height in the early nineteenth century. Shinjō, *Shaji sankei*, pp. 933–938. See also "Marugame hanjōki," in *Nihon toshi seikatsu shiryō shūsei*, vol. 7, *Minatomachi hen* 2, pp. 253–260.

136. Kiyokawa, p. 41.

137. Shinjō, *Shaji sankei*, pp. 947–950. There were more than 100 lodging places for pilgrims at Zenkō-ji in the late eighteenth century. These included firewood inns, full-service inns, and priests' lodgings. *Nagano ken shi tsūshi hen*, vol. 5, *Kinsei* 2, Nagano ken, ed., p. 327.

138. Iwashina Koichirō, *Fuji-kō no rekishi*, pp. 399–400.

139. On Ōyama, see Yamamoto Mitsumasa, "Soshū Yagurasawa ōkan ni tsuite," *Kanagawa ken shi kenkyū*, vol. 19, pp. 46–56 (1973); *Kanagawa ken shi tsūshi hen*, vol. 2, *Kinsei* 1, pp. 755–769. On Fuji, see also Inobe Shigeo, *Fuji no shinkō* and Martin C. Collcutt, "Mt. Fuji as the Realm of Miroku," in Alan Sponberg and Helen Hardacre, eds., *Maitreya, The Future Buddha*. For Chichibu, see Shinjō, *Shaji sankei*, pp. 98–99, and a guide to the circuit written by a monk from Akita in 1744, Takebe Ayatari: "Chichibu junrei hitori annaiki," in *Takebe Ayatari zenshū*, Takebe Ayatari chosaku kankō kai, ed., pp. 84–110.

140. Conversation with Yamamoto Mitsumasa, June 13, 1986. One notable exception is Murao Karyō's record of short trips the author took in the Edo area over the years 1821–1831, *Edo kingō michi shirube*.

141. Alcock, vol. 2, p. 316.

142. *KKSS*, vol. 10, pp. 12–13.

143. Shinjō, *Shomin to tabi*, pp. 110–111.

144. Fukuzawa, p. 31.

145. Igarashi, *Kinsei sekisho seido*, p. 529.

146. In rural Japan the number of cooperative groups declined and many types of dependent workers were able to establish independent households. See Thomas C. Smith, *The Agrarian Origins of Modern Japan*, especially 108–156.

147. Shinjō, *Shomin to tabi*, p. 107. One record from Aizu domain indicates that seventy-one townsmen and forty-six villagers left for Ise during the second month of 1652. *Aizu han kasei jikki*, p. 403. See "Ise sangū dōchūki," pp. 497–518, for an Ise diary kept by one member of a group of eleven merchants from Aizu domain.

148. Kiyokawa, p. 5.

149. Shinjō, *Shomin to tabi*, p. 158.

150. The specific figures are as follows: 1804–1817, fifty-two men and forty women; 1818–1830, seventy-one men and eighty-eight women. *Kagawa ken shi,* vol. 4, *Kinsei* 2, p. 325.
151. Shinjō, *Shaji sankei,* p. 954.
152. Maruyama Yasunari, "Kaidō, shukueki, tabi," p. 230.
153. Some Ise pilgrims are said to have converted the alms they collected in copper coins to silver before returning home because it was lighter in weight. "Ise-san okage no nikki," in Jingū shichō, ed., *Daijingū sanpaiki taisei,* p. 445. "Ukiyo no arisama," p. 83 lists items alms-givers donated during the *okagemairi of* 1830 such as money, fans, straw sandles and hats, tea, pounded rice cakes, and rice.
154. Shinjō, *Shaji sankei,* p. 1027.
155. Kaempfer, vol. 2, p. 338.
156. *Hachinohe shi shi shiryō hen, Kinsei,* 12 volumes.
157. Satow, p. 225.
158. Kiyokawa, p. 183.
159. *Kanagawa ken shi shiryō hen,* vol. 4, *Kinsei* 1, no. 335, p. 894.

CONCLUSION

1. Henderson, pp. 214–215.
2. John F. Sears, *Sacred Places. American Tourist Attractions in the Nineteenth Century,* p. 3. According to Sears these requirements "were not fully met in America until the 1820s." (p. 4.)
3. Takeuchi Makoto, *Bunka no taishuka,* is devoted to an exploration of this theme.
4. *Sankin kōtai* is the subject of the author's current book project, entitled, *A Year in Edo: The Alternate Attendance and Japan's Early Modern Experience.*
5. In one of Saikaku's stories he recounts how, after the death of one character, Yorozuya, and his wife, "their daughter-in-law made a pilgrimage to Ise, and on her return did some sightseeing in Kyoto and Osaka. Observing the elegant attire of the people, she remodelled her own dress in imitation." Ihara Saikaku, *The Japanese Family Storehouse,* p. 125. A merchant of Yodo, as well, "copied the extravagances he saw in the capital." (Ibid.)
6. Irokawa Daikichi, *The Culture of the Meiji Period,* pp. 196–207.
7. Jippensha, *Hizakurige or Shanks' Mare,* pp. 323–328.
8. Fukuzawa, p. 31.
9. Jippensha, *Hizakurige or Shanks' Mare,* p. 237.

List of Works Cited

Unless otherwise noted, the place of publication is Tokyo.

Addiss, Stephen, ed. *Tōkaidō: Adventures on the Road in Old Japan.* Lawrence: The University of Kansas, Spencer Museum of Art, 1980.

Aida Nirō. *Chūsei no sekisho* (Barriers in the Medieval Period). Unebi shobō, 1943.

——. *Odawara gassen* (The Battle of Odawara). Meichō shuppan, 1976.

Aizu han kasei jikki (True Record of Aizu Domain), vols. 1, 7, 8. Toyoda Takeshi, ed. Yoshikawa kōbunkan, 1975, 1981, 1982.

Akada Mitsui. "Kō to ohenro" (Confraternity Groups and Pilgrimage), in Kimura Motoi, ed., *Edo to chihō bunka* (Edo and Regional Culture), vol. 2 (q.v.).

Akamatsu Noriyoshi. *Akamatsu Noriyoshi hansei dan* (Record of Half the Lifetime of Akamatsu Noriyoshi). Akamatsu Han'ichi, ann. Tōyō bunko, 317. Heibonsha, 1977.

Akimoto Norio. "Ryōshu kenryoku to shuku, sukegō" (Post Stations, Assisting Villages, and Seigneurial Authority), *Shakai keizai shigaku,* vol. 27, no. 1, pp. 44–63 (1967).

Akita han machi fure shū (Collection of Regulations for Urban Areas in Akita Domain). Imamura Yoshitaka, ed. 3 vols. Miraisha, 1971–73.

Albert, William. "Popular Opposition to Turnpike Trusts in Early Eighteenth Century England," *Journal of Transport History,* Third Series, vol. 5, pp. 1–17 (1979).

Alcock, Sir Rutherford. *The Capital of the Tycoon: A Narrative of a Three Years' Residence in Japan.* 2 vols. St. Claireshores, Mich.: Scholarly Press, 1969.

Amino Yoshihiko, Tsukamoto Manabu, Tsuboi Hirofumi, and Miyata Noboru. "Rekishi to minzoku gaku" (History and Folklore), *Rettō no bunka shi* (Cultural History of the Japanese Archipelago), vol. 3, pp. 1–78 (1986).

Anzai Kazutoshi. "Shinagawa shuku ni okeru sukegō kayaku" (Shinagawa Post Station and the Overland Transport Corvée Levy), *Hōsei shigaku*, vol. 17, pp. 77–88 (1965).

Aoki Kōji. *Hyakushō ikki no nenjiteki kenkyū* (A Chronological Study of Peasant Movements). Shinseisha, 1966.

Arai chō shi, bekkan: sekisho shiryō (History of Arai, Supplemental Volume: Documents of Arai Sekisho). Arai: Arai chō shi, 1987.

Arai chō shi, bekkan: sekisho shiryō (History of Arai, Supplemental Volume: Documents of Arai Sekisho). Arai: Arai chō, 1987.

———. vol. 8. Yamamoto Mitsumasa and Watanabe Kazutoshi, eds. Arai machi: Arai machi kyōiku iinkai, 1976.

Arai Hakuseki. *Oritaku shiba no ki* (Tale Told Round a Brushwood Fire). Nihon koten bungaku taikei, 95. Iwanami shoten, 1964.

Arima onsen shiryō (Documents on Arima Hot Springs Resort), vol. 2. Kazahaya Jun, ed. Meichō shuppan, 1988.

"Arima nyūtō miyage-e nado" (Souvenirs and Other Items From a Stay at Arima Hot Springs). Gotō Family Documents no. 930, 1730. Aki City Library, Aki.

Asai Naohira. *Ōigawa to sono shūhen* (The Ōi River and Its Environs). Izumi shuppan, 1967.

Asai Ryōi. *Tōkaidō meishoki* (Tale of Famous Places Along the Tōkaidō). 2 vols. Tōyō bunko, 346, 361. Heibonsha, 1979.

Asakawa Masusaburō. "Tabi no kozukaisen ni tsuite" (Travel and Travel Expenses), *Shinano*, vol. 3, no. 5, pp. 44–47 (1951).

"Baiō zuihitsu" (Miscellaneous Writings on a Venerable Plum Tree), in *Nihon zuihitsu taisei*, Second Series, vol. 11, Nihon zuihitsu taisei henshūbu, ed. (q.v.).

Beier, A. L. *Masterless Men: The Vagrancy Problem in England 1560–1640*. London and New York: Methuen, 1985.

Bendix, Reinhard. *Kings or People: Power and the Mandate to Rule*. Berkeley: University of California Press, 1978.

Berry, Mary Elizabeth. "Public Peace and Private Attainment: The Goals and Conduct of Power in Early Modern Japan," *Journal of Japanese Studies*, vol. 12, no. 2, pp. 237–271 (Summer 1986).

Bird, Isabella L. *Unbeaten Tracks in Japan*. 2 vols. New York: G.P. Putnam's Sons, 1881.

Bix, Herbert P. *Peasant Protest in Japan, 1590–1884*. New Haven: Yale University Press, 1986.

Black, John R. *Young Japan: Yokohama and Yedo 1859–79*. Tokyo, London and New York: Oxford University Press, 1968.

Bolitho, Harold. *Treasures Among Men: The Fudai Daimyo in Tokugawa Japan.* New Haven: Yale University Press, 1974.

Boulton, W. H. *The Pageant of Transport Through the Ages.* London: Benjamin Blom, 1969.

Braudel, Fernand. *The Perspective of the World: Civilization and Capitalism, 15th–18th Century.* 3 vols. New York: Harper and Row Publishers, 1979.

Bresler, Lawrence. "The Origins of Popular Travel and Travel Literature in Japan." Ph.D. diss. New York: Columbia University, 1975.

Broadbridge, Seymour. "Economic and Social Trends in Tokugawa Japan," *Modern Asian Studies,* vol. 8, no. 3, pp. 347–372 (1974).

Brown, Philip C. *Central Authority and Local Autonomy in the Formation of Early Modern Japan: The Case of Kaga Domain.* Stanford: Stanford University Press, 1993.

"Bunsei jūsan toradoshi Ise okagemairi jitsuroku kagami" (A True Record of the Ise *Okagemairi* in the Thirteenth Year of the Bunsei Era), in Jingū shichō, ed., *Jingū sanpaiki taisei* (A Collection of Ise Pilgrimage Diaries), vol. 10 of *Daijingū sōsho* (q.v.).

The Cambridge Economic History of Europe, vol. 2, *Trade and Industry in the Middle Ages.* M. M. Postan and E. E. Rich, eds. Cambridge: Cambridge University Press, 1965.

———, vol. 6, *The Industrial Revolution and After.* M. M. Postan and H. J. Habakkuk, eds. Cambridge: Cambridge University Press, 1965.

Chambliss, William Jones. *Chiaraijima Village: Land Tenure, Taxation, and Local Trade, 1818–1884.* Association for Asian Studies Monograph 19. Tucson, Arizona: University of Arizona Press, 1965.

Chigasaki shi shi (History of Chigasaki City), vol. 4. Chigasaki shi, ed. Chigasaki: Chigasaki shi, 1981.

Chikamatsu Monzaemon. "Yosaku from Tamba," in Donald Keene, ed. and trans., *Major Plays of Chikamatsu.* New York and London: Columbia University Press, 1961.

Clark, Gordon L. and Dear, Michael. *State Apparatus: Structures and Language of Legitimacy.* Boston: Allen and Unwin, 1984.

Coaldrake, William H. "Unno: Edo Period Post Town of the Central Japan Alps," *Asian Art,* vol. 5, no. 2, pp. 9–30 (Spring 1992).

Cohen, Erik. "A Phenomenology of Tourist Experiences," *Sociology,* vol. 13, no. 2, pp. 179–201 (May 1979).

———. "Who Is a Tourist? A Conceptual Clarification," *The Sociological Review,* vol. 22, no. 4, pp. 527–555 (1974).

Cohen, Stanley and Scull, Andrew, eds. *Social Control and the State.* New York: St. Martins Press, 1983.

Collcutt, Martin, "Mt. Fuji as the Realm of Miroku," in Alan Sponberg and

Helen Hardacre, eds., *Maitreya, the Future Buddha*. Princeton: Princeton University Press, 1988.

Cooley, Charles H. "The Theory of Transportation." Special edition of *Sociological Theory and Social Research*. New York: Henry Holt and Company, 1930.

Cooper, Michael, comp. *They Came to Japan: An Anthology of European Reports on Japan, 1543–1640*. Berkeley: University of California Press, 1965.

Cortazzi, Hugh, ed. *Dr. Willis in Japan, 1862–67: British Medical Pioneer*. London and Dover, N.H.: The Athlone Press, 1985.

———, ed. *Victorians in Japan: In and Around the Treaty Ports*. London: Athlone Press, 1987.

Crofts, J. *Packhorse, Waggon and Post: Land Carriage and Communications under the Tudors and Stuarts*. London: Routledge and Kegan Paul, 1967.

Davis, Winston B. "Pilgrimage and World Renewal: A Study of Religion and Social Values in Tokugawa Japan," *History of Religions*, vol. 23, no. 2, pp. 97–116 (November 1983); vol. 23, no. 3, pp. 197–221 (February 1984).

de Vries, Jan. *Barges and Capitalism: Passenger Transportation in the Dutch Economy*. Utrecht: HES Publishers, 1981.

Deane, Phyllis. *The First Industrial Revolution*. Cambridge: Cambridge University Press, 1965.

Defoe, Daniel. *A Tour Through the Whole Island of Great Britain*. 2 vols. London: Penguin Books, 1983.

Descharmes, Leon. "Itinerary of a Journey from Yedo to Kusatsu, With Notes Upon the Waters of Kusatsu," *Transactions of the Asiatic Society of Japan*, First Series, vol. 2, pp. 25–54 (1874).

Dunbar, Seymour. *A History of Travel in America*. New York: Tudor Publishing Company, 1937.

Dyos, H. T. and Aldcroft, D. H. *British Transport: An Economic Survey from the Seventeenth Century through the Twentieth*. Leicester: Leicester University Press, 1969.

Edmonds, Richard Louis. *Northern Frontiers of Qing China and Tokugawa Japan*. Department of Geography Research Paper 213. Chicago: University of Chicago, 1985.

Eigashira Tsuneji. *Ōmi shōnin: Nakai ke no kenkyū* (Ōmi Merchants: A Study of the Nakai Family). Yūzankaku, 1965.

Ekiken kai hensan, ed. *Ekiken zenshū* (The Complete Works of Ekiken), vol. 7. Ekiken zenshū kankōbu, 1911.

Etchū shiryō (Documents on Etchū), vols. 2–3. Toyama ken, ed. Toyama: Toyama ken, 1909–1910.

Evans, Peter, Rueschemeyer, Dietrich, and Skocpol, Theda, eds. *Bringing the State Back In.* Cambridge: Cambridge University Press, 1985.

Foard, James H. "The Boundaries of Compassion: Buddhist and National Tradition in Japanese Pilgrimage," *Journal of Asian Studies,* vol. 41, no. 2, pp. 231–251 (1982).

Fruin, W. Mark. "Labor Migration in Nineteenth Century Japan: A Study Based on Echizen Han." Ph.D. diss. Stanford: Stanford University, 1973.

"Fūdo zakki" (Notes on Climate), in Ono Takeo, ed., *Nihon nōmin shiryō shusui* (Collected Documents on Peasants in Japan), vol. 2. Sakai shoten, 1970.

Fujimoto Toshiharu. *Kinsei toshi no chiiki kōzō: Sono rekishi chirigakuteki kenkyū* (Regional Patterns of Early Modern Cities: An Historical and Geographical Study). Kokon shoin, 1977.

Fujino Tamotsu. *Shintei bakuhan taisei shi no kenkyū* (A Study of the History of the *Bakuhan* System: Revised Edition). Yoshikawa kōbunkan, 1975.

Fujisawa Hiroshi. "Sukegō no sōsetsu katei to sonzai keitai" (The Development and Form of the Overland Transport Corvée Levy), *Shigaku zasshi,* vol. 77–79, pp. 187–200 (1960).

Fujisawa shi shi (History of Fujisawa City), vol. 2, *Shiryō hen* (Documents). Fujisawa shi shi hensan iinkai, ed. Fujisawa shi, 1973.

Fujitani Yoshio. *'Okagemairi' to 'eejanaika'* (*Okagemairi* and *Eejanaika*). Iwanami shinsho, 680. Iwanami shoten, 1968.

Fujiwara Morohide. "Fude makase" (Leave the Writing to Me), in Takeuchi Toshimi, Mori Kahei, and Miyamoto Tsuneichi, eds., *Nihon shomin seikatsu shiryō shū,* vol. 3 (q.v.).

Fukai Jinzō. "Sekisho yaburi to onna tabi" ("Sekisho Smashing" and Women's Travel), *Kōtsū shi kenkyū,* vol. 27, pp. 12–23 (1991).

—— "Sukegō no seiritsu to sono sonzai keitai" (The Development and Form of the Overland Transport Corvée Levy), *Bunka,* vol. 42, nos. 1–2, pp. 1–16 (1978).

——. "Yoshimune seiken ni okeru shukueki, sukegō seisaku" (Policy On Post Stations and Assisting Villages During the Reign of Yoshimune), *Nihon shi kenkyū,* vol. 272, pp. 27–54 (1985).

Fukushima ken shi (History of Fukushima Prefecture), vol. 10, *ge, Kinsei shiryō hen* (Documents of the Early Modern Period) 4. Fukushima: Fukushima ken, 1968.

Fukuzawa Yukichi. *The Autobiography of Fukuzawa Yukichi.* Eiichi Kiyōka, trans. New York: Columbia University Press, 1960.

Furukawa Koshōken. "Saiyū zakki" (Notes on Travel to the West), in *Tanken, kikō, chishi* (Exploration, Travel Accounts, and Topography), *Tōgoku hen,* (The Eastern Provinces), Takeuchi Toshimi, Mori Kahei, and Miyamoto Tsuneichi, eds., vol. 3 of *Nihon shomin seikatsu shiryō shūsei* (q.v.).

———. *Tōyū zakki* (Notes on Travels to the East). Tōyō bunko, 27. Heibonsha, 1964.

Furushima Toshio. *Furushima Toshio chosaku shū* (The Collected Writings of Furushima Toshio), vol. 4: *Shinshū chūma no kenkyū* (The *Chūma* System of the Shinano Area). Tōkyō daigaku shuppan kai, 1975.

Futagawa Yoshifumi. "Echigo no sekisho" (The Sekisho of Echigo), *Shinano*, vol. 22, no. 8, pp. 23–32 (1969).

———. "Edo bakufu hō to saiban kara mita sekisho no honshitsu" (The True Nature of Sekisho as Revealed in the Law and Legal Proceedings of the Edo Bakufu), *Nihon rekishi*, vol. 271, pp. 58–66 (1970).

———. "Kōzuke no sekisho" (The Sekisho of Kōzuke), *Shinano*, vol. 22, no. 12, pp. 31–42 (1970).

———. "Tōkaidō no sekisho" (The Sekisho of the Tōkaidō), *Nihon rekishi*, vol. 295, pp. 41–60 (1972).

Gifu ken shi shiryō hen (History of Gifu Prefecture, Documents), *Kinsei* (Early Modern) Gifu ken, ed. Gifu ken, 1970.

Goeki benran (Handbook on the Gokaidō Post Stations). Komazawa daigaku kinsei kōtsū shi kenkyu kai, ed. Kinsei kōtsū shiryō, 1. Komazawa daigaku, 1980.

Gokaidō sono hoka bunken mitori nobe ezu (Detailed Maps of the Gokaidō and Other Roads). 130 vols. Kodama Kōta, ed. Tōkyō bijutsu, 1977– .

Graburn, Nelson. *To Pray, Pay and Play: The Cultural Structure of Japanese Domestic Tourism*. Aix-en-Provence: Centre des Hautes Etudes Touristiques, 1983.

Graham, Patricia J. "The Political and Economic Importance of the Tōkaidō," in Stephen Addiss, ed., *Tokaido: Adventures on the Road in Old Japan* (q.v.).

Griffis, William Elliot. *The Mikado's Empire*. 2 vols. New York: Harper and Brothers Publishers, 1903.

Gunma ken shi shiryō hen (History of Gunma Prefecture: Documents), vols. 9–12, *Kinsei* (Early Modern) 1–4. Gunma ken shi hensan iinkai, ed. Gunma: Gunma ken, 1977–1982.

Gunma ken shi shiryō shū (Collected Documents on Gunma Prefecture), vols. 5–6, *Nikki hen* (Diaries) 1–2. Yamada Takemoro and Hagiwara Susumu, eds. Gunma: Gunma ken bunka jigyō shinkō kai. 1970–1971.

Gyōda shi shi (History of Gyōda City), vol. 2. Gyōda shi shi hensan iinkai, ed. Gyōda: Gyōda shi yakusho, 1964.

Hachinohe shi shi shiryō hen (History of Hachinohe City: Documents), *Kinsei* (Early Modern). 12 vols. Hachinohe shi shi hensan iinkai, ed. Hachinohe: Hachinohe shi, 1972–1982.

Haga Noboru. *Shukubamachi* (Post Towns). Yanagiwara shoten, 1977.

Hagiwara Susumu and Chijiwa Minori, eds. *Takayama Hikokurō zenshū* (The Collected Writings of Takayama Hikokurō). 5 vols. Takayama Hikokurō ikō kankō kai, 1943.

Hakone gosekisho nikki kakinuki (Excerpts from the Official Diary Kept at Hakone Sekisho). 3 vols. Hakone komonjo o manabu kai, ed. Hakone: Hakone machi kyōiku iinkai, 1976–1978.

"Hakone onsen michi no ki" (Record of a Trip to Hakone Hot Springs). 1763. Mitsui Collection. University of California, Berkeley.

Hall, John W. "Rule by Status in Tokugawa Japan," *Journal of Japanese Studies*, vol. 1, no. 1, pp. 34–50 (Autumn 1974).

Hall, R. B. "The Road in Old Japan," *Studies in the History of Culture*, pp. 122–155. Menasha, Wis.: American Council of Learned Societies, 1942.

Hamamatsu shi shi shiryō hen (History of Hamamatsu City: Documents), vol. 1. Hamamatsu shiyakusho, ed. Hamamatsu shi, 1967.

Hanley, Susan B. "Migration and Economic Change in Okayama during the Tokugawa Period," *Keio Economic Studies*, vol. 10, no. 2, pp. 19–36 (1973).

—— and Kozo Yamamura. *Economic and Demographic Change in Tokugawa Japan, 1600–1868*. Princeton: Princeton University Press, 1977.

Hanpōshū (A Collection of Domain Laws), vol. 1: *Okayama han* (Okayama domain). Ishii Ryōsuke, ed. Sōbunsha, 1959.

——, vol. 4: *Kanazawa han* (Kanazawa Domain). Ishii Ryōsuke, ed. Sōbunsha, 1963.

——, vol. 6: *Zoku Kanazawa han* (Kanazawa Domain: Supplementary Volume). Ishii Ryōsuke, ed. Sōbunsha, 1966.

——, vol. 9: *Morioka han* (Morioka Domain), pt. 1. Ishii Ryōsuke, ed. Sōbunsha, 1970.

——, vol. 11: *Kurume han* (Kurume Domain). Ishii Ryōsuke, ed. Sōbunsha, 1973.

Hara Masaoki. "Tamakushige futatsu ideyu michi no ki" (Guide to Two Hot Springs in Tamakushige), in Itasaka Yōko, ed., *Edo onsen kikō* (q.v.).

Haraguchi, Torao and Sakai, Robert K. *The Status System and Social Organization of Satsuma: A Translation of the Shumon Tefuda Aratame Jomoku*. Honolulu: University of Hawaii Press, 1975.

Harasawa Bun'ya. "Annaka shukueki to sukegō to no kankei" (The Relationship Between Annaka Post Station and Its Assisting Villages), *Nihon no rekishi*, vol. 128, pp. 33–48 (1959).

——. "Edo jidai ni okeru shukueki to wakimichi ōkan to no kankei" (Post Stations and Branch-Road Traffic), *Nihon rekishi*, vol. 119, pp. 33–48 (1958).

Harootunian, H. D. "Late Tokugawa Culture and Thought," in Marius B. Jansen, ed., *The Nineteenth Century*, vol. 5 of *The Cambridge History of Japan*. Cambridge and New York: Cambridge University Press, 1989.

Harris, Townsend. *The Complete Journal of Townsend Harris.* Introduction and Notes by Mario Emilio Cosenza. New York: Doubleday, Doran and Company, 1930.

Hart, Roger. *English Life in the Eighteenth Century.* New York: G. P. Putnam's Sons, 1970.

Hayami Akira. "Labor Migration in a Pre-industrial Society: A Study Tracing the Life Histories of the Inhabitants of a Village," *Keio Economic Studies,* vol. 10, no. 2, pp. 1–18 (1973).

———. "Thank You Francisco Xavier: An Essay in the Use of Micro-Data for Historical Demography of Tokugawa Japan," *Keio Economic Studies,* vol. 13, pp. 65–81 (1976).

Hayashi Miwako. "Kinsei zenki no sukegō yaku futan" (The Overland Transport Corvée Levy During the Early Part of the Early Modern Period), *Yokohama kaikō shiryōkan kiyō,* vol. 2, pp. 35–59 (1984).

Hayashi Razan. "Heishin kikō" (Account of a Journey in 1616), in Yanagida Kunio, ed., *Zoku kikō bunshū* (q.v.).

Hayashi Reiko. "Kasama jōkamachi ni okeru josei zō" (Portrait of Women in Kasama Castle Town), in Kinsei josei shi kenkyū kai, ed., *Edo jidai no joseitachi* (Women in the Edo Period). Yoshikawa kōbunkan, 1990.

Henderson, Dan Fenno. *Conciliation and Japanese Law: Tokugawa and Modern,* vol. 1. Seattle: University of Washington Press, 1966.

———. "The Evolution of Tokugawa Law," in John W. Hall and Marius B. Jansen, eds., *Studies in the Institutional History of Early Modern Japan.* Princeton: Princeton University Press, 1968.

———. *Village "Contracts" in Tokugawa Japan.* Seattle: University of Washington Press, 1975.

Hillier, Jack. *Suzuki Harunobu: An Exhibition of His Colour-Prints and Illustrated Books on the Occasion of the Bicentenary of His Death in 1770.* Philadelphia: Philadelphia Museum of Art, 1970.

Hirakawa Hajime. "Sukegō seido no seiritsu to tenkai" (The Establishment and Development of the Overland Transport Corvée Labor System), *Hōsei shiron,* vol. 4, pp. 16–37 (1976).

———. "Sukegō seido no kakuritsu katei" (The Establishment of the Overland Transport Corvée Labor System), in Kodama Kōta sensei koki kinen kai, ed., *Nihon kinsei kōtsū shi kenkyū* (q.v.).

Hiramatsu Yoshirō. "History of Penal Institutions: Japan," *Law in Japan,* vol. 6, pp. 1–48 (1973).

———. "Tokugawa Law," Dan Fenno Henderson, trans. *Law in Japan,* vol. 14, pp. 1–48 (1981).

Hirao Michio. *Kinsei shakai shikō* (A Consideration of Early Modern Society). Kōchi: Kōchi shiritsu shimin toshokan, 1962.

——. *Tosa han nōgyō keizai shi* (Economic History of Agriculture in Tosa Domain). Kōchi: Kōchi shiritsu shimin toshokan, 1958.

Hirasawa Kiyoto. *Hyakushō ikki no tenkai* (The Development of Peasant Movements). Azekura shobō, 1972.

Hiratsuka shi shi (History of Hiratsuka City), vol. 4, *Shiryō hen kinsei* (Documents: Early Modern) 3. Hiratsuka: Hiratsuka shi, 1984.

Hiroe Kiyoshi. *Kinsei Tosa no shūkyō* (Religion in Early Modern Tosa). Kōchi: Tosa shidan kai, 1980.

Hirosaki shi shi (History of Hirosaki City), *Hansei hen* (Domainal Period). Hirosaki shi shi hensan iinkai, ed. Hirosaki: Hirosaki shi, 1963.

Hiroshima ken shi (History of Hiroshima Prefecture), *Kinsei shiryō hen* (Early Modern Documents), vol. 4. Hiroshima: Hiroshima ken, 1975.

Hiroshima ken shi tsūshi hen (History of Hiroshima Prefecture), vol. 4, *Kinsei* (Early Modern) 2. Hiroshima: Hiroshima ken, 1984.

Hosoe chō shi shiryō hen (Documents of Hosoe). 2 vols. Hosoe: Hosoe chō, 1980–1981.

Hufton, Olwen H. *The Poor of Eighteenth Century France, 1750–1789*. Oxford: Clarendon Press, 1974.

Humbert, Aimé. *Anbēru bakumatsu Nihon ezu* (The Late-Tokugawa Illustrations of Aimé Humbert). 2 vols. Takahashi Hōtarō, trans. Shin ikoku sōsho, 14. Yūshōdō shoten, 1969–1970.

Hurstfield, Joel. *Freedom, Corruption and Government in Elizabethan England*. London: J. Cape, 1973.

Ibaraki kenritsu hakubutsukan, ed. *Nikkō sankei no michi* (The Pilgrimage Route to Nikkō). Ibaraki: Ibaraki kenritsu hakubutsukan, 1984.

Ichinomiya shi shi shiryō hen (History of Ichinomiya City: Documents), vol. 8. Ichinomiya shichō, ed. Ichinomiya: Ichinomiya shi, 1968.

Igarashi Tomio. *Kinsei sekisho no kisoteki kenkyū* (A Basic Study of the Sekisho System in the Early Modern Period). Taga shuppan, 1986.

——. *Kinsei sekisho seido no kenkyū* (The Sekisho System in the Early Modern Period). Yūhō shoten, 1975.

——. "Kinsei sekisho tegata no kenkyū" (Study of Sekisho Travel Permits of the Early Modern Period), *Jōmō shigaku*, vol. 16, pp. 80–95 (1965).

——. "Kinsei watashibune no sonzai keitai: Nakasendō Yanase watashibune o jirei to shite" (Ferry Boats in the Early Modern Period: the Case of Yanase on the Nakasendō), *Shinano*, vol. 22, no. 5, pp. 17–28 (1970).

——. *Nikkō reiheishi kaidō* (The Nikkō Reiheishi Road). Kashiwa shobō, 1977.

Ihara Saikaku. *Five Women Who Loved Love*. Wm. Theodore de Bary, trans. Tokyo and Rutland, Vt.: Charles E. Tuttle, Company, 1956.

——. *Hitome tamaboko* (A Glimpse of Life on the Road). Kinsei bungaku shoshi kenkyū kai, ed. Benseisha, 1975.

——. *The Japanese Family Storehouse: Or the Millionaires' Gospel Modernised.* G. W. Sargent, trans. Cambridge: Cambridge University Press, 1959.

——. *Some Final Words of Advice.* Peter Nosco, trans. Tokyo and Rutland, Vt.: Charles E. Tuttle, Company, 1980.

——. *Tales of Samurai Honor.* Ann Callahan, trans. Tokyo: Monumenta Nipponica, 1981.

Ikeda Yasaburō, Noma Kōshin, and Minakami Tsutomu, eds. *Nihon meisho fūzoku zue* (Illustrated Guide to the Customs and Famous Places of Japan). 18 plus 2 supplementary volumes. Kadokawa, 1979–1988.

Imai Kingo, ed. *Ryokō yōjin shū* (A Collection of Travel Precautions). Yasaka shobō, 1969.

——. "Shomin no michi" (Roads Used by Commoners), in Yamada Munemutsu et al., eds., *Michi no bunka* (The Culture of Roads). Kōdansha, 1979.

Inobe Shigeo. *Fuji no shinkō* (The Fuji Cult). Kokon shoin, 1928. Meichō shuppan, 1983.

Inoue Tsūjo. "Kika nikki" (Diary of a Journey Homeward), in *Inoue Tsūjo zenshū,* Inoue Tsūjo zenshū shūtei iinkai, ed., (q.v.).

——. "Tōkai kikō" (Account of a Journey to the East), in *Inoue Tsūjo zenshū,* Inoue Tsūjo zenshū shūtei iinkai, ed., (q.v.).

Inoue Tsūjo zenshū (The Collected Works of Inoue Tsūjo). Inoue Tsūjo zenshū shūtei iinkai, ed. Marugame: Kagawa kenritsu Marugame kōtō gakkō dōsō kai, 1973.

Irokawa Daikichi. *The Culture of the Meiji Period.* Marius B. Jansen, ed. Princeton: Princeton University Press, 1985.

Ise dōchūki shiryō (Ise Travel Diaries). Tōkyō to Setagaya ku kyōiku iinkai, 1984.

"Ise sangū dōchūki" (Diary of a Pilgrimage to Ise Shrine), in Tanigawa Ken'ichi, ed., *Nihon shomin seikatsu shiryō shūsei,* vol. 20, *Tanken, kikō, chishi: Hoi* (q.v.).

"Ise sangū kondate dōchūki" (Diary of a Pilgrimage to Ise Shrine), in Tanigawa Ken'ichi, ed., *Nihon shomin seikatsu shiryō shūsei,* vol. 20, *Tanken, kikō, chishi: Hoi* (q.v.).

"Ise sangū nikki" (Diary of a Pilgrimage to Ise Shrine), in *Ise dōchūki shiryō,* Tōkyō to Setagaya ku kyōiku iinkai, ed. (q.v.).

"Ise sangū oboe" (A Recollection of a Pilgrimage to Ise Shrine), in Tōkyō to Setagaya ku kyōiku iinkai, ed., *Ise dōchūki shiryō* (q.v.).

"Ise sangū shoshinsho" (Ise Pilgrimage: An Act of Original Intent), in Koike Masatane, ed., *Edo no ehon: shoki kusazōshi shūsei* (Edo picture books: *kusazōshi* of the Early Tokugawa Period), vol. 1. Kokusho kankō kai, 1987.

"Ise-san okage no nikki" (Diary of a Pilgrimage for Thanksgiving to Ise), in

Jingū shichō, ed., *Jingū sanpaiki taisei*, vol. 10 of *Daijingū sanpaiki taisei* (q.v.).

Ishiodori Kazuo. "Tosa han shoki no 'hashirimono' taisaku ni tsuite" (The Problem of Runaways in Tosa Domain in the Early Tokugawa Period), in Yamamoto Takeshi, ed., *Tosa shi no shomondai.* Meichō shuppan, 1978.

Itasaka Yōko, ed. *Edo onsen kikō* (Accounts of Trips to Hot Springs in the Edo Period). Tōyō bunko, 472. Heibonsha, 1987.

Itō Yoshiichi. *Edo no machi kado* (The Gates of Edo). Heibonsha, 1987.

Iwashina Koichirō. *Fuji-kō no rekishi* (History of the Fuji Cult). Meichō shuppan, 1983.

Iwate ken shi (History of Iwate Prefecture), vol. 4–5, *Kinsei* (Early Modern) 1–2, Iwate ken, ed. Iwate: Iwate ken, 1963.

Iwatsuki shi shi (History of Iwatsuki City), *Kinsei shiryō hen* (Early Modern Documents), vol. 4, *Chihō shiryō* (Local History) 2. Iwatsuki: Iwatsuki shi, 1984.

Jansen, Marius B. "Tosa in the Seventeenth Century," in John W. Hall and Marius B. Jansen, eds., *Studies in the Institutional History of Early Modern Japan.* Princeton: Princeton University Press, 1968.

Jingū shichō, ed., *Jingū sanpaiki taisei* (A Collection of Ise Pilgrimage Diaries), vol. 10 of *Daijinjū sōsho* (Series on the Great Shrine at Ise), 1947.

Jippensha Ikku. *Hizakurige or Shanks' Mare.* Thomas Satchell, trans. Tokyo and Rutland, Vt.: Charles E. Tuttle, 1960.

———. *Tōkaidō Hizakurige* (Riding Shanks' Mare). Asou Isoji, ann. Nihon koten bungaku taikei, 62. Iwanami shoten, 1974.

Jones, Joseph. *The Politics of Transport in Twentieth-Century France.* Kingston and Montreal: McGill-Queen's University Press, 1984.

"Jōshū Kusatsu dōhō" (Account of a Journey to Kusatsu in Kōzuke Province), in *Gunma ken shi shiryō shū*, vol. 6, *Nikki hen* 2, Yamada Takemoro and Hagiwara Susumu, eds. (q.v.).

Kaempfer, Englebert. *History of Japan, Together With a Description of the Kingdom of Siam, 1690–1692.* 3 vols. J. G. Schnechzer, F.R.S., trans. New York: MacMillan Company, 1906.

Kaga han shiryō (Documents on Kaga Domain). 18 vols. Heki Ken, comp. Ishiguro Bun'kichi, 1929–58.

Kagawa ken shi (History of Kagawa Prefecture), vol. 4, *Kinsei* (Early Modern) 2. Kagawa: Kagawa ken, 1989.

Kagoshima ken shiryō kyūki zatsuroku tsuiroku (Documents of Kagoshima Prefecture: A Supplement of Miscellaneous Old Records), vol. 6. Kagoshima ken ishin shiryō hensanjo, ed., Kagoshima: Kagoshima ken, 1976.

Kagoshima ken shi (History of Kagoshima Prefecture), vol. 2, Kagoshima ken, ed. Kagoshima: Kagoshima ken, 1940.

Kallard, Arne and Pederson, Jon. "Famine and Population in Fukuoka Domain During the Tokugawa Period," *Journal of Japanese Studies*, vol. 10, no. 1, pp. 31–72 (1984).

Kamiya Masashi. *Hime kaidō* (The Princess Road). Kokusho kankō kai, 1984.

Kanagawa ken no rekishi. Kanagawa ken kenminbu kenmin sōmushitsu, ed. Kanagawa: Kanagawa ken, 1984.

Kanagawa ken shi shiryō hen (History of Kanagawa Prefecture: Documents), vols. 4, 5, and 9, *Kinsei* (Early Modern) 1, 2 and 6. Kanagawa ken kikaku chōsabu ken shi henshū shitsu, ed. Kanagawa: Kanagawa ken, 1971, 1972, 1974.

Kanagawa ken shi tsūshi hen (History of Kanagawa Prefecture), vol. 3, *Kinsei* (Early Modern) 2. Kanagawa ken kikaku chōsabu ken shi henshū shitsu, ed. Kanagawa: Kanagawa ken, 1974.

Kanbashi Norimasa. *Shimazu Shigehide* (Shimazu Shigehide). Yoshikawa kōbunkan, 1980.

Kankō kiga kenkyū shochō, ed., *Tabi to shuku: Nihon ryōkan shi* (Travel and Post Stations: A History of Japanese Inns). Kokusai kankō ryokan renmei, 1977.

Kanzaki Noritake. *Monomi yusan to Nihonjin* (Sightseeing and the Japanese). Gendai shinsho, 1,064. Kōdansha, 1991.

"Kateyama ke monjo" (Records of the Kateyama Family), in *Gunma ken shiryō shū* (Collected Documents on Gunma Prefecture), vol. 5, *Nikki hen* (Diaries) 1, Yamada Takemoro and Hagiwara Susumu, eds. (q.v.).

Katō Toshiyuki. "Sekisho yaburi no shin monjo" (New Documents Concerning *sekisho yaburi*), *Hakone sekisho tayori*, vol. 6, pp. 5–7 (1984).

Katsu Kokichi. "Musui dokugen" (Musui's Story), in his *Musui dokugen, hoka* (Musui's Story and Other Accounts). Katsube Mitake, ed. Tōyō bunko, 138. Heibonsha, 1968.

Kawai Kenji. "Okagemairi e no ryōshu shihai no taiō" (Seigneurial Control and Management of *okagemairi*), *Chihō shi kenkyū*, vol. 224, pp. 1–24 (1990).

Kawaji Toshiakira. *Nagasaki nikki, Shimoda nikki* (Nagasaki Diary, Shimoda Diary). Fujii Sadafumi and Kawada Sadao, anns. Tōyō bunko, 124. Heibonsha, 1968.

Kawana Noboru. *Kinsei Nihon suiun shi to kenkyū* (Research on Water Transport History in Japan's Early-Modern Period). Yūzankaku, 1984.

Kawasaki shi shi (History of Kawasaki). Kawasaki: Kawasaki shiyakusho, 1968.

Keene, Donald. *Travelers of a Hundred Ages.* New York: Henry Holt, 1989.

Kenshōbo (Compendium of Laws), vols. 4–5. Yamamoto Takeshi et al., eds. Kōchi: Kōchi kenritsu toshokan, 1982, 1985.

Kimura Motoi. "Bakuhan seika no seikatsu no tenkai" (Changing Lifestyles under the *Bakuhan* System), in Morisue, Hōgetsu, and Kimura, eds., *Taikei Nihon shi sōsho,* vol. 16, *Seikatsu shi* pt. 2 (q.v.)

———, ed. *Edo to chihō bunka* (Edo and Regional Culture), vol. 2. Bun'ichi sōgō, 1978.

Kinsei kōtsū shiryō shū (Collected Documents on Communications in the Early Modern Period). 10 vols. Yoshikawa kōbunkan, 1965–1980.

Kishii Yoshie, ed. *Gokaidō saiken* (A Detailed View of the Gokaidō). Seiabō, 1959.

Kitajima Masamoto. *Edo bakufu no kenryōku kōzō* (The Power Structure of the Edo Bakufu). Iwanami shoten, 1964.

Kitazawa Fumitake. *Meiwa no dai-ikki* (The Large-scale Peasant Disturbance of the Meiwa Period). Hato-no-mori shobō, 1973.

Kiyokawa Hachirō. *Saiyūsō* (Account of a Journey to the West). Oyamatsu Katsuichirō, ann. Tōyō bunko, 140. Heibonsha, 1969.

Knollys, Major Henry. *Sketches of Life in Japan*. London: Chapman and Hall, 1887.

Kobayashi Keiichirō. "Kinsei makki no Zenkō-ji sankeisha ni tsuite" (Pilgrims to Zenkō-ji During the Late Tokugawa Period), *Shinano,* vol. 13, no. 12, pp. 778–782 (1961).

———. *Zenkōji-san* (Zenkō Temple). Ginga shobō, 1973.

Kobayashi Kuzufuru, "Gochi mōde" (A Pilgrimage to Gochi), in Yaba Katsuyuki, ed., *Edo jidai no Shinano kikō shū* (q.v.).

Kobayashi Shigeru. "Nissha" (Wheeled Vehicles), in Nagahara Keiji, et al., eds., *Kōza Nihon gijutsu no shakai shi,* vol. 8, *Kōtsū, unyū* (q.v.).

Kōchi ken shiryō (Documents on Kōchi Prefecture). Kōchi: Kōchi ken, 1924.

Kōchi ken shi (History of Kōchi Prefecture), *Kinsei shiryō hen* (Early Modern Documents). Kōchi: Kōchi ken, 1975.

Kodama Kōta. "Edo jidai no shukueki seido" (The Post-Station System in the Edo Period) *Nihon rekishi,* vol. 95, pp. 56–62 (1956); vol. 96, pp. 38–42 (1956); vol. 97, pp. 52–56 (1956); vol. 98, pp. 52–56 (1956); and vol. 99, pp. 54–56 (1956).

———. "Efu no fusei shiyō ni tsuite" (The Illegal Use of Baggage Tags), *Kōtsū shi kenkyū,* vol. 8, pp. 80–89 (1982).

———. *Kinsei nōmin seikatsu shi* (History of Peasant Life in the Early Modern period). Yoshikawa kōbunkan, 1958.

———. *Kinsei shukueki seido no kenkyū* (Study of the Post-Station System in the Early Modern Period). Yoshikawa kōbunkan, 1957.

———. *Shukuba to kaidō: Gokaidō nyūmon* (Post Station and Road: An Introduction to the Gokaidō). Tōkyō bijutsu, 1986.

———. *Shukueki* (Post Station). Shibundō, 1960.

———, ed. *Nihon kinsei kōtsū shi kenkyū* (Study of Japan's Early Modern Communications History). Yoshikawa kōbunkan, 1979.

——— et al., eds. *Edo jidai no kōtsū to tabi* (Transport and Travel in the Edo Period). Rekishi kōron bukkusu, 15. Yūzankaku, 1982.

——— and Toyoda Takeshi, eds. *Kōtsū shi* (History of Communications). Taikei Nihon shi sōsho, 24. Yamakawa kōbunkan, 1970.

Kodama Kōta sensei koki kinen kai, ed., *Nihon Kinsei kōtsū shi kenkyū* (Studies in the History of Early-Modern Japanese Communications). Yoshikawa kōbunkan, 1979.

Kodansha Encyclopedia of Japan. First edition. 9 vols. New York: Kodansha, 1983.

"Konpira sankei dōchū nikki" (Pilgrimage Diary to Konpira Shrine), Yamamoto Mitsumasa, ann., *Kokuritsu rekishi minzoku hakubutsukan kenkyū hōkoku*, vol. 4, pp. 55–74 (March 1984).

Kondō Tsuneji. "Kinsei no hatagoya to sono hōkōnin: Tōkaidō Akasaka no baai" (Commoner Inns and their Apprentices in Early Modern Japan: The Case of Akasaka on the Tōkaidō), in Aichi daigaku sōgō kyōdo kenkyūjo, ed., *Kinsei no kōtsū to chihō bunka* (Communications and Regional Culture in the Early Modern Period). Meichō shuppan, 1986.

———. *Tōkaidō Arai sekisho no kenkyū* (Study of Arai Sekisho on the Tōkaidō). Hashiyoshi bunko, 1969.

"Kōshū kaidō Kobotoke tōge sekiban nikki" (Diary of the Guard at Kobotoke Sekisho on the Kōshū Road), in *Nihon nōmin shiryō shusui*, vol. 6, Ono Takeo, ed. (q.v.).

Kōtsū shi kenkyū kai, ed., *Nihon kinsei kōtsū shi ronshū* (Debates on Communications in Japan During the Early Modern Period). Yoshikawa kōbunkan, 1986.

Kumai Tamotsu. "Edo no ushi kasegi" (Ox-drawn Carts in Edo), *Kokuritsu rekishi minzoku hakubutsukan kenkyū hōkoku*, vol. 14, pp. 119–146 (1987).

———. "Nakagawa no kensa to kinmu" (Guard Duty and Inspections at Nakagawa), in Tsuda Hideo, ed., *Kinsei kokka to Meiji ishin* (The Early Modern State and the Meiji Restoration). Sanseidō, 1989.

Kumamoto ken shiryō (Documents on Kumamoto Prefecture), *Kinsei* (Early Modern) 2–3. Kumamoto: Kumamoto ken, 1965.

Kuroita Mototsugu. *Edo jidai shi* (History of the Edo Period). 2 vols. Kondō shuppansha, 1976.

Kurume shi shi, vol. 2. Kurume shi shi hensan iinkai, ed. Kurume: Kurume shi, 1982.

Kusatsu shi shi (History of Kusatsu City), vol. 2. Kusatsu shi shi hensan iinkai, ed. Kusatsu: Kusatsu shiyakusho, 1984.

Maeda Takeshi. *Junrei no shakaigaku: Saikoku junrei to Shikoku henro* (A Sociological Study of Religious Pilgrimage: The Western and Shikoku Circuits). Osaka: Kansai Ōsaka keizai-seiji kenkyūjo, 1970.

Maeda Yoshi. "Tabi nikki no josei" (Women and Travel Diaries), in Enchi Fumiko, ed., *Nikki ni tsuzuru aikan* (The Joys and Sorrows of Life as Seen in Diaries). Shūeisha, 1977.

Mamiya Hisako. *Tosa han no sanson kōzō* (The Mountain Villages of Tosa Domain). Kōchi: Kōchi shimin toshokan, 1978.

Manchester, Curtis Alexander. "The Development and Distribution of Sekisho in Japan." Ph.D. diss. Ann Arbor, Mich.: University of Michigan, 1947.

"Marugame hanjōki," (A Tale of Marugame's Prosperity), in *Nihon toshi seikatsu shiryō shūsei*, vol. 7, *Minatomachi hen* pt. 2, Harada Tomohiko, ed. (q.v.).

Marumo Takeshige. *Chūsei no tabibitotachi* (Travelers of the Medieval Period). Rokkō shuppan, 1987.

Maruyama Kazuhiko and Kobayashi Keiichirō, eds. *Issa shū* (The Collected Works of Issa). Koten haibungaku taikei, 15. Shūeisha, 1970.

Maruyama Yasunari. "Kaidō, shukueki, tabi no seido to jittai" (Roads, Post Stations, and Travel: Institutions and Their Actual Conditions), in Maruyama Yasunari, ed., *Jōhō to kōtsū*, vol. 6 of *Nihon no kinsei* (q.v.).

———. "Kinsei no rikujō kōtsū" (Overland Transport in the Early Modern Period), in Kodama Kōta and Toyoda Takeshi, eds., *Kōtsū shi* (q.v.).

———. "Kinsei no watashiba ni kansuru jakkan no mondai" (Various Problems Concerning River Crossings in the Early Modern Period), in Toyoda Takeshi kyōju kanreki kinen kai, ed., *Nihon kinsei shi no chihōteki tenkai* (Regional Development in Japan's Early Modern History). Yoshikawa kōbunkan, 1973.

———. "Kinsei sekisho oyobi bansho no kenkyū" (The Study of Sekisho and Bansho of the Early Modern Period), *Kyūshū bunka shi kenkyū kiyō*, vol. 19, pp. 1–28 (1974); *Shien*, vol. 112, pp. 437–451 (1980).

———. *Kinsei shukueki no kisoteki kenkyū* (Basic Study of the Post Stations in the Early Modern Period). 2 vols. Yoshikawa kōbunkan, 1975.

———. "Kyūshū ni okeru kaidō to shukueki (Roads and Post Stations in Kyushu), in Kodama Kōta koki kinen kai, ed., *Nihon kinsei kōtsū shi kenkyū* (q.v.).

———. *Nihon kinsei kōtsū shi no kenkyū* (Studies in the History of Early-Modern Japanese Communications). Yoshikawa kōbunkan, 1989.

———, ed. *Jōhō to kōtsū* (Communications and Transportation), vol. 6 of *Nihon no kinsei* (Japan in the Early Modern Period). Chūō kōron, 1992.

"Masuya Heiuemon Sendai gekkō nikki" (Diary of Masuya Heiuemon's Trip

348 *List of Works Cited*

to Sendai), in *Nihon toshi seikatsu shiryō shūsei*, Harada Tomohiko, ed. vol. 8, *Shukubamachi hen*, (q.v.).

Matanabe Nobuo, ed. *Miyagi no kenkyū* (The Study of Miyagi), vol. 5, *Kinsei* (Early Modern) 3. Seibundō, 1983.

Matsuida chō shi (History of Matsuida). Matsuida: Matsuida chō shi hensan iinkai, 1985.

Matsuura Seizan. *Kashiyawa, zoku hen* (*Kashiyawa:* Second Series), vols. 1, 4. Tōyō bunko, 360, 375. Heibonsha, 1979, 1980.

McClain, James L. *Kanazawa: A Seventeenth Century Castle Town*. New Haven: Yale University Press, 1982.

McEwan, J. R. *The Political Writings of Ogyū Sorai*. Cambridge: Cambridge University Press, 1962.

McKendrik, Neil, Brewer, John, and Plumb, J. H. *The Birth of a Consumer Society: The Commercialization of Eighteenth-Century England*. Bloomington: Indiana University Press, 1982.

Mendoza, Gonzalez de. *The Historie of the Great and Mightie Kingdom of China and the Situation Thereof*. R. Parke, trans. New York: Da Capo Press, 1973.

Meyer, John A. "Notes Towards a Working Definition of Social Control in Historical Analysis," in Stanley Cohen and Andrew Scull, eds., *Social Control and the State* (q.v.).

Michaelis-Jena, Ruth and Merson, Willy, trans. and eds. *A Lady Travels: Journeys in England and Scotland From the Diaries of Johanna Schopenhauer*. London: Routledge, 1988.

Mieczkowski, Bosdan. *Transportation in Eastern Europe: Empirical Findings*. New York: Columbia University Press, 1978.

Migdal, Joel S. *Strong Societies and Weak States. State-Society Relations and State Capabilities in the Third World*. Princeton: Princeton University Press, 1988.

Mitane ke monjo (Documents of the Mitane Family). Kōchi Prefectural Library, Kōchi, Japan.

Miyagi ken shi (History of Miyagi Prefecture), vol. 5. Miyagi: Miyagi ken, 1960.

Miyata Noboru. "Josei to minkan shinkō" (Women and Folk Beliefs), in Josei shi sōgō kenkyū kai, ed., *Nihon josei shi* (History of Japanese Women), vol. 3, *Kinsei* (Early Modern). Tōkyō daigaku shuppan kai, 1984.

Miyazaki Katsunori. "Osso daihyōsha no tabi" (Journey for Direct Representation) in Kōtsū shi kenkyū kai, ed., *Nihon kinsei kōtsū shi ronshū* (q.v.).

Mizushima Shigeru. "Etchū sekisho no tsūkō aratame" (Inspection Procedures for Passage through Sekisho in Etchū), *Toyama shidan*, vol. 38, pp. 25–40 (1967); vol. 39, pp. 1–27 (1968); vol. 40, pp. 20–25 (1968).

Moir, Esther. *The Discovery of Britain: The English Tourist, 1540 to 1840*. London: Routledge & Kegan Paul, 1964.

Morisue Yoshiaki, Hōgetsu Keido, and Kimura Motoi, eds., *Taikei Nihon shi sōsho* (Series on Japanese History), vol. 16, *Seikatsu shi* (Life and Livelihood) pt. 2. Yamakawa shuppansha, 1977.

Moriya Takeshi. *Mura shibai: Kinsei bunka no susono kara.* (Village Theater: A History of Early Modern Culture From the Bottom Up). Heibonsha, 1988.

Morris, Christopher, ed. *The Journeys of Celia Fiennes.* London: The Cresset Press, 1949.

Murakami Tadashi. "Kai ni okeru kuchidome bansho no seiritsu" (The Establishment of *Kuchidome* Bansho in Kai Province), *Shinano*, vol. 16, no. 1, pp. 44–60 (1964).

——. "Rokugō watashi" (The Rokugō River Crossing), in Kodama Kōta et al., eds., *Edo jidai no kōtsū to tabi* (q.v.).

——, ed. *Edo bakufu sennin dōshin shiryō* (Documents on the Edo Bakufu's Thousand-man *Dōshin* Force). Bunken shuppan, 1982.

Murao Karyō. *Edo kingō michi shirube* (Guide to Roads in the Edo Vicinity). Heibonsha, 1989.

Muta Takatoshi. "Shokoku kaireki nichi roku" (Daily Record of a Journey Across Japan) in Noma Mitsunobu et al., eds., *Zuihitsu hyakkaen* (A Compendium of Miscellaneous Writings), vol. 13. Chūō kōron, 1979.

Nagahara Keiji, et al., eds. *Kōza Nihon gijutsu no shakaishi* (Series on the World of Japanese Technology), vol. 8, *Kōtsū, unyū* (Communications and Transportation). Nihon hyōronsha, 1985.

Nagakubo Sekisui, "Nagasaki kōeki nikki" (Diary of Military Duty in Nagasaki), in Yanagida Kunio, ed., *Kikō bunshū* (q.v.).

Nagano Hiroko. "Bakuhan hō to josei" (Law and Women Under the *Bakuhan* System), in Joseishi sōgō kenkyū kai, ed., *Nihon josei shi* (History of Japanese Women), vol. 3, *Kinsei* (Early Modern). Tōkyō daigaku shuppan kai, 1984.

Nagano ken shi (History of Nagano Prefecture), *Kinsei shiryō hen* (Early Modern Documents), 18 vols. Nagano ken shi kankō kai, ed. Nagano: Nagano ken, 1971–1984.

Nagano ken shi tsūshi hen (History of Nagano Prefecture), vol. 5, *Kinsei* (Early Modern) 2. Nagano ken shi kankō kai, ed. Nagano: Nagano ken, 1988.

Nagoya shi shi (History of Nagoya), *Seiji hen* (Politics), vol. 2. Nagoya: Nagoya shiyakusho, 1968.

Nagoya sōsho (Series on Nagoya), vol. 3, *Hōsei hen* (Laws) no. 2. Nagoya shi kyōiku iinkai, ed. Nagoya: Nagoya shi, 1981.

Nagoya sōsho, Zoku hen (Second Series on Nagoya), vols. 9–11, *Ōmurō chūki*

(Record From a Parrot's Cage) 1–3. Nagoya shi kyōiku iinkai, ed. Nagoya: Nagoya shi kyōiku iinkai, 1968.

Naitō Jirō. "Bakuhan ki shomin ryokō to sono hogo" (Travelers and Protective Care During the Tokugawa Period), *Nihon rekishi,* vol. 175, pp. 17–25 (1957).

"Nakai Genzaemon Mitsuoki tabi nikki" (The Travel Diary of Nakai Genzaemon Mitsuoki), in *Nihon toshi seikatsu shiryō shūsei,* Harada Tomohiko, ed. vol. 8, *Shukubamachi hen,* (q.v.).

Nakai, Kate Wildman. *Shogunal Politics: Arai Hakuseki and the Premises of Tokugawa Rule.* Harvard East Asian Monographs, 134. Cambridge: Council on East Asian Studies, Harvard University, 1988.

Nakai Nobuhiko. "Edo jidai chūki ni okeru rikujō kōtsū no ichi danmen" (A Perspective on Overland Communications During the Mid-Tokugawa Period), *Shigaku,* vol. 34, no. 1, pp. 15–44 (1961).

Nakami Hideo. "Sukegō yaku to murai zaisei" (The Overland Transport Corvée Levy and Village Economy), *Rekishi kyōiku,* vol. 4, no. 12, pp. 49–56 (1956).

Nakamura Shin'ichi, ed., *Takada hansei shi kenkyū* (A Study of Takada Domain History). 6 vols. Kazama shobō, 1967–1971.

Nakamura Shizuo. "Hakone sekisho tatemono kankei shiryō ni tsuite" (Documents Related to the Buildings of Hakone Sekisho), *Hakone sekisho tayori,* vol. 6, pp. 1–5 (1984).

――― and Iwasaki Munezumi. "Hakone sekisho tōmi bansho to Hakone kanetsukidō ni tsuite" (The Lookout Tower and Signal Bell at Hakone Sekisho), *Hakone sekisho tayori,* vol. 5, pp. 1–4 (1982).

Nakasendō kōtsū shiryō shū (Collected Documents on the Nakasendō). 3 vols. Hatano Tominobu, ed. Yoshikawa kōbunkan, 1982–1985.

Nakasendō Kumagaya eki, josukegō kokon shushi kakidome (Historical Record of Kumagawa Post Station on the Nakasendō and Its Regular Assisting Villages). Ibaraki kenritsu Urawa toshokan, ed. Ibaraki ken shiryō shū, 5. Urawa: Ibaraki kenritsu Urawa toshokan, 1972.

Namihara, Emiko. "Pollution in the Folk Belief System," *Current Anthropology,* vol. 28, no. 4, pp. S65–S74 (August–October 1987).

"Naniwa kō teishuku chō" (Ledger of Inns in the Naniwa Confraternity Association), in Imai Kingo, ed., *Ryokō yōjin shū* (q.v.).

Nash, Dennison. *Tourism in Pre-Industrial Societies.* Aix-en-Provence: Centre des Hautes Etudes Touristiques, 1979.

Neville, Edwin L. "The Development of Transportation in Japan: A Case Study of Okayama han, 1600–1868." Ph.D. diss. Ann Arbor, Mich.: University of Michigan, 1958.

Nihon gakushiin Nihon kagaku shi kankō kai, ed. *Meiji mae Nihon doboku shi* (History of Civil Engineering Before the Meiji Period). Revised edition. Inoue shoten, 1981.

Nihon kōtsū shiryō shūsei (Collected Documents on Japanese Communications), vol. 1, *Goeki benran* (A Handbook on the Gokaidō Post Stations); vol. 2, *Eki kanroku* (Post Station Records). Hibata Sekkō, ed. Jukai shorin, 1985.

Nihon meisho fūzoku ezu (Illustrated Guide to Japanese Customs and Famous Places). 18 and 2 supplemental vols. Ikeda Yasaburō, Noma Kōshin, and Minakami Tsutomu, eds. Kadokawa shoten, 1979–1988.

Nihon nōmin shiryō shusui (Collected Documents on Commoner Life in Japan), vol. 6. Ono Takeo, ed. Iwamatsudō shoten, 1942.

Nihon shomin seikatsu shiryō shūsei (Collected Documents on Commoner Life in Japan), vol. 1, *Tanken, kikō, chishi. Nantō hen* (Exploration, Travel Accounts, and Topography: The Southern Islands). Miyamoto Tsuneichi, Haraguchi Torao, and Higa Shunchō, eds. San'ichi shobō, 1968.

——, vol. 2, *Tanken, kikō, chishi. Saikoku hen* (Exploration, Travel Accounts, and Topography: The Western Provinces). Miyamoto Tsuneichi, Haraguchi Torao, and Tanigawa Ken'ichi, eds. San'ichi shobō, 1970.

——, vol. 3, *Tanken, kikō, chishi. Togoku hen* (Exploration, Travel Accounts and Topography: The Eastern Provinces). Takeuchi Toshimi, Mori Kahei, and Miyamoto Tsuneichi, eds. San'ichi shobō, 1970.

——, vol. 11, *Sesō* (World Conditions) pt. 1. Tanigawa Ken'ichi, ed. San'ichi shobō, 1970.

——, vol. 20, *Tanken, kikō, chishi. Hoi* (Exploration, Travel Accounts, and Topography. Supplementary Volume). Tanigawa Ken'ichi, ed. San'ichi shobō, 1972.

Nihon toshi seikatsu shiryō shūsei, vol. 2, *Santo hen* (The Three Metropolises), pt. 2. Harada Tomohiko, ed. Gakken. 1976.

——, vol. 7, *Minatomachi hen* (Port Towns) pt. 2. Harada Tomohiko, ed. Gakken, 1977.

——, vol. 8, *Shukubamachi hen* (Post Towns). Harada Tomohiko, ed. Gakken, 1977.

Nihon zuihitsu taisei (Compilation of Japanese Miscellanea), Second Series, vol. 11. Nihon zuihitsu taisei henshūbu, ed. Yoshikawa kōbunkan, 1974.

Niigata ken shi shiryō hen (History of Niigata Prefecture: Documents), vols. 6–7, *Kinsei* (Early Modern) 1–2. Niigata: Niigata ken, 1981.

Nishigori Gohei, "Tōbu nikki" (Edo Diary), in *Nihon toshi seikatsu shiryō shū*, vol. 2, *Santo hen*, Harada Tomohiko, ed. (q.v.).

Nishiyama Matsunosuke. "Edo bunka to chihō bunka" (Edo and Regional Culture), *Iwanami kōza Nihon rekishi* (Iwanami Series on Japanese History), vol. 15, *Kinsei* (Early Modern) 3. Iwanami shoten, 1963.

———. *Kinsei fūzoku to shakai* (Customs and Society in the Early Modern Period). Vol. 5 in his *Nishiyama Matsunosuke chosaku shū* (Collected Works of Nishiyama Matsunosuke). Yoshikawa kōbunkan, 1985.

Nomura Katsu. *Ise no furuichi are kore* (This and That About Furuichi in Ise). N.p.: Mie ken kyōdo shiryō kankō kai, 1976.

Ofuregaki Kanpō shūsei (Collected Regulations of the Kanpō Era). Ishii Ryōsuke and Takayanagi Shinzō, eds. Iwanami shoten, 1934.

Ogunremi, Gabriel Ogundeji. *Counting the Camels: The Economics of Transportation in Pre-industrial Nigeria.* New York: Nok Publishers, International, 1982.

Ogyū Sorai. *Seidan* (Political Writings). Tsuji Tatsuya, ann. Iwanami shoten, 1987.

Ōishi Shinsaburō and Chie Nakane, eds. *Tokugawa Japan.* University of Tokyo Press, 1990.

Okayama ken shi (History of Okayama Prefecture), vol. 7, *Kinsei* (Early Modern) 2. Okayama ken shi hensan iinkai, ed. Okayama: Okayama ken, 1979.

———, vol. 25, *Tsuyama monjo* (Documents on Tsuyama Domain). Okayama ken shi hensan iinkai, ed. Okayama: Okayama ken, 1981.

Ōme shi shi shiryō shū (History of Ōme City: Collected Documents), vols. 19, 23. Ōme: Ōme shi kyōdo hakubutsukan, 1974, 1978.

Ōmi Katada, "Saiban nikki" (Year-End Diary) in *Nihon toshi seikatsu shiryō shūsei*, vol. 7, *Minatomachi* pt. 2. Harada Tomohiko, ed. (q.v.).

Onishi Gen'ichi. *Sangū no konjaku* (Pilgrimage Then and Now). Jingū shichō, 1956.

Ono Masao. *Gokaidō fūzoku shi* (A History of Customs on the Gokaidō). Tembōsha, 1979.

Ōshima Nobujirō. *Honjin no kenkyū* (Study of Daimyo Inns). Yoshikawa kōbunkan, 1955.

———. *Sekisho: sono rekishi to jittai* (Sekisho: Their History and True Nature). Shinjinbutsu ōraisha, 1954.

Ōta Nanpo. *Ōta Nanpo shū* (The Collected Works of Ōta Nanpo). Yūmeidō shoten, 1918.

Ōta Shokusanjin (Nanpo). "Jinjutsu kikōshō" (Account of a Journey in 1742), in Sugiura Minpei, *Ōta Shokusanjin* (q.v.).

Ousby, Ian. *The Englishman's England: Taste, Travel and the Rise of Tourism.* Cambridge: Cambridge University Press, 1990.

Ōwada Kōichi. "Bunka ki Odawara shuku ni okeru sukegō funsō ni tsuite" (Disputes Between Odawara Post Station and Its Assisting Villages During the Bunka Period), *Hōsei shigaku*, vol. 33, pp. 29–40 (1981).

——— and Itō Jun. "Hakone kyūkaidō" (The Old Road at Hakone), *Kōtsū shi kenkyū*, vol. 20, pp. 66–67 (1988).

Ōyama Shikitarō. *Kinsei kōtsū keizai shi ron* (Debate on the Economic History of Communications During the Early Modern Period). Kashiwa shobō, 1967.

Pawson, Eric. *Transport and the Economy: The Turnpike Roads of Eighteenth Century Britain.* London and New York: Academic Press, 1977.
Plumb, J. H. *Georgian Delights.* Boston and Toronto: Little, Brown, 1980.
Plutschow, Herbert and Fukuda, Hideichi, trans. *Four Japanese Travel Diaries of the Middle Ages.* Cornell University East Asia Papers 25. Ithaca: Cornell University, 1981.

Redesdale, Algernon Bertram Freeman Mitford, Baron (Lord). *Memories.* 2 vols. London: Hutchinson and Company, 1915.
Reischauer, Edwin O. *Ennin's Travels in T'ang China.* New York: Ronald Press, 1955.
Robbins, Michael. "The Progress of Transport History," *Journal of Transport History,* Third Series, vol. 12, no. 1, pp. 74–87 (March 1991).
Roberts, Luke Shepherd. "The Merchant Origins of National Prosperity Thought in Eighteenth Century Tosa." Ph.D. diss. Princeton: Princeton University, 1991.
Rozman, Gilbert. "Edo's Importance in the Changing Tokugawa Society," *Journal of Japanese Studies,* vol. 1, no. 1, pp. 91–112 (Autumn 1974).
Rubinger, Richard. *Private Academies of Tokugawa Japan.* Princeton: Princeton University Press, 1982.

Sakai sekisho shi (History of the Sekisho at Sakai). Sakai sekisho shi hensan iinkai, ed. Asahi: Asahi machi yakuba, 1968.
Sakurai Kunio. "Kinsei ni okeru Tōhoku chihō kara no tabi" (Travel From the Tohoku Region During the Early Modern Period), *Komazawa shigaku,* vol. 34, pp. 144–181 (1985).
Sakurai Tokutarō. *Kōshūdan no kenkyū* (A Study of Confraternity Groups). Sakurai Tokutarō chosaku shū, 1. Yoshikawa kōbunkan, 1988.
Sandler, Mark H. "The Traveler's Way: Illustrated Guidebooks of Edo Japan," *Asian Art,* vol. 5, no. 2, pp. 31–55 (Spring 1992).
Sansom, George. *A History of Japan, 1615–1867.* Stanford: Stanford University Press, 1963.
Sarugakyō sekisho shiryō (Documents on Sarugakyō Sekisho). Harazawa Yasunosuke, ed. N.p.: Niiharu mura shiryō shū hensan iinkai, 1973.
Satow, Sir Ernest. *A Diplomat in Japan: An Inner History of the Meiji Restoration.* Rutland, Vt. and Tokyo: Charles E. Tuttle, 1983.
Savage, Christopher I. *An Economic History of Transport.* London: Hutchinson University Library, 1966.

Scott, James C. *Weapons of the Weak: Everyday Forms of Peasant Resistance.* New Haven: Yale University Press, 1985.

Sears, John F. *Sacred Places: American Tourist Attractions in the Nineteenth Century.* New York: Oxford University Press, 1989.

Shaku Keijun. *Jippō anyū reki zakki* (Miscellaneous Accounts of the Peregrinations of an Ascetic). Edo sōsho kankō kai, 1916.

Shiba Keiko. "Kinsei josei no tabi nikki kara—tabi suru joseitachi no sugata o otte" (In Search of a True Picture of Early-Modern Women Travelers as Seen through Women's Travel Diaries), *Kōtsū shi kenkyū,* vol. 27, pp. 31-51 (1991).

——. "Tabi nikki kara mita kinsei josei no ikkōsatsu" (A Consideration of Women in the Early Modern Period as Seen in Travel Diaries), in Kinsei josei shi kenkyū kai, ed., *Edo jidai no joseitachi* (q.v.).

Shiga ken shi (History of Shiga Prefecture), vol. 5: *Sangyō shiryō* (Documents on Industry). Shiga: Shiga ken, 1928.

Shima Takeshi. *Ōmi shōnin monogatari* (Tales of Ōmi Merchants). Kokusho kankōkai, 1976.

Shimada shi shi (History of Shimada City), vol. 2. Shimada shi hensan iinkai, ed. Shimada: Shimada shiyakusho, 1978.

Shimazaki Tōson. *Before the Dawn.* William E. Naff, trans. Honolulu: University of Hawaii Press, 1987.

——. *Yoake mae* (Before the Dawn). 2 vols. Shinchō bunko, 1954.

Shinagawa ku shi tsūshi hen (History of Shinagawa Ward), pt. 1. Shinagawa ku, ed. Tōkyō to Shinagawa ku, 1970.

Shinagawa ku shi shiryō hen (History of Shinagawa Ward: Documents). Tōkyō to Shinagawa ku, 1970.

Shinpen Saitama ken shi shiryō hen (The New History of Saitama Prefecture: Documents), vol. 15, *Kinsei* (Early Modern) 6: *Kōtsū* (Communications). Saitama ken, ed. Saitama: Saitama ken, 1984.

——, vol. 11, *Kinsei* (Early modern) 2: *Tenma sōjō* (The Tenma Disturbance). Saitama ken, ed. Saitama: Saitama ken, 1981.

Shinjō Tsunezō. "Kinsei no Ise sangū" (Ise Pilgrimage During the Early Modern Period), in Nishigaki Seiji, ed., *Ise shinkō* (The Ise Faith), vol. 2, *Kinsei* (Early Modern). Yūzankaku, 1984.

——. *Sengoku jidai no kōtsū* (Communications During the Warring States Period). Unebi shobō, 1943.

——. *Shaji to kōtsū* (Pilgrimage and Communications). Shibundō, 1960.

——. *Shomin to tabi no rekishi* (History of Commoners and Travel). NHK bukkusu, 143. NHK, 1975.

——. *Shaji sankei no shakai keizaishiteki kenkyū* (Social and Economic History of Pilgrimage). Revised edition. Hanawa shobō, 1982.

Shinshū Shiojiri Akabane ke Genroku ōjōya nikki (Diary of the Regional Headman of the Akabane Family of Shiojiri in Shinano Province During the Genroku Period). Keiyūsha, 1974.

Shirabyōshi Masako. "Kōshidō no ki" (Account of a Journey in 1720), in Yanagida Kunio, ed., *Zoku kikō bunshū* (q.v.).

Shizuoka ken shi shiryō hen (History of Shizuoka Prefecture: Documents), vol. 13, *Kinsei* (Early Modern) no. 5. Shizuoka: Shizuoka ken, 1991.

Siebold, Philipp Franz von. *Edo sanpu kikō* (Account of a Journey to Edo). Saitō Makoto, trans. Tōyō bunko, 87. Heibonsha, 1967.

————. *Manners and Customs of the Japanese in the Nineteenth Century.* Rutland, Vt. and Tokyo: Charles E. Tuttle, 1973.

Sigaux, Gilbert. *History of Tourism.* London: Leisure Arts, 1966.

Sin Yu-han. *Kaiyū roku* (Record of a Journey Across the Sea). Kang Chaeon, trans. Tōyō bunko, 252. Heibonsha, 1974.

Skocpol, Theda. "Bringing the State Back In: Strategies of Analysis in Current Research," in Peter Evans, Dietrich Rueschemeyer, and Theda Skocpol, eds., *Bringing the State Back In.* Cambridge: Cambridge University Press, 1985.

Smith, Thomas C. *The Agrarian Origins of Modern Japan.* Stanford: Stanford University Press, 1959.

————. "Farm Family By-Employments in Pre-industrial Japan," *Journal of Economic History,* vol. 29, no. 4, pp. 687–715 (1969).

Smith, Valene L., ed., *Hosts and Guests: The Anthropology of Tourism.* Philadelphia: University of Pennsylvania Press, 1977.

Spinks, Charles Nelson. "The Tōkaidō in Popular Literature and Art," *Transactions of the Asiatic Society of Japan,* Third Series, vol. 3, pp. 1–26 (1954).

Stamp, A. H. *A Social and Economic History of England From 1700 to 1970.* London: Research Publishing Co., 1979.

Staples, William G. *Castles of Our Conscience: Social Control and the American State, 1800–1985.* Cambridge (U.K.): Polity Press, 1990.

Sugae Masumi. *Sugae Masumi yūranki* (Travels of Sugae Masumi). 5 vols. Heibonsha, 1965–1967.

Sugiura Minpei. *Ōta Shokusanjin.* Nihon no tabibito, 8. Dankōsha, 1974.

Sumption, Jonathan. *Pilgrimage: An Image of Medieval Religion.* London: Faber and Faber, 1975.

Tachibana Nankei. *Tōzai yūki* (Account of Journeys East and West). 2 vols. Munemasa Isō, ann. Tōyō bunko, 248–249. Heibonsha, 1974.

Takagi Zensuke. "Satsuyō yukikaeri kiji" (Account of a Trip to Satsuma and Back), in *Nihon shomin seikatsu shiryō shūsei,* vol. 2: *Tanken, kikō, chishi. Saikoku hen,* Miyamoto Tsuneichi, Haraguchi Torao, and Tanigawa Ken'ichi, eds. (q.v.).

Takahashi Junji, *Nihon-e sugoroku shūsei* (Collection of Japanese *Sugoroku*). Kashiwa shoten, 1980.

Takayama Hikokurō zenshū (Collected Works of Takayama Hikokurō). Takayama Hikokurō sensei itoku kenshōkai, ed. 4 vols. Hakubunkan, 1943–1952.

Takebe Ayatari zenshū (Collected Works of Takebe Ayatari). Takebe Ayatari chosaku kankō kai, ed., Kokusho kankō kai, 1987.

Takechi Mitsuaki. *Ōigawa monogatari* (Tales of the Oi River). Takeda shuppan, 1967.

Takeuchi Makoto. "Edo ni okeru hō to minshu" (Law and the People in Edo), unpublished paper presented at the conference "Edo-Paris: Political Governance and Urban Society," Tokyo, June 4–11, 1990.

———, ed. *Bunka no taishūka* (The Popularization of Culture), vol. 14 of *Nihon no kinsei* (Japan in the Early Modern Period). Chūō kōron, 1993.

Tamamuro Fumio, ed. *Yūkō nichikan* (Daily Log of a Meandering Journey). 3 vols. Kadokawa shoten, 1977–1979.

Tamura Eitarō. *Edo jidai no kōtsū* (Communications in the Edo Period). Formerly published as *Kinsei Nihon kōtsū shi* in 1959. Yūzankaku, 1970.

Tanaka Kyūgu. "Minkan shōyo" (Economies of the People), in Takimoto Seiichi, ed., *Nihon keizai taiten* (Series on the Japanese Economy), vol. 5. Kenmeisha, 1928.

Tanaka Tomojirō. *Tōkaidō Enshū Mitsuke shuku* (Mitsuke Post Station on the Tōkaidō in Tōtōmi Province). Iwata: Iwata shi shi hensan iinkai, 1974.

Tanaka Yoshio. *Kaga hyakumangoku* (The One Million *Koku* Domain of Kaga). Kyōikusha, 1980.

Tanji Kenzō. "Kinsei shukueki ton'yasei no kakuritsu katei" (The Establishment of the *Ton'ya* System in Early Modern Post Stations, *Nihon rekishi*, vol. 220, pp. 42–59 (1966).

Tatsurō Akai, "The Common People and Painting," in Ōishi Shinsaburō and Chie Nakane, eds., *Tokugawa Japan* (q.v.).

Thunberg, Charles Peter. *Travels in Europe, Africa, and Asia.* London: W. Richardson, Cornhill and J. Egerton, Whitehall, 1785.

Tilly, Charles. *The Contentious French.* Cambridge: Harvard University Press, 1980.

Toby, Ronald P. *State and Diplomacy in Early Modern Japan: Asia in the Development of the Tokugawa Bakufu.* Princeton: Princeton University Press, 1984.

Tochigi ken shi shiryō hen (History of Tochigi Prefecture: Documents), *Kinsei* (Early Modern) 1–2. Tochigi ken shi shiryō hensan iinkai, ed. Tochigi: Tochigi ken, 1974–1976.

Tochigi ken shi tsūshi hen (History of Tochigi Prefecture), vols. 4–5, *Kinsei* (Early modern) 1–2. Tochigi: Tochigi ken, 1981 and 1984.

"Tōkaidō gojūsan eki no zu." 2 vols. (Illustrated scroll of fifty-three post stations on the Tōkaidō.) Sumi, color and gold on paper. The Hofer Collection, Sackler Museum. Cambridge: Harvard University.

"Tōkaidō gojūsantsugi." 7 vols. (Illustrated handscroll of the fifty-three post stations on the Tōkaidō.) Sumi, light color and gold on paper. The Hofer Collection, Sackler Museum. Cambridge: Harvard University.

Tōkaidō Hakone shuku, sekisho shiryō shū (Collected Documents on Hakone Post Station and Sekisho). 3 volumes. Hakone sekisho kenkyū kai, ed. Yoshikawa kōbunkan, 1972–1975.

Tokuda Ken'ichi. *Chūsei ni okeru suiun no hattatsu* (The Development of Sea Transport During the Medieval Period). Yūnandō, 1936.

Tokugawa jikki (True Record of the Tokugawa Reign). 10 vols. Kuroita Katsumi, ed. Shintei zōho kokushi taikei, 38–47. Nichiyō shōbō, 1929.

Tokugawa kinrei kō (Consideration of Tokugawa Regulations). 11 vols. Hōsei shi gakkai, ed. Shōbunsha, 1958–1961.

Tokushima ken shi (History of Tokushima Prefecture), vol. 4. Tokushima ken shi hensan iinkai, ed. Tokushima: Tokushima ken, 1965.

Tokutomi, Kenjiro. *Footprints in the Snow.* Kenneth Strong, trans. Rutland, Vt. and Tokyo: Charles E. Tuttle, 1971.

Tōkyō hyakunen shi (History of Tokyo's Century), vol. 1. Tōkyō hyakunen shi henshū iinkai, ed. Tōkyō to, 1979.

Tōkyō to komonjokan, ed. *Edo no ushi* (Oxen in Edo). Toshi kiyō, 32. Tōkyō to, 1989.

Totman, Conrad D. *Politics in the Tokugawa Bakufu, 1600–1843.* Cambridge: Harvard University Press, 1967.

———. *Tokugawa Ieyasu: Shogun.* San Francisco: Heian International, 1983.

———. "Tokugawa Peasants: Win, Lose, or Draw?" *Monumenta Nipponica,* vol. 41, no. 4, pp. 457–476 (Winter 1986).

Tottori han shi (History of Tottori Domain). Vols. 2–3. Tottori ken, ed. Tottori: Tottori kenritsu Tottori toshokan, 1970.

Tottori ken shi (History of Tottori Prefecture), vol. 4, *Kinsei shakai keizai* (Early Modern Society and Economy). Tottori: Tottori ken, 1981.

Toyama ken shi shiryō hen (History of Toyama Prefecture: Documents), vols. 4–5, *Kinsei* (Early Modern) 2–3. Toyama: Toyama ken, 1974, 1978.

Toyama ken shi tsūshi hen (History of Toyama Prefecture), Toyama ken, ed., vols. 3–4, *Kinsei* (Early Modern) 1–2. Toyama: Toyama ken, 1983.

Toyoda Takeshi. *A History of Pre-Meiji Commerce.* Kokusai bunka shinkō kai, 1969.

Tsukamoto Manabu. "Murabito no asobi to tabi" (Travel and Play in Peasant Society), in Nihon sonraku shi kōza henshū iinkai, ed., *Nihon sonraku shi kōza* (Series on the History of the Japanese Village), vol. 7, *Seikatsu* pt. 2, *Kinsei* (Early Modern). Yūzankaku, 1990.

Tsurugi Ryōichi. "Tsugi hikyaku no tsugitate hōhō to sono mondai ni tsuite" (The Relay Messenger System), *Hōsei shigaku*, vol. 23, pp. 27–40 (1973).

"Ukiyo no arisama" (The Way of the World), in *NSSS*, vol. 11, *Sesō* (World Conditions) pt. 1 (q.v.).

Usami Misako. "Bakumatsu ni okeru sukegō futan no tenkai" (Change in the Overland Transport Corvée Levy During the Late Tokugawa Period), *Hōsei shigaku*, vol. 42, no. 1, pp. 60–83 (1990).

——. "Odawara shuku ni okeru sukegō futan" (The Overland Transport Corvée Levy at Odawara), *Hōsei shigaku*, vol. 36, no. 1, pp. 26–60 (1984).

——. "Tōkaidō shukueki ni okeru meshimori onna no sonzai keitai" (Serving Women in Post Stations on the Tōkaidō), in Kinsei josei shi kenkyū kai, ed., *Ronshū kinsei josei shi* (Debates on the History of Women in the Early Modern Period). Yoshikawa kōbunkan, 1986.

Usui gun shi (History of Usui District). Usui: Usui gun shi kankō kai, 1973.

"Usui sekimori nikki" (Diary of the Guard at Usui Sekisho), in *Gunma ken shiryō shū*, vol. 5, *Nikki hen* 1, Yamada Takemoro and Hagiwara Susumu, eds. (q.v.).

Vance, James E. *Capturing the Horizon: The Historical Geography of Transportation Since the Sixteenth Century.* Baltimore: Johns Hopkins University Press, 1990.

Vaporis, Constantine N. "Caveat Viator: Advice to Travelers in the Edo Period," *Monumenta Nipponica*, vol. 44, no. 4, pp. 461–483 (Winter 1989).

——. "The Early Modern Origins of Japanese Tourism," *Senri Ethnological Studies*, 1994 (in press), National Museum of Ethnology, Osaka, Japan.

——. "Post Station and Assisting Villages: Corvée Labor and Peasant Contention," *Monumenta Nipponica*, vol. 41, no. 4, pp. 377–414 (Winter 1986).

Vlastos, Stephen. *Peasant Protests and Uprisings in Tokugawa Japan.* Berkeley: University of California Press, 1986.

Wakabayashi Kisaburō. *Kaga han nōsei shi kenkyū* (Study of Agricultural History in Kaga Domain). 2 vols. Yoshikawa kōbunkan, 1972.

Walthall, Anne. "The Life Cycle of Farm Women," in Gail Lee Bernstein, ed., *Recreating Japanese Women.* Berkeley: University of California Press, 1991.

——. "Peripheries," *Monumenta Nipponica*, vol. 39, no. 4, pp. 371–392 (Winter 1984).

——. *Social Protest and Popular Culture in Eighteenth-Century Japan.* Association for Asian Studies Monograph 43. Tucson: University of Arizona Press, 1986.

———, ed. and trans. *Peasant Uprisings in Japan.* Chicago: University of Chicago Press, 1991.

Watanabe Kazutoshi. "Edo bakufu no sekisho seido no kakuritsu to kinō" (The Establishment and Function of the Edo Bakufu's Sekisho System), *Nihon rekishi,* vol. 309, pp. 28–44 (1974).

———. "Edo bakufu rikujō kōtsū seisaku no hatten" (The Development of the Edo Bakufu's Policies on Overland Transportation), in Kodama Kōta sensei koki kinen kai, ed., *Nihon kinsei kōtsū shi kenkyū* (q.v.).

———. "Futatabi Edo bakufu no sekisho ni tsuite" (The Edo Bakufu's Sekisho System Reconsidered), *Nihon rekishi,* vol. 334, pp. 13–24 (1976).

———. "Imagiri sekisho ni okeru kaihen aratame seido" (The Coastal Inspection System at Imagiri Sekisho), *Aichi daigaku bungaku ronsō,* vol. 92, pp. 37–78 (1990).

———. *Kaidō to sekisho. Arai sekisho no rekishi.* (Road and Sekisho: The History of Arai Sekisho). Arai: Arai machi kyōiku iinkai, 1982.

———. "Kinsei sekisho no chihōteki tenkai" (Geographical Development of Sekisho in the Early Modern Period) *Aichi daigaku bungaku ronsō,* vol. 74, pp. 1–48 (1984).

———. "Kinsei sekisho no shokeitai" (The Various Types of Early Modern Sekisho), *Hōsei shigaku,* vol. 23, pp. 17–26 (1973).

———. "Sekisho, kuchidome bansho no kinō to unei" (The Function and Operation of Sekisho and Bansho), in Maruyama Yasunari, ed., *Jōhō to kōtsū,* vol. 6 of *Nihon no kinsei* (q.v.).

———. "Shukubamachi jūmin no seikatsu" (The Life of Post-Town Residents), *Aichi daigaku sōgō kyōdo kenkyū kiyō,* vol. 30, pp. 109–135 (1985).

———. "Tōkaidō Arai shuku ni okeru shukueki zaisei no ichi danmen" (A Perspective on the Economy of Arai Post Station on the Tōkaidō), *Kōtsū shi kenkyū,* vol. 8, pp. 56–79 (1982).

———. "Tōkaidō no kinseishiteki igi" (The Significance of the Tōkaidō in Early Modern History), *Aichi daigaku bungaku ronsō,* vol. 86, pp. 1–37 (1987).

Watanabe Kei'ichi. "Edo jidai ni okeru Hokkoku kaidō no tokusei" (The Special Characteristics of the Hokkoku kaidō in the Edo period), *Shinano,* vol. 18, no. 1, pp. 69–85 (1949).

Watanabe Morimichi. "Ōtsu-e no haitatsu to denpa" (The Distribution and Circulation of Ōtsu Pictures) in Ōishi Shinsaburō, ed. *Edo no chihō bunka* (Local Culture in the Edo Period), vol. 1. Bun'ichi sōgō shuppan, 1977.

Watanabe Nobuo, ed. "Kaidō to suiun" (Roads and Sea Transport), *Iwanami kōza Nihon rekishi* (Series on Japanese History), vol. 10, *Kinsei* (Early Modern) 2. Iwanami shoten, 1976.

———. *Miyagi no kenkyū* (Research on Miyagi), vol. 5, *Kinsei* (Early Modern) 3. Seibundō, 1983.

Waters, Neil L. *Japan's Local Pragmatists: The Transition from Bakumatsu to Meiji in the Kawasaki Region.* Cambridge: Council on East Asian Studies, Harvard University, 1983.

———. "Local Leadership in the Kawasaki Region From Bakumatsu to Meiji," *Journal of Japanese Studies,* vol. 7, no. 1, pp. 53–84 (Winter 1981).

Weber, Eugen. *Peasants into Frenchmen: The Modernization of Rural France, 1870–1914.* Stanford: Stanford University Press, 1976.

White, James W. "State Growth and Popular Protest in Tokugawa Japan," *Journal of Japanese Studies,* vol. 14, no. 1, pp. 1–25 (Winter 1988).

Willman, Olof Eriksson. "Nihon ryokōki" (Account of a Journey to Japan) in Murakawa Kengo and Ozaki Yoshi, trans., *Serisu Nihon tokōki. Viruman Nihon taizaiki* (Series on Voyages to Japan. Willman's Account of His Sojourn in Japan). Shin ikoku sōsho, 6. Yūshōdō, 1970.

Yaba Katsuyuki, ed. *Edo jidai no Shinano kikō shū.* Nagano: Shinano Mainichi Shinbunsha, 1984.

Yamada Munemitsu et al., eds. *Michi no bunka.* Kōdansha, 1979.

Yamagata ken shi shiryō hen (History of Yamagata Prefecture: Documents), vol. 6 (2 pts.); vols. 16–18, nos. 1–3. Yamagata ken, ed. Gannandō, 1960, 1976–1983.

Yamaguchi Keizaburō. *Hiroshige* (Hiroshige). Tōyō bijutsu sōsho, 5. Sansaisha, 1969.

Yamaguchi ken shiryō (Documents on Yamaguchi Prefecture), *Kinsei hen* (Early Modern), *Hōsei* (Legislation), 2 pts. Yamaguchi: Yamaguchi ken monjokan, 1979.

Yamamoto Hirofumi. "Boshin ki no gunji yusō to sukegō saihensei: shukueki sei shūmatsuki no ichi kenkyū" (Military Transport and the Reorganization of the Overland Transport Corvée System During the Boshin War: A Study of the Post-Station System in Its Last Phase), in Kodama Kōta, ed., *Nihon kinsei kōtsū shi kenkyū* (q.v.).

Yamamoto Mitsumasa. "Bōsō dōchūki" (Travel Accounts of the Bōsō Area), *Tokei Chiba,* vol. 426, pp. 30–32 (1983).

———. "Kinsei no shiteki dōro shisetsu–dōhyō ni tsuite" (The Establishment of Roads in the Early-Modern Period: Road Markers), *Kōtsū shi kenkyū,* vol. 20, pp. 67–68 (1988).

———. "Shokokujin ni totte no Edo. Shaji sankeisha o chūshin to shite" (Edo as Seen by People From the Provinces: With a Focus on Religious Pilgrimage), *Kokuritsu rekishi minzoku hakubutsukan kenkyū hōkoku,* vol. 14, pp. 335–355 (1987).

———. "Soshū Yagurasawa ōkan ni tsuite" (The Yagurasawa Road in Sagami Province), *Kanagawa ken shi kenkyū,* vol. 19, pp. 46–56 (1973).

———. "Tabi nikki ni miru kinsei no tabi ni tsuite" (Travel in the Early Modern Period As Seen Through Travel Diaries), *Kōtsū shi kenkyū*, vol. 13, pp. 69–84 (1985).

———. "Tōkaidō ni okeru jimba chinsen ni tsuite" (Rates for Post Horses and Porters on the Tōkaidō), *Hōsei shigaku*, vol. 21, pp. 89–105 (1969).

———. "Watashibune" (Ferry Boats), in Kodama Kōta et al., eds., *Edo jidai no kōtsū to tabi* (q.v.).

———, ed. *Kinsei Aizu shi no kenkyū* (Study of the History of Aizu in the Early Modern Period), vol. 1. Rekishi shinjūsha, 1978.

Yamauchi ke shiryō (Documents of the Yamauchi Family), vol. 1: *Daiichidai Kazutoyo kōki* (Official Record of the First Lord, Kazutoyo). Yamauchi ke shiryō kankō iinkai, ed. Yamauchi jinja hōmotsu shiryōkan, 1980.

———, vol. 3: *Dainidai Tadayoshi kōki* (Official Record of the Second Lord, Tadayoshi). Yamauchi ke shiryō kankō iinkai, ed. Yamauchi jinja hōmotsu shiryōkan, 1981.

Yanagida Kunio, ed. *Kikō bunshū* (Anthology of Travel Accounts). Hakubunkan, 1912.

———, ed. *Zoku kikō bunshū* (Second Anthology of Travel). Hakubunkan, 1930.

Yasumi Roan. *Ryokō yōjin shū* (Precautions for Travelers). Tōto shoshi, 1810.

Yataka Kōjirō. *Kiso Fukushima sekisho* (The Sekisho at Kiso Fukushima). Revised edition. Bunken shuppan, 1977.

Yazawa Yōshi. "Bakumatsu ki ni okeru sukegō ninsoku yaku ni tsuite" (Porter Duty as Part of the Overland Corvée Levy in the Late Tokugawa Period), *Kōtsū shi kenkyū*, vol. 6, pp. 63–93 (1981).

Yokohama shi shi, vol. 1. Yokohama shi shi, ed. Yokohama: Yokohama shi, 1957.

Yokoyama Toshio. *Hyakushō ikki to gimin denshō* (Peasant Movements and the Tradition of Martyrs). Rekishi shinsho, 85. Kyōikusha, 1977.

Yoshioka Sakutarō. "Usui sekisho gaisetsu" (An Outline of the Sekisho at Usui), *Shinano*, vol. 16, no. 1, pp. 61–72 (1964).

Yujirō Hayami and Saburō Yamada. "Technological Progress in Agriculture," in Lawrence Klein and Kazushi Ohkawa, eds., *Economic Growth: The Japanese Experience Since the Meiji Era*. Homewood, Ill.: Richard D. Irwin, 1968.

"Zenkō-ji, Tateyama sankei tabi nikki," in *Gifu ken shi shiryō hen, Kinsei*, vol. 7, Gifu ken, ed. (q.v.).

Zufu Nihon kaisō roku; Fuisseru sanpu kikō (Hendrik Doeff's Reflections on Japan and F. van Overmeer Fisscher's Travel Diary). Saitō Abe, trans. Yūshōdō shoten, 1966.

Index

Konpira sankei meisho zue ("Illustrated Guide to the Konpira Pilgrimage"), 234
Kōshū dōchū, 19, 33–34, 75. *See also* Gokaidō; Sekisho
Kuchidome bansho. See Domain border posts
Kumagaya, 85, 88
Kumano, pilgrimage to, 204
Kumiai. See Assisting villages: cooperative bodies of
Kuniyakukin ("ad hoc tax"), 93. *See also Suke-gō* tax
Kusatsu, 89, 240–241
Kutsukake, 66
Kyoto, 3, 241
Kyoto Deputy (*Kyōto shoshidai*), 26, 103, 122, 139, 144, 159
Kyōto shoshidai. See Kyoto Deputy

Lake Ashi. *See* Hakone sekisho
Lake Hamana, 35. *See also* Arai sekisho: and Lake Hamana
Load limits, 27, 75, 275n42. *See also* Post stations; Transport

Machi hikyaku ("commoner messenger system"), 10
Magistrate of Finance. *See* Finance Magistrate
Magistrate of Road Affairs (*dōchū bugyō*), 34, 59, 61, 89–90, 185; and assisting villages' petitions, 82, 89–92, 293n170, 256; creation of position, 31, 272–273n4; duties of, 43, 93; judgments of, 88, 95; and road maintenance, 280–281n126
Magistrate of Rural Affairs (*kōri bugyō*), 138
Magistrate of Shrines and Temples, 150
Maisaka, 32
Maki Chūzō, 151–152
Marugame, 248, 330n135
Mashi sukegō ("supplemental assisting villages"), 63. *See also* Auxiliary assisting villages; *Sukegō*
Masu kata ("L-shaped bends in road"), 35–36
Matsuura Seizan, 186
Meibutsu ("famous products"). *See* Souvenirs
Meiji government, 52, 65–66, 69, 87, 91, 290n105
Meisho zue ("illustrated guidebooks"), 224, 234. *See also* Travel literature
Meiwa Rebellion, 93–94. *See also* Assisting villages: and Meiwa Rebellion

Merchants, 76, 319–320n4, 325–326n81, 326n88. *See also* Private transport
Meshimori onna ("serving girls"), 81. *See also* Inns: prostitutes at
Messengers, official (*tsugi hikyaku*), 30, 121, 320n8
Migration. *See Dekasegi;* Travel: and migration
Mikuni kaidō, 32
Minoji, 60
Mishima, 32
Mitsuke, 61, 91
Monomi yusan ("sightseeing"), 238. *See also* Hot springs; Pilgrimage; Tourism; *Yusan tabi*
Mount Fuji, pilgrimage to, 248–249, 328n119, 329n120. *See also* Pilgrimage
Muchin. See Free rate
Muta Taketoshi, 197

Nagakubō Sekisui, 150
Nagasakidō, 34, 40, 43–44
Naitō Shinjuku, 33, 79
Nakagawa, 171; bansho, 191–192
Nakasemura, 104
Nakasendō, 19, 27, 33, 42–43, 58, 73–74, 75; and *sukegō*, 60–65, 70. *See also* Assisting villages; Gokaidō; Roads; Sekisho
Naniwa-kō, 230–231, 322n53. *See also* Confraternity groups
Nanmoku, 149, 172. *See also* Sekisho
Negotiable rate (*aitai chinsen*), 27, 74, 81–82, 96. *See also* Transport rates
Nikkō dōchū, 19, 34, 43, 45, 64, 93, 276n69. *See also* Assisting villages; Gokaidō; Roads; Sekisho
Nikkō pilgrimage, 64, 93–94, 118, 287n40. *See also* Pilgrimage
Nikkō reiheishi. See Imperial Envoy to Nikkō
Nobunaga. *See* Oda Nobunaga
Norimono. See Sedans
Nukemairi ("stealing away on pilgrimage"), 173, 203, 206–207, 210–211, 213–214, 223, 257–258, 317–318n144; punishment for, 215, 318–319n165
Nukemichi. See Side roads

Oda Nobunaga, 28, 101, 218
Odawara, 21, 32, 42, 79, 118–119, 125, 146, 186. *See also* Hakone sekisho

Harvard East Asian Monographs

93. Robert Repetto, Tai Hwan Kwon, Son-Ung Kim, Dae Young Kim, John E. Sloboda, and Peter J. Donaldson, *Economic Development, Population Policy, and Demographic Transition in the Republic of Korea*

94. Parks M. Coble, Jr., *The Shanghai Capitalists and the Nationalist Government, 1927–1937*

95. Noriko Kamachi, *Reform in China: Huang Tsun-hsien and the Japanese Model*

96. Richard Wich, *Sino-Soviet Crisis Politics: A Study of Political Change and Communication*

97. Lillian M. Li, *China's Silk Trade: Traditional Industry in the Modern World, 1842–1937*

98. R. David Arkush, *Fei Xiaotong and Sociology in Revolutionary China*

99. Kenneth Alan Grossberg, *Japan's Renaissance: The Politics of the Muromachi Bakufu*

100. James Reeve Pusey, *China and Charles Darwin*

101. Hoyt Cleveland Tillman, *Utilitarian Confucianism: Ch'en Liang's Challenge to Chu Hsi*

102. Thomas A. Stanley, *Ōsugi Sakae, Anarchist in Taishō Japan: The Creativity of the Ego*

103. Jonathan K. Ocko, *Bureaucratic Reform in Provincial China: Ting Jih-ch'ang in Restoration Kiangsu, 1867–1870*

104. James Reed, *The Missionary Mind and American East Asia Policy, 1911–1915*

105. Neil L. Waters, *Japan's Local Pragmatists: The Transition from Bakumatsu to Meiji in the Kawasaki Region*

106. David C. Cole and Yung Chul Park, *Financial Development in Korea, 1945–1978*

107. Roy Bahl, Chuk Kyo Kim, and Chong Kee Park, *Public Finances during the Korean Modernization Process*

108. William D. Wray, *Mitsubishi and the N.Y.K., 1870–1914: Business Strategy in the Japanese Shipping Industry*

109. Ralph William Huenemann, *The Dragon and the Iron Horse: The Economics of Railroads in China, 1876–1937*

110. Benjamin A. Elman, *From Philosophy to Philology: Intellectual and Social Aspects of Change in Late Imperial China*

111. Jane Kate Leonard, *Wei Yuan and China's Rediscovery of the Maritime World*

112. Luke S. K. Kwong, *A Mosaic of the Hundred Days: Personalities, Politics, and Ideas of 1898*

113. John E. Wills, Jr., *Embassies and Illusions: Dutch and Portuguese Envoys to K'ang-hsi, 1666–1687*

114. Joshua A. Fogel, *Politics and Sinology: The Case of Naitō Konan (1866–1934)*